THE PURITAN INVENTION

Goraka's Memoirs of Infamy

A STRANGE CASE OF BAD FAITH

THE PURITAN INVENTION

Goraka's Memoirs of Infamy

A STRANGE CASE OF BAD FAITH

Dr. Delridge Laveon Hunter

Copyright © 2023 by Dr. Delridge Laveon Hunter

All rights reserved. No part of this publication may be reproduced, distributed, or transmitted in any form or by any means, including, photocopying,recording, or other electronic or mechanical methods, without the prior written permission of the copyright owner and the publisher, except in the case of brief quotations embodied in critical reviews and certain other noncommercial uses permitted by copyright law. For permission requests, write to the publisher, addressed "Attention: Permissions Coordinator," at the address below.

ARPress
45 Dan Road Suite 5
Canton MA 02021

Hotline:	1(888) 821-0229
Fax:	1(508) 545-7580

Ordering Information:
Quantity sales. Special discounts are available on quantity purchases by corporations, associations, and others. For details, contact the publisher at the address above.

Printed in the United States of America.

ISBN-13:	Paperback	979-8-89330-573-9
	eBook	979-8-89330-575-3
	Hardback	979-8-89330-574-6

Library of Congress Control Number: 2024900956

Contents

Chapter 1 1
Chapter 2 9
Chapter 3 19
Chapter 4 24
Chapter 5 25
Chapter 6 27
Chapter 7 31
Chapter 8 32
Chapter 7, Again 39
Chapter 9 46
Chapter 10 55
Chapter 11 57
Chapter 12 60
Chapter 13 61
Chapter 14 71
Chapter 15 80
Chapter 16 85
Chapter 17 93
Chapter 18 97
Chapter 19 104
Chapter 20 109
Chapter 21 111
Chapter 22 113
Chapter 23 120
Chapter 24 123
Chapter 25 129
Chapter 26 136
Chapter 27 147

Chapter 28 156
Chapter 29 164
Chapter 30 173
Chapter 31 184
Chapter 32 192
Chapter 33 203
Chapter 34 212
Chapter 35 222
Chapter 36 223
Chapter 38 231

THE PURITAN INVENTION
GORAKA'S MEMOIRS OF INFAMY

A Strange Case in Bad Faith
DELRIDGE LA VEON HUNTER

A FICTION

THREE
WORLDS
WARS

A PURITAN
INVENTION

Characters of Goraka's Memoirs of Infamy

Goraka, Prodigal Prodigy, Barrister-General	Congregation
Story Teller	Council Member
Nigga Dred	Parliament
Neptune	Citizen Greer
Lost Scholar	MP-1
Gift Giver	Leader of the Opposition
Captain	Aero Guide
Sailor	Nailah, Priest of Priest, Prime Minister
Gentleman Don	Manila
Elder Lillieth	Idiot
Elder Grace Jones	Doubter
Esopus	Soweto
1st Advisor	New 1st Advisor
2nd Advisor	Judges of the Council
King-General III	Reporter on the Scene
King-General II	Radon
High Priest	Blood
Big Mouth	Killer Miller
Count	Phat Gorgeous
Duke	Pots
Baron	Gomora
Gate Keeper	Usher
Audience	Big Mamma Hunter
Citizen of New Republic	Yoni Informant Imposter
Citizen Two	Radio Aire Redefusion
Inga	Au-U-Khan
Prince Mother	Anee

Bandleader

CR16

Panthers

Angola

Roc Steadye

Dirty Spot

Fact

Security

Femiperson-in-White

Cry Baby

Look, See & Tell

General Too Crazy

Lightnin'

Blin' Lemmon

Comptroller

CEO

Judge, the Confessor

Passer-by

The Merciful

Dying Soul

Balal al Sudan

Yombe

Tutor

Learner

Lorenzo Lillie

Bekina

NeoScab

Steller Four

Krishna

Hip City Daddy

Blue, Abdul Malik

The Musician, Marimba

Audience

Cocky Brave

Smart Ass

Dip Ditty

Tattle Tale

Faugard

Ministers

Jom

Sharp

Captain-Fifty-plus-One

Yoni

A Strange Case of Bad Faith

This dialogue is a political satire of how power corrupts. The desire is to allow an extremely complex process called leadership to play itself out within the arena of the state, on stage. Why a dialogue? This is a satire. It is more comfortable doing this satire in dialogue. It is thought best rendered in dialogue. How did the idea of writing dialogue come about? It came out naturally. The characters told me that they were ready for presentation. The characters wanted to speak for themselves. They do not want a storyteller who dominates conversation all of the time. What are the influences? The influences are the black community theater; a black barber shop setting; the black community aesthetic of social commentary; the amphitheater of Anthems with plays such as Oedipus Rex; Plato's Socrates; the Elizabethan theater of Shakespeare; the Broadway playwright Lorain Hansberry; the black cinema; the street corner and black college campus signifying sessions. The aesthetic linguistic rules of engagement are that of black dialogue. Why should you want to read Goraka's Memoirs of Infamy? It is a very interesting read. The challenge is to not let the language defeat you. The language can be challenging when you do not pay attention to the dialogue as rendered by each character. This is a lesson of Goraka's life. This character Goraka is a collage of personalities who have ruled the state. It might be anywhere or during anytime. This satire is like but not quite like any thing you have read before.

A Basic Premise

We take as given the idea of distinction and the idea of indication, that in order to make an indication one must first make a distinction. We take therefore the form of distinction for the form. G. Spencer-Brown, 1979, Laws of Form, 1.

CHAPTER 1

Story Teller:

A wasteful wonder of the new world is the best way to explain this prodigal child of the new world colony called Fifty-plus-One. He had everything at his disposal. Well, just about. To the rest of the conscious world, he had everything. So I now make no apology for the overstatement. What made Fifty-plus-One so unbelievable yet envied beyond reason was what came from its time.

Scratch that! Make it, came to its time. As I said, what made Fifty-plus-One so extraordinary in its most dialectical sense was what it attracted to and sent away from its time. So who, what was the prodigal prodigy? Simple! He was a person from the old country who decided to go off to other times and claim them as his own. These new times were called the New World. Time was the product of discovery. Reason is how time was made operational. Everything was understood simply through time, it was reasoned. As transformed into a conscious form, we might simply call time the product of discovery through reason [DTR]. Young, intelligent, well educated in the beliefs of the New World Philosophy, this product of DTR knew no bounds to his ability. Time was a bound.

Time was everywhere. Through time, he ventured everywhere and as far as his vessel could take him. He was truly a Discoverer. An Adventurer! Thief! Don't get me wrong, I don't mean to imply that this prodigal child took everything, and then acted as though there had been nothing there before he arrived. Or, that others did not take what they saw when they might have. No, that is not my assertion. That would be preposterous.

No one can take everything. The point is, what he took was always saleable on the open market. If it could not be sold, it was declared worthless. 'We don't give anything away after we've taken it.' Ironically, this new explorer was not the prodigal child, nor was he a prodigy very often. He was the forerunner of the prodigal child who seemed to know what to take even if he did not know what to do with it. And, it would be the prodigal prodigy who would reason, 'take the whole thing, and find out what it is worth later when we have time to go through everything. If we find something valuable, so much the better, if not, we can always get rid of it. No problem! The best offer, it's yours.'

Nigga Dred: Overtime it rains, There's a dry spot on my window. No tear drops anymore, Only pain instead. Lust, Lust is everywhere, Greed too is forever There Yes, take what you see And defend your right To it while it is in your Possession. That is the first Principle of reason By the New World Prodigy. Possession is 9/10th of the law. And, under the principle, the possessor has first claim. Obviously, those who can lay first claim are those who "own" the property or thing. The best way to own Anything under the Claimants first principle is to possess it. To occupy it. To have it under your jurisdiction. Under your control, it is yours.

Neptune: The territory is mine. I own it. My claim is original. I have the first claim. First claim is the best claim. Your claim is a fraud. It is a fake. You are a fraud.

Nigga Dred: What's the basis of a claim?

The claim is in the name It is the name that lays the clai

Story Teller:

Yes, the prodigal prodigy though wayward was intelligent. Learned! Thus, as a way of proving ownership, he created a legal fiction of ownership by the individual. So, under ownership, one could do what he pleased. And, as he pleased, the prodigal prodigy planted other crops upon the soil he selected as his own. In doing so, nature's own indigenous crops were often supplanted with new plants derived from some place else. The indigenous peoples, who were responsible for the domestication and cultivation of the plants, were called upon to replace their own production activity, and begin another as servants of Goraka. The indigenous peoples could not believe what their eyes showed them, for they did not understand what they were told by the prodigal prodigy.

He communicated in a very confusing way for their senses, so they relied upon their visual abilities to arrive at a conclusion about what was happening to their crops and their culture. Not only did the prodigal prodigy change what nature was growing, he also changed the ecology in the process. He planted crops that required nature's vital energy to make them grow.

This was a radical change in that it changed how the indigenous peoples were expected to live. What was obvious was the balance the local people had learned to live within was no longer guaranteed. The indigenous peoples were amazed, and finally, appalled at what the prodigal prodigy had forced upon them. The funny thing is, reason was the idea, the process, if you will, that promoted this efficiency of activity.

Nigga Dred: Can I get a bid?

Do hear a bid?

One hundred million?

Did I hear one hundred zillion?

For this long standing property?

Can I get another bid?

Did I hear….?

Story Teller: It was called buying and selling on the open market. To buy on the open market, one had to be one of the New Natives, a believer in the New Way. A practitioner of discovery through reason, an adherent of rational thought, the new religion, a member of the new class. So, the new class had finally arrived. After centuries of evolution, practically speaking, the most favored had now become the new king makers. They were finally able to erect their own social arrangement and do this on a grand scale. Mind you, they did this on a scale bigger than heretofore seen by anyone before.

As the most favored, there was no place for remnants of the old upper class to thrive on. The upper class therefore had no insurance against its eventual demise. It also had no way of knowing that its replacement would use what had been learned to enact their new culture. However, in the meantime, the pass word was…

Nigga Dred: Death to the Monarch!

Death to the king!

Long live the Republic.

There was militancy among the new occupiers of the original position second to none. They were neither impressed with nor afraid of those who previously occupied the most favored position, the upper class of the old country. Ironically, no one expected to see the new occupiers of the most favored position to rise so quickly and forcefully. Not this soon. It was the cry that there should be a new world culture within the confines of a new world colony that became the cry. Power, culture and development were the thoughts of these New Nativists long before there was a founding of a new world colony, long before they founded Fifty-plus-One as a new world colony.

In other words the new occupiers of the most favored position began to reveal themselves long before they became the most rich and famous of the white position. In the end, there were elements of the new occupiers of the most favored positions present. They were the ones who lived to dictate their new way, thus qualifying themselves as the occupiers of the original position in the new world colony named Fifty-plus-One.

These new elitists became so vain as to be referred to, as 'bluebloods' Blue blood was a rather strange way to signify that you occupied the original and most favored positions of the new republic. What is even more interesting is to declare their way as the representative new positions model.

Nigga Dred:

My daddy is a bird; he owns the rights to the sky.

My daddy owns a lodge sitting on the rock in the sky.

My daddy as far as the mind can imagine knows all of the time.

My mother is a descendant of the first settler to arrive during the time the bird flew over the rock lodged in the sky.

Story Teller: As you can see, the Blue Bloods, the New Nativists of the New World Colony, Fifty-plus-One, authors of contracted land granted by the King General, authors of a new document of rules and regulations governing a nation state, and proprietors of a new way of life, were truly the occupiers of the original position as founders of Fifty-plus-One. They positioned themselves as occupiers of the most favored position; the most favored position as they would call it was the white position. Since there was no one to stop them, they became the ones to be. They were the top of the line.

Nigga Dred:

I am the alpha and the omega.

The beginning and the end

I am the alpha and the omega

The beginning and the end.

Story Teller: As things happened, the New Nativists were the child prodigies and prodigal children of the New Way. A lot had happened since travel in time had come about. This time travel made it possible to find volumes of worked authored by esoteric scholars of the past. But, even they were amazed at what they found out.

Prodigal Prodigy: My God! Holy Savior! I never dreamed, but why now? Why deny me so long? And, why now? To increase my insatiable thirst further into other's reaches?

Nigga Dred:

Every teardrop dries my pain.

Every raindrop reflects our reign.

Lust, lust is everywhere.

Lust is everywhere, everywhere.

Story Teller: Gratifying is simply too bland, too restrained an attempt to describe what was set into motion. But, gratifying is all one would hear from the new Nativists as they reflected on the significance of the discovery of a new knowledge hundred of millions of times beyond their knowledge base. In "languages" they never heard of and could not understand.

Prodigal Prodigy: My God! Are we that far behind? I've never seen any ideas like this before. At least, not stated this way. Interesting! But, why didn't I learn this before? Why did you deny me this body of knowledge so long? In preparation to enjoy the teachings!

Lost Scholar: I am Alpha and Omega. The beginning and the end. Can you imagine reading the compete text? In full! Ha! Ha! Can you imagine that? For the first time in the history of your learned society you are the first to read a trilogy thought to be buried by the infamous Alexandria fires. They weren't burnt. Amazing!

Prodigal Prodigy: No! I read it myself. I saw it with my own eyes. They exist. They really do exist. Oh, I forgot, guess what I brought back with me?

Lost Scholar: You didn't!

Prodigal Prodigy: Yes! It's a gift. Here, take it, it yours. No matter that hundreds of thousands of ageless beings died to bring about the process, It was a gift. Incredible! Communication between and within the Brotherhood of Literary Inquiry must have finally broadened or the Lost Scholar was lying. Who knows, maybe the works were thought to be worthless. After all, they were only books.

Gift Giver: Give them to the foreigner; they're worthless to us now.

Story Teller: The question, or better still, problem is what did they we receive in return?

Gift Giver: I give you what I never expect to receive in return. I give you our collection of valuable works. If a revolution comes, it will most likely occur over there where you're from. Change is in the wind. Nothing like you've ever seen before. Change is coming in the west. The works should serve you well. Good luck!

Story Teller: Although they sound a bit classic, these foreigners in their own land spoke in such riddles. What was that about the west? Why would there be change in the west?

Gift Giver: You'll need those works where you're going. Please read them carefully. Don't repeat our mistakes and misdeeds. It's all in script. You'll see.

Story Teller: As time passed, we moved down the road, and the lost scholar has stopped a passer-by. He seemed to be asking for information. Maybe lost or something, all out here alone.

Lost Scholar: Excuse me sir, do you speak Latin?

Prodigal Prodigy: [Startled that his coachman has stopped the carriage.] Yes, of course. What do you want? Are you lost

Lost Scholar: Yes! No! No! But, I was wondering if you could read this work, this book, and this manuscript to me. I would like to know what it is telling me inside of it.

Prodigal Prodigy: [Thinking, "is this fellow mad?"] Here, let me see. Hum! [After investigating the manuscript for quite some time…] No, I can't make out completely what it says. Why did you ask if I speak Latin? The language appears to be Greek, to me. That is not Latin.

Lost Scholar: But can you tell me what it says? Can you read any of it to me?

Prodigal Prodigy: No! I don't think so. I might recognize a word or two here and there, but nothing to brag about.

Lost Scholar; The one's you recognize, what…

Prodigal Prodigy: No wait, don't get me wrong. I don't want to misguide you. One word may have a meaning totally different when it is read in a sentence. Or, my inflection may be incorrect. Too many variables to contend with, besides these symbols are totally unrecognizable, to me, at least.

Lost Scholar: But you said that it looked like Greek.

Prodigal Prodigy: Well, I didn't mean that literally. I only meant that it looked like Greek. Not that it was Greek. That was simply a figure of speech. Besides, I don't read Greek, either. Sorry! Got to go! See you.

Story Teller: The lost scholar now greatly disappointed continued on down the road wondering how he might receive the knowledge contained within his newly acquired volume. Academe is truly a wonder built upon the ignorance of the knowledge it seeks to obtain, it would seem. It would seem.

Nigga Dred: Every time it rains,

There's a dry spot on my window.

No wonders anymore.

Pain instead.

Hunger for knowledge is everywhere.

A lost generation here,

More anti history there.

Hunger for knowledge is

every where, every where.

Hunger not knowledge is what is there, don't they dare.

Story Teller: Anyway, the prodigal prodigy was beginning—no, let me change that to, he had already begun to question his own ignorance. He had already begun to read the law, so, he knew Latin. But his knowledge of Greek was lost in his effort to learn the law. Besides, all Greek writing had been translated long ago. Legal codes on the other hand had remained only in Latin. But, things are changing now. The world was getting smaller and smaller. One could launch a vessel on one day and arrive in another planet world the next moment.

Ironically, this new ability to move about freely did not prepare the prodigal prodigy in how to interpret what he saw. As things turned out, he was more often wrong than right in his interpretations of what he thought he observed. For instance, on one occasion in a visit to a foreign land, the people were so giving that the prodigal prodigy advised the captain of the vessel to take all he needed. As far as the prodigal prodigy was concerned, these beings obviously were nothing but heathens or fools. No one but fools allow someone to take food off of their tables. So, when the prodigal prodigy advised the captain to take everything needed, the captain responded,

Captain: Oh, yes sir, my dear prodigy, what do we do with the books? They seem to know how to write. Should we take theirs books, too?

Prodigal Prodigy: [Overseeing the whole process.] Take as many as we can, burn and destroy the rest.

Captain: Burn them!

Prodigal Prodigy: [Sometime later] Not all of them you fool. We are to keep as many as we can take back with us.

Sailor: Ah, Ah sir. The Captain said to burn them.

Prodigal Prodigy: Yes, but not all of them. Don't forget to keep some. They may have some valuable information inside.

Captain: Oh, yes, my dear scholar wants us to keep some of those, what do you call them books?

Sailor: HA! HA! HA!HA!HA!AH!AH!HA! Most of them are burned. They are gone; we've burned most of them books, HA! HA!HA!HA, already.

Captain: Well, what ever. Save what you can. Sorry about that,...

Prodigal Prodigy: Based on my educated guess, I'd y say they are not worth very much.

Captain: Might be good to see how they lived, no one will ever know.

Prodigal Prodigy: At least we got a few. Who knows , maybe someday they might be worth something.

Captain: Yes sir. They do look very primitive, don't they?

Story Teller: Some centuries later, we discover otherwise. However, things are different. You see, the prodigal child has just begun to break out of his poverty of culture. So, things have not begun to make sense yet. That will have to come later. Right now, the search for money is his greatest ambition. His desire for money is the motive force that has promoted a further inquiry into what might be contained within the books.

Gentleman Don: My child, where are the books? We've allowed you to roam the world over. Did you find them? How was your search? We are dying to see what you have for us.

Prodigal Prodigy: Wait now! I made no promises about finding anything of value. I only said, if....

Gentleman Don: If, my ass. You didn't say nothing about that when you ask us to invest in your grand venture. You told us all these stories about how things were so different in the other world that each one required a separate passage. You told us about new passages to the other world. You said……

Prodigal Prodigy: I only said that this night be the breakthrough we are looking for. I said that it might be promising.

Gentleman Don: Promising my ass, you said nothing about 'might be' when you painted those beautiful pictures of library museums in the other worlds out there…where are the books?

Prodigal Prodigy: Well, I did bring something back. They might be what you want. They might be nothing. At least I brought them back....

Gentleman Don: Tell us what they say? What do these books you brought back say? Yell us what they say. Tell us what we have invested our capital in.

Story Teller: It was one thing to talk about knowledge conquest, another to see one fountain when it is facing you. Nothing could be more difficult. When there's a poverty of thought in a particular cultural surrounding, there is a tendency to deaden the senses to what constitutes knowledge. There's am underdevelopment of thought in other words, as I said, a poverty of culture. By now, however, it was the ability to go places that opened everyone's eyes to their lack of information. It was this ability to go places that had broken this poverty of culture, they thought.

All of this would happen at a great cost to those who once occupied what was to become the New World Colony. With the New world Colony having settlers and slaves, the old country inhabitants had a new relationship to cultivate and develop. To their surprise there was a serious malady operating within the new colony. There was a poverty of culture among the intellectuals, scholars and critics. This was the compliment that the offspring of the old country paid to their ancestors.

The refusal to understand the inhabitants they replaced, if you will, simply allowed the new nativists to become the most ardent exponents of the new way, as the only way. This they learned in the old country. It is always a sad outcome when those who are just discovering themselves culturally have the technology to conquer others.

Inadvertently, nothing is learned in the conquest. It is only sometime after the conquered have long vanished that the conquerors recognize their gifts to universal understanding. I guess the question comes down to this, what is the responsibility of a new civilization to all previous civilizations that gave it new life? How far does that responsibility go? Nowhere? HA!HA! HA!HA!HA!HA! For instance, when a new civilization places its academy atop a grave site of a previous civilization, and the inhabitants it slaughtered on that site, what does that say about the new civilization's respect for the old? Tell me, what respect should it have? Should the conquered expect their conquerors to honor their slain? Not according to Goraka's Memoirs of Infamy. His, Goraka's, that is, motto was:

Nigga Dred: Treat a giver with disdain.

Take their goods and lay your claim.

The greatest claim is in the name.

Our claim and our name are the same.

Story Teller: Lost, a bit off track? Don't worry everybody is lost at this point, including the adventurers, especially, the adventurers. They don't know whether to wind their Asses or scratch their watches. You recall? The old country lost control over its new adventurers. They travelled where they pleased, and took what they could, and, most importantly, they burried the souls of the slain. The people of the NewWay did not believe in ancestral worship as they mistakenly called it. What better way to do this than to build your institution of learning atop your foes burial ground?

When the conqueror controls the victim's burial site it is a pure and clear sign of non-recognition and denial, at the same time. Total extermination is the order when this occurs. Your refusal to recognize another's right to exist can be expressed no better than by placing your knowledge base atop their burial ground. Total disrespect! But, this was the life of the prodigal child, Goraka.

Chapter 2

Story Teller: I know! You've heard it all before. It was really an oversight, poor judgment, at best. Besides, change is inevitable. After all, the prodigal prodigy was already moving to establish a New World. Did you hear me? Not simply a new civilization, but a completely new world. The only problem was, there were already conscious inhabitants living there. Also, these inhabitants were not having the opinion that it was necessary to change what they had already established. Not only that, the original people called this, space, this place home, there home. For over thousands of eons we are told.

As a visitor, the old inhabitants paid the prodigal child no attention. What harm could he bring? They could not phantom this new world concept. Under new world definitions, it was not enough to claim that you 'are' the original inhabitants of a given space, place. You must maintain that position against all challenges or your position and claim will die with you.

It goes on to say, your death, in turn, is forever because your very existence as social beings has been brought to an end. This is what makes it possible for the new inhabitants to claim yours as theirs as long as they possess it. This is what makes it possible to create a new way of doing everything, including defining the original inhabitants as non people, and as such you are not entitled to any benefits awarded to the new inhabitants. Non-people of the New World Colony called Fifty-plus-One were thus replaced with New Nativists who could make there adopted home into a place of unbelievable wealth and advancement.

As the settler inhabitants of this new colony, they renamed themselves, and everybody else according to how they named themselves and thought others should be named. This was done according to who came within their defined jurisdiction. And, what was their newly defined territory? All of the New World of course, of course! What else could it have been? Using logic and reason one questions how could it have been otherwise? As I said, this was a new day, a new time, and things were different, totally different.

Under new world definitions things were very simple. If an old native killed a new native, the New World Tribunal had jurisdiction over the accused. On the other hand, if a New World Citizen killed an old world native the New World Tribunal still maintained jurisdiction over the accused. This monopoly over everybody and everything defined as falling within one of the jurisdiction made things simple. This monopoly was made possible by superior firepower.

But, again, you know all of that don't you? I know! I know! If you've seen the cowboys and injuns stories a thousand times over. This is nothing new to you. Anyway, at no time was the old country or old world system of justice considered legitimate. At no time was either recognized. Obviously one cannot exercise such restrictions unless one has the firepower to do so, that's understandable. What is not understandable is how these settlers, new nativists if you will, mistaken superior force for superior justice, morality and intellect. That, I do not understand.

Yet, the New Nativists actually believed that they enjoyed a super intellect and culture simply because they overthrew the old world natives and did not have to follow the dictates of the old country. What culture, you ask? Were they not too young to claim a culture all their own? Yes! I would agree. I understand your point. The fact that the old world culture was simply too dynamic and fluid for most of us to pin down is just as accurate an assessment of this new world prodigy's citizens creation as it is about that of the old world culture.

The fact that the New World Citizens were slow to pick up on how advanced other cultural forms were or are does not deny that the New World Colony possesses a viable culture all it own, too. Again, that is not the point. The point is the prodigal prodigy actually believed that he was intellectually superior to all others. Again, using the science of reason as a basis of a new belief system, these new natives were correct in their logic. As you see, this is really the only concern I have. They were not incorrect in terms of what they were measuring, but they were overstating the case when they applied that logic to the measurement of other's progress. For, as long as they measured their won progress, their logic was correct. To go beyond that was not justified. So, the old country was caught nappin.

The old rulers did not know whether to wind their Asses or scratch their watches. Everyone within the old country was at a loss as to how to deal with this wayward child. In the meantime, the prodigal prodigy became more ruthless in his interpretation of the law. For him there was no other way. No opposing view or concepts were tolerated. That was the Law. And that meant everybody. No acceptable alternatives were permitted. NONE! Not one. Any views that contradicted the New World Colonial were outlawed. Further, if your view strayed too far away from the colonial policies, death was the only logical solution.

The infamous 'YOO DUM' trials are the best examples of the above point, although later revisionists scholars tried to cover the real happenings during that period. These scholars attempted to say that the participants were crazy or suffered from depression or hysteria as a means of excusing behavior of everybody who participated in lynching during that period. That was a bit too much. The trials in fact were a cover of the activities that were, going in else, i.e., taking the indigenous peoples lands while the trials were going on, and killing old natives to take their land.

The rulers were clear. Don't get me wrong; there were mobs all over the New World Colony. And, vigilante rule was rather common during the decades following the Great Awakening. So, the VouDun trials were denied and never recognized as ever happening. We call it denial and non-recognition. Some say that it was our of and. Others sat that it was fear. It was also greed and desire to won others property without purchasing it. It was a need to exercise control over other's lives: I'm sure that the list is endless. The question is, what happened? What really happened to the New World Colony that caused it to force total conformity onto its residents, all of its citizens, too?

Nigga Dred: Every time it rains

There's a dry spot on my window.

(Pause)No opposition from the floor

No opposition any more

Lynching, Lynching

Lynching everywhere

Everywhere

Story Teller: As I said, the prodigal prodigy was making his way up the ladder of what was expected. When he returned home, they wanted to hear adventure stories. But, they also wanted to know where the wealth was, too.

Gentleman Don: Damn, Goraka, how many did you have to kill to get this? I know they did not give it up without a fight. How much did it cost? And, where's the rest of it? I know that this is not all of the wealth you brought back. Somehow, I feel much better if I know that I have the wealth in hand while you tell me the stories about your conquests. After all, it's been quite some time since we've seen you. We thought you were dead. Then we received word from this New World Colony that you were alive and prosperous. So, where's all that wealth I understand you have?

Story Teller: A very simple request, don't you think? The prodigal prodigy had been away exploring, traveling all over the eternity and now he had returned home, rich. And, what was this talk about a New World Colony?

Gentleman Don: What is this about a New World? Does it really exist? Is there really a better life in the New World? Of course, there must be Look at all the wealth you brought back. Tell me, why does everybody talk about a wilderness? Do you really mean to tell me there is no civilization out there? Any where around? Amazing! Simply amazing! Nowhere to be found. You are truly a pioneer. I never would have thought. You lucky scum.

Story Teller: Now, isn't that ironic? Back home, the prodigal prodigy is awarded the highest honors one can bestow upon a new class citizen. The indigenous peoples who occupied the territories called Fifty-plus-One think of him as a thief. The two awards were obviously complementary. But, how can someone called a thief in one place be a hero in another? Obviously, there must be a difference of opinion here. Come to think of it, everywhere we turn, there were differences between the prodigal prodigy and his new world neighbors. I guess that's why he decided to colonize everything. The principle is this; you tend to feel much safer when everything is done according to what you are accustomed to. That makes sense. And, since might make right, that can correct all differences of opinion that might arise other wise. It's just a matter of cracking the whip.

Nigga Dred:

Why would Antoine lettered as a new class

Intelligentsia find violence so necessary

To keep other people in line?

Story Teller: Well, I'm sure that reason was tried first. No one in their right mind would attack a virtually defenseless group of resident inhabitants. Such behavior would certainly get the New World Colony off to a wrong start. I am sure that reason was employed. Force must have been employed as a last resort. Apparently, no one listened to reason. The prodigal prodigy had to use force. That is logical, isn't it? No one in his right mind would use force unless, absolutely necessary.

Nigga Dred: Can a group of resident inhabitants wreck havoc on a growing population of foreign settlers when the settlers control the supply of weapons the resident inhabitants need simply to survive against their invading conquerors?

Story Teller: So, why was force so necessary? The New World concept certainly had a following, small at first, but rather dedicated lot. Yes, but that was in the old country. In the frontier where the new World would grow by leaps and bounds, hardly anybody showed any interest. All who did were considered outcasts, radicals. Thus, all adherents were transplants. I recall a story of the New World Colony erecting its first university college to serve the new nativists, and the settlers approached their old world ancestors and neighbors. They told them that the university college was created to serve both the settler population and the indigenous peoples as well. Upon hearing the offer, I am told one of the elders inquired about the value of this university education to his community, of which he was informed, that:

Prodigal Prodigy: Of course, it will help. Your sons—only the boy child qualified to attend the university at the beginning—will benefit greatly.

Elder Lillieth: What will they learn?

Prodigal Prodigy: Oh, language, music art, the classics, ancient studies, mathematics, rhetoric, grammar. KNOWLEDGE!

Elder Lillieth: Yes, but what will they know how to do when they finish?

Prodigal Prodigy: They will be educated, learned.

Elder Lillieth: Educated? Learned? What does educated mean?

Prodigy Prodigy: You know, you learn lots of important things.

Elder Grace Jones: Like how to grow crops?

Prodigal Prodigy: No!

Elder Lillieth: Like how to hunt, maybe?

Prodigal Prodigy: No!

Elder Lillieth: Like to fish and make fertilizers?

Prodigal Prodigy: NO!

Elder Lillieth: Then, what is this education? What is it for? What does it do?

Prodigal Prodigy: It's how we obtain knowledge.

Elder Lillieth: Knowledge? Knowledge! What is knowledge?

Prodigal Prodigy: Knowledge is when you know lots of things.

Elder Lillieth: Like how to find your way when you are lost?

Prodigal Prodigy; Yes! No, Exactly how you mean it. Yes, I mean. That is knowledge, but we don't learn that in the university.

Elder Lillieth: But we taught you how to farm.

Prodigal Prodigy: That 's true. You did, didn't you?

Elder Lillieth: And, we taught you how to fish.

Prodigal Prodigy: Yes, you let us try em, too.

Elder Lillieth: We helped you to survive, it that not true?

Prodigal Prodigy: That you certainly did and we are certainly grateful. That is why we want to repay you. We've set up this institution that we want to share with you and your off spring. We've set aside scholarships so you won't have to pay for your sons schooling, that's our way of showing our gratitude.

Elder Lillieth: So, tell me, why do you build a university?

Prodigal Prodigy: To teach your children and ours how to become good New World citizens of the great land of ours.

Elder Lillieth: OURS? And, what do you want to teach us? How to become good new world citizens, too, in this land of ours?

Prodigal Prodigy: Yes, exactly!

Elder Lillieth: Then, who will reach us how to survive? How to live with Mother Nature, and, what about our children?

Prodigal Prodigy: I don't know. I guess you will. That is, as long as there is no conflict with our teachings, as long as it does not conflict with our schedule.

Elder Lillieth: And, what do we gain? You take away our land. You force us to learn your language, and now you tell us that you want to teach our children, but they will not know how to survive when you finish. What do we gain?

Prodigal Prodigy: A better knowledge of the great philosophers, our great thinkers.

Elder Lillieth: My ancestors have lived on and worked these lands for over seventy thousand eons. We now have the exact balance the formula calls for, as you might say. Why would we give up our way for yours? We live in harmony with nature. We taught you how to survive in your wilderness, as you call it. Why should we give up our way for yours?

Prodigal Prodigy: Why, because we are the wave of the future. Without us you cannot survive.

Elder Lillieth: You're saying that we will not survive; yet, we don't know anything about your way of doing things, except what we see you do. You seem to want to cross over to the other side before you have completed your assignment on this side. We gave up those ways long long ago. More that you can count. You, on the other hand, are still searching. Tell us, what are you looking for?

Story Teller: "The wave of the future," interesting! The prodigal prodigy has trekked all the way to the end of the world only to become the wave of the future. Who is the wave of the future? Why was it so difficult for the old world natives to hear what the New Natives said? No frame of reference? No playback machine? No records of the past? No forecasting of the future? Wait! Did the elders not say that their legend goes back seventy thousand eons, is that what they said? So, how would they know? Unless they traveled to the other world over, they would not have a framework in which to judge from that is, unless they employ a different kind of record keeping system than the one we have come to rely on. [Pause] But isn't that the point? The system they used as opposed to the system we use to educate the future. The question now is who holds the authority?

    Clearly the New Natives believe they do. They reason, "We have the weapons, we have the power. We are the authority." Authority was shown when the New Natives started to make and enforce public policy. They did not influence policy; they made it and enforced it. The New Natives made policy and the first thing they did was legitimize their culture as the culture. The old world natives were allowed to keep their old "games" only if they made them competitive. That is, to be played by everybody currently left out. Coming from a culture of egalitarian practices, can you imagine such a decision for anyone to ponder? No one from the old world culture knows what the prodigal prodigy is talking about. Is it double talk? No one had thought of what they were hearing before. It simply did not compute. To keep a game by making it competitive must have seemed utterly ridiculous, such an uncivilized way of enjoying play activity, so unnecessary, but give it a try, either that or find the names of the old natives on the play teams of the New Natives' games.

Nigga-Dred:

Here lies a great civilization of the ancient past, where are its inhabitants today?

Story Teller: Adjust or die. It was very clear, that simple. Everything that the old world had existed for centuries and centuries was now it greatest opposition.

Nigga Dred: Its greatest for, their death blow!

A most devastating for A most devastating blow

Seventy thousand peons and they almost exist no mo almost no mo.

Story Teller: Was that the deathblow to old world dominance, to old world knowledge, to old world culture? [Pause] The New World Colony dates its civilization with the advent of "Ancient Civilization" that began with the Greeks in Egypt. To choose such a time and location is an obvious effort to date New World History as having begun with the invention of rational thought as a new theoretical frame. Obviously this was their plan to try something new, and dynamic. Up to this point, the old world natives had lived in harmony with nature for over seventy thousand eons. During that time, the old world natives must have grown tremendously intellectual: their sages predicted their own demise to the very day of when it would happen, seventy thousand eons later, amazing. What made it so bad was they predicted who the foe would be and nobody believed them. What is the lesson to be learned here? Is it, don't become complacent with your old way of life? The question is, is this a dirty trick played by nature against the old natives? Maybe there is no lesson to be learned here. Maybe things just happen that way. If that is true, then the prodigal prodigy must have happened onto his story accidentally. Obviously, there can be no lesson there.

Nigga Dred:

It's just a storyof fame love and glory of a man whose a simple story

Story Teller: This prodigal prodigy was really a wrangler of the modern university, a contender of the gods.

Nigga Dred:

That's my line, Story Teller

However. I would say,

I was a wrangler for higher knowledge

A contender of the gods

A prodigal of the old world

A prodigy of the new world.

Story Teller: Who was he, this prodigal prodigy? We know that he left home and eventually declared himself the occupier of the original position in the New World. But? How did he arrive at that declaration, you ask? He did so by finding the written documents on property ownership. Who owns the property? Possession is nine-tenths of the law. Ownership of the actual papers offering ownership does the rest.

Prodigal Prodigy: Yes, I own this piece of land. Here is my deed. This is a contract. This one here is a paper of incorporation and that one over there is my constitution of the state. Here is one abolishing form of slavery. The one over…

Story Teller: First is everything. This was the prodigal prodigy. He had assumed the advantage. This gave him first claim to the birth right of the New World Colony. In the process, he killed the great majority of the old world inhabitants. What this showed was how willing the prodigal prodigy was to go to any length to "own his property." This was his right to be free. Ownership of property meant freedom.

Prodigal Prodigy: A dead civilization is always underneath the new.

Story Teller: Yes, and advancement is always the reason given.

Lost Scholar: Yes, I know! I know! So what?

Prodigal Prodigy: Cynics, all of you, nothing but cynics.

Lost Scholar: And, skeptics, too. Don't forget the skeptics, but, so what?

Prodigal Prodigy: Long live the Republic! I, in my worst moods, never become cynical about anything. Well, not for very long. A bit of skepticism is warranted, however, tends to keep you honest. But, I could not entertain either for very long. Too time consuming. My time must be devoted to building my new world. I have no time for ungrateful like yourselves.

Nigga Dred:

He may have been idealistic and patriotic but he was never as ungrateful as you. never as ungrateful as you.

Story Teller: So, the party line began its evolution here with the new class, nationalistic and intellectual. Democratic centralism is what he would call it. Representative democracy is the official name he used to sell it. Majority rule is how they would choose; for citizens, innocent until proven guilty. Others had no rights that were enforceable under the law.

Nigga Dred:

The old world natives claimed happiness before the New Natives came.

Now, they claim they are sad, what's left of them, that is.

Prodigal Prodigy: You're just not being honest. If the old world natives were honest, they'd admit that it was their way of life that destroyed them. They practiced living in common for so long that they could never grow. They never leaned how to compete. We didn't kill all of them off they destroyed themselves through their own in inertia.

Story Teller: Of course idleness did the job. Non-activity was the reason the old world natives died of their out in large numbers after the new World Natives arrived on their shores. Simple idleness! This was the party line as spoken by the intellectuals of the new philosophy called reason. In time reason became the basis of the new teachings. In time what was said was true. The old natives certainly did die from the own in inertia. What a masterful use of physics, the most successful science of reason to date, by the new natives. Social inertia killed the old world natives. Social inertia destroyed Old World Civilization,

Nigga Dred:

Every time it rains

A dry spot clouds my window.

Sticks of madness drum my head

Drums of music bring pain instead.

Rural decease from urban disease.

Yet, everywhere social idleness

Is practiced with ease.

Story Teller: So, it was social idleness that made the New World possible. Some say necessary. Thus, according to this thesis, the cities of the old country were becoming unbearable for decent new class people to live. Too many, there were too many idle subjects in the capital city of the kingdom. The idle were crowding into the cities with no saleable skills and nothing to do. They thereby became the vagabonds, criminals, nightwalkers, and entrepreneurs Streets were unsafe for decent people. Within the New World Colony, things would be different. For,...

Prodigal Prodigy: ...anyone caught out past curfew will be hanged, that is, unless that person can read. Under those circumstances, you may migrate out to the Great Valley, and start a new life. Then it may be possible to incorporate your own jurisdiction. Do we have any volunteers? Anybody want to take their chances within the Great Valley, and start a new life? Remember if you choose to go you will not be able to return home. Anyone who tries will be hanged on the spot. I repeat, do we have any volunteers?

Story Teller: So, the prodigal prodigy and his motley crew needed more than warm bodies. But, not much more it seems. They needed people who either had a stake in the future or no stake in the past. Although the former was preferred, they'd take the latter. No problem, hence, the need for Democratic Centralism. It was imperative that the right policies were enforced. It was no accident that the original declaration of independence was enforced over one hundred and fifty years before the "official" Declaration of Independence was signed by its authors. These signers became the ones who would occupy the original position as the New World founders. They in turn became the ones who would occupy the most favored position. These were the New Natives who set out to and assumed control over the New World Colony. Simply put, it was there for the taking. They had the only workable solution: a modern state, a mixed market economy, a new religion, and a nascent culture that would develop from the creative labor for the least favored. In short, this was the new world, with new people who would make a new society.

Nigga Dred:

New life for me and for you.

A new place for life with baby, too.

This is our landform shore to shore.

If we don't stop, we'll have more and more.

If we can, we'll own as much as we can.

Elder Lillieth: Phew! Can you imagine? The prodigal prodigy left home not very long ago, and he's acting as though he's had no home training. None at all.

Nigga Dred:

A sin

Stars fell

No loss mainland

No loss to thee

No loss to thee

Story Teller: Can you imagine three worlds occupying the same space in complementarity? Can you imagine that, all revolving around each other as triplets? How did it happen, you say? Well, in this case, the most favored of a highly technologically advanced society made contact with a society that had existed at a very high level, and split into three, as you shall later see. When they arrived, everyone had plenty of food, clothing, and shelter. This encouraged a beautiful sense of belonging, and a universal free spirit.

Esopus: May all evil that engulfs my land come before itself in reverse destruction? Destroy thy self, evil child. Destroy thy wickedness. You stole our land, took our birthrights, claimed direct ancestry from my culture, became the beginning of a new culture, and killed my people. May all the evilness that you visited upon my land cease and desist, immediately. Destroy thy self, evilness.

Story Teller: So what was he to do? Invest in the guaranteed success that came before him? Or, return to the old country to live.

Prodigal Prodigy: No! I don't intend to return to the old country. There're too old in their ways back home. I'm sorry that the civilization I'm going to build won't be there. But, I won't return. Besides, Beside, I have more potential for advancement where I am. And, if I'm lucky, I'll be rich. You know, I think I'm going to be rich, very rich.

Story Teller: Now, what we obviously have here is the original switch hitter. He can bat both ways. Conversion and annihilation would go on interchangeably with the final solution being the complete removal of a people from their land, their culture, and their home for seventy thousand eons. Now, these people were gone, forever. Unlike the prodigal child, the adventurer, this was not an adventure. Their very existence was at stake. Can you imagine trying to sort out things while you are being displaced from your home in the middle of the night? Can you imagine that? I'm sure you cannot.

Prodigal Prodigy: Birthright? What birthright? What are you talking about, birthright? Ha! You must be kidding. This is our land. We have the deed to prove it. No one was here when we arrived. We were and are the only occupiers of this land. You came here after we had already established a civilization on this soil. You age latecomers. You are highly mistaken. You are the newly arrived.

Esopus: What? What was that? Did I hear you correctly, that, I arrived after you settled here? Is that what I heard? Is that what you said? Then damn you. May the orishas damn you for your blasphemy?

Story Teller: The war was on. Yet, it was no contest. I mean no contest. The old world tactics and strategies although innovative and original, were no match for the firepower of the new settlers. Ironically the old world natives were considered to be in rebellion. And, rebellion was not tolerated. Put differently, the existence of the old world natives within the New World Colony was considered a rebellion. To you, this might sound extreme, but everything the old world natives did that contained practices of their culture, was considered in rebellion of the New Way. Thus, in the end, the old world people lost. They lost everything. There was no more. They were no more, except through the offspring they were able to create by intermarrying with others brought to the New World Colony as slaves. They were the future new world. Other than that, they no longer exist.

Prodigal Prodigy: Yes, but you can't blame me for that. That's not my fault. We were only taking advantage of what was free space. Our God directed us here. This is our space, our land. We own it title free.

Story Teller: And, so it began, A New World Colony soon to be called Fifty-plus-One was now born. It all happened on the space once occupied by other conscious beings that we might say laid the groundwork for others to build upon. However, these beings could no longer claim what was theirs as their own. They were the victims of the prodigal prodigy and the New Way of Life.

CHAPTER 3

Story Teller: The best way for us to describe how the New World Colony called Fifty-plus-One, actually came about is to unravel the policies of these creatures that were called "New Native." How did they assume that statute? Acquire such a contradictory position? How can one be "new" and 'native' simultaneously?

Apparently it all began when the King-General Matthew III signed a document giving the prodigal prodigy full autonomy on all matters "domestic" as long as he paid the King-General Mathew III his expected due. Agreeing, the New World Colony could pass laws and collect taxes. As an autonomous jurisdiction, the power to experiment with a new economy—free market, state regulated—to see how it might function as a system when allowed to operate exclusively was the first assumption the new colony made. All other systems were outlawed. Of course, by the regulatory agency established to regulate such matters.

The art of mastery of the political economy was at work. Brilliant idea! In addition to the autonomy granted by the King-General Matthew III, the provincial state was permitted to recruit openly within the halls of academe for immigrants who believed in the "New Way" and were willing to risk their lives in a far away place to see that this "new way survives and flourishes." These new immigrants would give up their old names and their titles in the old country. In turn, they would be granted full title fee simple. Thus, a new type of inheritance would begin. The immigrants accepted and moved immediately. The first thing they did was to meet at their old Alma mater the Academe Par Excellence [APE].

There they finalized their document of incorporation and decided whose names would appear on the final draft. The appearance of names on the final document of incorporation was determined by who was going to the New World Colony to live permanently. All those going as the New Natives to establish a permanent residence were allowed to become the signers of the charter approved by King-General Mathew III. Only their names would appear on the document that was to remain in the colony in perpetuity.

At the meeting, the Board of Trustees of the Corporation established an election procedure that would allow others to serve on the board. Criteria, every new member must move to the New World Colony. The deed of ownership would accompany them. After the new board members were elected, they, in turn, elected new members to the executive committee, and the chief executive officer (CEO). All of the executive committee would accompany the contract along with the new membership to the New World Colony, brilliant, absolutely brilliant.

After the officers of the corporation arrived in the New World Colony, they declared that autonomy meant that as long as legislation was to be enforced locally, only, the new provincial state could enact any law the corporation chose: the corporation chose to declare itself a provincial state with powers to establish its own institutions within its own body politic. What did the new interpretation of the contract mean? It simply meant that the New Natives had decided that they had the right to enact any legislation as long as it did not interfere with the King-General Matthew III receiving his rightful due. Their first act as a provincial state was to decide that the local body had the authority to decide how it wanted to congregate itself religiously. The

King-General Matthew III was furious when he heard the news about this action by his subjects. To further complicate matters, it was decided that this new congregation would not have any attachment to the old country's church.

Following the dictates of the government, the congregation declared itself autonomous from any other body and elected its first Minister of the Gospel. This new minister was by church tenets a graduate of the Academe Par Excellence and a member of the Corporation Board of Trustees. The appointed minister then proposed that the congregation should not depend on the old country to fulfil its quota of trained Ministers of the Gospel. The training should be carried on locally. Since this was a new church, there was no place else to offer training for its Servants of the Gospel but within the Hall of their own Academe Par Excellence. The congregation agreed. After agreeing to the idea, a new institution of higher learning was established locally to train members of the ministry as well as the instructors for the learning institutions needed to train the offspring of this nascent middle class colony. To assure that no one misunderstood the intent of their action, the congregation agreed that they would only accept graduates from their own institution into the pulpit of their new church.

Being elders and members of the original congregation of the New World Colony, the provincial state called a meeting at the Town Hall to decide how this new institution of higher learning would be funded. It was decided to establish a university-college as the first institution of higher learning within the New World Colony. This would be the first of its kind in the New World. The ruling elite of the old country hit the roof. "What the hell was wrong with King-General? Was he out of his mind? He gave those thieves the autonomy to do that?" Another said, "That's not the half of it." When the old country's ruling circles heard what the legislation said they were dumbfounded. Here is how it read in part, "every community of one hundred families or more must fund and build a facility to educate its offspring so as to provide the New World University with an educated pool of applicants. The education is to be geared to providing a trained corps of entrepreneurs who are well versed in the principles of enterprise." It further stated, "If any community of one hundred or more families fail to carry out this legislation, that community will be fined enough to pay the costs of educating their offspring in the neighboring community. Fines will be based on the budget costs of educating additional youths from the neighboring jurisdictions."

Legislation was passed immediately in all of the New World Colony communities requiring citizens to pay taxes to the local school districts for the support of their schools. The effect was enormous. No body wanted to loose out on the windfall that they could gain by declaring themselves autonomous. The old country's ruling circles were very disturbed by these activities of their old neighbors. These quick successions of legislation had to be addressed lest the old country find itself without a colony to govern. The King-General Matthew III ordered an emissary to visit the new World Colony immediately, and bring back a personal report.

In the meantime, anticipating that the old country would probably be concerned with what was happening in the New World Colony, the prodigal prodigy took it upon himself to make the great trek back "home" to explain that "everything was O.K." His first stop was with the King-General Matthew III.

King-General Matthew III: Mr. Barrister-General, what are all of these rumors going about my Kingdom regarding your newfound colony, something about you setting up an assembly? And, that you are encouraging the New World Colony to become independent? To become a nation-state in its own right, are all of these allegations true? Please tell His Majesty that this is not true.

First Advisor: Our report states that the New World Colony is about to declare itself capable of tending to all of its affairs without any assistance from the "old country," as we hear that you speak of us, all affairs foreign and domestic. I am sure that you recall the conditions that were agreed to before you left the old country as His Majesty was told you now refer to you home.

Second Advisor: Why would you want to leave the Kingdom? How do you expect to make it? I can understand how many of our other colonies might petition His majesty, the King-General Mathew III, for rights equivalent to the ones you possess, but it dumbfounds me how you can speak of independence.

First Advisor: ...And, so quickly. My, my how ambitious.

Prodigal Prodigy: Your Highness, I must say, it is a pleasure to be in His presence once again, and find Him in good health. May Your Divine will rule forever. Long live the King-General Matthew III.

Story Teller: Long live the Prince. Long live the Prince. My, how things have changed.

Prodigal Prodigy: ...His Grace, the New World Colony has no intention of leaving your Kingdom. I assure you. There is no reason to do so. You have been so kind and gracious. You have shown so much generosity we could never show all of our appreciation. Independence has never been discussed in any of our meetings. Although there have been many, the topic of independence has never been raised from the floor. I assure you...

Story Teller: So, tell me, and I know that this might sound like a digression to you, but who gave the King-General Matthew III authority to grant permission to anyone within His jurisdiction to "colonize" another people's land? Where did he derive such authority? Well, apparently he took it. And, the prodigal prodigy simply decided that it was His authority to offer contracts to the old natives for that land. Each simply assumed that he had the authority to do so. Remember, possession is nine tenths of the law. In any case, the prodigal prodigy was asked to explain what was happening out in that new territory everyone was talking about, but no one had visited. So, as we resume,...

Prodigal Prodigy: His Grace, please forgive any misunderstanding we may have caused. I take full responsibility. I am sure that you will find my report in order. Everything is contained there.

First Advisor: I advised His Majesty against it, I'd remind you. I never did think that it was a wise decision, and I have not seen anything to change my opinion so far. I think what they are doing in the New World Colony is treason.

King-General III: Now! Now! Mr. Court Advisor we must review the facts first. I signed the original charter because I thought that it was a rather novel idea. Not only that, the place seems incapable of giving us the kind of income my tropical colonies can offer. I'm not certain that we'll ever get the—uh! What's that word?

Prodigal Prodigy: Returns on development, Your Highness.

King-General Mathew III: Yes, that's it. Development, I like that word. Where did you pick such a word, in the New World? HA!HA!HA!HA! My, my, you never cease to amaze me. One of my advisors predicts that in less than a hundred decades you'll have your own language. He said, for you, it is natural, and, here you come with "Development," amazing. HA!HA!HA!HA! Anyway, Mr. Barrister-General please do not leave before I have a chance to review your report. Leave word where we might reach you. Where are you staying, anyway, at your uncle's estate? I would think so,

Prodigal Prodigy: Yes, His Grace. I can be reached at my uncle's estate.

Story Teller: Now that the prodigal prodigy had completed his first leg of the "official" inquiry in the old country, he had to prepare for the other reasons that brought him home. Their reasons, yes, three to be exact: The University of the New World; the new political economy; and, the New Church. Why, three? Where three, you say? Well, starting with the new university, it needed an endowment and operating funds to supplement the budget provided by the colonial state. Also, the new university needed a library-museum with works collected from the old country and of the people now deceased. Then there was that need for a Chief Academic Officer [CAO] who class offspring, who would assume the responsibility of developing curricula for the new class offspring, the future leadership of the New World Colony. Remember, the intent was to assure as much as possible that all development would take place on the soil of the New World Colony.

Two: The development of the New World was expected to coincide with the changes organized to take place in the old country over the next one hundred years, or so. The Goraka was therefore anxious to see how the events scheduled to encourage these changes to come about were doing. In other words, he wanted to know if everything was still moving according to plans. It was important to find out where things were because the prodigal prodigy had learned that the King-General Matthew III was aware of "don't let me think such thought lest the King-General Matthew III or one of His Court Advisors overhear me."

Three: The State Church was about to require the New World Colony to establish a parish that incorporated the whole territory, or stand accused of promoting blasphemy of the highest order. Blasphemy of the highest order is the greatest offence one may commit against the State Church. Anyone found guilty of such a crime is automatically punished by death. So far, the New Natives had successfully argued their case. However, more time was needed until the new church had established its foundation. The only thing, the old world natives were not cooperating. Things were not progressing as well as the Goraka would like, thus, the need for more time.

In the meantime, the fact that the New Natives had declared themselves an autonomous congregation, founded a new church, elected a pastor, eliminated the roles of a hierarchy that contained positions such as a Pope, Archbishop, Bishop or other corresponding positions to the State Church. The New World Colony recruited the first missionary to enter, is what was troubling the High Priest. It was not the fact that the New Settlers had requested their own pastor and missionary, or that they wanted to convert the old natives from the old world to their new religion, it was their insistence on recording their own Rules of Worship that had everyone in the old country talking.

The local issue involving the refusal of the old world natives to cooperate and their insistence that they teach the New Nativists has gone unnoticed, however. Their real concern was their offspring, and how they were disobeying their old teachings. Matters worsened back home when it was reported that not only had the New Settlers founded their New Church as their own church, they refused to allow the State Church to enter on the grounds that a State Church violated the rights of the New Nativists to practice freedom of beliefs.

High Priest: How dare they! I am offended, but I know not what to do.

Story Teller: Blasphemy, this is pure adulterer blasphemy. Who did these new world heathens think they were? How dare they go against the State Church? Needless to say, the High Priest was very angry, very angry. The anger was so deep that the only thing that could come from His mouth was,...

High Priest: How could they? How could they? I'll ban them too forever.

Story Teller: Obviously the New World Nativists were either out of their minds or were out of touch with reality. Remember, they sent the prodigal prodigy back home to settle matters to everybody's satisfaction. Now, with out "hearing" charges that were lodged against them, preparation was under way to assume control of the New World Colony before its new settlers got out of hand. This idea had been on the high Priest's mind ever since the New Natives left the old country. He had predicted along with a few others that the prodigal prodigy would betray the trust of the Monarch.

High Priest: How dare those pagans! Just, who do they think they are? The King-General Matthew III will never allow them to...

Story Teller: But, what could the old country people do? Send an army over to the New World Colony? That's obviously very costly in transpiration costs alone. So, what could they do? In the meantime, the prodigal prodigy had become engrossed in his own thoughts about the New World Colony. He was home sick. But, I thought that he was at home in the old country.

Nigga-Dred: Land of enchantment

Place I call home

Place that I roam

Look forward to seeing you Land that I love.

Look forward to being there

Fairy tales do come true.

CHAPTER 4

Story Teller: In the New World Colony, the December calm was unsettling to the New Natives and the old world inhabitants alike. Maybe, this was not where he was going, after all. Back home in the country, the prodigal prodigy was headed out to his uncle's estate when he came upon a lonely traveller who was hitch hiking a ride in the same direction.

Prodigal Prodigy: Driver, stop the coach, how do you do, sir?

Lost Scholar: How do you do?

Prodigal Prodigy: It seems mighty mysterious that you would be travelling this way at this time. Where are you headed? May I offer you a lift some place? May I help you in some way?

Lost Scholar: Yes! I'll take a lift. [Pause looking exactly at the prodigal child] Do you read Latin?

Prodigal Prodigy: Yes, as a matter of fact I do.

Lost Scholar: Good! Can you read this work to me? I am searching for someone to tell me what it says.

Prodigal Prodigy: Here, let me see.

Lost Scholar: Well, sir? What does it say?

Story Teller: What the old esoteric work said in a language long since discarded was too unbelievable that the prodigal prodigy invited the wonderer home with him.

Prodigal Prodigy: Sir, how much time do you have? I think that this work is going to take some time to translate. Do you have the time?

Lost Scholar: My time is devoted to finding someone who can translate this document because I long to know what knowledge it contains.

Prodigal Prodigy: Then, come with me to my uncle's estate, and I'll translate it for you on the way. I have a translator here with me. Please, come. Come! Unbelievable! Unbelievable! Incredible!

Lost Scholar: Sorry? What did you say? Did you say something?

Prodigal Prodigy: No! Yes, I only said that it is not Latin. The language, I mean.

Lost Scholar: Oh! I understand. But, you can read this language can't you?

Prodigal Prodigy: Yes! Of course! I can read this language. I'll be more than happy to accommodate you. It is my pleasure.

Chapter 5

Story Teller: As the prodigal prodigy began to read this last document that he had returned to the old country to find, the winter was operating in full force in the New World. February was upon the landscape and the people were cold, real cold. The February wind chill was extreme by now and the Settlers were really beginning to doubt their decision to migrate to this part of the world. Soon, before anyone realized, the prodigal prodigy was into the basic thesis of the book.

Prodigal Prodigy: My God, this is going to go on forever, and I must prepare to respond to any possible questions the King-General Matthew III might want to ask me, especially after he reviews all of those documents from the New World Colony. I don't know! I'm not so certain this was a wise idea to come back here, but the Council said that I should show signs of good faith by returning and letting Him read everything. I'm not so sure that everything will be understood the way we meant it. But, what can I do?

Lost Scholar: Sorry sir? What was that? Are we going to finish the work? I do not quite understand everything you read, but it seems as though it's about a new colony that was lost forever. How could that be? How could we know about something that nobody has ever found, sounds weird, to me.

Prodigal Prodigy: Yes, my mysterious visitor, we are going to finish the work. It does seem weird doesn't it? Rather odd.

Lost Scholar: And unsettling?

Prodigal Prodigy: Yes, very. Parts of it send chills throughout my body. Yes, you are right, it can be very unsettling.

Story Teller: I guess the most unsettling "parts" of the discourse the prodigal prodigy was referring to the part about a "new colony that was lost to forever." Somehow he attributed the thought to the esoteric work rather than it reader.

Prodigal Prodigy: How can nation that is in the process of evolving get lost?

Story Teller: Unaware of what the lost scholar was really referring to his remarks seemed more telling than intended.

Lost Scholar: This nation did exist once upon a time. Stories have circulated our world for centuries about a new world colony that existed a long time ago and somehow got lost. No one can prove that it ever was, but many believe that this is not a myth.

Prodigal Prodigy: No! It seems to be talking about now. Right now!

Lost Scholar: Right now? No, this story is about some time and place in the fantasyland.

Prodigal Prodigy: No! You don't understand this is going on right now. Just like the work says.

Lost Scholar: Good! If you think so, then maybe you'll learn what mistakes not to make while you are going through it. Your timing is perfect. You seem to have such perfect luck. Things always seem to go well for you. How do you manage? I admire your ability to be at the right place at the right time.

Prodigal Prodigy: How do you mean? You speak as though you know me, or have seen me before. What made you say that? I don't know you, do I?

Lost Scholar: No, you do not know me. At least you do not remember. But, there is no reason to. You were too busy at the time. My! My! My! You left such a notorious trail. What price for learning? But, continue. Excuse my digression. I am sorry. I seem to have got lost in my thoughts.

Prodigy Prodigy: I must say that at this point, I am confused. Somehow, you feel familiar, but I cannot place you anywhere. Yet, you seem to know so much about me, I mean, and in general, too.

Lost Scholar: Do not fret! No need to worry yourself about who I am. You have other more important things to ponder at this point, many more important things than the likeness of me. But, continue. I want to hear more…

Chapter 6

Story Teller: As the teachings would have it, the most important event in the story of the new world occurred in the eon zero with the discovery of the calculus. I TON presented her famous discourse on the Calculus of Mathematics in what is now considered the eon when it all began. Others may disagree by alleging the most important events to change the world occurred with the discovery of the new world as a settler colony, the invention in new world time [NWT], and the founding of the New World Colony, Fifty-plus-One. To those adherents, Zero time is the founding of Fifty-plus-One. Whatever! After all, it was events like these that made it possible for intellectuals and scholars like I TON to make such discoveries...

Enough of that! Where were we? Oh, yes. While the prodigal prodigy was reading about himself, and the future from a document many thousands of eons old, things were coming alive at the Palace of the King-General Matthew III. So much material was brought forward by the Barrister-General Goraka that the King-General Matthew III partitioned different documents out to His respective Councils of Advisors. The response was uproar. Never in their lives had they worked so hard. The volume was enough to cause the counselors to call for a trial. What it contained made it even more so, they want a trial. Everybody wanted to ask the prodigal prodigy some questions.

First Advisor: King-General Matthew III, you must send for your Barrister-General Goraka at once. From the documents I have examined, there is a clear case of treason. Therefore, I urge you to send for him at once.

King-General Matthew III: Those are sharp accusations my dear council. I hope you have sufficient evidence to support that claim.

Story Teller: The King-General Matthew III was adamant about this point. He had personally signed the Charter against the wishes of his favorite Advisors, and now they have come forward with allegations that this most favored and trusted subject had betrayed the Monarchy, They better be able to substantiate these claims or some heads will roll.

The question now is, will this independence on the part of the King-General Matthew III bring about His downfall. Ironically, prior to this adventure on the part of King-General Matthew III, He rarely exercised any independence. However, this venture seemed so novel and beside, it required no venture capital on the part of the Monarch so the King-General gave it His approval, personally. His decision was controversial because He acted against the advice His most respected council, the First Council of Advisors. It now appears as though the decision might go down as a bad one.

All the King-General Matthew III needs now are more rumors that He supports more change than permitted under their system without first coming before the Parliament of the Old Country.

Big Mouth: Obviously He has not been forthright with us. He supports more change, and appears that the Members of the Ruling Circle are going to call for His Royal Head, literally.

Story Teller: Members of the Ruling Circle are the ones who occupy the original position therefore the most favored people. They occupy that position because they became by creating the anti-story of the indigenous people.

Big Mouth: First, He allows the Assembly to convene more than a decade ago, now, Shortly there after, He permits the prodigal child, Garaka, to go away to some foreign land and experiment with a whole new way of life. That's blasphemy. Unhindered unhampered blasphemy...

Out of Touch: Somebody needs to tell me what the hell is going on, here?

Big Mouth: And, now things seem to have backfired. In fact, in terms of recognizing the assembly, He had no choice. If He had not created this new chamber as the Assembly, a Civil War was threatened.

Baron: We have had nothing but trouble since those New Class Radicals were given the Assembly.

Duke: Yes, I agree! The King-General Matthew III must realize that one cannot reason with Fanatics. You, you give them a break and they get the Monarch to give Garaka a new land he will make into a Republic. A Democratic Republic.

Count: We must talk to the King-General Matthew III at once. Immediately!

Story Teller: At the prescribed time, the Members of the Ruling Circle who had been selected convened upon the King-General Matthew III's Palace at once only to be informed that the Monarch is not available to receive visitors at this time.

Gate Keeper: Gentlemen, Ladies. I must inform you that the King-General Matthew III is not receiving anyone right now.

Story Teller: The King-General Matthew III is livid when he gets word that His Ruling Circle is angry about His decision to allow the Barrister-General to migrate to a new land unsupervised, and ty receive him with open arms when he returned.

King-General Matthew III: "How dare them. Do they know who I am?"

Story Teller: ...He's thinking. He is even more alarmed that they are surprised that He locked them out. He has never acted so strangely before. So, everybody some body is locked around the gate asking each other with the obvious question that was less than profound,

The Court: Why?

Story Teller: Why? Whatever the puzzlement, they begin to gossip and speculate more. No matter. It got to the point where by the Duke said.

Duke: I understand that as soon as the King-General Matthew III had summoned one of His Most Trusted, the Most Respected, Sir H. N I.C. to take the trip to the New World Colony, the Barrister-General from guess where appeared?

Count: Just like that. HEE! HEEE! HEEE!

Duke: Just like that. Out of nowhere.

Count: Are you sure that he was not summoned by His Majesty the King-General Matthew III? HEE! HEEE! HEEEE!

Duke: Positive! Absolutely, positive. The order has not been signed, yet.

Count: HA!HA!HA!HA!HA!HA! Simply hilarious.

Story Teller: I am sure that this is an understatement but the Count is extremely entertained by the story being told by the Duke.

Duke: NO! No, not yet, at least. No, let me correct myself. The King-General Matthew III has signed the order but He did not expect to see the Barrister-General before/while the document is being delivered to the Estate. As the Barrister-General arrives at the Palace,

Story Teller: By now, everyone within listening distance of the Duke is dying with laughter. Becoming all demonstrative the Duke assumes a character role as he begins...

Duke: [Mimicking the Count in a very hilarious laughter] HA!HA!HA!HA!

Story Teller: Then, in a very loud voice to be heard all over the place, THE PRODIGAL PRODIGY, Barrister-General Goraka appears, Ping, presto. HA!HA!HA!HA! THE KING-GENERAL MATTHEW III HAS JUST COMMANDED THE NOTED PHILOSOPHER NEPTUNE TO BOARD THE NEXT VESSEL OUTWARD BOUND, HEADED TO THE NEW WORLD COLONY, FIFTY-PLUS-ONE. WHEN PING. HA!HA!HA!HA!AH! The Barrister-General Goraka Appears.

Count: HA!HA!AH!HA!HA! Presto, like presto, like magic. A new world was right here with us in the Old Country.

Duke: HA! HA! A new world vessel—mind you—I said, a new world vessel that was built in the New World Colony called Fifty-plus-One has appeared with the prodigal prodigy, as the Barrister-General, Goraka on board.

Count: Amazing!

Duke: Yes, too amazing for em. Something smells funny.

Count: What'd you mean, sir?

Duke: I mean, I think there's a spy in the Court of the King-General Matthew III.

Story Teller: The Duke is right about there being a spy in the court, but he has no idea of how it is configured. He is not even in the vicinity

Duke: Besides, the New World Colonies were not supposed to be capable of that level of development for at least four of five hundred eons.

Count: So, King-General Matthew III was furious, not giving in to anyone.

Duke: No, not really! He was amazed.

Count: And, what about the vessel? What did he say about the vessel?

Duke: Did he say anything? He couldn't believe it. It was too amazing. Too over whelming!

Count: Oh, my! This is getting interesting. Back to the spy, how did they communicate?

Baron: [Still referring to the spy statement.] Yes? How? I understand that the decision to summon Neptune was designed to coincide with the only vessel leaving the port headed for the New World Colony, Fifty-plus-One. That was the only vessel the spy could board.

Count: Thus arriving in the New World Colony at the same time.

Baron: Almost Exactly!

Duke: That's true, except, the prodigal child would land here before the spy could reach him back in the New World Colony. No, it must be something else. I find his luck a bit too good because of this. Too good. Look at how they seem to equal us already in only fifty-seven eons.

Count: Equal? HA!HA!HA!HA! That's a joke. That vessel is far superior to any thing we have ever seen in these parts, or would expect for the next five hundred years. I've never seen anything like it before. And, I know nobody else has. Anyone who says otherwise is lying.

Duke: Yes, that's true. They seem to anticipate everything the King-General Matthew III is about to do.

Count: I'm beginning to see your point. It was rumored that many of the signers who migrated to the New World Colony were in the forefront to create an Assembly here before they left. They were the ones who migrated; the handwriting was on the wall.

Duke: And, what did the King-General Matthew III do?

Count: What did He do? What did He do? We all know what He did,..And, now we all know what He did. The Council is now ready to take off His head. They are tired of His Rule. They wanna see some heads roll, now.

Baron: Yes, I see your point. We must do something, and soon. He's still our one and only King-General.

Chapter 7

Story Teller: So, the monarchists proceed to organize a party to see the King-General Matthew III, and establish themselves as legislators as the House of Lords at the same time. Of course, the King-General Matthew III is fuming at the heart and foaming at the mouth. I mean He is MAD. One has never heard so much profanity. So much cursing. So much swearing, and carrying on.

King-General Matthew III: I want to see that bastard, immediately! No sooner! [In a very high tone but loud.] I want his ass here right now or some heads are going to roll across my throne.

First Advisor: Who, His Majesty?

King-General Matthew III: WHO? WHO? That TWIRT, THE BARRISTER-GENERAL GORAKA, WHERE THE HELL IS HE? I THOUGHT I TOLD YOU I WANTED TO SEE HIM NOW. I MEAN RIGHT NOW. WHO GAVE HIM THE SID-DI-TY TO THINK THAT HE COULD GET AWAY WITH THIS? I WANT HIS ASS IN FRONT OF MY FACE. I WANT HIM RIGHT NOW. DID YOU HEAR ME, RIGHT NOW!

First Advisor: But, His Majesty, his uncle's estate is three days travel at best. And, during this season, who knows?

Story Teller: Without any sign or warning,...

Prodigal Prodigy: Sir, I understand that you want to see me?

Story Teller: Although Goraka's arrival on the spot on the dot, has scared the shit out of Second Advisor and just about everybody else, including the King-General, he recovers with...

He's almost insultingly solicitous, you know like, "can I kiss your butt His Majesty?" but he makes his point.

Second Advisor: His Majesty, he said "SIR." Only treason is a greater crime. That should not be allowed in His presence His Majesty.

Story Teller: So tired of how the prodigal child had been insulting him, without warning, Goraka was arrested and taken to his quarters where he was treated with the care of a prince. As a matter of fact, things were so friendly that he did not realize it when someone slipped a sleeping pill into his liquid. Thus, without knowing it, the prodigal prodigy got a chance to rest without even requesting it. They in fact did him a favor. While asleep, the prodigal prodigy found himself in the dreamtime of the discovery of silence in the new World Colony, Fifty-plus-One. Little did he know that his visitors were reading his dreams while he slept? Little did he know that they learned more from him while he slept than when he was awake; that being awake allowed them to verify what they learned from him while he slept. At first they found it impossible to believe what he dreamed. It seemed some fantasy within his imagination. But, then they felt the scream. It frightened them terribly. They were convinced that he truly lived another life some place they could not yet comprehend. Excuse me; I am getting ahead of the story.

Chapter 8

Story Teller: Once upon a time—as things came to pass—people thought that music was only explained by reference to itself. As it came to pass, the prodigal prodigy upon landing on the New Found Land declared Music a sin thus to be outlawed in secular life, as well as in the New Church. Correspondingly, legislation was passed outlawing the playing of Music in any form or fashion. Instruments designed to produce Music were outlawed, also.

Audience: Say what? What was that again?

Story Teller: HA!HA!HA!HA! Yes, I know. It's hard to believe, but it's true. All forms of making Music were outlawed. With the New Found Land serving as the headquarters of the New World Colony, Fifty-plus-One-, a" Musical Instruments were banned from the New Church. In turn, Music was defined as secular. Secular Music not being from the church was opposed to the teachings of the Devil. And, since the Devil was known to use Music as a way of reaching His victims, the new provincial state passed laws outlawing music in the New World Colony. As the story was told, the Settlers had stopped listening to God. They had stopped talking to God. So, the Prodigal Prodigy was instructed to seek the banning of Music as a Secular Art Form. All instruments were removed from the church halls. First the Bells, then the Chimes, and then came the Organ. What had happened was, the prodigal prodigy felt that the best way to teach the New Way was to have everyone's complete attention. He wanted them to talk about it. Argue about it. Fight about it. And, the only way to do that was to keep all distractions to a minimum. The results were disastrous. A near Civic War broke out.

Prodigal Prodigy: No killing! No killing! I said, killing. Those are the rules. Anyone accused of a capital offence will therefore be considered innocent until shown otherwise.

Story Teller: The place was in shock. New ruin set in. An open rebellion was barely averted. Barely, averted!

Prodigal Prodigy: We said we would form a union. Our charter from the King-General Matthew III is a written testament to say that. We agreed. That's our contract.

Story Teller: Howl How! What had he done? Didn't he tell them? This was for life. There was no return. The contract said, all who agree would be bound forever.

Citizen of New Republic: I don't give a damn what is on that piece of paper, your almighty charter. We came here of our own free will to set up plantations. We are going to own land no differently than they do in the other colonies.

Story Teller: Had the prodigal prodigy done one of his tricks, again?

Prodigal Prodigy: No! That is not the way things are. We are going to doings differently here in this new land of ours. We didn't come over here simply to become rich absentee landlords. No Big Man here. If that had been our desire, we never would have gone to so much bother to come this far away from home. I know we are some adventuresome mothas, but you also want POWER. I figure why not go for broke. Why don't we create our own state? HA!

Story Teller: At first, the New World Settlers laughed. Jumped up and down! Sang halleluiah, and, carried on as though this was a major holiday. I mean that if you had been present you would have thought that these young people were just given their freedom.

Citizen Two: THE STATE! THE STATE! THE STATE! THE STATE!

Story Teller: Then someone joined in by repeating, THE REPUBLIC! THE REPUBLIC! THE REPUBLIC! A complete silence fell upon the place. Not a word was uttered for one whole year. Total silence rang upon the new landscape. Total silence! It was during this time the experiments began in telepathic sensory processes. This is where/how the prodigal prodigy discovered how he would get his "Republic." Although he didn't say it, that day was the day that brought on the silence. Everyone felt it. That's what bought on the silence. They knew it was his energy that allowed some to dare talk of a new state, a national state. A REPUBLIC!

(This—the enclosing parenthesis of this sentence—symbol represents silence. Names inside of parentheses communicate through   language telepathically.)

(Citizen Two:) THE REPUBLIC!

(Audience:) Is this language communicated through speaking telepathically, i.e., silently or is it communicated through telepathic language? Or just telepathic thought? Thoughts communicated telepathical- ly? You know what I mean. [Pause] Don't you?

(Story Teller:) Yes, I understand the question. I do not however have an answer to any, right now. Sorry 'bout that. 'Am sure that you can understand. Oh, I am not sure how two can communicate telepathically without a language, a telepathic language "spoken" in silence.

(Audience:) We understand. I understand.

(Story Teller:) What are telepathic sensory processes? Well, you just saw it at work, now. The last comment made by the New World Citizen was communicated with a telepathic language, so to speak. So, simply stated telepathic sensory process is the ability to employ direct communication with another being thus allowing brain to brain and the respective nervous systems to speak to each other. This mode of communication allows the brain to contact through its most efficient mechanism, unspoken wave transference by use of the nervous system at its core. How does it work? Each subject must align self with the object to receive communication. That alignment must allow the liquid formation that provides complementarities between the "brain" and its nervous system to reach equilibrium with a comparable mechanism in the object.

The whole process was thought to be induced by a drug they called "loco weed." You'll note I said, "Was thought." Well, was that the cause? Or, a facilitator, if you will! Or, was it not? It was not according to the latest scientific research. According to WE SCIENCE, the new found way of communicating probably occurred this way: at the same time that silence was self imposed, the congregation discovered a substance they would later identify as "loco weed." Out of the silence grew a great desire to communicate. To talk! As the desire grew, the substance became more plentiful. Finally, out of a desire to deplete the substance, which had become as plentiful as silence, the congregation began to consume it.

It was reasoned that if the congregation consumed locoweed, their silence would go away. At first, they began to chew it raw. However, the experiences were so frightening that the congregation reasoned that the best way to consume the substance was by inhaling and exhaling it as a gas. In other words, they decided to "smoke" it. That way, silence would have to compete with vapor created by their newfound substance. Silence, it was reasoned, would be consumed by vapor thus allowing the congregation to speak again. As fate would have it, as the congregation experimented with the many ways to consume locoweed, one member found herself "Talking" to her distant cousin over two hundred kilometers away. Everyone was amazed. At first, they thought it was a vision. Then she realized, otherwise.

(Inga:) Cousin Rita, is that you? If your voice were not so clear, I'd be frightened. However, when it happened, I immediately knew what it was. I quickly remembered our grandmother telling us how she and her twin sister could take to each other without making a sound, -- without movement of the lips. I knew that's what it was. Cousin Rita…

(Story Teller:) By the time Inga communicated her reaction to what she discovered, the whole congregation knew, too. They overheard. It was weird. No one knew what to do what to say. Like I said, it was weird. Silent screams were heard everywhere. It was a "Panic Attack." The congregation thought that it—the congregation, that is—was mad. At first everyone thought that Inga was mad. Then, they thought it was not her who was insane but it was they. They were crazy, stone cold crazy. No one knew how to handle this new found, UH, being able to hear each other without anyone saying anything verbally, without anyone making a sound. Something had to be done, and quickly. The prodigal prodigy knew what to do. It was simple. Everyone had to be shown what they are doing is possible. The congregation had to be shown through demonstration that they were "talking." to each other; that they were "hearing" each other, while no one said a word. Spoke a sound. Not one sound or word! Unbelievable! Simply, unbelievable!

(Prodigal Prodigy:) unbelievable! We've finally done it. This is our show of faith. Our silence has brought us this gift. Yes, my congregation, it is true. We can now talk to each other without making a sound. As much as making a sound. Can you believe? It is miracle. Yes, Faithful, it's a miracle. Now how do we know? I KNOW! AND I KNOW WHY YOU ARE HERE, TOO. Everyone came to be filled with the word. You want proof. You want verification.

(Story Teller:) The place was now near bedlam. They simply could not take it anymore. And, as soon as someone was about to…

(Prodigal Prodigy:) Don't scream! Please, don't scream. You're not mad. Did you hear me, you're not mad. You hear every word every word I say. You can hear me. Now, hear this, it is not really "hearing" we are doing, because hearing requires sound. And, we're not making sound, any sound. I am sure that you have already picked this up. I cannot explain, but somehow they have learned how to…

(Prince Mother:) Don't say it! Don't say what I think you're thinkin'…

(Prodigal Prodigy:) No! It does not seem as though we've learned how to read each other's thoughts. Not yet, anyway. You're supposed to laugh! That was a joke.

(Prince Mother:) How do we laugh?

(Prodigal Prodigy:) How did we scream silently?

(Prince Mother:) I don't know. You stopped me just as I was goin' to…

(Prodigal Prodigy:) Someone did! Who did? Who screamed?

(Story Teller:) The whole congregation had screamed the moment they felt the voice speak. Whatever! Only it wasn't a voice. It was like a voice. Strange! Gradually, two teenage girls, one fifteen, the other sixteen, came forward. Everyone looked on in wonderment.

(Prince Mother:) That's Brother Del's second daughter. But, I don't know who the other one is......They must be related. I've never seen her around here before.

(Story Teller:) The other one was the girl who caused a near panic not to happen. She's the one who spoke to her cousin Inga 2000 kilometers away. She's the one who did not panic. She avoided the panic just about everybody else fell right into. It was of epidemic proportions now. Inga, however literally stopped the screams, silent though they were. A scream is still a scream. By confirming that she heard her cousin speak, Inga forced everyone else to see that they had in fact learned a new way of communicating. It was amazing! It was the realization that the voice Inga heard was not within their immediate surroundings. That information allowed everybody to know that they had made a new discovery.

Now one could remember the screams. Oh! How they screamed. But there was a problem. Screams could not occur without noise. So they reasoned. By now, none could remember. After all, how can one scream without making noise? How does one scream without making noise? How does one scream without showing visible fear? Fear visible? So, everyone screamed, nobody heard, except those far far away. There were reports back in the old country of strange noises coming from afar. The old country people thought that this noise came from other neighboring countries, though even that idea seemed a bit UH! Strange!

Lots of gossip flowing throughout was made about the "happenings" some place else. Silent noises. Everyone heard it but no one could verify where this strange noise came from. Meanwhile back at the New World Colony Inga and her cousin, Rita, came to witness to their respective congregations simultaneously

(Prodigal Prodigy:) Are you the ones who screamed?

(Inga:) No!

(Rita:) No, I saw the message.

(Inga:) I received the message. The message cousin Rita sent. I received it. And, so did you. It was so clear you screamed. I nearly did also, then I realized that was Cousin Rita doing what our grandmother use to talk about

(Prodigal Prodigy:) What did she use to say, dear? Please, say more.

(Inga:) Well, our grandmother often talked about her twin sisters being able to "talk" to each other without making a sound, without movement of lips. I knew what it was as soon as I heard Rita. It was just a little frightening, that's all.

(Prodigal Prodigy:) What do you mean? Dear? Go on.

(Inga:) Obviously Rita wasn't at home with me. I hadn't seen her in a while. So, I knew it was she. And, at the same time, I knew she wasn't here with me.—I mean when I was at home—and, I knew I wasn't dreaming either.

(Story Teller:) Those were the thoughts that brought calm upon the congregation. Now, they knew definitely: fear of their own girl was unnecessary, totally unnecessary. The problem was how to regulate it, how to create order, how to guarantee freedom of expression, and the privacy of the individual. The individual's thought, you know what I mean.

(Prodigal Prodigy:) And, tell us, our little wonder, how do we regulate our gift?

(Congregation:) THE GIFT1 THE GIFT! THE GIFT!

(Inga:) Simply! We are never to speak or scream—out loud or in silence—again, with one exception.

(Prodigal Prodigy:) Yes, child! Go on...

(Inga:) When we give the death scream.

(Congregation:) What do we do when we?...[Speak outside the congregation.]

(Prodigal Prodigy:) We talk so everyone can hear us. We make noise. Sound. Act Normal. But the way the outsiders mean it. In the presence of others, we speak in their tongue, their language. Their voice!

(Congregation:) But Minister, I must question, who is this person who has explained our happening so clearly? And, so youthful? What is your name?

(Inga:) Inga!

(Congregation:) Inga! How did you come to know about our dilimma?

(Council Member:) Barrister-General, minister, as our Barrister-General...

(Prodigal Prodigy:) Yes, First Elder? What do you want?

(Council Member:) I strongly suggest that you as the minister of our congregation and Barrister-General stop this backwardness immediately

(Prodigal Prodigy:) I agree! Go on, Inga...

(Congregation:) Barrister-General...

(Prodigal Prodigy:) Please, inquirer we must go on. Inga as you were...

(Congregation:) Cal for the question!

(Inga:) Not even a thought is necessary. It's like everything operates according to a whole other—another—system. We talk, but it's not talking, at all. It's not even thinking, as we know it. It's scary. That's why I didn't scream.

(Congregation:) There she goes. Why is she raising the question, again?

(Inga:) You asked!

(Congregation:) Child, mind your elders.

(Inga:) Sorry! Anyway, as I was about to say. I didn't scream because I thought it would make Cousin Rita scream because I thought it would make cousin Rita scream, too.

(Story Teller:) So?

(Prodigal Prodigy:) If Cousin Rita had screamed the silence would never have lasted. The mystery would never be learned.

(Congregation:) No old country will stop our emerging order from its growth and development. We have struck our precious metal. The new order will need a complete informed citizenry.

(Prodigal Prodigy:) And, we got it. Let's not throw it away. What is the question?

(Congregation: [Singing lyrics in the style—in minor tones—of a favorite tune of the least favored people, the blacks, so named after the black king in chess. Some call the music, blues-gospel. Others call it gospel-blues, whatever..] How does an outsider know our dilemma? Yes, I want to know, also. We want to know? [Repeat]{Remain singing while Prodigal Prodigy is about to deliver a sermon on silent communication called telepathy.}

(Prodigal Prodigy:) The whole: contem-porary world knows about the silence. The point is, no one has guessed who it is, or why. I suspect that Inga got involved much later. Please, members do not torment this bright, attractive youth for bringing us the gift. Let's avoid others misfortunes. We must avoid others mistakes. Remember, we swore! We swore!

(Story Teller:) Silence was again upon the congregation.

(Prodigal Prodigy:} We don't need to return to that level of silence again. There is some place in between total silence and audible sound. It must be possible to communicate lower than a whisper.

(Inga:) …Nor for the ears to hear, or the voice to say. It cannot be spoken.

(Prodigal Prodigy:) …Even lower than a whisper.

(Inga:) Yes, it is there, we must not loose it.

(Story Teller:) As the New World Intellectuals began their research to unravel how this accident happened, it became apparent that a research institution was necessary to carry on this investigation scientifically.

(Council Member:) Barrister-General, why don't we begin to build that university we have talked about over the last ten or twelve years. Maybe a good place to start would be to start by building that institute we need so badly. The research institute might serve as the first department within the university.

(Council Member, II:) Madam Council Member, do you mean faculty? You said department, and I was wondering if you meant faculty become the first faculty of the new university.

(Prodigal Prodigy:) Whatever!

(Council Member:) I mean department. Under the new system, things are going to be better organized, better defined. We prefer the term department. This research institute will allow us to study how we have come to communicate without so much as a word. You see, if what you and the young lady said are correct, we no longer need a language to communicate. If it violates the form we know, then our knowledge of all old forms of communicating offer us no assistance in understanding how we communicate now. I say, let's erect a research department as the first academic department at our new university.

(Prodigal Prodigy:) First, we must create a university and in outward appearance, it must look like the university of the old world. They would never understand otherwise.

(Story Teller:) The congregation built it's first of many thousands of universities all across the New World. All would be devoted to the study of some aspect of knowledge of the New World Colony would be based on the prototype founded by the New World Settlers, the New Nativists. The prototype university was simply named the First University of the New World. All others were named in some way as a response to that name. All were governed according to the new traditions, the new laws governing the New World Colony officially called Fifty-plus-One. New tradition had it that all charters that did not deal with interstate activity, when passed locally, could be enforced without approval from the old country. The founding and chartering of the First University of the New World was thus, according to this understanding.

Obviously, word got back to the King-General Mathew III. Such an act was treason. So, yes, obviously it got back. That part of the reason why the prodigal prodigy returned to the old country, it's also the reason why the s talking about how the prodigal prodigy managed to arrive at the Palace just before the order could be given to arrest him. His or her concern was that since it is always considered to be in the favor of someone if he or she can appear before the King-General III before the order is given for an arrest of that person, the prodigal prodigy would get off for a sure crime against the State. This no one from the ruling circle wanted to happen. This, they were determined would not happen. Even if it meant that the King General III had to go, too.

CHAPTER 7, AGAIN

(Story Teller): Characters are speaking with voice again. This is the old country.} Oh, I'm sorry, I can speak with voice now.

Prodigal Prodigy: Sir, I understand that you want to see me?

StoryTeller: Somewhat stunned/ surprised at the unexpected appearance of the Barrister General Goraka, but not wanting to give that surprise away.

King-General Mathew III: Yes, Barrister General Goraka, what an unexpected appearance. It is like you are reading my mind, and we know that that is impossible. In any case, please explain to me what is going on. I should think that some type of explanation is in order, now. Do you not think so?

Prodigal Prodigy: Yes, of course, King General Mathew III. But, may I inquire as to what I am being asked to explain? His Majesty!

First Advisor: The King-General,. . .

King-General Mathew III: I can raise questions in my own behalf, thank you, First Advisor. Please do not interrupt.[Now facing and directed to Prodigal Prodigy] Tell us about the silence and all of those laws you've passed in your Town Council meetings. And, what is the name Fifty-plus-One suppose to mean?

Prodigal Prodigy: THE SILENCE KING GENERAL???...Was simply a fear of the unknown.

King-General Mathew III: I simply love this man's answers to my questions, then, why the missing persons, any ideas, my wayward child?

Story Teller: There is total silence over the Chamber. Everyone is present, including Parliament. Everyone is present who is important, that is. And, because of the circumstances, it is certainly important that the Parliament was invited to this gathering. Obviously the King-General Mathew III considered this point in making his decision. Of course, the landed gentry and the urban aristocracy are present, too. They had arrived days before to see the King-General Mathew III about 'related' matters.

According to the reporters, timing is perfect, a coincidence only possible at the correct moment. Though simple and seemingly insignificant, timing must be mentioned because each member present in the Chamber represents a different time. And, each believes that his/her time is the most important time in the political evolution of their story. Being at such auspicious—no, make that, suspicious! --Gathering, some members find the timing too perfect. Never has such gathering gathered together before, in these numbers, with the statute. Never, in recent times, I am speaking of. You know that the crowning of the King General Mathew III draws a like crowd. Just about, I should add, but not quite. Not even close. HA! HA! HA! Anyway, let us return to the Chamber.

Baron: Something is wrong, here, Have you noticed that every since the prodigal child, Goraka, has returned home, his appearance has always been unexpected. Then everything begins to happen differently. Something is definitely wrong.

Story Teller: Is it true? Or, is this simply the suspicious nature of all the politicos involved? Is the King-General's most important advisor once upon a time acting paranoid? Is this former advisor too cynical about everything? Maybe he is simply too skeptical about those things he does not clearly understand. After all, no matter how astute, the most candid advisor has no way of knowing, no way of comprehending what he sees, or, feels.Anyway, enough speculation, back to the real activity. Where were we? Oh yes, the question put on the floor by His Majesty, the King General Mathew III....

King-General Mathew III: I thought I told everybody that I should do all of the talking. I shall ask all of the questions. It is I who must be satisfied with the answer. Now, please answer the query on the floor my child. Where are all of the missing persons no one can account for?

Prodigal Prodigy: Now wait a minute. I cannot account for events I have no control over. All I can say, and remain truthful to His Majesty is that they must have decided to settle elsewhere. Some that is. The others must have, UH, vanished. I know that you will perhaps find that answer rather hard to believe, but it is true. I am telling you the truth.

Story Teller: The whole chamber shakes. Everybody has something to say by now, everybody, but members of the Parliament. They or I should say, it remain silent, they say nothing, absolutely nothing.

Baron: And, look at our Parliament, not one word has been uttered during the entire proceedings. AMAZING! Your Majesty, don't you find that rather odd? Not a simple word from our most verbose crowd?

Story Teller: The place shakes with laughter, as the Baron's comments seem to act as comic relief to a very tense situation.

King-General Mathew III: Yes, yes, and my moody trusted advisor, one thing at a time, however, one thing at a time. Now, back to my child, quiet everybody, quiet in the Chamber. I shall conduct this inquiry in my private chambers alone if you cannot cooperate. Is that clear? I'd like to commend our Parliament for being so cooperative....

 Now, my child, where were we? Oh yes, the silence....

Story Teller: By now, everyone is looking at each other with a question mark on their faces. What silence? Does he mean the silence of the Parliament? What exactly is he talking about?

First Advisor: NO! YOUR MAJESTY! DON'T...

King-General Mathew III: Good! Now, continue my child.

Story Teller: What to do, and, what to say? No one can or will believe his story. Besides, he swears everybody in the Chamber to secrecy, including himself.

Prodigal Prodigy: His Majesty, I can only repeat what I said earlier. The silence was brought on by our fear of the unknown. It was caused by a fear of things we had never witnessed before. That is all I can tell.

First Advisor:A!HA!AH!HA!HA! HA! His Majesty, Goraka has one everywhere, and has seen everything. Now, he claims fear of the unknown. What unknown? I suppose he'll tell us about the mysterious practices of these creatures that occupy the space they took to found the New World Colony, Fifty-plus-One. What a joke. HA!HA!HA!AH!HA!HA!AH!

Prodigal Prodigy: As a matter of fact, it was something the natives did that caused fear to be inflicted upon the New World Settlers. You see, His Majesty?

First Advisor: HA!HA!AH!HA!HA! HA!AH!HA!HA!HA!HA!HA!

Story Teller: By now, everybody is dying with laughter. People are falling all down on the floor, slapping each other on the backsides, slapping fives, and carrying on as though they are watching a comedy hour show, that is, everybody, except the Members of Parliament. They fail to see the humor.

Prodigal Prodigy: Please! Please! These have been trying times. You must show some consideration. After all,...

King-General Mathew III: SILENCE! SILENCE! I SHALL NOT REPEAT MY SELF AGAIN! IS THAT PERFECTLY CLEAR, THANK YOU! CONTINUE MY CHILD. SPEAK! SPEAK!

Prodigal Prodigy: I was about to reveal what brought on the silence, and we suspect, what caused some of the settlers to disappear, and others to settle elsewhere.

First Advisor: Did you hear that? HA! HA! HA! HA! AH! AH! HA! Watch him lie, right through his teeth.

Prodigy Prodigy: I heard that remark.

King-General Mathew III: FIRST ADVISOR, ONE MORE WARNING..

Prodigal Prodigy: Thank You.

King-General Mathew III: Continue my child.

Story Teller: The story that unfolds is fascinating. The important thing is, however, it is believable. After he thinks about it, he said that he might as well have told the truth. They would not have believed him anyway. For the moment, the story he weaves will suffice. It is believable for the moment. What makes it so fascinating is how poetically he weaves fact with myth to build his fantasy. In other words, what makes the prodigal prodigy so believable is his ability to tell stories. By the time he has finished, the prodigal prodigy has recreated the horrible "witches trials" more like burning, with a new twist.

Prodigal Prodigy: Well, you see His Majesty, on the last night of this ritual a faceless creature appears out of nowhere and begin to sing this song,

Nigga Dred: Every time it rains,

There's dryness inside of me.

Deep-seated guilt is everywhere.

Trouble rests just over the horizon.

Guilt covers our land.

Chorus: We are faceless creatures,

Who will our sun god more?

We faceless creatures,

Who will our sun god no more?

Prodigal Prodigy: Of course, the settlers take that to mean a bad omen. All of sudden, the festive occasion becomes quiet and somber. People begin to drift away, one by one. Then we receive word that one followed by three then five, etc, etc., of our settlers are missing. Every time one of our settlers is found missing, one of the native creatures is also missing. Always the same. Then we panic, yes we did,-- finally, I get everybody to calm down, and organize a group of armed settlers to confront the natives. They get word we are coming to attack, and all hell breaks loose. We suffer heavy casualties. Nine-tenths of the whole New World Colony is wiped out. All dead.

First Advisor: And, what about your enemy creatures?

Prodigal Prodigy: They were wiped out

King-General Mathew III: I suppose you mean destroyed.

Prodigal Prodigy: Excuse me sir, I mean destroyed.

First Advisor: Wiped out! Have you ever heard that before, Your Majesty? I suppose by that he means the slate was wiped clean. No more native creatures to occupy the New-Found-Land. In effect, all potential opposition was removed by the song and dance of a faceless creature one can never verify ever existed.

Story Teller: The question is, did it work? The prodigal prodigy is very gifted at improvising. And, today he is at his best. Even the skeptical first advisor do not laugh when he asked the last question. But, the King-General Mathew III is not fooled as his rhetorical question indicates.

King-General Mathew III: So, my prodigal prodigy, what is a just reward for a cutthroat, silence?

Story Teller: Everyone is caught by surprise. No one expects the King-General Mathew III to be so blunt, at least, not so soon. As a matter of fact, the prodigal prodigy had to do a straight act to recover. The first thing he makes sure not to do is to clear his throat even though it needed clearing for different reasons. You see, the prodigal prodigy has developed a sinus congestion problem. So, at the most in opportune time he needs to clear his throat. Rather than do so, and appear as though he is hiding something, he selects to do otherwise. To do so, meant he has to appear as though nothing is wrong. The thing is how to do it? Then, it comes to him.

Prodigal Prodigy: As I said, His majesty it was fear. And, out of fear, temporary insanity set in. I don't really know when it happened. It happened so fast. Everything was over so quickly, not one reasonable being had any opportunity to act. Everything happened in a flash. Then, there was a long moment of darkness. At that point, the congregation must have suffered a panic attack. It was probably during the time of darkness that all of the UH! Errors were made.

King-General Mathew III: Errors?

Prodigal Prodigy: The silence, His majesty

King-General Mathew III: Silence? Errors? What in the King's name are you talking about? Are you trying to imply that the silence was the result of a mistake? What kind of mistake? Going mad and the massacre of all those—what do you call them? Native Creatures? Is that what I am to believe brought the silence on? What were you, in mourning?

First Advisor: The Cut Throats, Your Majesty. How did the settlers get their throats cut, by the native creatures?

King-General Mathew III: Yes, Mr. Barrister-General Goraka, how did? How exactly did the settlers die?

Prodigal Prodigy: Many died with their throats cut, sir. Others died from...

First Advisor: Never mind the others. Tell us about those who died with their throats...

King-General Mathew III: ...wide open. Was it true? Who were the suspects, and how were they punished?

First Advisor: NATIVES CREATURES!

King-General Mathew III: Are you saying that the Native Creatures committed the wicked crimes?

Baron: Your Majesty, the documents speak of how the native creatures helped the new settlers to survive, showed how to plant and graze. Why would they want to help you to survive then destroy you? Were they, too, mad?

King-General Mathew III: Mr. Barrister-General Goraka, what creatures would teach you how to survive only to take that life from you later on?

Baron: Maybe he had too much freedom, too much freedom to experiment with those new faulting ideas floating out there in the new urban classes.

King-General Mathew III:--Yes! You were granted complete freedom, were you not? You were given a buyers contract; I believe you merchants call it.

Prodigal Prodigy: No different than any of the other contracts of incorporation issued at the time. Everyone had at least the freedom to determine how their society should look. How it should be ordered, so to speak. As a matter of fact, His Highness, we had more restrictions placed on us than anywhere else.

Baron: He means about the slaves, Your Majesty.

Kings-General Mathew III: What about the slaves?

Baron: They couldn't have slaves in the New World Colony. Remember, Your Majesty. That was your idea.

King-General Mathew III: That was only a period of...

Second Advisor: ....No Your Majesty that was removed at your request.

King-General Mathew III: By whom?

Baron: Your Majesty, mind me, we don't get side tracked. Can't we address that later?

King-General Mathew III: Yes, you are right. Thank you!

Prodigal Prodigy: There's no need.

King-General Mathew III: What was that?

Prodigal Prodigy: I said, there's no need to address the slavery question later. Your First Advisor withdrew the timetable. His rationale was, and I quote, "Since you want to experiment Mr. Barrister-General, why don't you start from the ground up? Why don't we simply delete the whole section on slavery? No slaves will be permitted in the New World Colony. That way, you can start fresh, from the beginning. Start from scratch. You know, Old Scratch, as you would say, unimpeded."

[Pause] Obviously, we are placed at a considerable disadvantage.

King-General Mathew III: Is that true?

First Advisor: Your Majesty, I only did that to save the Empire. Your Rule was my only concern.

King-General Mathew III: Yes, but in the process, we have one less ally.

Prodigal Prodigy: No His Kinship. The New Settler Colony would never betray His Trust. We are still Loyal Subjects of His Majesty, the King-General Mathew III. God Save The King!

Baron: Then, where does the name, Fifty-plus-One emanate?

Prodigal Prodigy: It's simply a nickname.

King-General Mathew III: Nickname? What is a nickname? My, how you do amaze me with your ability to concoct these new words. What are you doing, making a new language?

Story Teller: Little does he know? That's hitting the nail on the head.

Prodigal Prodigy: A nickname is a name people prefer to call someone or something or someplace. You remember the places we call by other names. That does not mean that that is their real name. It's simply what we choose to call them. Fifty-plus-One is the same thing. No different.

King-General Mathew III: Yes, of course, very good.

Baron: Sure! So, Fifty-plus-One is simply a nickname. And, it was nicknamed Fifty-plus-One because its Founders believed that one day all of the New World Colony would be governed as one.

King-General Mathew III: Is this your dream, my prodigal child? Do you want to build your own empire? Excuse me, civilazation? Is that your dream?

First Advisor: From North to South. From East to West.

Prodigal Prodigy: That is a thought, now that you mention it His Kindness. However, I must admit, it is not one we have discussed.

Baron: Sure! So, Fifty-plus-One is simply a nickname.

Prodigal Prodigy: Fifty-plus-One is the nickname we have for our New World Colony because everyone got tired of calling it New World Colony.

King-General Mathew III: Why Fifty-plus-One?

Prodigal Prodigy: Because fifty members of our original colony of fifty thousand survived the trip, and one died after we arrived.

First Advisor: That should be Fifty -minus-One. Or, better still, Forty-Nine, if one died. That seems logical to use your term. Wouldn't you agree?

Prodigal Prodigy: No! She was there but in spirit. You know what I mean? She became our reason to be, to go on. She really held on in spite of the odds. Everybody was moved.

First Advisor: To do what?

King-General Mathew III: Create a new civilization.

Story Teller: Although you will not see it in print because this machine disallows it, Goraka uses the "i" rather than "I." His preference as a way of passive resistance to the old country's rigid use of language.

Prodigal Prodigy: No. No. His Majesty! We want to create an extension of our land, our culture, our language, and our heritage. It's simply that in the New World, things are different. You know what I mean. You don't know?

Second Advisor: How different?

Story Teller: As the night had gotten late, and the King-General Mathew III needed to confer with His Advisors, as well as members from the Ruling Circle and the Parliament, the prodigal prodigy was returned to his quarters within the Palace. Being so tired, although the prodigal prodigy had been offered the comforts of a companion, he went right off to sleep after being bathed and oiled by a masseur. No sooner had the prodigal prodigy fallen asleep than he began to dream about his first encounter with the King-General Mathew II. So caught up in his dream, at some point he leaves his dream process and enters reality: the moment acts as the bridge between the two processes. The two are operating simultaneously and in complementarities. This means the interaction between dream and consciousness is Omni-present. Such a process is taxing to the psychic, especially the psychic of these beings of consciousness.

Chapter 9

Story Teller: The encounter with King-General Mathew II is Dream Time.

Prodigal Prodigy: Oh, Lord, you sent us into the chaos of activity while you retired to the inner sanctum of Her Womb. You told us that we are two, that you are, too. Which is true? Are we one? Are we, two, too?

King-General Mathew II: You know the rules, my child. Every third child of the reigning king-general must leave at age seven to begin anew. You are required to formulate and construct your own empire.

Baron: I do not follow you my Lord.

King-General Mathew II: Civilization! My prodigal prodigy doesn't want an empire in the sense that we think of empires. No, he wants a UH! Tell them what you want, my child. Go ahead, tell them.

Prodigal Prodigy: I have decided to build a New World from Old Scratch.

King-General Mathew II: Say it louder. No one can hear you.

Prodigal Prodigy: I have decided to build a New World from Old Scratch, from the ground up.

First Advisor: HA!HA!HA! Me Lord's child decided to go out and build himself some pyramids.

Prodigal Prodigy: No! They will not be pyramids. They will have tall buildings, with live creatures living and working inside. These buildings will be as tall as technology will allow.

Story Teller: For the first time, the Parliament moves forward in their seats with a desire to hear. Everyone wants to hear about this plan to build a new world with tall buildings that are not pyramids in the honour of the dead.

Prodigal Prodigy: There will be time vessels that move about the stars.

Story Teller: Of course, everyone begins to laugh. At first, shyly, then with real robust, and finally derisively, HA! HA!HA!HA!AH!HA!

First Advisor: HA!AH!AH!HA! Your Majesty, Your prodigal child is going to destroy our empire. He will bring about ruin and shame. He's mad!

Prodigal Prodigy: Ruin? Shame? Mad? All of you have seen the vessel I arrived in. You saw it destructive capabilities.... That is just the beginning.

Second Advisor: He works for the Devil.

Prodigal Prodigy: I work for myself! [As he turns toward the Parliament he surprises everyone with] TO THE NEW CLASS! [Parliament brakes out in pandemonium. Yells and cat calls can be heard everywhere. They begin to dance in the isle, sing, and laugh. The whole place is in an up roar.]

Parliament: THE NEW CLASS! THE NEW CLASS! THE NEW CLASS!

First Advisor: Your Majesty, we should arrest these conspirators. They are going to cause a revolution some day, if we don't stop them.

King-General Mathew III: My First Council, most favored, can't you see? He said what they want to hear; we can't fight then, and win. They control the wealth, the industry, and the land. We are simply figureheads. What a joke. HA!HA!HA!HA! WE GIVE THEM PRESTIGE. THEY GIVE US MONEY AND WEAPONS!

First Advisor: Your Majesty, they take what belongs to the Empire as private property that belongs to themselves. They are thieves. Nothing' but thieves! All of 'em, yell, and scream and carry on. UH! I just hate those sleazy bastards.

King-General Mathew II: Most favored, does that include my son?

Story Teller: For thousands of eons the old country has willingly given the lives of their children in mortal combat for the privilege of being declared a child of the Monarch; regions outside of Sha Sha Faso, that is. The inhabitants of Sha Sha Faso have long considered the contest too cruel and too uncivilized, so they, being learners of jurisprudence, opted not to participate. As it turns out the Kinshasha people do not participate because a godchild never came from their region, anyway. It is always the Northern Regions that provide the best seventeen year olds for mortal combat. Therefore, when the Sha Sha Faso name appeared next on the list, everyone laughed. "What a joke," everyone thought. So when the Sha Sha Faso Council asked for an audience with the King-General Mathew II, he was advised ahead of time as to what to do.

First Advisor: They do not know how to play the game fairly. They expand upon the rules.

Second Advisor: Yes, that is right, The King-General Mathew II will do well not to select any one from Sha Sha Faso. They only provide good legal advice, those Kin Sha Shas. They are too over built for combat.

King-General Mathew II: Nor for leading an Empire.

Second Advisor: Yes, you are right Your Highness.

Story Teller: As I said, the Kin Sha Shas were not well thought of as a breed that could produce warriors.

King-Generals Mathew II: They, in turn, decided to use their talents in jurisprudence to engage in the kind of combat advantageous to them. They began by having the Barrister-General speak first.

Prince-Mother: King-General, we request that you allow a very unusual thing to happen.

King-General Mathew II: And, what might that be?

Prince-Mother: The Council of the Kin Sha Shas request that you accept its rather unusual decision as to how we should conduct the contest.

King-General Mathew II: Contest? What contest?

Prince-Mother: We request that you change the rules of contest?

King-General Mathew II: What was that, no mortal combat? So, how is my third child to be chosen?

Prince-Mother: The Council of the Kin Sha Shas request that the child we have selected be sent out in to the Real World to bring back new ideas and gifts of advancement from afar. He shall be required to exist on his own part from us, and without our support.

Council Member: Yes, His Kinship, we thought that since it takes three generations of intense instruction to produce a King-General. If Your New Son survives in the Real World, HE should be more than prepared to assume HIS new post when you are no longer with us. We are simply attempting to expedite the matter, it is your will.

Prince-Mother: Also, all of the fears that everyone has about the ability of the Kin Sha Shas to Rule an Empire can be tested.

Council Member: We thought this would be more than a fair test, His Kindness.

King-General Mathew II: And, whom have ou chosen for this experiment of yours?

Prince-Mother: MY SON, YOUR MAJESTY.

Council Member: It was unanimous. All was one. One was all...

King-General Mathew II: Of course! First Council, what do you make of this newfound scream? My, my, the Kin Sha Sha never cease to amaze me, what will they think of next?

First Advisor: I think it is a trick, Hour Highness. Beware of the Kin Sha Shas.

King-General Mathew II: Yes, but you must admit that this is not a bad idea. Times are changing. And, you must tell me more than I should not trust them. Beware of what?

Second Advisor: Their entrepreneurial schemes. They are always trying to realize a profit, at any cost. Just look how they are willing to sacrifice the Barrister -General's child.

Citizen Greer: Mind you, I know she's is doing it out of necessity, the only way we thought that we might, that the only way we might convince you of our total belief in the idea and the process. Not because we are sleazy and conniving cowards.

[Ignoring Citizen Greer's defense]

First Advisor: HUH! Yes sure, I don't trust them.

[Continuing, Citizen Greer...]

Citizen Greer: ...not because as you say, "we are sleazy and conniving cowards."

[Complete negation of Citizen Greer]

King-General Mathew II: Whom do you trust, First Advisor?

First Advisor: I simply don't trust anyone from Sha Sha Faso. They are into too many deals and other to weird things for me. Who would have ever thought..?

King-General Mathew II: ...Of a prodigal prodigy? That's what he'll be, if he lives.

Second Advisor: If he lives.

Council Member: If not, banishment to another world is what we request.

King-General Mathew II: nd, if he succeeds?

Council Member: Grant him what he requests, what ever it may be.

Story Teller: The Chamber shakes with amazement. Everyone is stunned. Only the Kin Sha Sha people from Sha Sha Faso dare to talk to the King-General Mathew II in that manner. And, they are hated for it. But, the King-General Mathew II always tolerates their unusualness. Some say that if it were not for the King-General II, the Kin Sha Sha people would be dead. Extinct! And, as a reward, they say, the King-General must watch them embarrass and insult Him frequently.

After the prodigal prodigy was granted the King-General's permission to embark on his conquest, the Kin Sha Sha people disappeared permanently. However, according to custom, no one is allowed to occupy that land until the original inhabitants are either contacted or relinquish title. So the land has remained vacant now, nobody knows low long.

Rumor has it that their "main" enemies, the Akuyu people, exterminated the Kin Sha Sha people of Sha Sha Faso. No one can verify that allegation, however because not one trace of anyone having lived there can be found. Not one trace. Legend has it that the Kin Sha Sha people—what or whom ever they were—were sent out of the old country because the population was dying out. You see, the games were devastating to the male population. It was the Kin Sha Sha dying, so they stopped the killing.

After they left, the killing stopped because the games were declared illegal. No more games, no more killing.... Not quite! The energy was directed elsewhere, outside. So, the Great Bear, the Great Wolf and the Great Elephant came within the death throws of the Empire. The Great Lion was felled, too. So was the Great Whale.

So, the legend of how the Kin Sha Sha people stopped the killing, then disappeared, after putting up their most favored child to waywardness rather than put all of their off spring through the cruelty that lay ahead, i.e., they did not want to watch their seventeen year olds die in combat until one was chosen as the god-child of the King-General. Now, legend has it that the prodigal prodigy does not exist, that he cannot be found any where, that no one can find traces of the Prince-Mother and the Barrister General any where, and that the Kin Sha Sha never existed.

How can that be? The prodigal Prodigy has been reported everywhere, but no one can find him anywhere. Occasionally, there was talk of an elderly woman being seen with a handsome young man, but no one has been able to verify his where a bouts until today.

{Please recall all of the above was in dreamtime now we have the transition between dreamtime and reality in the present. Also, the tendency of the old country was to allow for a continuum of the monarch in that the replacement was seen as a continuation of the ones who followed before therefore there was no need to act like there was a break in the chain. This means that the new monarch was addressed it was he or she was the person who made the original decision. That decision may have been arrived at generation eons ago. Following that tradition, the present monarch was treated as though he or she has ruled forever, that that king-general had ruled all the time. Thus it was not out of character or sink for the king-general to ask,}

King-General Mathew III: Who is the elderly woman?

Prodigal-Prodigy: My mothe

King-General Mathew III: Your mother? How could that be?

Prodigal Prodigy: She is a disguiser. She uses various disguises.

King-General Mathew III: What happened to the Kin Sha Sha people?

Prodigal Prodigy: They now occupy the New World Colony, Fifty-plus-One. I am the Barrister-General. My mother is Barrister-General, Emeritus.

King -General Mathew III: How?

Prodigal Prodigy: We travelled from empire to empire, until we discovered....

Second Advisor: They learned to fly

King-General Mathew III: What was that? No one except birds and spirits can fly. Do you also claim to be a spirit, a god? My, my, what is it you have not accomplished, my way ward child?

Prodigal Prodigy: No!! I am not a god, a spirit, or a representation of our ancestors, His Fun ness. As a matter of fact, I've come to believe there are no gods, except the ones we create.

{Audience is stunned, Ahhhhhhhh. Goraka did not say that!}

Story Teller: The moment the prodigal prodigy makes his declaration of independence with, a there is no god thesis, the whole place signs with disbelief. Some hold their heads down in shame. The prodigal prodigy stands and looks, as though to say, "what is the problem did I say something wrong?" What he gets for an answer is....

Second Advisor: ...He flies Your Majesty, yet he claims no equality with the gods and spirits. Instead, he negates their existence. I wonder, does that apply to the Supreme, OLODUMARE, The Creator?

Prodigal Prodigy: [Pissed! With cynicism!] If you insist. [Piss ass!!]

Story Teller: The place is busy with conversation, as each tries to tell the other what he or she has just heard. Total disbelief is registered on everybody's face. No one has ever heard any one talk like that before. Just the idea is difficult to comprehend. That alone with what he said is almost too much.

The fact that he would make such a statement was unbelievable. The fact that he said it in public and for the King-General Mathew III to hear was beyond discussion. No one could believe it. Not even the King-General Mathew III, or, should I say, and most of all, the King-General Mathew III.

King-General III: If you insist? Did I hear you correctly, my child? "If you insist?" Am I missing something here, child? Is there some point to this discussion?

Prodigal Prodigy: Did I hear a bit of authority, my Great Father? Am I considered out of order, rude?

King-General Mathew III: You know, my child, I get the distinct impression that you are teasing us? It is simply a joke to you. What gives you to such foolishness? I'd like to know. What possesses you, my child?

Second Advisor: He is possessed by Evil thought and an avarice mind.

King-General Mathew III: SPEAK, MY CHILD! SPEAK!

Prodigal Prodigy: I find your logic so fascinating, if you get my meaning. It's like thousands of years out of the lost future. I find your questioning full of evil. If not in deed, in intent.

King-General Mathew III: Do not get too carried away, my child. I am still the King-General Mathew III. You still have to report to me. Now about this "Lost Future?" I have not understood a word you have said, my child, so far. It is as though you are saying the words we use but they do not mean the same thing currently.

Like words that do not sound the same, coming from you. They do not mean the same, coming from you. It is as though I am looking at the future standing right in front of me. I feel as though I have entered another world totally lost.

Story Teller: PHEW!

Prodigal Prodigy: Disrespectful, or, bright? This is knowledgeable!

Second Advisor: This is a cunning, arrogant, deceiving, demonic plague standing before us.

Prodigal Prodigy: And, just what have I done to deserve such libel? I've only returned out of a desire to bring you up to date.

Second Advisor: Bring us up to date about what? Why? How? How do you bring us up to date?

Prodigal Prodigy: [Amazed at such an uniformed group of leaders and advisors...] ...What we've done as the New World Colony, so far.

Count: And, just how did you know that we wanted a report, right now?

Baron: Yes, especially since the correspondence never had a chance to reach you....

Prodigal Prodigy: It's simply a coincidence, nothing but a coincidence.

Count: Then explain how you know to return to the capital?

Prodigal Prodigy: Where else would I go? I simply calculated that you should be ready too raise what ever questions you might have about the documents I have left in the care of the King-General Mathew III: So, I returned

Baron: Right on time. I could not have timed it better myself

King-General Mathew III: What questions would you raise after reading your documents for the first time? I must add, they are very well put together, and coded. We might learn much from the system you have employed here, very impressive. Our Parliament might gain a great deal by studying your system.........that is why you have come back, is it not, my child?

Story Teller: Up to this point, the Members of Parliament have managed to remain quiet and attentive --- except for that brief surprise. Now, one member decides to speak. Of course, everybody is listening

MP-1: His Majesty, Her Majesties son, does this mean that you are going to share those documents with this legislative body?

King-General Mathew III: IN DUE TIME! IN DUE TIME!

StoryTeller: MP-1 EMBARRASSED, INSULTED, AND NOT SATISFIED WITH HOW KING-GENERAL HAS HANDLED THE LAST INQUIRY, MP-1 CONTINUES HIS STATEMENT.

MP-1: THOSE DOCUMENTS RIGHTFULLY BELONG TO TO/IN PARLIAMENT...

[All of the Members of Parliament give out loud grunts so as to emphasize

{Not at all disturbed by the "Show of Force" by Parliament, the King-General Mathew III repeats His statement another way.}

King-General Mathew III: You shall receive every opportunity.

MP-1: In due time.

Second Advisor: Your Excellency, aren't they going a bit too far? After all....

Story Teller: There is never so such tension in the air before underneath so much silence. No one has dared to question the King-General Mathew III like that before...

Second Advisor:. . . How does Goraka receive such special treatment?...

Story Teller: . .He has always been in charge. This is always His Day. But, that is not all. Parliament is still steaming over the continued insults directed toward their section of the Chamber by the King-General's Advisors. They shall see. Things will be different in the future. Is that not what the prodigal prodigy has shown them? Despite all attempts to discredit Him?

King-General Mathew III: I can handle these things my worthy advisors. The question is not out of order. Although I do not like the way it was asked. I do not share your concern. Now, back to my question to you my wayward fellow. What would you do having read your document for the first time.

MP-1: [Loud and forceful] I must object your Lordship! None of us has had an opportunity to examine the documents in question.

[Ignoring a Member of Parliament as though she is not there, has not said a word; Goraka's attention is directed solely and totally at the King-General Mathew III.]

Prodigal Prodigy: Well, sir, obviously the answer I give depends on the documents I have read and what areas I might not fully understand.

First Advisor: [Loud and forceful] Stop all of that jawboning and lollygag. Talk. Stop trying to confuse the issue. Answer the question.

Prodigal Prodigy: [To First Advisor] I am answering the question, but, if you want an answer in relationship to what kinds of questions you might ask, I would raise some definite questions regarding what you have in your possession

King-General Mathew III: What questions?

Prodigal Prodigy: Oh, like who granted us the authority to initiate and pass laws on territory that does not legally belong to the King-General Mathew III? But first, I would like to examine the original charter to see if the authority is contained there too.

Baron: And, what if you were not satisfied that such authority was given?

King-General Mathew III: Please, please. I must ask you again to hold down the commentary. I must conduct this hearing.

Prodigal Prodigy: [Ignoring the King-General] Oh? I cannot allow you to make such an allegation without a challenge. Authority was granted in the original charter to do exactly what we have done. Read the charter! It's in the contract. It's all-legal. We have not violated any code of conduct, or Common Practices Acceptable to the King-General Mathew III.

Story Teller: By now, the Members of Parliament are furious. Not once has Goraka looked to them for support, or even bothered to address them in any way. How foolish, they think. Protocol is one thing, rejection is another. Does he not know all the things that Parliament has accomplished since he and his clan left decades ago? Is he not aware of all the laws they have passed granting basically the same types of things to the old country? Does he not know that they are responsible for him being present? After all, it is Parliament that has demanded the prodigal prodigy receive a fair hearing. It is Parliament that has made it possible for a new world colony to exist.

MP-1: And, this is his thanks! Ghees, thanks, Goraka.   Thanks a lot. [Jack ass dune!]

Story Teller: In fact, the prodigal prodigy and Parliament were natural allies. Instead, they were treated as non-entities. They did not exist. So, he did not know that the King-General could not help him.

Leader of the Opposition: [He whispers to his neighbor.] The New World Colony will need venture capital to develop, and there is only one place with kind of liquid assets. Parliament better still, the Members of Parliament who represent the new capital formations taking place in the old country. So, I guess we might say that for all practical purposes, the King-General Mathew III god home is an illusion, a mind-set, a symbol, an artefact: the kingdom is dead. The kingdom is dead.

Prodigal Prodigy: [He hears the comment. Very loudly he said,] live the King-General Mathew III, ruler of the empire for Life. Long lives our Divine Ruler.

King-General Mathew III: Now those words are very clear to me. Every time there's flattery, I understand you clearly. When your New World Colony is discussed, however, I fail to understand a word you say. Why, my child

Second Advisor: He has a way with words

King-General Mathew III: I should say, go ahead, my child. Tell me how that is. When you flatter me, you words are as clear as the sun shinning on a clear day, but when you tell me about your home, your words become cloudy as on a foggy day. Why is that, my child?

Prodigal Prodigy: I cannot explain His Lordship. Maybe it is because you can invision what I am talking about when I mention you, but cannot when I discuss some far away place like the New World Colony. [Pause] Why don't I do this, His Grace? I'll take Neptune back with me to the New World Colony, and he can bring home a personal report.

First Advisor: Your Lordship how does this foreigner know who you have selected to visit our colonies? No one knows this but us. My Lord, he should not be allowed to leave the Palace Grounds until this matter had been settled. And, ...

MP-1: Your Majesty, we, Members of Parliament, reserve the right to question Mr Barrister-General at another time, and in another venue. That is our privilege.

King-General Mathew III: Don't worry about questioning Mr. Barrister-General I am still in charge of this Kingdom.

MP-1: Your Majesty, we, Members of Parliament, do not question him staying here, we simply want to make it known that we need to question our guest at another time and location. We do agree that he should remain in the old country, however, with free movement as long as he does not try to board his vessel.

King-General Mathew III: So it shall be done. Neptune shall leave immediately for the New World Colony and the Barrister-General Goraka will remain here with me. Or at one of my palaces.

MP-1: No movement shall be permitted, your majesty?

King-General Mathew III: Yes! Movement shall be permitted.

Second Advisor: But, your Lordship!

King-General Mathew III: But, only within the confines of the Parliament.

CHAPTER 10

Story Teller: It is not difficult for this prodigal prodigy to see what has happened. Members of Parliament had won a victory without firing one simple word. All they wanted was access, and now they had it. They sat, never interrupted the King General, raised only procedural questions, and still ended up with the prize. But, are they in any position to understand what they have won? That we do not know. What we do know is this; Parliament convinced the King General that they ought to send their own representative to visit the New World Colony.

The person have chosen to represent parliament is the noted Parliamentarian and new jurist scholar, Manila. Manila is not only considered brilliant, she also possesses a charisma that is hard to ignore. She is just the person to counteract Neptune who is an objective, but loyal follower of the King General. Now, two of the most brilliant politicians will have access to Fifty-plus-one for the first time. The first lesson learned is in the politics of travel, i.e., the only way they can get to this New World Colony is by a vessel provided by the Barrister General. The whole matter took longer than expected because until this vessel is shown, no one believed that the old country vessels owned by a local merchant are capable of making the journey. The real surprise comes when everyone finds out how long it will take to get there. In the process, it is discovered that none besides the New World crew know how to read the log on how to make the journey. They also discover that no one in the old country had any way to determine how the vessel is supposed to move. As to what it cost to build such a vessel, they have not the faintest idea. But these are trivial points because no one believes it will move, let alone fly.

King General Matthew III: My Astute Advisor was right, I suppose.

Prodigal Prodigy: Yes, he was correct!

Story Teller: The astute advisor the king General is referring to is the one who initially theorized that the prodigal prodigy knew how to fly. His only problem was, he had no way of verifying his theory. So, everyone laughed, but not any more. No, not any more. It is truly unbelievable who this person is. Is he really a person? Who is he? A god dressed up like a man? No one human can accomplish so much in so little time. Impossible! Simply unbelievable! This can not possibly be the child wonder of the Kinshasa people. He was dead. They were jurists. Jurists could not have possibly produced this unusual creature that calls himself a person, too. What ever happened to them anyway? I know that a few remained, scattered throughout the countryside, and the Empire at large, but now we discover that are the New World Settlers, also.

Leader of the Opposition: The Kinshasa people are the representative new class. They are the ones responsible for the new whatchacallit, Fifty-plus-One. What is their aim for coming back here? Especially if what they have looks just like what the new class is doing in the country? If that's what they have, they did not have to go away for that. So, why are they here? It has to be more than that, but, what?

Story Teller: The capital city has never seen so much activity in its many eons of existence. The streets—so to speak—are buzzing with activity and conversation. Traffic is operating at a virtual standstill. No rooms are available for out of town visitors who got there too late. Everybody some body is trying to get an audience with the King General. No one is successful. King General remains unavailable to everyone. The most of the most favored are completely ignored. Those who occupy the original position have spoken.

King General Mathew III: No visitors.

Story Teller: His Majesty is unavailable, that means everybody somebody talking to everybody somebody about everybody somebody. They are all nobody, now. Even to them. They now know how the least favored feel. For a moment, that is. Nobody knows what is going on. Those who do, are not talking to anybody, somebody or otherwise. What we see operating is PURE SPECULATION. So, nobody knows what is going on than 'those in the know.' You know, like 'I know. 'Yea, like 'I know, too.'

In the meantime, Parliament is sequestered until Manila and Neptune return home. Everybody expect a long journey, a long visit, and a long inquest. This allows, members to send messages back and forth that are meaningless and without foundation. Some Members even complain of being under a virtual house arrest. The protest mounts as the constituents and families pressure the King General to break the siege on Capital City. This opposition makes the King General even more determined. He becomes very angry at Parliament. He feels—and rightfully so, of course—that Parliament is exploiting the situation, thus deceiving their constituents.

   Everyone within Capital City knows that the Members are having the best time of their lives. Many are partying every night, getting up late the next day and missing the roll call, although Parliament is not in session. It is the point of it, the citizens thought. And they let this criticism become public information for all of the citizens to see. Hardly anyone pays this critique any attention. It is treated as passé. For the King General it is treason. The countryside thought that a Civil War is in order, so they collected their rations, weapons, ammunition and march off to war, so to speak. The fire works begin when King General sets up a hearing to expose the grievances the citizens have against Parliament. This notion is strongly and vehemently opposed by the most of the most favored.

Duke: The least favored should not have been invited to this hearing of King General. It was a mistake. Only His loyal supporters should have been there.

Count: That is how I feel, also. I do not agree with this hearing. But, it is too late, now. However!

Baron: Aren't you being a bit unrealistic? King General had no choice. Didn't you hear Hum? Things have changed. Can't you tell? Any of you?

Count: Then what are we suppose to do?

Duke: Wait! Simply wait!

Story Teller: We all know how that works. Intrigue and deception runs rampant. King General Matthew III is nearly assassinated six times that we know of. His name becomes 'nine' lives after the last attempt failed. They mean it. There's no way he's suppose to survive the last attempt. NO WAY! Somehow He survives although He losses one of His most trusted Advisors. Rumor has it that……

Chapter 11

Story Teller: Only the miracle of modern technology saved Neptune from becoming a casualty of the journey. A journey it was. An indescribable journey. The only way to understand what happened is to have experienced it, and that's impossible. Neptune may never recover, completely. It was exceedingly too much for him. He saw it, but could not believe what he saw. 'It just did not make sense. 'It did not may any sense,' he kept thinking. Then, after a while, he fell into a kind of confusing confusion. 'He,' what's the old saying, 'didn't know whether to wind his ass or scratch his watch.' Neptune was lost clearly lost. Being lost was fascinating and frightening. Yet, surprisingly, on the surface, he kept his cool. The way he did it was too keep asking questions such as, 'how did you do that?' And. 'what was that we just saw?'

Aero Guide: How do I do what? What was what?

Neptune: Make all of the imaginary things appear? Ho do you do that?

Aero Guide: All of those things you see, or saw, are real. None of this you see is imaginary unless, you question our reality, too. Everything you've seen is real. Every sound you've heard is real when we complete the journey, twenty-six million real.

Neptune: HUH?

Story Teller: The thing that did it was the last statement, accentuated by one million years of radiation showers that occurred within a flash. Can you imagine? A Big Bang! Out of nowhere, just like that, and without any warning white light, and continuous bombardment of the psychic with indescribable pain followed by nothing. Pure Dee nothing! Finally, there was a passage, a creation, a-rev-solution, and presto, the New World Colony all in a matter of mini-secs, at most, 10secs. Without a doubt that was beyond anything Neptune could fathom let alone comprehend, without faith, that is. Complete faith.

Neptune: Yes! God, I   Believe! I Believe! I Believe! I....

Story Teller: It all had to be done within the time span, I am told, or we would perish. However, to allow Neptune and Manila to see the voyage, time was slowed down, but, only within their minds. This process allowed them to see what others dared not look at. Neptune and Manila saw what no homo sapiens had ever seen. Would they tell antibody? Would you? Before swearing before the god forces, Neptune went between the inquisition and plague, the Holy Wars backwards, the early empires, prehistory, no history as though he was riding on a wing. The huge animals he saw get larger and larger as man became smaller and smaller were unbelievably slow as they moved along in reverse while they devoured their prey. Then without warning, there was a big explosion that drew the vessel into it at an unspecified velocity that made us feel as though we were not moving. Neptune thought that he was in Lucifer's Heaven. Anyway you stretch it that means Hell for you people. Of course, Neptune panicked. He literally flipped out.

Neptune: I'm in hell! I'm in hell. I don't wanna go to hell, please? Please! Please! Please! Save me! Save.....

Story Teller: Manila immediately slapped Neptune across the face. Neptune started to go into shock. Out of nowhere, the bio technicians appeared and corrected the matter quickly by touching him on the bottom of his foot. I cannot remember which one. In any case, as easily as Neptune had flipped out, he was well again. Something was different. Now all Neptune talked about was repenting and seeing the Lord. Neptune expressed that he had been born again. And, he was right, but not the way he thought. Neptune had no way of comprehending what he had passed through.

Twenty-six million years on the other side of the world is hard to comprehend by just about anyone. To expect to see living creatures in this new world is even more incomprehensible. But, to see living creatures that look like you and talk like you --, just about! -- On the other side of your world is a bit too much. I'm sure you can see why he went crazy, even if it were just for a moment. When Neptune and Manila landed on the other side -- as the New Worlders called it—they had entered a world that was considerable different from anything they could envision in their utopias. None of Neptune's models approached what he saw. That coerced Neptune to believe that he was now in God's heaven. Manila looked on in disbelief.

Manila: Where'd they choose this fool? Dumb clut

Story Teller: Well, obviously Manila was a bit harsh on Neptune, Manila could never have possibly understood what he felt or saw. What Neptune saw was the burning of the old country, how it looked before the fire, and all of the other reminisces brought to mind. So profound was this experience, Neptune regressed into a past that allowed him to see the Old Country appear again in the future, but who were these people? They were people weren't they? They certainly appeared to be.

Neptune: My child, no one would ever believe what we've just experienced.

Manila: Yes, I know. Thought we had lost you for a second, there.

Neptune: You did. You did, my child. I was in Hell for a moment. I never want to experience that again. Never!

Manila: It was a fantasy.... The change was too drastic. You failed to adjust in time. You moved beyond your mind for a moment, there.

Neptune: But, --then I saw light again, and I know that I was being tested on my way to Heaven. Everything was so beautiful a changing. I guess we had to pass all of those places to get to the New World Colony. The prodigal prodigy was exactly right. We never would have found the place

Manila: So, why bother to come back?

Neptune: What, my child?

Manila: Why would the Barrister General return to the old country? We would never have arrived here. They are civilizations beyond us.

Story Teller: It's true. There's no way anyone from the old country might have landed on the New World, except the same way the prodigal prodigy discovered this New World Colony, by accident. However, unless one was extremely venturesome, the likelihood of it happening was virtually nil. So, why bother to return? What's the point? Glory? Power? Wealth? What was the necessity for a Barrister General living in another time space to return to his old time and place? Why go to the trouble? Risking lives, to return through millions of years, our time, to a time and space that people would never comprehend what had transpired on any comprehensible level, except belief? Oh, sure, obviously later on someone—as a matter of fact a whole body of scholar scientists—would speculate about the possibility of such a happening, but during the time under discussion here, this happening was utterly impossible, so, why, to make a scientific point, a neurotic joke on fate, to save people kind, like in general? To show that if you know a complementary law to the one you are operating within, you may crossover to the other worlds and live? To see if their wave becomes the particle becomes the wave once the unity and particular of the force field is understood? Yes, that is why. It is believed, but, why all the way into another Earth Life Epoch? All the way back to the original position by passing through a new life epoch seems almost like choosing to play a game with a toy you've just learned to operate. You, know, like uh, let's see, why don't I try to arrive in 1984, C.E.? Yea, that seems like a good idea. No one could be that far gone. No, something more important to the future is about to happen. What other reasons could the prodigal prodigy claim at this point? What other rationale would there be to give? What other claim could one make?

CHAPTER 12

Story Teller: since the prodigal prodigy had nothing but time on his hands, what do you suppose he did? He got special permission to invite the lost scholar to the Palace. Reason given? To finish reading documents brought to him by lost scholar. Finding the story too hard to believe, the King-General Mathew III had the lost scholar invited to the Palace to see these documents himself, first hand. After finding out what these documents were about, the King-General thought that the whole Court should be invited to hear the prodigal prodigy read his translation of this document entitled The New Native.

Of course, queries were raised about the prodigal prodigy being the only one capable of translating this document. After every linguist of the old country and there a bouts had tried and failed, it was conceded that the prodigal prodigy could continue to fulfill his charge. Then, one idiot blotted out....

Idiot: How do we know if he's telling the truth? Ho do we know he's not simply making up what he says as he goes along?

Story Teller: No one saw the necessity to respond to this wild out burst, because every one knew that none of them could understand a word, not even one character.

Doubter: So, why make a fool out of one's self by asking such a question? You know how some of us are.

Idiot: Well, say what you may, but you never can tell about these matters. You never can tell, besides, it's my right to ask if I want to.

Story Teller; In the meantime, the prodigal prodigy looked on in amusement. He was amazed that so much time could be wasted on such trivial issues while lives were at stake.

Idiot: Wait now that wasn't me there with the last statement. Who said that?

King-General Mathew III: Was that you prodigal child. Who said that? What was the meaning?

Prodigal Prodigy: Yes, His Lordship. I was simply stating a fact. May I go one with the reading?

King-General Mathew III: Yes, of course. We'll discuss this other matter later

Chapter 13

Story Teller: At first, no one paid it any attention. As a matter of fact, it went on for quite some time before any one really noticed. Then by coincidence, one of the overseers was reported missing and within a matter of traveling time the whole country heard about it. But, what was it? Why were so many people missing lately? Who was responsible?

New First Advisor: I think that the Barrister-General Goraka has something to do with it.

King-General Mathew III: Impossible, my child. He's right here with someone observing him all the time.

Story Teller: You know when you are right about something, but because you are still unable to correctly identify what it is everybody thinks you are crazy? Well, that's how the New 1st Advisor felt after the King-General Mathew III gave his response. The New 1st Advisor's new job was not easy, now that he had finally received the recognition he rightfully deserved.

[Get the point?]

It was very difficult to follow in the footprints of the First Advisor, as the New 1st Advisor began to learn. After all, the First advisor had been with the King-General Mathew III from the time His Reign began. And, that was along time ago. Believe me. So, the New 1st advisor devoted his spare time trying to figure out how to get the King-General to have confidence in his advice. In the meantime, on arrival in the New World Colony, Fifty-plus-One, Neptune speaks,

Neptune: Civilizations beyond us? You blasphemous agrarian class bitch. This is heaven. And, I am alive. HA!HA!HA!AH!HA! I know I'm alive because I see you. HA!HA!HA! You little fool.

Manila: Me? In heaven with Neptune? HA!HA!HA!AH!AH!HA!HA! That doesn't hardly sound like Neptune's Rational Logic. HA!HA!HA!HA!

Story Teller: After Manila made her blasphemous statement; Neptune became puzzled because nothing happened to her after she spoke. He immediately went into a depression of faith.

Manila: Neptune, please, we did not come all the way here for you to think you're in heaven. What happened to you? My you look old. How dare you call me dirty names, you old bastard prartz?

Story Teller: Neptune immediately regenerated himself upon hearing this very negative picture recited to him by a teenage prodigy. Neptune always took pride in his appearance. He was a very distinguished looking philosopher of impeccable authority. Neptune was editor of the Learned Society Journal a very old and prestigious journal of interdisciplinary studies. So, nothing made Neptune more determined than when someone told him that he was looking his age. Somehow, at age 375 old country time (OCT), Neptune would within a single day make you forget a comment you made the day before. Also, at age 375 OCT, he was actually older than the New World Colony by over one hundred and fifty years OCT and older in New World Time (NWT) than the New World Colony, also. Still Manila could not keep from showing her admiration at how he literally transformed himself.

Manila: You know if you gave up all of your old fashion notions, you would probably be able to carry a great deal of information back to your King-General Mathew III.

Story Teller: Neptune despised Manila for the frankness and her refusal to call the king-general her monarch. Oh, I forgot to tell you. Manila is 15 OCT. She represents the university students in Parliament. Her brilliance seems to know no bounds, "leave no bounds" Neptune always retorts. Twice when Manila made statements, she has been right. And, Neptune is no old fool. He can count very well so without a question, he dropped all of his old country ways.

Manila: I'm...

Neptune: No comment. No comment my dear comrade child.

Story Teller: Manila obeyed without comment or the slightest hesitation or sign of resentment. Neptune was completely thrown by this unusual sign of obedience, After all, she had slapped him, cursed him out, laughed at him, and then without hesitation, Manila obeyed Neptune. Neptune did not really know what to do at this point so he looked out though the screen for the first time since he overcame his depression. Everyone in the Capitol District of Fifty-plus-One was informed that the Barrister-General Goraka had returned from the old country, possibly with visitors. The body had gathered to welcome everyone. Only the new visitors were present, however. The Barrister-General was nowhere to be found. The most immediate thing that the new visitors felt was the silence. It was deafening. Neither Neptune nor Manila was prepared for it, that silent noise. Neptune immediately forgot his promise to discard all of his old notions and requested to be returned to the old country. Neither noticed that there was no official to greet them and take them to the official house so that their credentials may be inspected and verified. They were supposed to be there on official business, however.

Neptune: In the name of the King-General Mathew III, I request that you return my cohort and me to our place of origin safely immediately.

Manila: Speak for your self old man, I'm staying. We have official business to take care of.

Story Teller: The welcoming crown began to applaud in support of Manila. Neptune felt like a coward and a fool. Manila realized that everyone heard their conversation, so she inquired,

Manila: Is here no privacy here? And, where are we exactly, anyway?

Soweto: You are in the New World Colony. We call it Fifty-plus-One.

Manila: Yes, I've heard the story from the Barrister-General Goraka of your newfound land. That is why we are here. Who's in charge? We must meet with them. Who is you chief executive officer?

Saweto: Where is the Barrister-General? Why is he not with you?

Manila: He is our guest while we pay an on sight visit to his new home place.

Saweto: I am the spokes voice. You may address me for all your inquiries

Manila: Are you in charge? Who is the deputy here? Who is in..?

Saweto: I am the one --- the only one—you may address all of your inquiries to. I am here to serve you. Every thing you require is at your disposal. All you need is to say so.

Manila: You do not seem to understand, this is an official visit. I want to speak to who ever are in charge. I would appreciate that. Thank you.

Saweto: That is impossible, as you would say. We have no such person. No one person here is so vested. You must make all inquiries through me, sorry.

Manila: And, who are you?

Saweto: I am Saweto.

Manila: I am Manila, Member of Parliament, an Official Representative of that August Body. My cowardly associate over there is Neptune. He represents the King-General Mathew III.

Saweto: Yes, we know.

Manila: What do you know? How can you know before we have told you? This was a secret mission. No one from here was to know that we were coming. Who are you people anyway? You don't sound or look like us. Who are you? You are not from the old country, are you?

Story Teller: Any explanation now, thought Saweto, was simply too soon. They need time.

Saweto: Please let me begin tomorrow by taking you on a historical tour. We shall begin there. That seems like the wisest thing to do. Do you agree?

Manila: What kind of, never mind. I don't know anything about this place anyway, so, I might as well start some place. O.K. Tomorrow.

Saweto: Tomorrow.

Story Teller: With nothing else to do but see the sights, Manila and Neptune went along with the program and enjoyed the wonders they had never before seen. Things they really could not imagine, let alone understand. [Pause] The following day Manila's first question was,...

Manila: Why is your city so quiet? It's even quieter than it is at home on a late Sunday night. Yet, your city is active all the time. No one ever seems to sleep. How is that?

Story Teller: Knowing that this question most certainly would be asked, and also that the city had changed so radically that not even the prodigal prodigy would recognize it; Saweto gave what became a standard response.

Saweto: I don't know! I guess maybe because we live here and never think about it that way. Also, as I am sure you saw, the city is large. We have over thirty-five million people here, you know. We are active all the time. No one ever seems to sleep.

Manila: I'm sure you saw. You said, "I" sure. Anyway, I understand. And, what is the name of your city. What do you call this place?

Saweto: Capital District 17.

Manila: Yes, I know.

Saweto: You do? How?

Manila: Well, I don't mean I know its name. What is its name? You know what I mean. Every place has a name. What is it?

Saweto: Yes, you are correct. We call it Capital District 17. This is our name for our...

Manila: Metropolis. King-General Mathew III metropolis

Saweto: Yes, exactly! Capital District 17 houses the local governmental beau racy and political offices.

Manila: What do the numbers mean?

Soweto: That makes it easy to identify when exactly where is.

Manila: Wha… Excuse me, what did you say? Would you repeat that, again? I seem to get lost when you speak. I must pay closer attention

Saweto: It makes it easy to identify when where is.

Story Teller: Neptune, who has recovered, except for the spacey feeling he projects, becomes more attentive as he looks into the yonder. Frankly, he is trying to figure out what the hell Saweto is talking about. He wonders, "Did he say what I thought I heard?" while constantly looking away from Saweto. Neptune figures that if he looks away from Saweto, constantly, he'll relax. There's something about Saweto Neptune wants to study. The time does not seem right, however. So, he simply listens. Besides, Manila has some interesting questions she's raising anyway.

Manila: What? I don't understand you. You talk like us, sort of, but I don't understand the words you use, the way you use your words. Everything seems different. Why so?

Saweto: You see, when we are at this time, we are in this space.

Story Teller: As Saweto spoke, he pointed to a "map" suspended in space after appearing out of nowhere. Manila and Neptune were amazed at the appearance of this "map" but Manila did not let on that she has never seen such occurrences before. By now, she was aware that Saweto did not know nor understood that they could never hope to figure out most of what he was talking about, thus, as if nothing was wrong, she inquired...

Manila: ...And, in what time and space do we presently exist?

Saweto: The time is Century 21 A.D The space is Fifty-plus-One, Capital District 17.

Manila: Century 21, A. D. After Death

Saweto: No! Century 21, A. D. means Another Dimension. You see we are twenty-six million years on the other side of where you originated. As the guardians of the word "silence" have told us, the only way we can make contact with our past is to move ahead in time rapidly. It is now possible for our society to continue forever.

Manila: How long is forever

Saweto: It never ends.

Manila: Is that possible?

Saweto: As long as we observe certain basic principles.

Manila: Prin-ci-ples? WHAT PRINCIPLES?

Saweto: We take as given the idea of distinction and the idea of indication. In order to make an indication we must first make a distinction. We take therefore the idea of distinction for the form. Applying this tool, we transformed into antimatter while we were going through the radiation showers then back into matter again once the stream was passed.

Manila: So, what are principles?

Saweto: Those are simply laws we must follow if we want to transform one process into another. We take as given the idea of distinction and the idea of indication. That in order to give an indication we must first make a distinction. We take therefore the form of distinction for the form.

Manila: You mean like the middle class is doing with the King-General Mathew III?

Saweto: How do you mean?

Manila: You know? The way Parliament is set up to make the laws that were once made by the King-General Mathew III. Isn't that transformation? Of some sort?

Saweto: Yes, I suppose, but only after you have completely assumed total authority of all relations can you say that a transformation has occurred.

Manila: If we are 26 million years on the other side of where you are, why is it only Century 21? Why not millennia 26,000,000? Or...

Saweto: I see what you mean. Well, in a way the number is arbitrary. It really has no relation to how far we are from you. Or, what time/space this is.

Manila: Oh! How was it decided?

Saweto: Well, we decided to number our civilization from the time we landed on these shores, that was...

Manila: 21 centuries ago, but how can that be when you say that...

Saweto: ...We are 26 million years on the other side of where you came from?

Manila: Yes!

Saweto: Those are two separate space-times. In fact, the new world civilization is only...

Manila: ...21 centuries old, but its 26 million years some place else. So, why does it appear as though it only took a few days to reach here?

Saweto: ...Because of how you traveled through time. f you had only traveled the distance you think the New World Colony is from the old country, you never would have reached here.

Manila: Not in a million years.

Saweto: Precisely!

Manila: Then, how fast did we?...

Saweto: Beyond anything you can imagine.

Manila: How fast?

Saweto: More than twenty-six million miles a frame

Manila: Twenty-six million miles a what?

Saweto: "Frame."...

Manila: What's a frame?

Saweto: Less than a second. An example is light travels at about one hundred and eighty-six thousands miles per second. The vessel you were traveling in moved faster than light.

Manila: Faster than light? Faster than light? Impossible! Nothing is faster than light. That should make you go backwards. HUH? Say, how do you know all this?

Neptune: Incredible! Incredible! Simply incredible!

Saweto: Because of science we have discovered with the technology we invented.

Manila: Technology?

Sewato: All of the things you see around you, that's technology transforming nature to allow nature to offer people the real value of its gifts.

Manila: How does this technology work?

Saweto: That depends!

Manila: On what?

Saweto: On what it is? Living quarters are made one way out of one type of technology, while working space is made another way out of another type of technology. So, it depends.

Manila: What about the vessel that brought us here? What?...

Saweto: HA!HA!HA!HAHA!

Story Teller: The laugh of Saweto was very unusual. Obviously, he did not laugh a lot. Matter of fact, he laughed as though this was the first time he had had the occasion to.

Saweto: That was not; well I guess you might call it that for now. Yes, let's call it a vessel, very original. That "vessel," as you call it operates according to our laws of time-space. In other words, the time period you are in creates your space. Here, it could not be otherwise. Whereas in the old country, you operate according to the laws relevant to your time-space and this is where we hook up. Is that not how you say it?

Manila: No! We'd say, it's here we meet up. Whatever!

Saweto: [Thinking to himself] (Hum, what period was that quoted from?)

Manila: I beg you pardon?

Saweto: I didn't say anything! (Did she hear me thinking?)

Story Teller: Saweto was caught totally by surprise. But so was Manila. If Saweto had not said anything when Manila questioned what he had said, she might have thought that she really did not hear anything. This brief dialogue caught Neptune's attention, because he heard it too. Neptune however was still in a daze, so he thought nothing of it until Manila raised questions. Then he perked up. Maybe, he was not crazy after all. Just by chance, I caught Neptune giving Manila a "What?" look on his face.

Manila: Oh! I'm sorry. I thought you were trying to say something, or, figure something out.

Saweto: I was, but I didn't say anything. (Darn, how does she know that?)

Manila: Know what?

Story Teller: Neptune looked at Manila then Saweto. Neptune was very perplexed. Saweto and Manila were total question marks for him, then Saweto commented,…

Saweto: I did not know that you knew how to hear our silence.

Manila: Did I read your thoughts? Is that what I did?

Saweto: You can read our sublevel frequencies…. So accustomed to no one being able to hear us from your world, I did not realize your heritage was Kin-Sha-Sha.

Story Teller: Neptune now looked at Manila in utter amazement. Now Neptune knew what he could not stand about this little twerp. "She is a Kin-Sha-Sha" is what went through Neptune's mind, but he didn't speak, yet.

Neptune:" Yes that's it. A KIN-SHA-SHA! I thought that the prodigal prodigy was lying when he told that story.

Manila: Kin-Sha-Sha? I thought they were just legend, stories. I never knew what they looked like.

Story Teller: So Manila found out that she did not know her linage. She also did not know that she was chosen by Parliament because of her alleged heritage. To Manila, she was a member of the New Classes evolving in the old country. To Parliament she might be a long shot. Manila might be one of the remaining…

    Interesting, because no one from Parliament ever dared say so. Beside, it was outlawed to ever, use the name Kin-Sha-Sha after they disappeared. Those who remained assimilated or were banished. Some were even slaughtered. The myth was no one knew that or where they were banished. I find that hard to believe. The more likely possibility is, no one cared, and was therefore surprised when the Barrister-General appeared at the Palace gates. I think that it never dawned on the Ruling Circle that Kin-Sha-Sha people might survive. Seems dumb to you? Well, this was all new to the people from the old country. They were bound to make mistake, even the King-General Mathew III, Himself.

Saweto: They look like you, they look like me.

Manila: WAW! I'm a Kin-Sha-Sha! WAW!

Story Teller: Now, that's treason. Clear and simple this is treason back in the old country. No one was allowed to use the name "Kin-Sha-Sha." But, in Fifty-plus-One they're in control.

Saweto: The only way we can tell is by constantly lowering the frequency. You are our first Kin-Sha-Sha to arrive from the old country. Every one else…

Manila: EVERYONE???? WHAT, EVERY ONE? I THOUGH?…

Story Teller: Neptune raised the identical question. He continued to say nothing, and interestingly enough they ignored him. Not in a rebellious kind of way, but as teenagers who had become so interested in their conversation that they simply forgot that he was there.

Suddenly, Manila surprised Neptune by looking his way. She immediately caught his eyes staring at her. She disarmed him so quickly that Neptune attacked with uncontrolled anger. For the first time, Manila was frightened. Saweto saw the fear, and challenged Neptune. Manila restrained Saweto. Within an instant, Council of Judges appeared out of nowhere: the New World Colony had a law, justice immediately, or set the accused free. Reason for hearing, local jurisdiction required all persons who attacked anyone else out of anger to be tried immediately.

Judges: [In unison.} What precipitated the attack?

Saweto: I was angry. I was simply defending Manila.

Manila: I became frightened for a moment, and, I guess....

Judges: What was that Ms. M.P. ? How was that Mr. M.P.?

Manila: I caught Neptune staring at me. As he approached me with anger as though he was about strike me, I got frightened for a moment. I guess Saweto must sense what happened because as soon as the fear rose within me, Saweto sprung into action. Amazing!

Judges: "Amazing how Saweto must have read my fear," is that what you're saying?

Manila: Yes! [Manila could not help smiling at the thought.]

Story Teller: At this point, it was too much for Neptune, he found himself saying,...

Neptune: Is all of this supposed to be some kind of drama or something? Whose in charge here? I want to see who's in charge.

Judges: We are in charge, at the moment, and we can assure you, this is no drama. We are here to see that justice is served. What are the charges?

Neptune: Well, I, Neptune, am the "Official Representative of the King-General Mathew III. I should think as Official Rep....

Judges..."preventative of the King-General Mathew III, I ought to be afforded some protocol?" Is this your next point?

Neptune: [Surprised at how easily they finished his sentence.] Yes, Exactly!

[Neptune acts as though nothing is unusual about what just happened. He still wants to know how they do it.]

Judges: You are being afforded the same courtesy all citizens of Fifty-one Plus are afforded. Consider yourself fortunate. An alleged crime has just been committed. We are here to sit in judgment, to interpret the law. There is no other protocol necessary in this preceding.

Neptune: Then, demand that Saweto—what ever 'is name is—be punished for assault and battery.

Judges: What is the nature of your complaint? What is the alleged crime?

Neptune: I was simply standing listening to Saweto—what's 'is name—tell our Distinguished Member of Parliament all of these fairy tales when suddenly without provocation, I was attacked by that young thug over there.

Judges: But, Saweto maintains that you frightened Manila in your launch to attack her, and that he came to her rescue.

Neptune: That's a lie. I never came near that young twerp. And, why would you believe them, these youngsters over me, an elder?

Judges: Yes, our only role here is to collect the facts. Somehow we get the impression that you would like for us to play another role.

Neptune: I only expect you to afford me—us!-- the privilege we deserve as representatives of the old country. We expect diplomatic privilege.

Judges: We thought that you were receiving such treatment. Sewato have you been remiss in your responsibility?

Neptune: No! That is not what I am referring to...

Judges: Then, we are confused....

Neptune: I mean [pause] when do we speak to your Deputy Barrister-General. We are here on Official Business at the request of...

Judges: The King-General Mathew III and the Parliament. Yes, you said that already. So, what is the nature of your problem?

Neptune: We haven't seen anyone in authority, yet. When do we see..?

Judges: CALM! CALM! It is not necessary for you to become excited. You might place too much stress on yourself. After all...

Neptune: After all? After all, what? I AM NOT CONFUSED!!!

Judges: Good! May we then get back to the preceding, thank you. Now!...

Neptune:....Wait a minute....

Judges: What is the problem, now?

Neptune: You have not addressed my concerns. I shall go on until you do. I do not have to be a party to this illegal gathering.

Judges: To what? This preceding is within the legal codes of this jurisdiction. According to our codes, everyone within our jurisdiction will receive the same respect be they citizen or visitor. If you have problems with this preceding, please be advised that you may call upon the Court of Appeals. But, only after you have exhausted all recourse, and the Court has ruled against you may you appeal.

Neptune: I don't give a damn about your preceding. Simply put, Saweto is a thug who should be in jail. So, put him there, and be done with it. Then, take me to your Deputy Barrister-General. My, god! I don't believe...

Judges: We are sorry. That is not possible. Do you want to press charges or drop this matter?

Manila: I suggest that we drop it because no harm was done.

Judges: Is it true? Was no harm done to Neptune?

Neptune: If you mean did he actually strike me, then the answer is no, but still he should be punished, on G.P.

Judges: CASE CLOSED! COURT ADJOURNED.

Story Teller: As soon as the Council of Judges were satisfied that the matter at hand was taken care of, they disappeared I suppose to another location to sit in judgment over some other matter in dispute. Now. What about the matter official representative of the King-General Mathew III, one from the mother country at that? I am sure that this will be reported when Neptune returns to the old country. Somehow, I do not get the impression that the people of Fifty-plus-One really care. At least it appears that way, to me that is. However, I am only the storyteller. My role in this activity is unimportant, except to report what I see and hear. Back to the point, did you see how they acted when they were told that the prodigal prodigy was not with the visiting party? Hardly any concern, can you believe? Can you imagine? What is going on. I thought he was the Barrister-General.

But, how did a colony become more advanced than its mother country in such a short span of time? And, what is this about living twenty-six million eons, or years, excuse me, apart from the old country? Are they real? I mean, come on, now. Give me a break. I am sure that someone can come up with a better line than that. The fact of the matter is, such a line is unnecessary. What do they have to gain? Or hide? Or, is this a joke designed to throw everybody off. They seem to be deliberately making their visitors angry. As an example, was it necessary for Saweto to attack Neptune? I mean virtually attack him. Of course that is not what he did. He did not attack him. He only made him back off of Manila. And, was that treason what Manila did? She does not seem to understand the serious nature of the matter. Someone more qualified, more experienced should have come, don't you agree? Audience, I am speaking to you. Manila has already forgotten her loyalty and they haven't been in the New World Colony a day yet. How does she expect to represent the old country?

Chapter 14

[Back in the Old Country. This reporter has placed Caps on "O" and "C" out of respect for the name Old Country]

Reporter on the scene: "I wonder what has happened to them?" has become a rather common question around the Old Country's Capital City of late. Everyone expected the trip to be long, but it has been quite a number of years. Just about eight years to be exact. And, because Neptune and Manila have not returned home, things have begun to heat up. Rumor has it that either the Duke, or the Count, or the Baron is responsible for a move to try the Barrister-General for High Treason.

The prodigal prodigy is actually afraid for a moment, just a moment. After all, he is the ultimate gambler. He bet that he could make the trip back to the Old Country before he died. That trip has taken 12 years non-stop. He never wants to make the trip again. So, this is to be his last trip before he returns to Fifty-plus-One to govern his congregation. The trip back is literally in no time, so, that is okay. He just had to make the trip back once, and it was worth the long voyage. Yet, nobody in the old country still has any idea why their prodigal child returned? Especially, if his New World Colony looks any way like he has shown us on this visual. It is an amazing contraption, almost real. But, why leave heaven? That's what everybody keeps asking. So, by now the "Readings" being shown all over the countryside, are the topics of discussion everywhere. Everybody keeps saying that he's really not telling us about where he came from, and that Lost Scholar is not even real, that he is one the Barrister-General's flunkies. As the reporter, I have no opinion.

Funny thing, nobody has bothered to mention that they did not have any visuals available to them before the prodigal prodigy arrived. Everybody acts as though they have had them all the time. So, the criticism deals only with those areas in which they fear or revere him, never about the new technology he brought back with him. No one would believe that just a few shorts years ago; hardly anyone from the old country had traveled more than twenty-five or forty kilometers away from their homes. Today, they can go virtually anywhere, except to Fifty-plus-One. So, most everybody is angry.

Obviously, no one realizes that the trip back for Neptune and Manila will take 8 years [which feel like 12 in relative time because of all the stops for this and that] and they may not return if they don't leave virtually as soon as they arrive. But, that's impossible!! What would they learn? Regardless of the time it takes, Neptune and Manila must be expected to stay as long as it takes. They must be able to bring back a complete report. That will take time. I would think.

What ever! The natives are restless because they have no way of communicating with their representatives who went to the New World Colony. Finally, the Barrister-General is summoned to appear at the Court, but not to read from this mysterious and esoteric book of ancient times.

King-General Mathew III: My child, we have not heard a word from Neptune as of yet, can you tell us why?

Member of Parliament, Forest State: And, MP Manila, don't forget about Manila.

King-General Mathew III: Yes, of course. In any case, we must communicate with Neptune and what's her name, Manila, immediately. I'm sure you understand the urgency of the situation, and will assist us in these matters of grave times.

Barrister-General: By all means, His Highness. As soon as you are ready. However, I can make no promises. The distance is very long and tricky. We must be at the right place at the right time.

King-General Mathew III: We should be ready within the moment.

Barrister-General Goraka: But, I must warn you. We still need to put in another system. That is, if we want to reach the New World Colony. Otherwise, you must send a currier. The problem with that is, you have no way of knowing if the currier ever arrived. We must install our new communications processes as quickly as our skills will allow us. In the meantime, let's send your curriers on their way.

King-General Mathew III: How long will it take?

Barrister-General Goraka: Round trip? At least, 16 to 20 years, relative time, sir.

New 1st Advisor: 16 years, as much as 20 years, maybe? Relative time? Your Majesty, we must. Pardon me! Your Majesty, we must make a decision soon. The provinces are beginning to wonder.

King-General Mathew III: You know, my New 1st Advisor, I think I know why I give the impression of ignoring you when you make a statement....

New 1st Advisor:...Yes? What is it, Your Majesty? I am here to serve...

King-General Mathew III: But, whom? Whom do you serve, my New 1st Advisor?

New 1st Advisor: You, you, Your Majesty. Of course! I have worked long hours for this moment, this privilege. If you mean about the "WE," I really meant WE in the Royal sense. The King-General Mathew III represents ALL of His Kingdom. He is WE. YOU ARE HE!

King-General Mathew III: Cut out the nonsense. The place is in near rebellion. You told me that only a short while ago. Beside, no one has used the Royal WE in so long, now, that it seems our-of-place.

New 1st Advisor: I'm sorry! Your Majesty, I thought that you did not hear me. So, you will decide?

King-General Mathew III: Decide what? What is there to decide?

New 1st Advisor: Your Majesty, I am sure you have heard that the prodigal prodigy is being called a traitor and a secessionist. Those are very serious allegations.

King-General Mathew III: And, what do I decide based on what? We have no evidence.

New 1st Advisor: We have what he brought here. That is enough by Your Wise Council. It is unanimous! All was one. One was all.

King-General Mathew III: I am still the King-General. The one and only. I still decide. And, the Barrister-General said that these were local matters only, that these decisions have no application outside of their jurisdiction, and I happen to agree. If that is so, then although we may not like what they have, we are not privy to go in and declare them null and void. That would be unwise. I am sure that everyone remembers the Preamble of Parliament. Interesting how self-serving all of a sudden, right Mr. Parliamentarian?

How self-serving to call upon the King-General to unite what all of you want to control. BUT! Until you assassinate me, I make all final decisions about everything. That includes your soul! And, don't you forget it. DID YOU HEAR ME????????

New 1st Advisor: Yes, Your Majesty!!!

Barrister-General Goraka: OH! SHIT!

Story Teller: No one can say that all the parties involved in the coming intrigue did not try. All tried in one-way or another to communicate. Each employed the procedure unique to its position within the hierarchy. That was the problem. By now, each position was so rigid that although the procedure was correct, the results were disastrous, a total disaster. It really did not matter that everyone wanted to cooperate. I mean that sincerely. Everyone sincerely tried and did cooperate, i.e., everyone did operate within the bounds of the law. Order was maintained. Strained but maintained. In the end, it really did not matter. The King-General Mathew III had to go, if the Monarchy was going to be saved. Otherwise, the Republicans were going to assume total control. That meant revolution. None of the aristocracy could afford a revolution on their hands. There were already hocked up to their estates in debt. The middle classes already control most of their assets. With a revolution, they would control their names, too. Their names were all they had left, and their names and titles would go over to the upper middle class if there were a revolution. So, as I said, the King-General Mathew III had to go

Baron: [The monarchist] The King-General must reassert the Divine Rule over His Kingdom Empire.

Duke: [The loyalist] I think it is time that the King-General should demand greater loyalty to the Crown.

Story Teller: Interesting, Baron did not mentioned His name. Nor the Duke. Interesting!

Count: [The Fascist] We need more law and order. Petty crimes are on the rise. This scum are becoming a menace. We must exterminate them. Stray Dogs. Kacha Roaches.

Member of Parliament Waun: [The Democrat] We need more liberty for our growing citizenry. More human rights practice.

Jurist Julia: [The Constitutionalist] We must be bound by the constitution of laws not men, especially men.

Sir Knight Kelley: [Reactionary, Protector of the Status quo] These new classes are trying to destroy our old way of life.

General Raul: [Counter-Revolutionist] we must destroy the Revolution, down with Parliament. We need a strong authority. Someone who can lead us.

Member of Parliament Tousal: [Republican Nationalist] LONG LIVE THE REPUBLIC. DOWN WITH THE KING-GENERALSHIP!

Story Teller: With that statement, the shit hit the fan, as they say out in the street. Every known weapon to people was brought out of the cellars and basements and caves and ground. These weapons were immediately put to use to kill the opposition. The opposition was the one who was holding the opposing weapon at the time he or she was killed. People were being killed with weapons no one had ever heard of before today. What kind, you say? I'd really prefer not to mention the things that were used, that were employed. You know how it is when you have a family affair for a war, no one offers mercy. What's the old saying? Some things are better left unsaid? You know what I mean, as for you freaks, in your imagination, I'm sure that you can concoct some death machinery as grotesque as that used in the Civil War of the Old Country.

Peasants died by the billions as many were slaughtered simply because they were peons in bondage on the oppositions land, many of them, that is. Others died as soldiers in the armies of those who slaughtered the peons. These peons slaughtered the other peons. As one slaughtered the other, each died namelessly. Those who lived became urban dwellers that learned how to survive through"black" markets of their wits. The rest became wage earners who toiled everyday just as they did out in the rural areas of the old country while toiling on the farm estates. After a while, someone began to notice that there were more people missing than the war could account for. Where were they, and, why so many missing?

Hold on a second, we are moving ahead of ourselves. We've gotten ahead of ourselves.

On the third day, it was obvious that the Civil War was going to last a bit longer than anyone expected, so they thought. As things turned out, the New Class Revolutionists were much better organized than anticipated by the King-General's Elite Forces. Matters were aggravated when the Monarchist surprised everyone by attempting a coup d' eater. That effort failed and divided the King-General's natural allies. That left him dependent on none other than the commercial sector and the conservative members of Parliament. Only the entrepreneurs who served in Parliament were in a position to allocate funds for new weapons the King-General needed to put down His Rebellion. So, things might work out for King-General Mathew III, after all.

With the advise of the Council of Advisors, the King-General conducted an induction ceremony. The purpose was to admit the old established commercial strata of the middle class into the official Order of the Court. They would become Upper Middle Class, just one step below the Upper Class rank they aspired too. By keeping their "middle" class status, they could continue to seek election to Parliament as members of the property owning convenience class and build the economy so badly needed at this juncture. By receiving their new titles they were now official members of the King-General Mathew III's court with rank and title. Obviously, loyalty was the price and it would cost the King-General mightily.

To say the least, that induction ceremony was unprecedented. Everybody was offended. The middle classes were offended because, how could one of their class allies and members betray them by leaving their ranks just when they could make the difference? The Forces of the King-General were angry because they thought that he had betrayed them again just when His most trusted supporters were questioning His Leadership. So everybody had a reason to be angry with the King-General Mathew III. They knew that the old linage system was forever, yet, surprisingly, nobody had a better idea of how to handle the situation if "you were the King-General Mathew III."

By now, matters had changed. Things were different. The King-General Mathew III's life as well as His Thrown was at stake. As a matter of fact, the Monarchy was threatened to be toppled. The Monarchists were working with the New Middle Class to overthrow the King-General because for the Monarchists He had no right to admit new members to the Court without their advice and consent. And for the middle class Democrats and Republicans, he would be overthrown, period. There should not even be a monarchy, again, period.

With knowledge that the New World Colony was in fact a state unto itself, the middle classes considered the King-General Mathew III a traitor. To which the Barrister-General always asked how is that? Of course, no answer was forth coming because he too was a traitor. This, the Barrister-General also found unbelievable. How could class siblings be enemies against the same cause each was fighting for? After thinking about it a bit, I am sure you'll agree that eventually the King-General and the conservative entrepreneurial strata would find it beneficial to hook up together. But, one would never have thought so soon. Too soon for the reactionaries.

Duke: TRAITOR! TRAITOR! TRAITOR!

Story Teller: Yes, but whom, for whom? The reactions it's looked on as by standards. It seemed like a joke to them. Had they not been the first to claim that the King-General Mathew III was guilty of sins against the state, so, why now.

Republican: Yea man, as far as I'm conceded, let the suckers fight it out among themselves. Both of them are the same. Who ever rules, it will still be oppression, and the violation of our liberty. They can kill each…

Story Teller: And, that's exactly what they did. When the King-General Mathew III knighted the Merchants of Foreign Trade, he declared war on His Old Guard. He had learned that the merchants were a very dangerous crew who would go all out to win a war where their interests were threatened. The Monarchists and Loyalists did not stand a chance. There was no match for the merchants of war. And, by now, the merchants of war controlled the warfare going on within the old country. Everybody who wanted weapons had to see one of the weapons merchants. Now that was their time to declare war, they would show no mercy.

If you have an enemy, destroy that enemy totally. That is the creed they fought by. Or, should I say, had their mercenaries fight by. The merchants did not actually fight wars themselves, even when they were officially at war with an enemy. This was an innovation over how the old country Monarchy fought its wars. Also, once you became the allies of these middle class entrepreneurs, they taught you all of the skills that once destroyed you amazing creatures these entrepreneurs who call themselves manufacturers. Amazing creatures! According to the representatives of their offspring, their godchildren, they would be even more amazing. Here's how one explained it.

Radon: When you are within the throws of the Devil's reach, you felt like a tick has set upon you. If the tick is persistent and has her way, you will eventually find yourself succumbing to the will of the tick, your Devil.… Eventually you succumb to the ways of the tick…Then, you to become the Devil, the tick.

Story Teller: GOTCHA! That was the point outlined by the theorists of the new revolution now brewing among the new class intellectuals and their teeming black market allies. These were to become the new masters of intrigue and counter-deception. For many, this was to be a game of wit. Others thought of it as a struggle to try out some new ideas regarding social engineering, e.g., market manipulation to see if the price of war materials could be controlled by distributors rather than manufacturers.

Out of this new movement grew the purists who argued that nothing good could happen until a Democratic Republic was founded on the ashes of the Monarch's Grave. For the Monarch and the Merchants of Foreign Trade, they were the real troublemakers. They did not listen to anybody, but themselves. One wonders how they could stand to hear their own rhetoric all the time. Their goals were very clear, however. KILL THE KING-GENERAL MATHEW III: They wanted to rid the emerging Republic of Him immediately. He must die if progress is to come, and continue unabated.

And, what was progress, the new machinery that would make everybody a New Person through organized leisure. Play would become the ultimate desire. And, play would be made possible for everybody who deemed it, through technology and science. No one was surprised at the radical nature of the revolutionists. That was to be expected. They were new in the struggle to unseat the Monarch. What surprised everybody was how easily these New Class Intellectuals got the masses to move into action. In their rhetoric, the New Class Intellectuals did not think that their army could understand what they were saying. So, I say stumbled, because up to now, they had succeeded in alienating just about everybody. That is, everybody who could understand them. Even they were surprised with their catch. Most had become satisfied with talking to themselves. They believed their ideas so much that they would sit around and talk and argue and fight all night. Then the police for disturbing the peace would arrest them. These arrests caused the black marketeers to pay more attention to what they said. Gradually, they started to address audience of thousands of people.

Why the sudden support? Well, there was the unsolved problem of the missing. The new urban dwellers and the remaining peons were insulted when they were put on twenty-four hour alert when one Overseer was reported missing. How unfair, they thought. Then when the Overseer was immortalized, they became incensed. They were pissed, to be more exact. Thousands of urban dwellers had been missing since the prodigal prodigy arrives; yet, no one uttered a word of concern. "NOT A WORD." Not one word. Now, with the inability of the police to locate the Overseer, a national crisis was at hand. [MP Lillieth: Well, we'll show them a national crisis. We'll give them a Civil War.] As days turned into weeks into months into years, the urban dwellers became uglier and uglier in their pronouncements against the Monarch and His concerns. How many Overseers equalled the number of common people lost in battle, and missing in action, how many?" "How many" became the battle cry.

Lead Solo: [Singing blues style] How many? How many? How many? How many? How many more will it be?

Chorus: [singing response] A lot more than you know, A lot more than we know, A Lot More Than You Know?

Story Teller: This old country choir could be heard singing all over the countryside. And, everywhere they stopped everybody joined. The King-General could not explain what was happening. Nobody could, except the prodigal prodigy. And, he was quiter than a church mouse: the King-General Mathew II had a problem on His hand. His enemies were now the Monarchists, the Republican, the Democrats, the Parliament, and the masses. Things did look rather dim by then.

The Revolutionists joined the Reactionaries in demanding that the King-General Mathew III should abdicate the Thrown, and retire the Crown. The Reactionaries did not know what to do. Their enemies were now their allies. The King-General Mathew III attempted a meeting with the representative fractions, but was betrayed when His contact was assassinated while trying to contact the contact for his contact to find out if their were any assassination plots on the King-General Mathew III life. Irony isn't it.

The Revolutionists in the meantime were promoting the notion of free universal education for all classes and genders. The masses were thrilled by this much attention.

Masses: This is the first time any one has ever left the other side to come over here. This is great.

Story Teller: ...Is how they expressed it?

Radon: A MONARCHY IS TOTALLY UNNECESSARY! WHO NEEDS A MONARCH! THE COURT IS TOO COSTLY! WHY DO YOU THINK HE BROUGHT THE MERCHANTS INTO THE COURT! MONEY! CLEAR AND SIMPLE! AND WEAPONS! THE MASSES NEED FREE SCHOOLS! THE UNIVERSITY ENTRANCE SHOULD BE BASED ON MERIT EXAMINATIONS NOT WEALTH! HOUSING IS A DISGRACE! SANITATION IS UNHEARD OF! AND WHAT ABOUT THE MISSING? HUH?

New 1ST Advisor: We must discover the cause of all these missing people, Your Highness. We must do something.

Story Teller: That evening while attending a rally, an attempt was made on Radon's life. The attempt failed. The masses became angrier. She became the star of the revolution.

King-General Mathew III: [Still talking to His New 1ST Advisor] and, what do you propose my New 1St advisor? And, please, don't mention the Barrister-General Goraka. It is pretence

New 1St Advisor: Yes, Your Majesty, but

King-General Mathew III: NO BUTS!!!

New 1ˢᵀ Advisor: …You do admit that we have a war going out there?

King-General Mathew III: There is no Civil War. It is Rebellion, maybe, but no Civil War. This is an attempted Rebellion that will be put down in do time. My Royal Elite Force [REF] is the best disciplined and trained on the Continent,

New 1ˢᵀ Advisor: Was this blind faith? Stupidity? Stubbornness? Everybody knowledgeable about the situation in the Palace and old country could not have disagreed with the King-General Mathew III more. The Royal Elite Force was nearly sacked in the attack on Parliament. The information received in the Palace was no more reliable than the reported on the streets of the Capital City. Thus, as a result of this fiasco called the "Parliament Affair" the King-General Mathew III became the laughing stock of the entire country. His Royal Elite Force was ridiculed all over the Continent. Mock battles were staged to poke fun at how badly Royal Elite Force performed in battle. People laughed in the streets when the Force was approaching. This behavior on the part of the masses only served to inflame the Loyalists and the "True" Monarchists more determined to save the Crown. By this point, everyone agreed that the King-General Mathew III must go. That was only way to save the Crown. The Crown was more important than one person, no matter who he was. The King-General Mathew III must go. NOW! Of course, every effort was made to get him to step down. These efforts were met with,…

King-General Mathew III: I have got everything under control. I am still in command. This is my Kingdom. I will never leave except over my dead body.

Story Teller: Not only did the King-General fail to hear the call for His resignation, he placed everyone who made the request for Him to step down under house arrest. He then issued a decree entitled, "A CRY AGAINST SOFTNESS." This is how it reads,

King-General Mathew III: During the last few months, we have witnessed an attempt to overthrow My Kingdom through malicious gossip, rumor, and terrorists acts of violence. It was the belief of those rumormongers and thugs that once the Kingdom was discredited, the King-General would crumble as a spineless snake. As you can see, nothing could be further from the truth. The Kingdom is alive and kicking with activity. We are still moving forward to our destiny and greatness.

As for the troublemakers who spread vicious rumors and bring harm to the King-General's subjects, they shall be executed. They shall be…

Story Teller: By now, the group that started the "Great Rebellion" was just about too tired of this King-General, Mathew III. And, who was now behind the Great Rebellion? Radon and her New Class Entrepreneurs as represented by the Black Marketers. And, who were these New Class Entrepreneurs? They were the God Children of the middle class barristers, schoolteachers, solicitors, clerics, artists, musicians, college faculty, merchants, and etcetera. Those were not bad credentials to bring to a show down. At least, one would think that with the kind of bargaining power, this new group of revolutionists would not loose in a show down with the King-General Mathew III. However, as things turned out, it was the God Parents who benefited greatly from this great outpouring of anger and pent up hostilities as expressed in the actions of the God Children. Although the God Parents, the middle classes benefited enormously, they did not initiate the actions that brought about their gains. Many participated to varying degrees, but the middle classes did not initiate any attempt at substantive change that came to benefit them. In other words, although it was the middle classes who stood to gain most by the overthrow of the King-General, they were not the ones who seriously challenge the status quo. That was left to the New Classes emerging from the urban blight and rubble everyone thought was only a refuge for the down and out of society. Ironically, these New Classes, or New Class despised their God Parents for not helping them in time of need, then benefiting from their struggle without "getting involved." The New Class position became, "why allow these elitists to shit on the only people capable of keeping them in their positions of prestige and acclaim?"

Radon: All the middle class wants is to be just like the "Duke of Grace?" What will they call themselves, the Duke of Ham? HA!HA!AHA!HA!HA!HA! AAH!...You dig? All they want is to be like them. They'll never be like them. AAH!HA!HA!HA!HA! Not in our life, HA! HA!HA!HA! HA! Time. AAH!HA!HA!HA!

Fumier: Maybe not my child, but it certainly will make life easier. Oh, I know that we'll have to attend banquets and balls, but we'll finally get exposed to the culture of the upper classes. That's the only thing missing. You see, my child, there are more things to life than making money. For instance, I'm in to horticulture. I collect exotic plants from around the world. You should see my botanic garden. I won first prize for having the most aesthetically beautiful design of all gardens in the old country. The architecture alone will probably change the whole nature of design from here to come. You must come by some time when your busy schedule permits, of course. The plants are beautiful, too. It's a place for romantics. HA!HA!HA!HA!HA! Not wanna bees like you. HA! AH!HA! AH!AH!!HA!HA!HA!

I know you think that in relationship to the upper classes, even the lowest raking of them; we will never really be accepted. That is probably true, but we have something else: MONEY, WEALTH, AND NOW, POWER. As a matter of fact, anyone appearing here for the first time would find it extremely difficult to understand how all of the wealth rests with us, while all of the cultural life and social status is reserved for the upper class. Only for the upper class! NO! NO! NOT ANY MORE1 NOT ANY MORE!

Radon: So why do you allow it to continue? You have the resources. More than enough, I should think.

Fumier: ...Enough to supply an army to defeat the Monarchy? Yes, we know that. We know....

Radon: But, why haven't you?????

Fumier: ....We have done something? Is that your question?

Radon: Yes! People are dying outside so that you may be rich and fame—ous...

Fumier: For me? A!HA!HAA! No, no, my child, I should never ask anyone to do that for me, nor asked anyone to do something I am not prepared to do.

Radon: What do you mean?

Fumier: I would never ask anyone to storm the King-General's Palace.

Radon: What about Parliament?

Fumier: I would be opposed to that completely.

Radon: The King-General ordered the invaders?

Fumier: OH that would be difficult, very difficult. That's a different matter.

Radon: Do you support law and order?

Fumier: Why yes! Of course! I would be appalled at such an undertaking, repulsed at such a thought.

Radon: Then why do you support…?

Fumier: …Listen, my child! I have no time for your idealism. The world is not divided in to clearly define black and white issues, although I'm sure that you think otherwise.

Radon: Don't be so naive, my father. We know exactly what our struggle is about. Nothing is all black and white.

Fumier: Yes, I've heard. You seem to be doing very well.

Radon: Yes, fortunately not everyone feels the same way you do about change. There are many from your ranks that feel otherwise.

Story Teller: With that point, we see that nothing was ever the same yet, what was, always remains. Father and daughter were going their separate ways, father into the Court and daughter into the urban ghetto.

Chapter 15

Story Teller: After spending what appeared to be days, ---in fact it was more like years --- conferring with the General Court, the decision making body of Fifty-plus-One, in the Capital District I7, Neptune and Manila were more than ready for some lively entertainment. Saweto knew of this great place to have fun. It was an underground entertainment complex called Hunter' Den. Within Hunter's Den were Nite Spots, Deli's, Ice Crème Parlors, Chocolate Candy Stores, Restaurants, Cinemas, and other pleasure spots not mentionable here. But I'm sure you get the point, after all it was underground.

For those in the know, I shouldn't have to explain because you know what goes on in the Underground. One particular Nite Spot called the Pathmark had a group, Black Uhuru, appearing the evening everyone was scheduled to go out on the town before the long journey back to the old country. Saweto though brilliant was still a teenager. He was a big fan of Black Uhuru and Third World. He really enjoyed the rhythms of the African-Caribbean musicians because they knew how to improvise in the minor tones with the screaming sax trumpet combo according to the tradition developed by their cousins the African Americans.

However, it was the African polyrhythm accented by a heavy hypnotic bass line layered under the political commentary that struck a special chord with Saweto. These lyric poets were bad. I mean bad. With such a dynamic pulsating, I should say penetrating, performance, Saweto knew without a doubt that Manila, and maybe Neptune too, who were both brilliant in the comprehension of the polity would be greatly delighted by this great work of musical art as a performance venue. He was more than convinced of his assessment when he discovered that Black Uhuru was performing its latest hit, "What is Life?"

Being a gofer, excuse me, aficionado, Saweto thought that nobody on the planet should miss this performance by Black Uhuru. Finding the African Fela Anikulapo-Kuti, the lyric poet who was a troublemaker, acting as a supporting cast with his 20-piece orchestra brought him to utter pandemonium. "Who could ask for more," he thought to himself while bathing in his glory. So, without so much as a consultation, Saweto ushered his visiting party of Manila and Neptune into their seats at Pathmark, and proceeded to enjoy himself immensely. As they sat, Fela was bringing to a close his masterpiece "Confusion Break Bone." The audience broke. Sewato said to himself, "right on time."

With that observation, Saweto immediately became engrossed in the performance. Interesting how Black Uhuru began the tune "What is Life" unlike anyone, including Sawcto, had heard before. They began slowly with a pulsating rhythm that before long had everybody in Pathmark mesmerized. It was like an old 45 RPM being played in 331/3-RPM speed. That is how they played the whole tune. It lasted exactly thirty minutes. In the meantime, a group of Fela's dancers, his wives, entered the stage and began to dance the Mighty Kwanzaa while a chorus sang the ritual lyrics as counter measurement to Uhuru's "What is Life?" composition. It was wild, different, and magnetic.

The Mighty Kwanzaa dance that was performed was from the thirteenth stanza of Kwanzaa Spiritual Hymn Ritual. The whole ritual is called, "In Search of the Vodoun." So in essence, "In Search if the Vodoun" was being performed while Uhuru performed "What is Life?" commonly thought of as a commercial tune. They were sung simultaneously and in complementarity. All of this, mind you, was taking place at a nite spot. Interesting! The sacred and the Secular were being performed side by side without conflict. Heavy. Did you hear me, "I said heavy." That was some bad stuff. It could not be duplicated again ever. Never ever! Not on this planet. Not in this lifetime. Never will you hear something like this performed in public at a nite spot again. I must say, I don't believe.

Manila: Everybody seem to be some place else. I can hardly make out the faces. Why is that Saweto?

Story Teller: Neptune and Manila looked to Saweto, their guide, for the answer. But, Saweto was dead silent just like the rest. He was faceless, too.

Neptune: We must get out of here, quickly, quickly, Manila.

Story Teller: For once, Neptune hoped that this smart teenager understood what he really meant. She did. Simultaneously they attempted to move from their seats only to find their minds running backwards at a rapid velocity. Immediately, they tried to panic simply to show themselves that they were alive. No panic. Not even from the fear that no panic had occurred. They could not even panic from the fear of not being able to panic.

Can you imagine, wanting to say "OH SHIT and not being able to? That's the exact position Neptune and Manila were in. Manila immediately remembered each trip they took and somehow told Neptune what was happening. Although it happened so fast that Manila found herself asking, "How did I do that?" only to have it seem as though everybody could hear every word without any difficulty.... Somehow Manila did not think she actually spoke, but she was heard. Amazing.

Manila: But how?

Story Teller: I thought that Manila knew, and Neptune, too. [Pause] Anyway, before Manila could release the words from her mind, she said,...

Manila: Look! Neptune, that's the old country. They appear to be fighting and killing each other. Who are those femipersons? What are?.... Are we back home, now? But, how? All we did was think it and we ended up back home, in the old country. Is this a trick? Ghee! What luck!

Story Teller: Is it interesting what you think people know sometime? I thought that Manila and Neptune had picked up the fact that they were reading Saweto's conversation, back when, only to find out that neither really knew what was going on. So now, they think what luck. HA!HA!HA!HA! How interesting. To the surprise of Neptune and Manila simply be thinking it they were back home in the old country.

Manila: But how do we enter? Or, land? Whatever!

Neptune: My child, there does not appear to be anyway for us to, UH! UH! I really do not know how to UH! What to say.

Manila: Yea, I know what you mean. I think!...Let's ask Saweto.

Neptune: Saweto! Saweto! Should Saweto be here if we are at home? *

Manila: I don't know exactly. I'm still trying to figure out how we're talking to each other.

Neptune: I don't know. This place is so strange.... who are these creatures? They are so unlike us. Yet, I thought we were the same. All the same.

Manila: Even the old country appears different. But, why? Saweto! Saweto! Is this all real?

Story Teller: Unknowingly, Neptune and Manila had reached the outskirts of what they called the "old country" but during another Earth Life Epoch. You remember. They were on earth. They were also operating during their time space. The problem was they were still 26 million years away from their point of origin..... To make a long story short, because Neptune and Manila were operating in another Earth Life Epoch, it was impossible for them to enter the one they observed. Can you imagine that? But, what they did not know was the same applied to Saweto, and the whole of Fifty-plus-One. You see, the trick was this, the prodigal prodigy, accidentally sorta backdoored into another epoch of earth. This was the Earth Life Epoch. In doing so, he established a passage for his compatriots to pass through time at a speed beyond imagination.

The trick was to pass through the radiation showers unharmed. Those who did literally recomposed in time of the Life Cycle from wince they came, but within another life epoch on earth. Learning how to do this allowed the prodigal prodigy to move freely back and forth through times far ahead or back as time permitted. The one problem was although the New World Colony could move back and forth in time-space; it could never recover new territory. It was always the same land space. Exactly! It was a different time, but the same space every time. Simply put, the Kin-Sha-Sha people crossed the barrier between Earth Life Epochs because life was measured in Linear Time Cone Sequences that were arrived at by counting 1,2,3,4,5, ad infinitum. They could enter no space except that found unoccupied at the time the first entered the Earth Life Epoch. All other "travel" had to be through space as time progressed.

The Kin-Sha-Sha people could visit and observe any space they chose. They could not enter any of these spaces, however. Returning to the Earth Life Epoch they originally left could only do that. There they could travel through space. So, Neptune and Manila were locked into a situation each willingly entered. How were they to know? Anyway! So, here Neptune and Manila struggled to understand what they should have been able to take for granted. The problem was their world got so caught up in destroying "Witchcraft" that they never learned what the old techniques and teachings were about. If they had learned the techniques these teachings offered, the puzzle to the riddle would have been solved. The witches so-called were not their enemies as they had come to believe.

The witches were the practitioners of the old science. This science had been defeated to create the New Science of Rational Thought. No one believed the old superstition any more. So, here they were caught up in their own contradiction. A new science had overthrown an old science without ever finding out what the old science really did. Or better still what these witches really knew. All of this came about at around the time the new science of reason was being revised, again. Particles so dense that they appeared as strings circling the universe became their preoccupation. I should say, one of their preoccupations. The other is why we are having this discussion today. It involves the prodigal prodigy name Goraka.

This preoccupation all came about around the time a new science of observation, and evidenced empiricism through scientific research were in vogue. The burning of the witches was thus an ironic and symbolic after thought to the real defeat of the old science. The dramatization however served as the official overthrow. By so doing, the adherents of the new science engaged in the same human sacrifice their old predecessors were condemned for. How ironic! How symbolic for denial of the old way to occur, the old science was overthrown literally by killing its adherents.

This was not the ways of the Kin-Sha -Sha people, however. There were different. They did not believe in human sacrifice under any circumstances. Nor did they believe in discarding old information. All things taught to the offspring were those teachings of the elders. The teachings of the elders said that one day a Kin-Sha-Sha would be chosen to assume the Crown. At that time, the child so chosen would be given a name and taught the secrets of the Great Texts. That would only occur with the Kin-Sha-Sha people present, the teachings said. The whole clan thus migrated with the prodigal prodigy until he had learned the complete text, except for that lost some place during the eons they were lost in the wilderness. Doing his studies, the prodigal prodigy was a brilliant student who always had creative ideas so much so that the tutors wanted to quit everyday for the first 12 centuries of his instructions.

Tutor: Ghees! Where'd they find this dumb lark?

Story Teller: In any case, the prodigal prodigy while chasing after one of his tutors one day fell down a well. Sounds simple and familiar don't it. How did it happen? Who knows? Maybe the well was about to dry out and was abandoned or something. Look, the story is second, O.K.? Anyway, while the prodigal prodigy was chasing a tutor out in the countryside, the child fell down an abandoned well. And, the rest is his story. He accidentally landed in to another world. That is the beginning of the myth of how the New World Colony was founded.

Learner: You know, I heard that story a long time ago and I always thought that it was…

Tutor: …Bull Shit! Pure unadulterated bull shit. Yes, I know, but that's what we're told to tell everybody. Sorry!

Lost Scholar: Bullshit or not, that's what you going to get when you try to unravel how the prodigal prodigy learned the secret of time travel. Unlike space travel, time travel permits one to cover no additional space travel within the time travelled. Thus, one may remain on earth after 26 million years of travel. As the equivalent to space travel, time movers may literally go from one life epoch to another without getting old. This outstanding feat made new discoveries as commonplace as life itself. Everyone came to expect inventions to occur as often as society wanted them to.

Story Teller: In terms of the human equation, only the specie can save itself from any possible extinction. That seems to be the message delivered here, but to whom, and, for what purpose? It has been stated some place in the old text that man's habitat would be destroyed twice: once by water, and the other by fire. Will there be an equivalent to the boat that saved the people before? This time, too? Uh! Huh! Now, we know the noble cause that allowed the Kin-Sha-Shas to give the Barrister-General permission to return to the old country, and most importantly, to expose them to possible detection. After being sold into bondage, the "lost tribe" regrouped some how and migrated across time. The concept of space as we know it was removed in the process. They had no choice. Why?

Legend has it, as the Kin-Sha-Sha people moved across in their Mirages---ones they had learned how to build to escape slavery---the realized that in order to avoid the permanent destruction of the human species as a life force, and as a form of life itself, they would have to learn how to return to the other side, i.e., the original side, their point of origin.

After experimenting for what many maintain and describe as forever, a passage was established. A time mirage was created to navigate the route. Of course, when a people assume such a mission, many lives are destroyed; excuse me, lost, in the process of transit. Is alleged that all of this might or could have been avoided but the pains of hatred died very slowly. And, the Kin-Sha-Sha people, it is said, hated the world they left behind. So everything that reminded them of their old world was destroyed and they left. Sounds familiar? And, after their arrival to the new time, the old mirage was destroyed, too, along with the blue prints used to design it. That proved to be another major mistake, a very critical error.

After much time to examine their anger and what it had led them to do, the Kin-Sha-Sha people realized that they had to return to the old country, and that they had in fact, to give the old country a chance to live, theoretical though the possibility may be, this was a chance they must take, other wise . . . So, in spite of themselves, they must return home to continue the species. Coincidently, the Kin-Sha-Sha people discovered that they existed in time but that they could not evade the space they occupied: that although life, intelligent life, existed by their findings, they searched back and forth, too and fro, time in and time out, that nothing, that is, no other space existed for them. It was only through the process of time that they existed. Therefore, they could never allow time to run out.

Interestingly enough, when the Kin-Sha-Sha people went as far as ten life epochs, it was discovered that human life reached high points then gradually became more settled with nature and found ways of transforming self for a reincarnation to the next life epoch. However, somehow, during the life epochs of the Kin-Sha-Sha people, turmoil was more the rule than the exception. Life was not treasured as much as a process of becoming. However, this idea of becoming, that of transcending the present became one of being. It was easier simply being. Being was now a commodity. But, so was death. With death always capable of bringing a high price as a commodity than becoming, what reason was there to reincarnate as another being? That became every Kin-sha-Sha's existential question. What reason was there to live?

The more humanist Kin-Sha-Sha people reasoned that spiritually this line of reasoning was mad. These prophets reasoned that this is what led to their willingness to destroy so mindfully, so willfully, and so easily. They reasoned that the above understanding of creation only led to human destruction, and the destruction of other life forms, too. That they reasoned was unforgivable to nature. And, nature awards a very heavy penalty for such a sin. This they already knew.

What to do? To be sure, the Kin-Sha-Sha people took their time mirage and moved ahead for the ten earth life epochs and discovered no humans. No homo sapiens? No homo sapiens anywhere? They also discovered that they could not enter the future that only the present was theirs to behold. Only the present was theirs. They could observe it, however, the future that is. That is how they discovered that it was at the time presently occupied by the old country that was the beginning point of the end of humankind on earth. That was the point that had to be reconstructed in time. Such a project was rather easy for the Kin-Sha-Sha people, now.

Neptune and Manila, Saweto and his people thought, had no way of knowing what was going on in the minds of their hosts. They could never comprehend the magnitude of the problems they faced, or the action necessary to resolve these problems. Furthermore, if by chance they did learn what they were thinking, the idea would sound too far fetched to be possible, to be real. Only the Devil's people could enjoy such medicine.

Chapter 16

Manila: Why did you take us to see that vulgar show and listen to that Devil Music?

Story Teller: As you can imagine, Saweto was now confused: Manila could not be talking about Black Uhuru, the singing band, or, the Katherine Durham Dancers. That was sacred music they were dancing to. That was a sacred dance that they were doing. They were performing something one does not see every day. The performance Manila was speaking about did not come from the Devil. It came from the ancestors. Maybe Manila was referring the "showcase" at Chicago's Poor House, that other nite spot Saweto took them to. If so, he apologizes. But, Decoding Society was performing there. They certainly did not perform Devil Music. And, no one was putting on a show, unless you want to call the Decoding Society a show. ODD! So Saweto's response was expected when he responded with....

Saweto: ...Manila, I am confused. What vulgar show are you talking about?

Manila: Don't play me dumb. You know where you took us. That first place called Pathmark must have been a House of the Devil.

Saweto: A Devil House? And, what is a Devil House?

Manila: You know what a Devil House of Worship is. That place where bad things go on. You know, like the dance those naked people were doing.

Saweto: Naked? People naked? Dancing? They were not naked. HA! AHA! HA! HA! HA! AH!AH! HA!

Neptune: Now, now Saweto. Let us be honest about everything going on here.

Saweto: I am being honest. Is this some type of game or joke you are playing with Saweto?

Story Teller: Now, there's a real dilemma. Neither knows what the other is referring to because the present time is different. The results here have to be disastrous. No other way.

Neptune: Are you trying to tell us that music we were listening to was not Devil Music?

Saweto: Yea, exactly.

Neptune: Then, please explain the dancing we saw. Why were those people dancing like no one I have ever seen? You know that Hoo che! Coo che! Dance. That perverse and vulgar dance the least favored people do. You know what I am talking about. The Black!

Saweto: The what?

Neptune: The Black.

Saweto: What is the Black? Who represents the Black?

Neptune: The least favored. You know, the least favored are called, "The Black in Western Art." As in chess, the black king occupies the least favored position.

Saweto: What is the least favored position?

Manila: The oppressed poor. Those who are still in and or have been freed from bandage.

Saweto: Bondage? What bandage?

Manila: In this instance slavery.

Saweto: So, the least favored are The Black who were slaves?

Neptune: The Black is referring to positions in chess, remember, not a color of ones skin.

Saweto: If one who occupies The Black position was a slave, why do you mention color, skin color and black in the same sentence?

Manila: At one time people who are considered black were slaves, also. But so were other people. Slavery was not limited to skin color. They too were held in bondage as peons, peasants, serfs and Slavs. So, as not confuse who occupy the least favored position, the positions of chess were selected. This way there is no confusion as to who occupies the least favored position.

Saweto: And, if there is a least favored, there must be someone who is more favored, yes? What is that person called?

Neptune: The most favored, as again, in chess. That is the white position....

Manila: ...As in the white king in chess.

Saweto: And, Manila what position do you hold? What position do the people you represent hold?

Manila: I represent the people who occupy the least favored position in the old country. These are my constituents. I am one of them. I am there only contact with authority.

Saweto: Uh, huh! And, you Neptune, whom do you represent? No, let me guess? You represent the most favored, the King-General Mathew III. You represent those who occupy the most favored position.

Neptune: Yes, you are correct. I....

Saweto: ... There must be an original position? Who occupies the original position? Is there an original position, or am I guessing in the wrong direction?

Manila: You are correct. There is an original position. That is held by the monarchy in the name of the people. We, the Parliament have since challenged that notion. Those of us from the least favored position that is.

Saweto: Have you been successful [Pause] in your challenge, [Pause] so far?

Neptune: [Interrupting this line of questioning quickly] What does this digression have to do with the question I have raised about that Devil Music you took Manila and I to see? You are confused if you do not know that King-General III forbids that type of dancing.

Saweto: Is this the son of King-General II.

Manila: And, Parliament.

Saweto: When did he assume power?

Neptune: Come, come now my child. Certainly your elders have told you of the King-General Mathew III and have laws governing dance. I am sure that you are aware of these laws. Your elders taught you no morals, no ethics?

Saweto: [To keep from bitch slapping the old phartz] If I may return to my original interest, my question was raised because I would never have suspected that a society who places such restrictions on dance would have progressed beyond the notion of color applying to a people's skin color. And totally amazed at how this notion would come from chess. It sounds like a new paradigm. Am I correct about this proposition?

Story Teller: No one had ever talked about Saweto's morals before. And, ethics? No one. Again, Saweto came within a hair's blow from striking Neptune. He caught himself in the thought process. No activity physical was committed. PHEW! Close. Real close! I guess that is why he continued with his line of questioning. You know, as a way of keeping his cool, like, chilling out. I am sure you can dig. This was a heavy line of reasoning thrown out there by the representa- tives from the old country. It surprised me, too. I have never heard anything discussed by the old country people about positions based on chess. Obviously, I am not privy to everything as much as I thought. School me.

Saweto: Oh, I see that you do not want to inform me about your concepts regarding people and the positions they hold in your society. You would rather raise questions with me about my morals and ethics using of all things dance and music as a way to do this. My elders told me that you would question me about my morals and my ethics once we reached the Youth Temple of Inquiry. I guess I did not believe anybody as knowledgeable as you would stoop so low. And, out of nowhere, mind you and, of all aesthetic manifestations, dance and music. That was the gift of the Kin-Sha-Sha people to the old country, I am told. [My Elders you are always so graphic and explicit. I guess this was my object lesson. But, how am I supposed to handle it? Them?

Story Teller: Remember, as Barrister-General, the prodigal prodigy, as one of his first "laws" passed, a sign of recognizing silence as the holy tenant of faith, outlawed all music and dance as Devil Activity. As in all societies that are closed, an underground existed where all of those things forbidden were conducted. Saweto, a staunch practitioner of the arts, lived in the underground when operating during his playtime. Playtime was the leisure time offered to the people of Fifty-plus-One when they were not required to do all things serious. Officially it was outlawed, but unofficially, everyone knew that it existed, everyone except those who considered this the den of iniquity. For them, they were always kept at in the dark.

Saweto, you see, was the Next Chosen. The Next Chosen was to be the best, period. He was picked after a contest that taxed brawn and brain passed their limitations. This was done simultaneously. The one who survived the contest was Saweto. He won out. Saweto, the Next Chosen. What an honor. Yes, but what to do next? Neptune was a Moral Philosopher in the old country. He was an atheist and a sceptic. He could pick arguments apart at the seams. Was this the test Saweto had been told about by the elders? Is this the test the elders said was bound to come? Would they put the life of the prodigal son on the line? A sixteen-year male child who is to replace the Barrister-General in case he does not return? Why would they allow him to go up against the master of Moral Suasion?

Neptune: And, what is this youth temple you have brought us to?

Saweto: This is where we come to chill out.

Neptune: I beg you pardon?

Saweto: You know, when spirits need a life, so to speak. Or, when you need to feel good about something you are depressed about.

Neptune: You receive a spiritual uplift in a nite spot? What is the name of that place?

Saweto: Which one?

Neptune: The first one, and the second one.

Saweto: The Pathmark was the first. Chicago's Poor House was the second.

Manila: ....And you worship in these places?

Saweto: Worship?

Manila: You know, pray to God. How do you pray to your God?

Story Teller: Saweto looked on in confusion. One did not pray to a god. Not in Fifty-plus-One, the New World Colony. One simply went into a nite spot and meditated. Meditation took as long as the spirit required. Since the youth found it very hard to relate to the Elders, and how the adults meditated, a code was passed allowing the youth to set up their own forms and places of mediation. Therefore, some youths engaged in physical development while others pursued other ways of reaching an oneness with self.

Saweto: OH! I get it. I take it you are referring to the oneness. You know, a unity with oneself. That is what we call it if I understand you...

Story Teller: Can you imagine? At this point, two youth unable to communicate, but Neptune understands. He finds it unbelievable that there are people who are practicing the form of worship he has always envisioned.

Neptune: AMAZING!

Saweto: What was that?

Manila: I beg your pardon?

Neptune: I said amazing. Simply amazing. And, what were all those gadgets your musicians were playing. I suppose you call them musical instruments.

Saweto: Yes, you are correct.

Neptune: And, where does the sound imitate?

Manila: I am totally lost. What are the two of you taking about?

Neptune: The Kin-Sha-Sha people apparently have advanced to the point whereby they can produce sound in ways we have yet to ponder. That seems to apply to everything we have seen so far. They are centuries ahead of the old country. How it that? You came from us, but you've advanced far beyond anything comprehensible to me. PHEW!

Manila: Yes, me too. I've never seen so much, what do you call it?

Saweto: Technology. Artificial intelligence! AI!

Neptune: Do you mean that steam engine has been responsible for all of this?

Saweto: Not really! We are located in time. We have had to modify everything we do accordingly. Everything is built to occupy time, not space. You see, we have no space, only time.

Story Teller: By now, Neptune an Manila were operating in a dream world. What was this Saweto person talking about? One did not occupy time except in terms of how it related to its surrounding space. Man could not live without land.

Neptune: How do you plant your crops?

Manila: Yes, if you have no space, how do grow your food?

Saweto: Well, I know it may sound strange and contradictory, but matter is mostly empty space. Through a system we have developed, we allow our plant life to occupy that empty space.

Manila: I know this is off the subject but, why did everyone look so blank when we were sitting in that nite spot, Pathmark?

Saweto: We were meditating. We speak in silence. Our conversations are carried on in the spaces unused by other transmission signals at the time.

Manila: So you do have space?

Saweto: Of course! However, it operates opposite to that you are accustomed to. For you, your time is organized around space.

Neptune: And, for you space is organized around time. AMAZING! UNBELIEVABLE! SIMPLY, AMAZING!

Manila: How? How do you do it?

Saweto: Well, if you recall, it took you less than two minutes to arrive here.

Manila: WHAT?

Neptune: What was that young man? It seemed like 8 years.

Saweto: We operate according to the parallax of one second. Parsec we call it. Everything is timed according to...

Neptune: ONE SECOND? There is nothing shorter than ones recond. Not as we know time in the old country.

Manila: Why did it appear so long to arrive here?

Saweto: WHAT????

Manila: It seemed to take so long to arrive here. Why?

Saweto: Probably because of how you travelled. It was roughly twenty-six million years of travel, your time.

Manila: I don't understand. What do you mean?

Saweto: You remember when Neptune yelled out we're in Hell>

Manila: Yes that was frightening....

Saweto: What happened is, you were passing over the bridge, so to speak.

Manila: Bridge? What bridge.

Saweto: Not literally! In fact, you were travelling through one million years of radiation showers upon the earth. That happens every twenty-six million years.

Manila: Was that Hell?

Saweto: I suppose so....

Neptune: Then, we're in heaven, now.

Saweto: HA!HA!HA!HA!HA! I suppose you may say that. It only lasted less than a flash, a frame. Anything longer would have annihilated you.

Neptune: Why???

Saweto: Your imagination would not have been able to take it.

Manila: But, you said it was real....

Saweto: Yes, I did.

Manila: Then, how???

Saweto: Neptune almost did not make it. But, we shut the window just in time.

Manila: Will it be the same going back?

Saweto: WHEW! HUM! NO! It will be quite different.

Manila: How so?

Saweto: For one, it will take longer.

Manila: Longer? I thought you....

Saweto: I know! Less than a Second Coming going back will take twelve years, your time.

Story Teller: A long pause covered with silence now entered everybody. Saweto never felt so inadequate before in his life. Here it was now time to go, and they were finally able to commutate. So much has remained unsaid. Like what has happened to those missing persons. And, why did the, prodigal prodigy return to the old country, and, take twelve years to do so? He certainly had a decided advantage over the citizens of the old country. Citizens? Did I say, citizens? My gosh, what happened to the Civil War going in the old country?

Reporter: Well, while they were touring the New World Colony, Fifty-plus-One, the Civil War in the old country was fought to completion. Yes, that's correct. The king-general was overthrown, and escaped to an unknown location, vowing to restore his kingdom. In fact, the king-general—notice that I use small caps, and refuse to call him by name—was given asylum in a far away dictatorship on grounds that he will never seek his thrown again. More pressing news: The prodigal prodigy was "rescued" by a fraction of the New Age Left. The New Age Left numbered no more than a handful of New Class Radicals set on beheading the king-general and creating a Republican form of government.

After holding the prodigal prodigy all winter, their urban hide out was discovered and raided. Ironically, it was the Middle Class lead Parliament that ordered the raid. All of the New Age Left members were brutally killed except for a handful that escaped. The Parliament's Army suffered large numbers of casualties, too. The prodigal prodigy somehow survived the attack. The plan was to assassinate him, but he escaped with the help of the survivors of the attack.

In the meantime, Neptune and Manila were given final instructions about the passage back to the old country: the mythological 12-year sojourn. As soon as the thought hit Neptune, he reverted to how he appeared after he had arrived in the New World Colony, Fifty-plus-One. It is reported that he appeared thoughtless, and psychotic. These were his thoughts heard coming from his lips, the lips of an atheist.

Neptune: Dear God, I know my soul looks out to thee. All of the ways I've erred. Please forgive me, Lord. Thy way is the light. I have seen the light. I have seen the glory. I have been to the Promised Land. So, please Lord, do not make me go back through Hell. Please Lord; do not make me go back through this Hell. Please! Please!

Story Teller: UH! HUH! I SEE! Neptune, the atheist, did not want anyone to know that he was praying to the god he says does not exist. He did not want the word out that he had gone mad, having to go back though hell was too much to bear.

Neptune: I might not make it back Lord, so, tell me what to do? What should I do to let you know that I believe in you? I was only kidding. You know that don't you, Lord?

Story Teller: Saweto spoke as though he had heard Neptune. He did. Neptune thought so, but could not stop his gibberish rubbish though his mind at the speed of light. Nor, could he prove it. This mystery became his alone here in Heaven. Where else could someone read you thought but in Heaven? And, give you a solution. After realizing that he was correct, that Saweto in fact read his thought,

[Neptune confided,]

Neptune: This is Heaven, Lord.

Saweto: [Knowing that he is only trying to relieve Neptune's fears.] Actually the trip back to the old country should not be as traumatic. You went through the reverse of it at a faster rate than you are going back so you should find it less stressful. [Then with caution] That is what our scientists suppose.

Neptune: That is what you suppose? That is what you suppose? You might as well have said nothing. You did not ally my fears.

Saweto: Well we were not sure that the Barrister-General had arrived in the old country until the two of you arrived here. That proves to us that we've found the formula for returning.

Neptune: The prodigal prodigy was sent home from Heaven? How poetic…

Saweto: This is not heaven though it may be to you. We would never claim to be Heaven.

Neptune: But you must be. You are grander than anything I dreamed of before. Are you testing our will? I know the prodigal prodigy is our salvation. And, we are going back home to bare witness. Why else would we be sent back?

Story Teller: Isn't it funny how we arrive at solutions? More luck than skill most of the time? Anyway, Neptune was about to make a fool of himself well intended though it may be. Let's see.

Neptune: The Barrister-General is really the Savoir returning as the prodigal child. Yes, I see now. Oh, my Lord. I hope they do not crucify Him before we return. We must return, immediately. I cannot afford to wait 12 years. He will be dead and buried by then. Why did you not give us some signal, Lord?

Story Teller: and, Neptune is worried about the prodigal child dying, HA! He must be kidding. Do you know how old Neptune is? Guess.

Saweto: I am totally embarrassed, Neptune.

Manila: Yes, so am I. Ghee, you are such a coward. Oh, how embarrassing.

Saweto: Don't worry Neptune, you'll arrive safely. Unfortunately, there is no way to change your mind.

Story Teller: At that moment Manila walked over to Saweto and whispered in his ear. His face lit up with a beautiful smile.

Manila: We'll be back in a little while. [Manila tells Neptune as she and Saweto walk away from him.]

Saweto: Manila, you won't believe the trip back, so I'm told. HA!HA!HA!HA!AH!

Story Teller: Now wait! How insulting can one be to dignitaries? First, some teenager who claimed that he is everything including their official guide met Neptune and Manila. Second, they were informed that they were talking to the Official Voice of the Government. Third, they were placed before a tribunal that closed the case because Neptune insisted that his official status be recognized before the take care of any other matters. To top it off, no official recognition had been given yet. For all practical purposes, this "Official Visit" from the King-General Mathew III was a waste of time. How insulting.

Chapter 17

Story Teller: Through Ife's Garden they traveled. A trip like none that ever behold the senses. "Before has passed. The rising tide of change" spoke Neptune exhilarated in his New Found Faith.

Neptune: [Thinking to himself] Time is change. Change is time. We are the rising tide of change. We are the endless bridge of time…. And the earth stood still, the world unfolded beyond our horizon. We shall be. Sorrow no more. Hardship no more. Pain no more. Glory be in thy name.

Lost Scholar: Is it not amazing how one acquires faith? But, in what? The Lord, you say? So who is the Lord? Who is Neptune's Lord?

Neptune: Yes, we must give Him a New Name. We shall call him Our Savior. Yes, Our Savior. What a Blessed name. He shall be the prodigal prodigy no more. Glory be in Our Savior's name.

Story Teller: Well! Neptune, in his New found Faith, could never have been better with his prognosis. He was never more right. The prodigal prodigy was now President Goraka. Yep! That's right! Goraka, the righteous! In the meantime, Neptune continued his prognosis as though he did not realize what he was saying.

Neptune: One movement Lord to be one continuous motion. Lord, forever and ever. It is so beautiful, Lord. Is it heaven we're in? I never knew there was a trip back home and that it was so beautiful. I thought it was a hoax, Lord. A dreamer's fantasy, Lord. I thought it was a dreamer's fantasy…But, the beautiful you reveal of the Heavens is beyond my wildest imagination…I'm free, I'm free, I am free.

Story Teller: Neptune had obviously gone off. The question is, was it for real? It probably did not matter anyway because for all practical purposes, Neptune was asleep. A deep sleep. How else could one endure 8 years of travel? Dreaming? If he was asleep, he was obviously dreaming. But, so what? That was Neptune's only reality at this point. Also, we have assured his that he was alive, not that there was any reason to assume otherwise.

Obviously freedom knows no bounds. Here in Neptune's sleep, he even delved into the mystery. How interesting. Earlier on, I told you that the King-General Mathew II had been advised not to grant the prodigal prodigy a Charter. Neptune was the drafter of that document. In it he recommended that, and I quote,

Neptune: Your Loyal, Trusted Advisors request and we that the prodigal prodigy Not, I repeat not, is granted a Charter to Colonize the New World….

Story Teller: How foolish these words seem, now…. But, does…

Neptune: That means that I was being tested? Oh, My Lord, I failed the test. No wonder they did not keep me back in heaven. I must make amends back home when return. That is my first task. How could I have been so dumb? A, to think I wrote the one and only draft. I know what I shall do when I get back. I'll proclaim my Sin, and ask forgiveness. Yes, I am free. I am free. I'll ask for forgiveness…HA!HA!HA!HA!HA!HA!HA!AH!AH!HA!

Story Teller: Where is "B"? While Neptune is planning his future, he hears as choir singing in the background. It frightens him in an unsettling way because he can hear but cannot recognize the lyrics.

Choir: me kai sai

> ye sai me kai
>
> me kai sai
>
> ye sai me kai

Story Teller: What are they saying became the recurring question Neptune asked until it became an inadvertent call-response of?

Neptune/Choir: Whadousai?

Whadousai? me kai ye sai.

ye sai me kai

Whadousai? Whadousai?

Story Teller: At some point in the dream world, the call-response becomes one continues chant. Neptune becomes so enchanted with the rhythm from the chant that he finds himself dancing. Yes, I said dancing, with the music. Not knowing how to dance or what to do, how to begin, Neptune begins to mimic the dancers he saw in the Pathmark nite spot. Every motion he pictured the Dunham Dancers make, he copies verbatim. That was a sight to behold. Oh, my goodness, what a sight to behold.

Eventually Neptune is in another world. The call-response never misses a beat while he lay transfixed listening to some kind of digital music being played by the other group he and Manila saw the night before they left Fifty-plus-One for home. After a while however Neptune finds himself going deeper and deeper into his fears. Finally, not being able to take it any more, Neptune tries to scream.

Neptune: {Dream thoughts of Neptune} (Oh, my Lord, it is beginning to get to me. I cannot stop. I cannot stop. me kai ya sai, ye sai me kai ya, what is happening to me? I do not seem to be in control. me kai sai ya, Please! Please! Somebody! Tell me what is going on. I am sinking. Oh my, Lord. Help me. Please help me. I am sink-ing I am....)

Story Teller: By now, Neptune was going through a kind of withdrawal process that created his mind, body and spirit for the long journey back to the old country. The sleep state he had entered was stage one. While in stage one, all of the Fears of Rest are exposed and eradicated. Fears of Rest were simply those fears during the journey in the Time Mirage. A restful state was necessary for a successful journey. The human body was not prepared to endure any kind of trauma of the magnitude a Fear of Rest could impose. So, all skeletons were let out of the closet by allowing free thoughts to float to the surface of the mind. One by one each fear was exposed a neutralized, one by one.

The withdrawal process was so taxing that the experience itself could cause irreparable damage to the psychic, if not death itself when handled improperly. And, here Neptune was approaching four hundred years, Old Country Time. "What a challenge" thought the technicians handling the preparation of Neptune's travel?" Oh! Oh! What is that? There he goes again." Neptune appears to be going through one of his dream conversations...."What did he say? What did he say? What was that?"

Neptune: {Still dreaming} (I've got it. I've got it. Man is placed here to assist nature. Not to rule this earth. Thus, when there's a genetic imbalance, we are to discover ways of correcting it. That applies to everything. I've got it! We are God's corrective tools.... We are not to destroy Mother Earth; we are to build upon it.... We are to build upon it...How does one build upon Mother Earth's, miracle? How does,....ya sai me kai ya, Me kai ya sai me kai ya. {Now other thoughts are surfacing} The Prince of Evil does not govern Joy, enjoyment of pleasure. It is desire that causes the pain. Evil pain! {Neptune then turns to lust.} Oh! Look at her. What beauty. What elegance. What a stream of joy she can bring. What pleasure, oh, what pleasure? What pleasure! {He suddenly stops} What need have I for such passion? What desire can such passion bring? Such desire! Such passion! {Now fear enters his dreams.} No, Lord! I take back these thoughts of passion, My Lord. They are not right. So, I was told. They are not right. So, I am told. They...ya me kai me sai me kai ya...)

Story Teller: By observing Neptune constantly throughout the withdrawal process, the technicians discovered.

Lorenzo Lillie: Apparently Neptune has a built-in code that he relies on in times of severe stress.

Bekina: He does not seen to be aware of it, however.

Lorenzo Lillie: Yes that is true.

Bekina: Should we allow him to discover its nature?

Lorenzo Lillie: I'm not so certain we'll have time.... The cycle begins soon.

Bekina: So what do we do?

Lorenzo Lillie: Wait!

Bekina: Why? Do you anticipate something?

Lorenzo Lillie: I don't know. I feel something.

Bekina: Should we postpone?

Lorenzo Lillie: No! That's not my worry.

Bekina: Then,...

Lorenzo Lillie: ....Let's just wait. I think we might hear {pause nothing said then,} ...somethng we never knew.

Bekina: No idea what?

Lorenzo Lillie: NONE!

Neptune: Me kai he kai. Ye sai me asi.

Story Teller: By now, Neptune surprising himself in the process slows the haunt down to a crawl. He was still trying to understand the lyrics. They sounded like, uh! So foreign, and in the process discovered that he could actually reason and control his senses while asleep.

Neptune: I slowed down the music. I actually slowed down the vulgar beat....ye asi me asi. me dai yee sai. I can control that enchanting music with those funny words.

Lorenzo Lillie: Did you see and hear that?

Bekina: You mean the appearance of those lyrics when Neptune used a negative to describe them?

Lorenzo Lillie: Yes! Interesting!

Bekina: It seems to be working.

Story Teller: What was that, did I read something into what the technicians said? How do I keep getting the impression that the Ken-Sha-Sha people are not revealing everything? Even to me. I am Story Teller.

Bekina: It seems to be working.

Story Teller: What was that, did I read something into what the technicians said? You might say that it is not their fault --- meaning the Kin-Sha-Sha people—since Neptune and Manila knew not what to ask. That is true. I shall not deny that. But, my question remains, what are they up to?

Neptune: ye asi me sai. me asi ye sai. What was that, again Something about man's role as the helper of Mother Earth? Oh, yes, we are here to keep the process going. Was that a wise choice in choosing men as Nature's assistant? Are there too many unfulfilled desires in man? I think men might have been delivered too soon. Granted too much responsibility.... Created too much confusion of thought...How does it go, ye sai me sai?

Lorenzo Lillie: There he goes again. Trying to figure out what it means. Interesting fellow, this Neptune. I think we might have something h

Chapter 18

Story Teller: I must say, I found these technicians to be very unusual. I found it hard to determine what they were about. I thought they were simply going to give final instructions before the take passage home. Then I found that they tested Neptune. Even that was not unusual in and of itself. After all, such a long journey required much preparation, I suppose. But why were they so interested in Neptune's thoughts? And, how did they read these private thoughts?

Lorenzo Lillie: Well, if you must know, we used what you might call a scanner. This scanner recorded and translated brain signals into our language: very simple, no, as to why? We needed to know everything. Period! We are scientists. That is our job.

Story Teller: Yes, but how did this scanner work? They obviously worked by reading the thoughts patterns, that is, the neurotransmitters, of its subjects. The question raised was, who gave the New World scientists the moral authority to literally go into the minds of other unsuspecting victims and learn their hidden thoughts. Thoughts these victims were not necessarily aware of? Huh? Who?

Lorenzo Lillie: Obviously the nature of your question reveals that you are not of our time. You are not of this world. The question of moral authority to read as you put it others thoughts was resolved by our Privy Council centuries ago. As you know, we do not have to use this technology you are talking about to accomplish that end: it is a moot question. For us, that is.

Story Teller: Then, what is the purpose of your technology? Why bother?

Bekina: The technology allows us to....

Lorenzo Lillie...Be more exact in our determination of where the thoughts emanate, and how they are developed.

Story Teller: Yes, but for what purpose?

Bekina: There are obviously many ways we may utilize this information.

Lorenzo Lillie: Our rules strictly forbid us from applying these skills to change,

Bekina:....A subject without his knowledge or consent.

Story Teller: Yes, of course! It's my scepticism of the old country. That is what I bring with me. Please, forgive my rudeness. Things got pretty bad for modern people you know. I am speaking primarily about the time we were celebrating when we left the old country. So, please excuse my lack of trust.

Lorenzo Lillie: Yes, we know. Our fore parents are from your world, we understand.

Story Teller: You are in fact scientists. I thought you were only technicians. Excuse my ignorance, now to the point, are you claiming altruism? Amazing, a world of altruists, unbelievable I must say. {With cynicism} Should we call your world heaven, as Neptune has typified it?

Bekina: Heaven? HA!HA!HA!HA! [Both Bekina and Lorenzo Lillie laugh hysterically.]

Story Teller: Excuse me, I know this is a digression, but why is your laughter UH! so, I don't know how to put it....

Bekina: Stilte?

Story Teller: Yes! That's it, exactly. Why so stilted, as you put it?

Bekina: Don't know!

Story Teller: You knew the correct term, yet you don't know why interesting.

Bekina: I knew that was the term you were searching for, but as to whether that is correct description...

Lorenzo Lillie: ...Most appropriate description....

Bekina: ...Is possibly another matter, but we were following your intent....

Story Teller...Are you telling me—in a non-threatening way, however, -- that you read my thoughts better than I do?

Bekina: In this instance, it was unnecessary.

Story Teller: How's that?

Lorenzo Lillie: We simply read your expression.

Story Teller: My expression?...

Bekina: All of you from the old country....

Story Teller: ....I'm not from the old country. I am the narrator ---I am Story Teller.

Lorenzo Lillie: You mentioned the old country, however, Bekina means everyone from the other time.

Story Teller: Yes, but you shouldn't be reading my thoughts as Story Teller. I should be creating yours. That is, your thoughts. The role is reversed. The role should not be reversed. I, Story Teller, know the story. I tell the story. I make up the story oftentimes, as I go along. Isn't that so? I mean, isn't that what it is suppose to be, to be so? Huh!? Ghee, what am I saying here. I do not believe this is happening to me. I am talking to my characters and they are reading me. Is this supposed to be real? You can't see....

Lorenzo Lillie: ...Every time you raise a question of us, we answer. You may hear us, but no matter how you choose to contact us....

Story Teller: Wait! Wait! Wait! Wait! Let me see if I follow you. If I draw you on a piece of paper, I'm communicating with you?

Bekina: Only when you ask us a direct question. Not until then. That applies to all of you, excuse me us. Which ever. What ever.

Story Teller: If I create you...

Lorenzo Lillie:…You open the window, the door, so to speak.

Story Teller: But, not until then? Not until I address you with a direct question?

Bekina: ….Can you enter our world? Is that your question?

Story Teller: Can you see me? I mean, before I talk to you….

Lorenzo Lillie: HA!HA!HA!HA!HA!

Bekina: Of course, sure. Why not? Aren't you standing or sitting there? Don't you exist?

Story Teller: But you do not exist, except in my mind.

Lorenzo Lillie and Bekina: OH? Really? We exist only in your imagination? Is that what you are telling us?

Story Teller: Yes, no. Yes. I create you. I imagine you as a thought. You are simply a thought that I put down on a piece of paper as a character. You are my characters.

Lorenzo Lillie: We talk, you listen, you write. If we do not talk to you, for you, you have no characters, to speak of, so, to speak. HA! HA! AH! HA! HA! Do you? HA!HA!HA! Well? We talk, you ease drop, you write. Right? We don't complain. You give us life. We could have our own storyteller, you know. But we like you. HA!HA!HA!HA!HA!

Story Teller: OH!

Bekina: Yes, but we don't mind you being here.

Story Teller: OH?

Lorenzo Lillie: Yes, of course. You are the only mechanism we have of entering your world.

Story Teller: You mean, by my imagination??????

Bekina: If you say so. HA!HA!HA!AH!HA!HA! What ever, we accept your description. These are your thoughts, remember?

Story Teller: Ghee, how generous you are, I thank you!

Lorenzo Lillie: Hey, what can we say? You are in us and we are of you. What can we say? You are Story Teller.

Bekina: And, you are pretty good at it. At least we think so. HA!HA!HA!HA! Don't we Lorenzo Lillie? {Hardy Laughter}

Lorenzo Lillie: Yea, he's okay. {Laughter, again}

Story Teller: So, let me get this straight. Every time I choose to describe something or someone, you accept it without question?

Bekina: We have no choice in the matter. This is your story.

Lorenzo Lillie: We have no quarrel with you or your language. It is ours, too.

Story Teller: Yes but you still have not told me how you read us. The people back home will not believe me unless you tell me how you do it. You still have not told me how you do it. That is the bottom line.

{As Story Teller argues with Lorenzo Lillie and Bekina, the scientists, Goraka begins to speak to Neptune.}

Goraka: {Remember Goraka uses the small case "i" for "I" for reasons only he can explain. Will he explain? I do not know.} When I/we were shown that great passage, I knew it was a gift. I knew that immediately: Not an accident, but a gift. Oh, I'm the first to argue that we actually did nothing to receive the gift, if you know what I mean. What can we present as our reason for being chosen? Fate? As the receivers of the gift, if it had been that, we blew it. First, we began by closing off the passage. Dumb foolery! Really, dumb. We wanted to be 'PURE." Example: the music! Did you hear the music, Neptune?

{At this point, Story Teller and his informants stop to take notes beginning with this last comment. Neptune is lying in a stupor trying to figure out what he is trying to figure out. Unaware of this entire goings on Goraka continues, that was our gift. Music! We were the culture and the art and the music of the old country. As a matter of fact it became the basis of all world popular music with a creative labor process. Today, I'm sure without a doubt you did not recognize any of the sounds during the concerts you attended. Did you? {Without waiting for Neptune to answer,}

That's because we wanted to be PURE. Our music now sounds nothing like the old country music. It is not suppose to. That is by design. The New Music is urban fi-pop. Fi-pop is to be futuristic urban interstellar sounds of artistic creation. It is to e urbane, par excellence. But you would never recognize that music as having the same origin as the music you listen to back home. It does, and, that's exactly what I mean. We left and decided that we wanted to build our civilization from the ground up...

Neptune:…Is, is that--- you--- my prodigal child? [I must be insane, am I?]

Goraka: Yes, of course, my mentor. Who else could it be?

Neptune: [Then I am not insane.] Okay, go on.

Goraka:.... Then, I remembered that book I found, but could not read. I had to return to find it to complete my training. It was on my return home that I realized why we were sent beyond our time. Ye sai me kai. Me sai ya kai.

Story Teller: What was that just went on there? Do not tell me your Barrister-General is back here, now?????

Lorenzo Lillie: No, he's not here. But, yes, that was he speaking to Neptune.

Story Teller: How did that happen? Isn't Neptune supposed to be asleep?

Lorenzo Lillie: We're not certain.

Story Teller: How's that?

Bekina: We've just witnessed the same event you did. We'll have to find out. That'll probably happen after you leave.

Story Teller: What do you plan to do? Why can't you do it now, so I may tell the people about it back home?

Lorenzo Lillie: First we must study the recordings. Then we'll go from there. That can take some time.

Story Teller: Is that a frequent occurrence?

Bekina: If you mean do we have access to the Barrister-General, yes we do.

Story Teller: How? Why haven't we been told? Why wasn't I informed?

Lorenzo Lillie: No big secret, you know. We do it by connecting our thought patterns. It's very simple.

Bekina: In your language, we simply tune into each other.

Story Teller: Tune in? Can I????

Lorenzo Lillie: Well, you already are.

Story Teller: Yes, of course. I am, but you do understand the question!?

Lorenzo Lillie: You mean that the only way you have access to us through your imagination. Of course! We have no control over that.

Bekina: We've discovered that the only way an outsider ---that is, someone who did not migrate with us through the First Passage—can use our facility to communicate non-verbally is by going into the Tranquillity Tank.

Story Teller: What was that? By doing what?

Lorenzo Lillie: That's a Tranquillity Tank. So named because it allows its inhabitant to delve into the deep recesses of the brain-nervous systems.

Bekina: At first, you think you are unusual, that something is wrong with you. Then, you realize that you are picking up voices that are making no sound.

Lorenzo Lillie: Thoughts really! It's not the voices you hear, but the thoughts.

Bekina: Yes, that's true.

Story Teller: Yes, sure I know! I know! So you placed Neptune and I suppose Manila in a Tranquillity Tank?

Bekina: Two! Two separate tanks! For different purposes.

Story Teller: OH?

Lorenzo Lillie: Well, not really.

Story Teller: I finally got the two of you disagreeing on something.

Bekina: We are not disagreeing. We are simply....

Lorenzo Lillie: Looking at it from different positions, that's all. Nothing more.

Storyteller: sure!

Bekina: If you insist on continuing to misread our comments....Yes? Threatening me? Huh? You said that we made contact with you was through my imagination. How can you stop me from imagining you? HA!HA!HA! AH!

[Story Teller disappears.]

Bekina: I lied.

Neoscab: Did it finally catch up with you, Story Teller? HA!HA!HA!HA! Was chapter eighteen too much for an ambitious migrant? [Now to the audience.] I'm afraid that I'll have to take up the story at this point. You see, Story Teller let his imagination run away with him. Get it? HA!HA!HA!HA!HA! He had really begun to believe that he was inventing what was going on. I'm sure that you know what happened. No? He was vaporized. They cut him off completely. As to whether it is a boycott or not is unknown at this point. Last I heard, hearsay of course, Story Teller was out chasing his imagination. Or, maybe it even ran away with him HA!HA!HA!HA! Whatever! HA! HA! HA! HA! AH! I got the job, now. HA! HA! HA! HA! HA!

Lorenzo Lillie: Now, that was cold, Bekina.

Bekina: Cold? Story Teller was becoming too anxious to know things we have not even begun to investigate. You saw what he did earlier. As a matter of fact, he has done that throughout the whole process.

Lorenzo Lillie: Yes, but what about our open and free access policy? The Council won't like that.

Bekina: He was a pest. Besides, he was only Story Teller, and he was from some place else. He wasn't even from our world. Besides,,,,

Council of Judges: No one has said a word. Not anything? Is that your next point, Bekina? We were simply allowing you to complete tour argument. In the meantime, ...Yep!

Bekina: .... Story Teller must return. Must return. [Story Teller reappears.]

Council of Judges: He is allowed to continue observing the process, and will be allowed to travel with Neptune and Manila on their journey.

Bekina: However?

Council of Judges: Our new replacement will assume the responsibility of keeping communi- cations open between Our World and elsewhere. Her role shall be a bit different. [Bekina and Lorenzo Lillie look at the Council of Judges with a surprised singleness,] Yes, our, your new observer shall report rather than editorialise. Or, tell stories if you will......Commentary, she has been informed, should be engaged in only when necessary...

Bekina: .....When necessary, my dear Council?

[Lorenzo Lillie said, "Oh?"]

Council of Judges: Yes, only when it is necessary to clarify points, or, add further dimensions to the discussion.

Bekina: That places her in the same role as the previous storyteller, Council. Coun.... [On their way out, the judges say,]

Council of Judges: Her name is Stellar Four.

Lorenzo Lillie: Come Bekina, let's get back to work. We don't have much time and we still have not studied Manila's results.

Stellar Four: Well, I guess this is where I come in. Uh! Umm! No! This is where they come in. As you know, Neptune and Manila are undergoing a series of tests designed to determine the problems they might encounter on their way back to the old country. During the process, Neptune has shown great facility for nonverbal communication. We don't know what that means at the moment, however.

Story Teller: So? How does it feel?

Stellar Four: You mean about taking your place? And, getting rid of Neoscab?

Story Teller: Of course, what else?

Stellar Four: I had nothing to do with it.

Story Teller: Yea, but you accepted.... don't you Feel..

Stellar Four: Don't spank me, someone was going to take the job. You saw the scab,

Story Teller: Neoscab, you mean. They never gave me a chance to fight back. I did not even see it coming. I was vaporized. [Snap finger] Just like that.

Stellar Four: Fight back? Is that how you see it? HA!HA!HA!HA! You never had a chance. Good thing the Council of Judges is always on standby. It was no contest. You were only a dream of your parents.

Story Teller: Hell, I thought I was writing the whole thing in my head. I didn't realize that I was a narrator, only someone who reads what others assign him as a job, as a functionary. I didn't realize the depth of their powers. I see why Neptune mistaken them for Heavenites.

Stellar Four: Heavenians.

StoryTeller: Heavenians? Heavenians? Not Heavenites, Heavenians. Now, I have heard it all.   HA!HA!HA!

Stellar Four: Not Quite!

Story Teller: Oh! You're smart. Murphy was funny!

Stellar Four: Not really. You know we are not supposed to carry on conversation. You also know that you are not supposed to be in the story. We are not its subjects. We are not to dominate it or the reader may think we're simply one of the characters.

Story Teller: Now, you're more interesting than they are. Where'd they dig you up from? So to speak, as you might say. By the way, why...

Stellar Four: So to speak is simply to let you know that what was said was only an analogy. Simply that! But, let us go on with the story.

Story Teller: I'm....

Stellar Four: .... I insist! We must go on. Events wait for no one to happen. Reader, audience, whatever! Please recall, these Kin-Sha-Sha people are not speaking literally. Please remember that they are telepathic, so no sounds are being made. Okay. I thought I would remind you in case you forgot. Thank you. Okay, here we go again. Lorenzo Lillie is speaking,...

Lorenzo Lillie: Well, that sparring between Story Teller and Stellar Four gave us enough time to get back into the swing of things, ask into what Neptune is doing.

Bekina: You're right! There's been no real change in the pattern he has established. At this point, he continues to delve into the intellectual; aspects of his metamorphosis

Lorenzo Lillie: Yes, he does have an inquisitive mind. Will he figure out the code? That he's changing?

Story Teller: Metaphors is? Aren't you going to report that, what 's going on in the Lab?

Stellar Four: NO! Not necessary again. What is there to report? Everyone can see what is happening. As long as I am here, everyone can see for themselves what is going on. Please, I beg of you.... We beg ...thank you!

CHAPTER 19

Stellar Four: Well, I think it is about time we explain what has been going on here in the New World Colony, Fifty-plus One. Briefly put, there are many things in the New World Colony, Fifth-plus-One. Most I do not think you would comprehend, maybe at another point in time, but not now. Right now, I think it might be appropriate to explain what our relationship to the old country is. I must be fair about this, so I shall try to convey the whole dynamic of "what's going on."

Since everyone is aware of the "passage," I shall focus on why we reopened it. Bluntly, we had to. We had no other choice. Our world is literally caving in all around us: that is something we had not planned for when we arrived. We thought we had it all figured out. When we arrived here, we found that there were limitations on what we could do by the amount of time we controlled. We also discovered that after your present Earth Life Epoch, human life is missing. We want to correct that magnetic mystique by placing delegates from old country in a New Earth Life Time Frame.

Apparently, another set of Settlers from the old country migrated to a New World Colony the called Acirema. These Settlers, Aciremans, inadvertently set off a new chain of destruction that spread faster than Nature could protect itself from. Life forms, as we know them ceased to exist in any meaningful ways after that point. We shall attempt to correct that imbalance. Our ability to travel through time passages allowed us to see exactly what happened, simply by going to the previous Earth Life epochs and comparing the results of all those investigated.

The results were all Earth Life Epochs following the catastrophe had many and varying forms of life, but no human life. It was the Great Migration of the Kin-Sha-Sha people that avoided human extinction we hope to bring about a Human Rebirth. The process should not be too difficult. After all, we are of the same classification. We simply followed different paths. They chose to exploit space, we chose to exploit time. We are caught in our world, in many a meaningful way, but there's no longer any exist. However, to be fair, many of our citizens believe that we are headed toward our own demise and much sooner than we think. That brings me to the next point.

Our real intent for migrating back home, and now to the New Colony, is to assure our continuation as a species. That is now primary. The greater goal has not been forgotten, but it is secondary to our survival as intelligent social beings that consciously seek pleasure. This would not be if it were no for the plague of DRY ROT. This DRY ROT has everybody cautious about contact. The problem is no one has been able to discover a sure cure. As a matter of fact, we do not even have a clue as to how it is contacted let alone how to stop it. So, we find ourselves living 'for today" everyday we live. The results have been devastating. No one has panicked, but the numbers of Rot victims have increased beyond our ability to save the species.

Now we need people. I know you will find this totally unbelievable, but we keep the passage open with our minds. I think you call it mind control. We simply have taken it further. And now, we pay the price. It is speculated by many noted scholars and scientists that DRY ROT is probably caused by the use of our minds to control the passage. They have suggested that we shut down the passage for a while to see what will happen. They say we have nothing to loose. The Council voted the idea down with a simple majority. It's rational was, "that passage may be our only way out of here. We had better not close of that notion."

Who knows, the decision of the Council may very well be the correct one. However, I must inform you that the last major decision they made about this same problem did not pan out too well: they decided to engage in forced migration. That is how the "Noners" from Xaire, excuse me, old country ended up staying here permanently. The problem is, the Noners refused to learn how to communicate silently and they provided no assistance in keeping the passage open.

They obviously are of no use value to us here. Fortunately for both our concerns, most have migrated to the New Colony, Global Village. They do not know how to rule however. There since of administration is lacking. We must therefore send our own leaders there to govern them until, who knows? Unfortunately, most of the Fifty-plus-Oners prefer to migrate back to the old country rather than to our New Colony, Global Village. They say that they are out numbered there, and it really would not work, anyway. They may have a point. I personally do not think the Xaire is any better.

In fact, they point out how the memory of the Noners seems to be underdeveloped as the reason why they do not want to migrate with the remainder of those who are about to leave our Capital District Seventeen. The problem is, they haven't much choice in the matter. We are not certain how much longer we can keep the passage open. Although we made many errors, our greatest error was our miscalculation of how much time these was/is. By racing through all of those times so quickly, we expended enormous energy. We literally burned our lights too fast. Too soon! At the time, time seemed limitless. It was so present that it appeared to replenish it, to last forever.

Theories were proposed on how "Extended Time" operated, e.g., time added to time equals extended time (t + t =et). Great honor was bestowed upon our great minds, all for explaining the Extended Time Process [ETP]. Then without warning, our time began to pass us by, so to speak. And, we were unable to occupy any more space. The ETP occupied our usable space. Space became a premium. Our numbers were not that great, but we consumed so much time so quickly that our space diminished. Our only choice was to return to Xaire for recruits. To that end Father, the Barrister-General volunteered to go back thereby opening the passageway for new settlements in the New Earth Life Epoch.

As it turned out, we made an error and many Xaireans came through the passage unexpectedly: they could not return. We tried, but to no avail. They remained here with us. That's where we got the idea of interning from. At least that's how it started. Now we have an over populated Capital District. Thirty million is a jump from eight million in a matter of fifty years, New World Time [NWT]. With most of the population unable to provide for itself, starvation is reported in many time zones. Thus, as of the last Assembly, nothing will be purchased on time any more. Every purchaser must show concrete evidence of space...

Back to the ROT, the DRY ROT is what we call it because one day a person is fine, next, the day after, a dry rot object is there. One interesting thing is that DRY ROT always forms into a shape of an abstraction said to be a compilation of the dead person's personality. Each abstraction looks like some form of nature with most assuming a tree trunk like characterization of abstractly carved features. When first observed by scientists, many thought this was the weirdest thing they had ever seen. They say that it gives them another perspective of how we evolve personalities. One neuroscientist attributes these unusual sculptures to a "lack of personality development commensurate with the person's ideal personalized ego expectation. Whatever! What it boils down this, no body has enough personalized time-space. [Pause] Oh, here comes the Council.

Council of Judges: Stellar Four, as our Reporter, we advise you to use a bit more discretion reporting; and, be more concise. Also, please stop misleading the audience. We are not going to collapse at the center. We are not going to unravel at the core, so, please do not cause undue concern with your pessimism. Please, be advised. [Council disappears]

Stellar Four: Thank you, Council! I, Stellar Four, Reporter for Capital District 17, have been given this news release; this release just arrived from the test lab of the Time Mirage: Because there is an energy shortage, Neptune and Manila will be unable to complete their journey back to the old country, Xaire.

   Instead, we have secured their recorded permission to migrate to The New Colony. That should read, "Recorded permission to migrate to the New Colony." Thank you.

Story Teller: Collapse? Your system is about to collapse, and you're sending an old man and a young girl away thinking that they are going home? AND, THAT THIS IS HEAVEN? SO, WHAT IS THIS ABOUT NOT REPORT....

Stellar Four: That is not true. [Council appears]

Council of Judges: Stellar Four, carry out your assignment. Execute your charge. [Stellar Four tries to object, but to no avail. she thanks Council as they disappear.]

Bekina: Okay, okay, Lorenzo, we now have Manila and Neptune hooked into each other. Should we prepare them for transit?

Lorenzo Lillie: Yes, but we have been advised to await the arrival of another passenger.

Story Teller: I thought they were already in the Time Mirage. What the hell's going on? I don't know whether to trust you or not. I want to know...

Stellar Four: We got your point....

Story Teller: Why do you always say "we?"

Stellar Four: Because we all hear you.

Story Teller: You don't mean all of you when you say all of you, do you?

Stellar Four: My god, I do not believe this person. Are you always like this? Yes, I mean all of us.

Story Teller: My god! My god! This is insane. What are they doing to us?

Stellar Four: HA!HA!HA!HA! US? Are you us, StoryTeller? You are not in this process. You are not a character here. You don't exist. Don't you know the uses of story telling? Please, no more digressions.

Story Teller: No More Digres...."

[Stellar Four "zaps" the storyteller, he disappears.]

Lorenzo Lillie: Oh, we almost forgot our third passenger.

Bekina: Do we have time to hook him in, too? Lorenzo?

Lorenzo Lillie: I have an idea I'd like to try, if what I suspect is about to happen, happens. We'll have to let our third passenger for through the process while they're in transit.

Bekina: Can he survive it?

Lorenzo Lillie: He'll survive. That's the least of my worries.

Bekina: Call for a council hearing. [Council appears]

Council of Judges: What is the nature of your concern, Our Scientists?

Lorenzo Lillie: I, frankly…

Council of Judges: Everybody is frank here, Lorenzo Lillie, strike the preliminaries.

Lorenzo Lillie: I recommend that Story Teller not be allowed to travel with Manila and Neptune to the New Colony. He represents trouble if he stays.

Council of Judges: And, what do you say Bekina? [Bekina agreed with Lorenzo Lillie on the grounds that StoryTeller asks too many questions.] My, My! Onc would never know that you and Lorenzo Lillie are our prized scholar-scientists. Does he ask too many questions? Recommendation denied for reasons of subjectivity on the part of the allegers.

Lorenzo Lillie: We are not barristers. We are not counselors-of-law.

Council of Judges: My, my Lorenzo Lillie, not only are you subjective, you are trying to rationalize you subjectivity.

Beknia: Not subjective, Council. Emotional not subjective. The two are separate.

Council of Judges: And, reinforcing!

Bekina: Not necessarily!

Council of judges: All right! Bekina state your case.

Bekina: The whole purpose of sending Neptune and Manila to the New Colony is to introduce some civil law, is it not?

Lorenzo Lillie: Yes, and to teach the New Settlers how to communicate non-verbally.

Council of Judges: Go on!

Bekina: Lorenzo and Bekina feel that StoryTeller may create so much confusion when they arrive, that the project may be jeopardized. This project is too important to allow a non-existent destroy it. If this fails, there is no future for the human species, as we know it. PHEW!

Council of Judges: Strong argument, strong argument, now, the evidence.

Lorenzo: Oh! [To himself.] Oh, Dudley squat! Hartz! Phartz!] Evidence! [Surprise] You saw everything we did.

Council of Judges: Exactly! Obviously you saw something the untrained eye cannot detect. Please, share your findings with us. [Bekina and Lorenzo Lillie wanted to "we feel" only to realize that that was even more unscientific.] Not enough! Story Teller may turn out to be our salvation.

Lorenzo Lillie: Council, I hate it when you start to sound…

Bekina:…Metaphysical…..

Council of Judges: Yes! And, the two of you sound like twins: one position; the other process. The answer is still no. [Council disappears.]

Stellar Four: As you know, I zapped Story Teller this time. I could not take it any more with the Council and all.

[Council appears.]

Council of Judges: Stellar Four, as our Reporter, tell us, how did you come embroiled in the wits of Story Teller, too? [Now, to the twins,] Your point?.... Yes, we have decided to approve Saweto taking the trip with Neptune and Manila if he so desires. [Sawato then appears to approach the Council.]

[Now to Saweto.] Saweto, the Council convened for another matter. Upon learning from Stellar Four that you want to approach the bench, we decided to remain until you arrived. Do you have a request?

Saweto: Yes, Council. I trust that your patience is our greatest strength. I must request that you grant me leave to travel to the New Colony with my friends and family. I shall be happy to look after Story Teller. I think I can satisfy both concerns, simultaneously.

Council of Judges: Granted! Safe journey. May the species continue? Be careful. When he discovers that the passage,.... He's going to raise holy hell. He can be very persistent. The Story Teller is a very clever person.

[Everyone breaks out in laughter, where upon StellarFour announces that Saweto wants to sing a song he wrote especially for this occasion.]

Council of Judges: Granted! Safe journey. May the specie continue? Be careful. When he discovers that the passage...He's going to raise holy hell. He can be very persistent. Story Teller is a very cleaver person.

Saweto: This is dedicated to the people of tomorrow.

Sing: What awaits the passion

      of the night.

      As we travel into the dawn.

Chorus: A light passage. A mirage

flight. What awaits ......

A night passage on a midnight

light through a time mirage

A night passage on a midnight flight through a time mirage

CHAPTER 20

Stellar Four: I could not have said it better. These were the parting of Saweto as we bade farewell to our Next Chosen. You see, Saweto is to govern in the absence of the Barrister-General. His choice as Barrister-General is based on ability and intellect. He governs by the Common Will. Everyone receives the same information as well as the same powers. That is the only way a republic can run democratically: by the will of the citizenry.

Just who are the citizens, you ask? Kinshasas—we say the word together and without the "h" in the last syllabus. We have no idea what prompted Story Teller to call us the way he did. Anyway, where was I? Oh yes, Knishasas automatically, if they can experience peace with silence as a mode and means of communication. This means that Manila automatically qualified upon arrival Fifty-plus-One. She immediately turned in to Saweto and read him well, although she did not know what she had done. All others become citizens by means of internment. The length of the internment is dependent on your ability to learn non-verbal communication.

I must say that many of our New Comers will never become citizens. They do not seem to possess the ability. It is a gift, you know. Only a few of us have the gift. All are Kinshasas. That is why the experiment with Neptune is important. We made a breakthrough that may save Fifty-plus One from the fate of its twin republic on the other side. The place called Carima. The problem we are going to face is this, people from the old country communicate with sound; noise is what we call it. Sound consumes a lot of energy and covers a lot of space. Too much for people who live in time rather than space. That is energy that may be used to keep our life cycle going. "Talking" creates a dissonance in the time particles that keep passages open. That dissonance has turned into a movement. In other words, the waves we have relied on are becoming too stormy for travel.

The people who were once peace loving are now talking about violence as the only solution, some even demand that all of the space in the Time Mirage transport system be used to transport the Noners to the New Colony, Global Village. Of course, that would certainly do if such attempts were made to remove them by that

Council of Judges: Mind your tone, Stellar Four.

Stellar Four: We do not wa to use time to leave, but we have no choice in the matter. We only regret that they cannot return home. How many, you say? We lost count when they reached over one hundred million. There is a good side, however. With the loss of such large percentage of its population has forced the old country to call upon us to help.

The Council corrected, "Assistance."] ...Assistance! Thank you, Council, in need of our assistance, as a kind gesture, we offered our own Council chair to assist this newly emerging nation-state. It has been a principality for so long that we have loaned our Chair to establish rule until normalcy has been restored. It now operates as nation-state: presently, under the leadership of the Chair. The Chair is the President Goraka I, and he is away in the old country. The old country as a new nation-state has adopted a name to signify it new status. The citizens call it Xaire [pronounced. without the "X" Aire].

In Reverence to the borrowed leadership, he new president is referred to as Our Savoir; this reverence does not set Goraka apart from his people. He is one of us always. He is one of them now. As our representative Goraka has pledged to end all hunger, starvation and poverty in Xaire. We are proud of this offering. What makes us even more proud is the fact that we have already given the New Beginning Two of Our Great Leaders: Goraka President of Zaire and Soweto Distinguished Ruler of Global Village, blessings to those who give willingly.

As our Blessing, the Noners are now productive citizens of; excuse me, residents of Fifty-plus-One. How did the Miracle occur? We discovered how to convert the Noners Sound into productive energy. Accidentally we discovered that the Noners make beautiful music with their voices. The musical groups that you saw in those Nite Spots are products of this discovery. Not only do they make beautiful music with their voices, they also invented unusual musical instruments that they play when they perform The music they play and sing is usually performed in many different times sequences using those minor tones they are so noted for. The way it works is all of the time sequences complement each other as an orchestration. Amazing.

What we learned is the Noners seem to be in rhythm with our motion. Did I say that right? Anyway, that's great but all they want to do is sing and play their music all the time. ALL THE TIME! That simply drives us up the clock. But it works, so what do we do? I know that this may sound or seem like it has nothing to do with what we are talking about, but that brings me to another situation that I have avoided. Well, Um! Okay, this is it.

We need—we think - blood transfusions from the Noners if we are to survive. We think, I said. It is so taxing to talk about, but here it is. The Kinshasas must call upon the Noners for help—sorry—assistance to survive. Up to now, many mistakes that we are not proud of have been made in trying to resolve this contradiction. At first, when it was theorized that Noners blood might mean our salvation, we panicked. Many lives were lost, Noners lives.

How? I must decline to answer that question. Humanity would suffer great traumatic stress if I revealed what some of the things are the Kinshasas did. Unspeakable! Let us leave it at that. In any case the Noners, now the majority at least, occupy the New Colony, Global Village. However, it has been determined by our Council that the Noners cannot govern themselves properly at this time. They have not been sufficiently trained to govern themselves, yet. Thus, to expedite her development it was decided by the Council that Neptune and Manila accompanied by a team of Kinshasas would constitute the new governing body.

This team will be lead by Saweto. It is thought that the experiences in Parliamentary Law that Neptune and Manila bring with them will prove more valuable in the Global Village, than in Xaire. Xaire has its leaders, Global Village has none. Get it??? None! Noners HA!HA!HA!HA!HA !HA!HA!AH!AH!HA! Isn't that funny? Time of the Noners.

Council of Judges: Stellar Four, Stellar Four. You have begun to editorialize again. Please, resume your duties as a reporter. As the Council cautioned, your commentary should only be given when required to provide information. That is, better insight into the matter. You are cautioned not to become subjective.

Chapter 21

Krishna: [Time switches to the New Colony, Zania. Hip City Daddy is giving a Nite Spot audience his interpretation of how they came to occupy this new virgin territory they call Zania. This the same place Stellar Four refers to as Global Village.]

{By now, everybody is laughing like mad.}

Hip City Daddy: Hold up. Hold up, I gots another joke for yah. Hold up, now. I gots another for yah! HA! HA!HA!HA! No wait. Wait.

still don't know how it happened, but the best thing that happened to us was to end up in Fifty-plus-One. No, serious! HA!HA!HA! I know you don't what I mean. But check this, living there taught us how to use sound to open the passage. HA! HA! HA! Ain't that nothin'? Funny, we had to end up in Fifty-plus-One to find out how to use our Music, our gift, to open the passage. It's been there all the time; we just didn't know how to get there.

The question is, is the gift from the Creator or the Kinshasas? It may very well be so, but it is good. No! Of course, all the lives we free. Free at last. HA!HA!HA! AH! HA!HA! OH! YES! FREE AT LAST! When I finally realized, I said to myself, either they are lying, or Hip City Daddy has found a way to get to the other side. HA!HA!HA! Did you hear what I said? HA!HA! But is this Heaven, I thought? I don't think so. I don't get the feeling that this Heaven. As a matter of fact, I find the place rather depressing. HA!HA!HA! You know what I mean?

There is something strange goin' on, I said. No body talks! HA! HA!HA!AH! AS soon as I said that, somebody said, "Hello." HA! HA! HA! HA! AHHH! HAA! I said what? What waz dat, I'm thinking to myself. I ain't said nothin' to no body, you hear me? I ain't said Dudley squat to nobody, and somebody says, "Hello." HA!HA!HA!HA! Then another person says, "Hello." NAW! NAW! She says, "Good Morning, may I help you?" HA!HA! HA! I said, oh shit. Did you hear that, they could hear everything you're thinking? Oh, shit! That's wild! HA!

So, I said, Okay you mothas, what's the trick? How do it work? You can hear me. So, I wants to hear yawl. How do it work? You see, whether you teach me or not, I'm gonna learn how to do it. I'm gone learn it some kinda way. You can do it, I can do it, bottom line. Bet. 'Sure 'bout dat. So tell me now or kill me right on the spot right now. Right on! HA!AH!HA! HA! HA! AA AH! ZAP! That's what it felt like. I was gone. But, I kept rappin' to'um. I just kept rapin.'…,

They crazy yo know! HA!HA!HA! Anyway, they stopped me here. By the way, I ain't no NONER NO MORE! Matter-o-fact, I ain't never been nobody's NONER. Never! This is our territory. It has a name and it has people just like you and me. The look just like us and are in the same position we're in. They were the least favored just like you and me in Fifty-plus-One. Now they're here. We're here. And here to stay. I don't care what nobody says. This is our territory. It has a name and it has us, people. The name of this territory is ZANIA. Let me hear it from everybody. [AT THIS POINT, HIP DADDY PAUSES TO LET EVERY SAY,]

Audience: ZANIA! ZANIA! ZANIA!

Hip City Daddy: This is how it works for us. If we want to open a passage let's say to Earth Life Epoch number fifteen, we gone play the music. We simply play the music. We play the music in the time required. We can go where we want…It is the sound that creates the form. It is the time that creates the passage. [At this point, someone from the audience speaks in support of what Hip City Daddy has just said.]

Smart Ass: Yea, our way is easier on the personality. The way the Kinshasas are using it, it collapses the personality. That's why the Kinshasas die from DRY ROT. They are simply burned out. [Audience goes into hysterics as they fall all over the floor laughing.]

Hip City Daddy: So, what will they say when they can no longer remain there? What will the Rot Tons do when the lights go out? HA!HA!HA!HA!HA!HA!

Cocky Brave: I say we prepare to greet them with open arms, cause they'll be coming home. HA!Ha!!HA!

Hip City Daddy: Greet them? Greet them? Greet them, how?

Cocky Brave: The way they greeted us, the way they treated us when they stole us away from our homeland.

Hip City Daddy: Yes, but don't that work out in our favor? Look at us, and look at the people who stayed behind. They're dead, or dying.

Cocky Brave: I git it, what you said, but I stand by what I said, too.

Hip City Daddy: Hold on brotha, we ain't here to fight. We're just makin' jokes. [The whole audience laughs due to the humor and partly due to the fact that nobody wants to deal with what may lie ahead.

Chapter 22

Krishna: [The setting is Xaire, a.k.a. the old country. Goraka who is President is walking briskly and thinking to himself.] {He is on the presidential grounds, which measures about thirty-five hectares. He is walking with his Cabinet of Ministers in his favorite section of the grounds, Ife's Garden, eventually speaks so the rest can hear him. He keeps forgetting that the people here do not communicate silently. So, it is only when one of his Cabinets speaks, usually with a question that he remembers to "talk."}

Goraka: {Thinking silently. I hope the message got to through to the Council of judges on Fifty-plus-One. Our energy has gotten very low, I can tell. They hardly know that things are bad here, too. Or, do they? Who else is taking all of our people? Where are they disappearing to? I wasn't satisfied with their answer.

If the Kinshasas are talking bull shit after we agreed that it would end, we must stop them. What do they need with so many? We've lost count.....six or seven million, at least.......I don't know how we'll get there now, however. The passage has been shut off. And, we have no defence against them if it opens again.}

Nailah: Goraka, may I help you with something? You seem perplexed. What seems to be the matter? The Cabinet is concerned.

Nailah: Yes, Goraka, you must let us know so we can help you.

Goraka: I never expected it to turn out like this.

Nailah: Yes, the aftermath has been tragic. We must keep trying thou Goraka. Don't you think?

Goraka: Of course, of course.

Krishna: Goraka's mind continues to wander. Or, is that wondering what to do? The Council of Ministers never told the truth about where Goraka came form. No, no, let me restate that no one could really understand where he came form. It seems right for him to lead the Council of Ministers, or Cabinet, as he prefers to call it, however. They do not care that he might be a foreigner. Now, he feels that he is failing them. Eight years it take to arrive back in the old country, now called Xaire, pronounced Aire, after another two generation of absence. Now, here he is President Goraka of the New Republic of Xaire, named after his people the most favored, occupiers of the original position the Kinshasas.

Goraka thought that the Kinshasas would be proud of him. Instead, there were pirating his people. Why? What would they gain by taking so many? It's in the millions now. But, the Kinshasas cannot possible house of these people, that's impossible. Fifty-plus-One could not have gown so big since he left there to return to his native soil, the place of his birth. Never. Not in such a short time.

Goraka: I just do not understand, Nailah.

Nailah: Yes, Goraka.

Goraka: Do you have someone...

Nailah:....That I thrust, implicitly? Yes, what do you want done?

Goraka: We need to go around the mass to find out what's going on.

Nailah: What information do we require?

Goraka: We need to know why so many of our mass are missing.

Dip Ditty: But Goraka, I thought that after my report, we had given up on that. You never requested to see it.

Goraka: That is true, but we simply cannot continue this way.

Dip Ditty: But what about my findings? What happen to my report?

[Ignoring Dip Ditty's question, which offends him to no end.]

Nailah: We'll expedite it immediately, Goraka.

Goraka: Thank you, Nailah.

Dip Ditty: And, what about my report? What will you do about my findings? Are you even going to ever read it? What will you be looking for?

Nailah: I don't really know. What would you suggest, Dip

Goraka: Dip, that is your constituency, what do you think? What do you suggest?

Nailah: Goraka. Maybe Dip would like to assume the charge.

Goraka: No, I thought about it, and I would rather have an unknown to the area go in right now.

Nailah: So what do you suggest? Dip? Where should I start? I know, I'll begin with your report Dip. Minister Dip Ditty.

Dip Ditty: I began at the Nite Spot. How old is that Nite Spot? It's only a few months old. The owner is one of the mass. He is very committed to their cause,

Goraka: OH? I see! Nailah have your informant to start with this Nite Spot, Global Village. And, I want a full report tomorrow. Please tell him...

Nailah: Her!

Goraka: Her? OH! Okay. Have her to be careful. We don't want her missing, too.

Krishna: There were many changes after the Civil War ended, when it was finally over. Finally, I said. It's not over yet, as quietly as it is kept. The most favored, as the middle classes, won for sure. The mass also won a few seats in the Parliament and a Cabinet Post. Dip Ditty now holds the Cabinet Post as Minister Without Portfolio. This means he has no departmental responsibilities and no one to supervise. He's just there. Since becoming Minister, he has lost many of his constituencies. They have simply disappeared. Dip Ditty took it upon himself to investigate the disappearance without any request from the President or Parliament. He went there and produced a report: A very extensive one. But no one would read it. That is, until Nailah said that there is where she will start.

Goraka had requested a copy but never commented on it until Nailah stated that she would take it upon herself to read it. Until today, it was never spoken of. And, no one is thought to have read it. The report is 532 pages, no wonder.

Knowing that Dip Ditty has done all of this research, and knowing that Goraka has not taken the time to read it, the mass call Dip Ditty the "mouth piece" because they say that he talks so much that no one listens. Already threats have been made against his life. The gossip around the District is that Dip Ditty was elected by the more votes than are registered has not helped matters at all. The fact that Goraka has called for an investigation has caused the mass to cry corruption. These cries have gone ignored. So, it is interesting --- some say insulting --- that Goraka has called Nailah, a stanch critic of Dip Ditty, to lead an investigation into the "missing." Those who call it insulting, base their remarks on the fact that it was Dip Ditty that first reported the people missing. Dip was in a good position to know because he was street banker before becoming a politician. As a street banker, he dealt with just about everybody on the urban street. No body listened, however. The critics said, HA! Who cares? They are only the mass. They are not like us. We can stand to loose some of those poor bastards, anyway. Here, they are a drain on the resources.

Not Dip Ditty. He feels otherwise. These were his clients, so to speak, his associates, his friends.

After the Civil War ended, no matter what precautions were taken, people would end up missing. The middle classes were blamed by the mass because many merchants had been engaging in the illegal slave trade before the old country became a Republic. The accusations against the merchants left Goraka unsuspected, except by the old line Monarchists and Loyalists who are now dead, due to the revolution. With His base of support all dead, King-General Mathew III, who was in hiding, surrendered and Parliament demanded that he be hanged for treason. A compromise was reached: "Let Mathew "live," and the prodigal prodigy can become your next King-General."

It seemed like a natural succession to power. After all, by law, the prodigal prodigy was the Next Chosen in line for the job. Isn't that something? For the duration of the Civil War, a price was on the prodigy's head. After the Revolution, he becomes the compromise candidate for the Presidency and the job as Head of State. So, the first thing he does when he assumes power is to discard the title King-General, and becomes Chief Minister of the Cabinet. For that, he is accused of betrayal. His enemies swear to avenge him. In return, Goraka declares that a monarchy no longer exists. To add insult to injury, this is done by decree. He then has Parliament, which is controlled by the Revolutionists, to pass a law to that effect. In the process, the old country is given the name Xaire, and declared a Republic. The nobility no longer exists as an official organ of the state. The Kingdom is no more and the Knighthoods are legal fiction. The New Class has won the Civil War. Through Goraka and Parliament, they control the state.

Not beset with enough controversy, the High Priest moves into the Presidential Estate to serve as the Spiritual Advisor to Goraka. Also, she retains her elected membership to the Parliament, which allows her to serve in the Cabinet.

Who is this femi-wonder? Nailah, Akuya, Kinshasa, Mother of Manila, High Priest of the Akuyus, and one of the "remainder," as those who stayed are called. Nailah is a member of the Family of Priests from the Hau de-no-sau-nee, who dates their linage over seventy thousand years. Nailah was selected to become Priest by birth. However, she became High Priest on her own. (By the way, the term "Priest" is used regardless of gender in Xaire.) Oh, one more thing, the owner of the Global Village is also a High Priest. He was a street banker before the Revolution, now he plays his music and runs his Nite Spot. Nobody I've talked to knows his real name so they all call him "Sharp." His imitates call him, "The Musician." They say when he performs—which is rare—the sky seems to open up like magic. Obviously, Nailah either knows or knows of Sharp, the Musician, so why the game?

Nailah: Goraka has asked me to find out all I can about the missing.

Blue: I thought you were going to tell him.

Nailah: I just can't seem to find the right occ

Blue: So what's the deal? Where do we start?

Nailah: With the Global Village

Blue: The Global Village?

Nailah: Yep! Dip...

Blue: ...The mouthpiece suggested it. That...

Nailah: Patience! Patience! Go over and warn the Musician. Something is up. Goraka has something else in mind.

Blue: How do you mean?

Nailah: Well, Dip Ditty was to report his findings about the missing, but Goraka has not called on him to do so. He was pissed when Goraka ask me to do the assignment. I think...

Blue: What's the report about? Did you read it?

Nailah: Yes, and it's not bad either. Too long, 532 pages, but extremely detailed and exact. It's about how many of the mass have been missing since the Civil War began.

Blue: Dip showed it to you?

Nailah: Yes, but it's public information, too. You should read it. He doesn't know anything about how the mass has grown.

Blue: How do you mean?

Nailah: Well, with the adventure we have going, any other time, somebody would have snitched. Somebody. But, nobody has..

Blue: Yes, but didn't you say that Dip suggested that you begin at Global Village?

Nailah: Yes, I did.

Blue: That's not snitchin'!

Nailah: Take it easy. He doesn't know. He only wants to. He knows something, but he can't figure it out.

Blue: Has he been inside?

Nailah: I am sure he has, but everybody knows who he is. There's nothing he can find out.

Blue: And, with us? Does he suspect?

Nailah: NO! Don't say it. You know the penalty. Don't say any more.

Blue: Sorry! Okay, I'll go over to the Global Village. When do you want a report?

Nailah: Tomorrow afternoon. 1300 hours. The Cabinet has a meeting at that time.

Blue: Okay. That should give us enough time to....

Nailah: .... Do further research if we need to. I'll check Dip out further in the meantime. Apparently, he's on to something.

Blue: And, what about....?

Nailah: Don't call any names...

Blue: But you called....

Nailah: I am the High Priest! I can do some things nobody else can do. I can block any intrusion, except from the Guardian. You do not believe. You do not have such powers.

Krishna: For your information, the Guardian is the protector and finder of the future. The role of the Guardian is to protect all High Priest from themselves and others.

Blue: Are you telling e that?

Nailah: I can read your mind...

Blue: How? What did you do? Nailah!

Nailah: Never mind! When yo're ready, you'll

Blue: .... Let you know. Yes, I know! Later!...

Krishna: As Nailah leaves her companion in EcoCentral Regional Park, we see Dip Ditty moving in the shadows of the trees toward the street. Obviously, I became so involved in Nailah's conversation with Blue that I was not ever aware of his presence. I wonder if he overheard the conversation. Better still, did he see who Nailah was talking to. On the other hand, if Nailah is so good at what she does, why didn't she...

Nailah: Hello Dip! What are you up to? What are you doing over here? {Startled at how quickly Nailah approached him Dip Ditty retorts,....}

Dip Ditty: I might ask you the same thing. What are you doing over here? {Realizing that she surprised Dip a bit more than intended Nailah apologizes.} {Also, she wants to maintain the advantage.}

Nailah: Sorry, did I startle you? I'm sorry; I really did not intend to do that. I simply saw you a while ago and was surprised that you were in the same vicinity as I. Sorry!

Dip Ditty: {Realizing that Nailah has read him, but trying to sound convincing so as not to loose ground.} NO! NO! {Now angry and ashamed at the same time.} {Nailah continues the conversation from the question Dip raised, as thou "ain't no big thing."}

Nailah: {Teasing} I live here. What your excuse?

Dip ditty: {Trying not to appear too doggish, Dip accepts Nialah's tease with visual reservations.} ...I was walking and just decided to....

Nailah: {Taking the tease too far Nailah adds, ...} ...to be in the area. Try another one...

Dip ditty: [Now really defensive, Dip retorts,...} Hey! This is my park, too. I'm in the Cabinet just as you are. I have a right to walk where I please. {Wrong word}

Nailah: {Now realizing that Dip Ditty's ego is injured a bit more than intended Nailah then responds in kind.} Go ahead! Go ahead! Go ahead and say it!... {Some how Nailah hopes to relieve some of the tension, but she really does not realize what she has unleashed. still she prepares for the worst, she thinks.}

Dip Ditty: You, you Black Bitch!

Nailah: {Surprised beyond belief.} What????? {Even more surprised than she thought.} {Dip doesn't stop there, however. So, Nailah is even more surprised, now.}

Dip Ditty: I'm tired of you mombo jumbo bullshit. I'm gonna cut yo ass to ribbons.

Krishna: Obviously, this is a bit too much at this point, so simultaneous to Dip making that statement, he drew his straight razor out of no where, and I know that Nailah is D-E-A-D! Stone dead! She didn't have a chance. It was just too quick. I wanted to help, but I was so shocked that I didn't know what to do. It was so fast that I saw it, but I didn't. I was still trying to phantom where the razor came from when I suddenly noticed that Nailah was walking away from Dip Ditty and me like nothing had happened. The only problem was Dip Ditty was nowhere to be found. He was gone. I swear. Dip! PHEW!

Now that was heavy. That shi' was heavy. I still don't believe it. I swear. Oh, my goodness, I forgot. I am not suppose to get involved. I am only here to tell the story. But, what happed to Dip? Nailah,.... what's going on?

Nailah: Look! Let me tell you what happened so that this storyteller does not loose his kool, snap and loose his job. You're not gonna believe me, but Dip caught me by surprise when he called me a Black Bitch. I got so angry when he said it that I zapped him right on the spot. The nerve. It blew my mind. He was caught with his razor in his hand, speechless. What he said was really uncalled for. I am not that kind of person. I am not to be called anybody's bitch. I am too nice a person for that kind of abuse from anyone. Even Dip Ditty. Especially, Dip Ditty. The nerve. I can't believe it.

Krishna: Yea, but what happen to Dip Ditty? Where did he go?

Nailah: You're the storyteller, you figure it out. Use your imagination. The think is, he's not here with us, is he? By the way, you are out of a tight one so you own me.

Krishna But, I don't understand. And, I am not suppose to be involved.

Nailah: That's your problem! You figure it out! Remember, you owe

Krishna: Wait-minute, you can't do this to me. You know the ruls. I'm the storyteller. You can't do anything without my knowing first

Nailah: Test me!

Krishna: I don't believe this. Look, I don't want this job. It's not worth it. It is simply not worth it. I don't get paid enough. I am not going through this, again. PERIOD! And, to think, I wanted to save your life.

Nailah: HUM! I suppose, but you were too indecisive. My life was at stake. He did have a straight razor, you know. And, that was a deathblow he had aimed at me.

Krishna: I mean.... do you let up? What happen to Dip Ditty? I know you did not kill him. Did you?

Nailah: I came close to striking that sucker dead. {Nailah demonstrates to Krinsha how close she came. Krishna still does not understa

Krishna: What happen

Nailah: {Realizing that Krishna does not know what she has just done to him, she precedes to answer the question he has asked.} My guardian stopped me just in time. I had already signed the death certificate. I thought this was his death wish when he called me a Black Bitch. So, I was about to oblige him with pleasure. Dip Ditty is a very lucky person. Somebody was looking out for him. He should read the signs and mend his ways. Soon! Any other High Priest may not be as giving. Or, even better, the Guardian may not get there soon enough. Anything can happen. And, next time it certainly may.

Krishna: Now wait! I saw Dip pull a straight razor out of now where…

Nailah: {Nailah wants to laugh, but she knows that Krishna is serious and that this is no laughing matter.} At least, to… Did you see that? What else did you see, after thinking about it? After that, I mean?

Krishna: I do not really know. I don't recall seeing anything. I simply knew that you were gone forever. There's no way that Nailah should be standing here now. No way. Yet, according to her, she performed this magic trick and instead of Dip Ditty being arrested for her murder, he's now "incapacitated" with Nailah walking away as though nothing ever happen. What the hell is going on? Anyway, this is you story teller Krishna on the job as always saying, see you later. It was a pleasure. I hope you like it. I have done my best. {Will somebody please tell me what is going on here?]

Chapter 23

Goraka: {Thinking, contemplating, reflecting, wondering} All I can do is to wonder. There is nothing more for me to do. I wanted to be the King-General of the country. I got that. I was almost -- what am I saying—it was gift. The position I hold I fell into. But, it's the prostitution I always wanted. It's the position I was trained for. Who could have received better training? I attended the best institutions of advanced learning in the universe, to my knowledge, of course. Who could have received better training?

I hold a doctorate of laws diploma. I discovered the passage. I found the lost work. I left a son in the Chief Council's seat. A position that requires a million times the responsibility of the one I hold, now. While in the other position, I accomplished untold knowledge, Knowledge that may be useful forever. Now, I have retuned home and brought the Republic together. I give it a name. The mass opposes it. What 's a name" old country," anyway. HA! That's not a name of anything, or, anybody. HA!HA! old country. Not even with capital letters.

......Yes, old country is now Xaire, and all I have is famine, war, bandits, revolutionists, and witch doctors, so, what is life? What does it mean? Now I have more problems on my hands. The passage is closed, which means that my community links with Fifty-plus-One are gone. On top of that, someone is raiding our republic and taking away the mass. The question is who? Saweto my son? Naw! Not my son, Saweto. .... You know, I really feel isolated. No one here generates that kind of energy I need to feel at home. Isn't that something?

I felt more at home in our new world creation than I do in my birthplace. Five generations can do that to you. So I've tried to build a replica of Fifty-plus-One in the old country. Excuse me, Xaire. And, of all people, the mass has given the most resistance. Amazing isn't it? They are the ones who stand to benefit most; something about they lived better, grew taller, and enjoyed, more freedom as hunter-gathers.

What nonsense is that, something else about not wanting to learn how to from here. What makes them so special? So they happen to be taller than everybody else so what? Diet has nothing to do with it. Besides, there are now too many mouths to feed, to everybody reaming around the countryside hunting for food.

To top that off, now, I learn that my administrative services are rotten to the core. Nothing gets done without a fee going into somebody's pocket. Our new technology does not work for a lack of spare parts. So, it sits idle and rots. When I ask about the matter, I am always told unequivocally that parts are on order. Upon checking further, I learn that the treasury is empty: we cannot order because we have no money. Everybody wants to be paid in cash.

To make matters worse, we cannot produce anything, food or consumer good. All of this has happen after we decided that it would be best for all to allow the urban mass migrate back to the farms because they would be much happier. It now means that we have no choice but to modernize through automation. I can only wonder, where will we get the wealth? I should think, what would be next?

Tattle Tale: Goraka, Dip is dead, and Nailah is accused of committing the crime. She allegedly murdered him.

Goraka: Dip? Dead? Dip, Dead? Nailah, the murderer? Have we gone mad? Where? When?

Tattle Tale: Now nobody knows...matter-o-fact, no one has found his body. It happens over in the EcoCentral regional park, near to where both live. It happen just a while ago. They say that Nailah must have used her voodoo on him. Apparently, Dip Ditty pulled a straight razor to cut her throat, and no one has seen him since.

Goraka: Is this a joke, two Cabinet members fighting in public? It is a New Republic. This is not the old country. We do not carry on in witchcraft, superstition, and street crime. We are supposed to be beyond that.... where is Nailah? I want her at my Cabinet meeting, and Dip Ditty had better be there, too. And, I mean that.

{Specially called Cabinet Meeting is in session. Goraka is speaking.}

Okay, now that we have finished our regular meeting, I ask the Cabinet to remain convened so that we might inquire into the matter of straight razors and voodoo. {The Cabinet ministers all laugh at the way Goraka announces the agenda.} Who wants to begin? And, I expect this forum to remain....

Faugard: ....Cut the bull Goraka, go on with the show. {No matter how often it happens, Faugard always surprises everyone, including Goraka, with his bluntness.} [What is even more amazing to the Cabinet is how Goraka does exactly that.]

Goraka: Who wants to begin? Nailah, you firs

Nailah: I was put walking to my District, a while ago and I ran into Dip Ditty coming toward me. I greeted him, and ask, not really serious, if course...

Faugard: ...Of course!

Nailah:...What are you doing in this neck of the woods, or something like that, and Dip, excuse me, Minister Ditty [Everyone except Dip and Goraka laugh.] got angry and called me a "Black Bitch!"

{Ministers groan in disapproval, all looking at Dip Ditty.}

Faugard: Wha? Did that? Dip? What's the matter Dip? Got a problem or something? {Goraka calls for order.}

Goraka: Continue Nailah, Ministers you must refrain from editorializing.

Nailah: Then, he pulled a straight razor, and I had to protect myself.

Goraka: And, what did you do?

Nailah: I placed him under suspension until now.

Goraka: Okay! Is that all, Nailah? {Nailah signals that that is all.} [Ministers object vigorously.]

Ministers: How despicable.

Faugard: Dip! Dip! What's the matter you? You know he rules, get out. We don't need no crisis over some nonsense like yo

Goraka: All right, Faugard. Let dip Speak. Watch your language Dip. By the way, why were you in Nailah's neighborhood?

Dip Ditty: I was checkin' upon something...

Goraka: Oh? What?

Dip Ditty: I wanted to see if Nailah would follow up on that matter we discussed yesterday.

Goraka: Oh? And, what did you discover? {Ministers object to allowing Dip Ditty to talk about his spying on Nailah.} My, this gets more interesting all the time. Go on, Dip, And Continue. {Objections get loud.}

Dip Ditty: any way....{Faugard interrupts Dip Ditty to ask Goraka what matter, Goraka answers Faugard leaves Dip Ditty alone, and goes right back to Nailah.}

Goraka: I simply asked Nailah to conduct an inquiry into why we are missing so much or our population so rapidly. And, without a trace. She is to check it out for me, and report back when she has some pertinent information. Oh, by the way, excuse me Minister Ditty; is it too soon for you to give us a report, Nailah? Did you check that Nite Spot, Global Village, out? Did you find anything, yet?

Chapter 24

Jom: Nailah has never gotten herself caught in this situation before, except, when they requested that her daughter, Manila become the first representative of Parliament for the secondary and university scholars when that same august body requested that Manila be allowed to become the first Member of Parliament to be represented in the New World Colony. Since Manila was from an original ancestor and occupier of the most favored position, as a Kinshasa, it was thought that she might be able to make the communication between the two jurisdictions positive and rewarding to both sides.

Although honored, Nailah had mixed feelings about allowing her only daughter, the youngest representative ever to become elected to Parliament at age eight, to go so far away at only age fourteen and, on such a dangerous mission. But, being a patriot, Nailah consented. Then she realized that Neptune and Manila were not going to return. It was too late then, so? By then Saweto Goraka's son, had wedded her daughter.

Nailah did not appreciate that turn of events at all. Before the trip, Nailah had approached Goraka personally and inquired extensively about the journey. It was then that she learned about the passage. The guardians of the word had long talked about the passage, and now, through no doing of her own, Nailah's only daughter was about to take a journey every priest dreams of taking daily. What an honor.

Nailah knew of Goraka through family relatives who lived in "Kinshasa Ville," as outsiders called it. The stories she heard always sounded so strange, and mysterious. Yet, she found them interesting as a people. True! Nailah was a Kinshasa, but her clan practices were of a different order. "Her family was sho nuf Vudoun.

In any case, Goraka assured Nailah of a safe passage to and for. He totalled the round trip travel time to be about twelve years: six years there and six years back. Nailah discovered this t o be not quite accurate. She was pissed. NO! That's not correct. Nailah was insane with anger and rage. She could have ZAPPED Goraka right there on the spot. However, her better judgment warned her against it. So, she waited. She even worked as part of the conspiracy to keep Goraka alive when there was a bounty on his head.

You see, Nailah's tradition says that the mother must see her daughter before she goes on to another existence. That is a must. If not done, Nailah must live her existence as this life forever. That is the worst form of punishment that can be brought to bear upon a High Priest of the Akuyu Kinshasa people. Nailah knows therefore that she has no choice but to find her daughter. She knows that Goraka has to remain alive, too. So, she protects him. To do so, she has become his most trusted ally, his Companion-in-Residence, and a Minister in his Government.

On Goraka's part, he has long forgotten the ways of the New World Colony. He has even stopped practicing ease dropping. He has really gotten lazy. Tired. Complacent. Alienated. As a result, Goraka has chosen to resort to violence/force too often for the people's taste.

They have gotten rid of Mathew III, and they can certainly do it again if Goraka is not too careful. I'm not certain how much power Goraka has over that, however. The thing is, he's done what leaders who assume power the way he did tend to do, i.e., he got cocky. Anyway, let's return to the question on the floor. What was it now?

Goraka: Did you check out the Nite Spot, Global Village, Nailah?

Nailah: I've had someone to investigate the matter.

Goraka: And, what have you learned? What did your informant say?

Dip Ditty: Ask her whom it was she talked to? Ask her who her informant is?

Faugard: {Cabinet is very disturbed about the loss of confidentiality grumble and moan. Faugard speaks out} YOU KNOW THAT'S CONFIDENTIAL INFORMATION, DIP DITTY. GORAKA IS THIS AN INQUEST

Goraka: NO! NO! NO! Faugard, please? Later, Dip.

Dip Ditty: NOW! I SAID N-O-W!

Goraka: Well, that puts me in an embarrassing position. Obviously, this matter between Dip and Nailah goes deeper than I realized. Can you be rational and accommodate us Nailah.

{Cabinet Ministers scream}

Cabinet Ministers: WE OBJECT! WE OBJECT!

Goraka: We overrule.

Jom: Minister Faugard demands the floor.

Faogard: Goraka, you'd better watch your Parliamentary procedure.

Goraka: Sure! Go on! Answer the question, Nailah.

Jom: By now everybody sees this as a set up with Nailah no way out but to explain. If she is right, the Ministers will go after Goraka's head. But, if she is defenseless, however, Nailah does not stand a chance. This is pure improvisation on the part of Nailah. She knows what the stakes are: this is strictly the "Big Leagues" here. Her very life is at stake.

Nailah: I'll tell you what I learned, but I refuse to divulge any of my sources to anyone even Goraka, in public.

Goraka: That leaves it up to Dip Ditty and, Dip it's your ass if you don't have something to do.

Jom: Dip Ditty knows he has the upper hand, so, he plays it for what it is worth., [Pause] Nailah's life.

Dip Ditty: Nailah's contact was Abdul Malik.

Jam: The whole place went silent.

Minister of Agriculture: Abdul Malik

Minister of Community Development: I thought he got killed in the raid where they tried to assassinate Goraka over there. Somehow not aware of the contact between Abdul Malik and Goraka, Faugard questions Goraka.

Faugard: You know Abdul Malik, Goraka? You know that revolutionist?

Goraka: BANDIT!!!!

Minister of Community Development: Who held Goraka prisoner for almost, how long was it Goraka?

Goraka: TOO LONG! IS THAT TRUE NAILAH? THE MOST WANTED CRIMINAL IN ALL OF XAIRE, AND YOU WERE TALKING TO HIM IN OUR REGIONAL PARK IN PUBLIC? THIS WAS YOUR FEMIPERSON INFORMANT? ARREST NAILAH!

Jom: The Cabinet opposes Goraka's move to arrest Nailah. Faugard speaks.

Faugard: You do, and you've got a Civil War on your hands. Go ahead, leave Nailah.

Jom: After a brief impassé everyone heads for the door. Dip Ditty immediately moves toward Nailah to block her way.

Dip Ditty: Stop that voodoo Queen. Goraka, she can't leave this room, she's dangerous. Stop her. Stop, you bitch.

Jom: Just as Dip Ditty yells out to Goraka, he pulls his straight razor and approaches Nailah. Minister Faugard sees him and jumps in the way as Dip Ditty swings his arm down and across. Faugard drops to the floor bleeding profusely: his throat is cut from ear to ear. Within the same instance Nailah releases a force that strikes Dip Ditty with such impact that he tries to fight back. In his effort to remove his attacker, he moves uncontrollably toward Goraka. The Security Force, confused as to what to do or whom to detain, sees Dip Ditty's irrational movements toward Goraka and fires point blank at the frame of his body. Dip Ditty is killed instantly.

Funny thing is, Nailah disappears during the fracas. After all of that, se manages to escape, and unharmed. Goraka is furious, needless to say. He sends his Security Force scrambling after her, but apparently they are too late, because Nailah is nowhere to be found. Some how she has escaped the Presidential Grounds undetected.

The first thing Nailah does when she leaves the Presidential Grounds is head for the Nite Spot, Global Village. Upon arrival, Nailah informs the Musician and Blue – A.K.A. Abdul Malik --- about the incident, and what transpired before. Garaka immediately issues a Hugh reward for her capture, DEAD OR ALIVE! The Musician and Blue decide that Nailah had better go underground, now.

Blue: They should be on their way here shortly, we'd better act fast. Should she take the "A" train or the #2?

Jom: Take the "A" train is the signal for someone to be shipped out immediately. No #2 means that she will do directly to Zania.

Sharp: It's up to Nailah. However, if you want myvote, I'd say that she might was to take No.#2. Ship her out, and now.

Nailah: I MUST STAY! I UNDERSTAND THE DANGER!

Sharp: Okay, it's up to you, Blue. UH! Abdul Malik! HA! HA! HA! HA! That's your territory. But, we need a signal. HUM!

Jom: After everybody thinks for a while, The Musician speaks.

The Musician: Hey! I GOT IT! GIANT STEPS! That'll be our signal. When I play Giant Steps, listen for how I improvise to receive the message.

Nailah: OH, BOI! INTELLECTUAL HA!HA!HA!HA!HA! I like that. I like that very much. That's such a beautiful tune. Thanks Sharp.

Sharp: That was The Musician who suggested that idea.

Nailah: Oh, yes. I meant The Musician, sorry. My blood is pumping so hard and fast, I Uh, Never mind. You all understand.

Blue: John Coltrane!

Nailah: Cultural Feeling!

Sharp: Okay, now. Let's go! We don't have time to waste. Remember once per week on the weekend every Saturday night.

Blue: When you see us again, even you won't recognize us.

Nailah: OH? Master of disguise I'm traveling in fast company. I think I'm gonna have some fun.

Sharp: HA!HA!HA! OUTA HERE

Jom: The moment Blue and Nailah disappear, the Security Force arrives. The Global Village is jumping with people the moment they enter. Upon entering, the Security Force creates an, "I ain't gone lighten up off yo ass 'till I gets what I'm commin' for, and that's Nailah. Any body wanna say something, speak now 'cause from here it's yo ass."

Blood: Yo! Wha u hit her fo, man? Yo mamma ain't teach u nothin'? She ain't teach u no mannas?

Killer Miller: Take them goddamn muthas off, and I kick all u muthas ass.

Jom: Now, this is funny. The Security Force lightened up. The tension was so high and rose so quickly that the Security Force forgot why they were here. You could hear a rat pee on concrete it was so quiet.

Captain: WHERE'S THE OWNER? WHO'S IN CHARGE HERE? WHERE'S THAT MUSICIAN. SHARP?

Jom: We're looking over around them. The soldier knows that there is no chance that he will get out alive if he fires his weapon. There is no way out, but to leave peacefully. By now, you can see the beads of sweat crawling down everybody's face. Finally, without thoroughly searching the place, the Captain pulls his force out as quickly as he can reassemble them. Once on the out side of the Global Village, it is another story.

Captain: ABOUT FACE! READY! AIM! FIRE!

Jom: The soldiers fire on the Global village point Blank. They fire and throw everything they have at the place. This goes on for a good three of four minutes non-stop. The place sounds like a major offensive has been launched at the enemy in a surprise attack. Under the cover of the very darkness that allows the Security Force fire at will toward the Global Village, Blue and Nailah look on at the joy expressed as the soldiers take pride in the slaughter of others lives mercilessly. They are very troubled at what they see. For the moment, each thinks of the times this tragedy could have been prevented or avoided simply by killing Goraka. Each has had the opportunity. Each declined. Now, their close friends are being ruthlessly murdered while they watch. Nailah suddenly asks…

Nailah: My Guardian, should I have given up? What are you doing to me? I could have avoided this tragedy simply by killing Goraka. Tell me, what am I to gain in this insight now that I have saved Goraka? Please, tell me…

Jom: Simultaneously, Blue thoughts are…

Blue: I have lost all of my comrades because of Goraka. All of them, and all we ever requested was one person one power. We saved his ass, and his first executive order is to declare the LEFT WINGERS OUTLAWS. We were not only out of the Party – Our Party – we were outside of the law. He made us Outlaws and then put a reward on our heads collectively. So no matter that all but one was assassinated, if one is still alive, he is still an Outlaw, forever means as long as I'm alive, I am an Outlaw. And, now I witness this pogrom. My god, must the price always be so high? Must the prize be so costly?

Jom: At last, it's finally over. The bombardment has finally ceased. What? What is that I hear, Music? Is that music I hear? Coming from the Global Village? NO! That's impossible. How could they? Who could be playing that music inside of the Global Village after that, that deplorable exhibition of humanity at its worse?…Oh, my God, I'm responsible for this madness. I should have allowed Nailah to go on after I didn't see Dip ditty. It's all my fault. I have failed! Nailah told me. Now, she's wanted for treason and murders she did not commit…And, are they really that mad, too? Who would play music on an occasion like….? But, listen. What are they saying? What are they saying, Nailah? Opps! I am not supposed to be talking to Nailah.

Global Village Choir: {Sing;} Me-di-ca-tion for some kind of peace. Ye sai me kai. Kai ye me asi kai. Ye sai me kai. Kai ye asi kai.

Jom: Listen! Shssss! Listen! They are repeating it louder and louder. Look at the building. It looks like nothing has ever touched it. I do not believe this. Nothing has happened to the Global Village. Impossible! Improbable! Come on, now. I see it with my own eyes. I did not think about something else this time. I was alert. I see what is happening. There is no way that this place called Global Village is supposed to be standing. No way! Look!

Whom ever is responsible please tell me why things are not what I see, what they appear to be. I see a person pull out a straight razor. Next, thing I see is like nothing ever happened. Now, I see some military soldiers shoot their best shots and they are singing and playing and dancing like nothing ever happened. Is this real? Is this psychological warfare going on here?

How am I suppose to tell the story and not have it appear to be that I am making it up if you continue to do that? Do you want me to act as though it is not real? Is that the point? Anyway, by the time I regroup, the soldiers are walking up to Global Village—each of them—and touch it to see, as if in total disbelief. They're walking away like zombies. Their weapons drop to the ground for lack of attention. The Captain has fallen to the back of the pack as though it is a natural place for him there. He has his rear end exposed as though this is his only gesture left of defiance. He shows in utter defeat he can still show contempt.

Blue: You see that?

Nailah: Yes, but isn't that symbolic, the letter "X" dragging along in the rear with his bare ass exposed for all to see?

Blue: Symbolic? That appears a show of utter defeat. It goes back centuries. Many centuries back. The exposed backside is dishonor and infamy. They will all die when Goraka hears. That is part of the old country tradition that still remains.

Nailah: …You mean, there is also vengeance after such an embarrass- ment?

Blue: UHHH! Yes, that is true. That is certainly true. One thing is certain, that's the safest place to be, now: Global Village, the Nite Spot. Glad Sharp and the rest are okay. Okay, Nailah, let's go while we have the advantage. We need to strike right away. We can keep them off balance until we hit them with the whammy.

Jom: And strike they did, every time Goraka turned the other way, they would smack him. Every time he turned, SMACK! Goraka has already arrested all of his former Cabinet Ministers after forcing them to resign. Now, he is going after their relatives, friends, ands associates, accusing them of consorting with the enemy. Blue and the Panthers have increased their attacks upon the military targets to the point whereby he has sought and received military support from the Limited Fascists States of The Old World.

Sharp, in turn, has opened up the "pipeline" as more recruits may enter Zania-on-the-other side, as it is called by the Opposition to undergo training in small group tactics designed for urban warfare. Zania as you may recall exists in another Earth Life Epoch. So, sharp the Musician refers to it as "Zania-on-the-other side of Zaria-in-the-otherworld." Within a matter of months, another full-fledged civil war has erupted all over Xaire. Goraka has been so stunned and confused that he has suffered from bouts of depression that have lasted weeks on end. Part of his problem is, he knows where his enemies are coming from: Paid mercenaries from all over the continent.

Goraka: But where are the Rebels getting their military personnel and supplies? Some how there seem to be more people in Xaire during warfare than during peace. But, is this possible or am I suffering from battle fatigue? How can it be a nation that is suffering a population loss, have enough people and energy to fight a domestic war?

Jom: So, in continuation of the madness, Goraka recesses Parliament and issues s decree renaming the mass the Akuyu people, since according to Garaka, their misguided leader Nailah is an Akuyu. Nailah, in turn, has been elected President of Parliament, and, except Goraka's supporters, have remained within Parliament Hall in defiance of Goraka's executive order. Goraka, so as not to be outdone, declares Parliament Outlawed as an enemy agent of a foreign Republic to be named.

Parliament passes a bill naming Abdul Malik "Hero of the State." Goraka reportedly goes stone cold mad upon hearing about this action. According to other reliable sources, he literally "goes off" killing at random those who dared to disagree with his pronouncement no matter how irrational they are. As an example of his madness, a noted Barrister-General is murdered in broad day light today for no apparent reason except that he is in the wrong place at the wrong time.

In retaliation, Parliament declares Goraka an "Outlaw of the People" just a while ago. A reward of .25% of the state treasury is posted to encourage "some law abiding citizen to capture and bring this 'mad dog killer' to justice. There are already reported attacks on the newly reinforced Chief Minister's Palace walls. It seems to be a matter of time before someone finally gets through, simply a matter of time? It does not matter that the treasury is empty; they want his ass, now. How they get it, they do not seem to care: Goraka is leaving office, period. The place is in serious Rebellion; and, Goraka is madder than that is at all possible.

Suddenly, out of nowhere, Goraka remembers that he has not used the "Gift." Remember? Goraka has the gift that he as a Kinshasa receives as a reward for accomplishment. The question is can he use it? Does it work? It has been quite some time since he has attempted to use it. Matter of fact, he has been so engrossed in all of his trials and tribulations that it might not work. I am not sure that that is such a good idea at this point. It may well just back fire on him. Why? Nailah possesses the same gift. And we know that hers works, don't we? Anyway, whatever?

Chapter 25

Yani: The economy of Xaire {called, Aire} has never fully recovered from the previous Civil War. The public treasury is broke, in other words. So, obviously, the state needs capital, venture capital to be exact. It also needs an operating budget which means that receiving venture capital is out of the question: Xaire is too debt ridden to attract investments from the rich Kinshasa living abroad, the place the new republic has to go to get enough capital to clear up the mess the first Republic in civil war, now the second Republic after its civil war has caused. When you must call on your classmates, and they tell you, "sorry, can't help you, that's your problem," what do you do? Tell them, "go fuck yourself?" Then, what?

Obviously you fight another civil war, because somehow you have not resolved where you want to go, and how you expect to get there, or no group has established dominance – hegemony – over the operation of the state. So, you'd rather fight than talk. To resort to a military solution is in this case a belief that you can defeat your enemy in the end. Or, you have no choice, i.e., you are backed into a corner. Whatever the reasons, no one wants to give up now, no matter the costs.

What is the Kinshasa abroad saying? [As an aside, I still prefer calling them the Kin-Sha-Sha people. It sounds more distinct, however it has been agreed that we should recognize the integrity of a people's name, and they prefer to be called the Kinshasas. After all, what's in a name, the basis of its claim? Now that I have got that off of my chest, where was I?] As I said, what are the Kinshasas abroad to say about all of these wars that have plagued old country since Goraka arrived, especially, those living in Fifty-plus-One? Why have they refused to enter the conflicts? Or, tried to bring about a resolution, to bring about a peace? I guess one might respond that everyone who or that has involved themselves in the conflict have gained nothing and are now worse off. They have gained nothing and lost much, many everything, including their families and wealth. And, the question nobody ever asks is, whose going to take responsibility for the dead bodies? "Nobody, you said. That's why nobody has asked the question."

Now, take that.

Blue: You know Nailah; I hope the people don't think Goraka's the cause of our hardship.

Nailah: They do! But I know what you mean.

Blue: We'll never straighten the situation out as long as we think that. Well, I guess that's a task for the New Revolutionary Council, don't you think?

Nailah: Yes, I guess it is.

Yoni: At this stage "of the Revolution," the Revolutionary Council seldom disagreed on matters of importance. As a matter of fact, foreign correspondents began to make too much out it; saying things like, "Blue has total control over the New Revolutionary Council." And, "nobody ever discusses Revolutionary Council matters outside the Global Village." Global Village is now the "Official Headquarters of the New Revolutionary Party." Nailah is listed as the Prime Minister, Abdul Malik is Minister of External Relations, Sharp is Minister of Culture, Communications and Aesthetics, etcetera, etcetera, etcetera.

Everyone is wondering why it is taking so long for the Revolutionary Council, or, simply the Council as it is commonly referred to, to select a location as the symbolic "Headquarters" for the opposition, and a place for Nailah as Prime Minister to meet with her Cabinet. Anyway, the day the New Revolutionary Council announces that it has founded a new political party, and has chosen the Global Village ass the sight of the official headquarters of this new political party, a Congress held to elect the members to the new House of Parliament will convene within the next six months.

This will give each District an opportunity to conduct their local elections to decide whether the people selected at the Congress are acceptable. However, as reported by NOWCAST, the major focus of the twenty-eight hour debate is over what constitutes the correct revolutionary approach to the Revolution. According to that report, "it was finally agreed that propaganda should be the major emphasis of the struggle." I could not help thinking at that point, "here goes the rhetoric."

Blue: Where do we begin?

Nailah: What about starting right here, at Global Village.

Blue: What do we do? Ain't no time for dancing, you know.

Nailah: No problem! We'll let Pots perform, free.

Blue: Pots? I thought Pots and Trevor were artists. I didn't know they did speaking engagements, too.

Nailah: This is not a speaking engagement. Pots is going to humor the people.

Blue: NO! NO! I said Pots, not Pots and Trevor. And, this will not be a speaking engagement. Pots is going to humor the people.

Nailah: Humor the people? Hey, I thought we were discussing politics. How?

Blue: Who said you cannot do both. There is no law that says we cannot have a comedian at the Global Village. Pots is the best political satirist around today. Who would be better?

Yoni: Blue sees the logic and agrees. Nailah knows that Sharp will be easy to convince: he suggested the idea. She was correct, so, the next evening Pots was asked to "speak" at a special meeting that had been called just for him to speak. He could not refuse. Besides, the mass needs to know what is going on. What better way to inform them than with homor? If anyone can do it, Pots can.

Sharp: Look, Pots. Isn't that Pot coming down the street? What is that? Are those people? Damn, it we'd gotten word out sooner, the place wouldn't hold anybody. Look at that mass. Ain't that something? They all coming to see Pots.

Yoni: Now, this should be very interesting, people.

Blood: YO! SHUT UP STORY TELLER YANI AND LET POTS HAVE DE FLOOR.

Killer Miller: YO! Hey, Maine, bee kool, chill out. Leave the Story Teller Yani alone. She has a right to be here. How else is anybody going to know in the future? HUH?

Yani: Looks like Pots is going to be bad tonight. Look out!

Pots: Naw! I ain't necessarily gone be sassy tonight…I don't know what mood I'm in to tell you the truth. And, frankly, I don't give a damn. You know me, if it passes you by, bye.

Yoni: By now, the audience has begun to laugh.

Pots: I gotta tell you a story about something I saw the other day. It's about Story Teller, Yani. She didn't see 'cause I did what she does. You know, pick out a wall, and watch the story unfold. UH! HUH! You didn't know that I watch you, too, did you? There's somebody even watching Story Teller, Yani. See! You never know. Ain't that right, brotha man? Right, Blood? [Pause]

Blood, don't look now, but, there's a gorgeous sumptuous phat mama about two tables over to yo' right, right behind you. Don't look! She's looking you way, don't look. UH! HUH! Guess what? Mam? Is that you escort sitting there with you? He plays what sport? How tall is he? And, how much did you say he weighed? [The place is rolling with laughter.]

NAW! NAW! Blood ain't nobody with her. I was just teasin'. What you say, Blood? You too shame to look, now? NAW! Seriously, you can look. What u say honey?

Phat Gorgeous: You shouldn't embarrass him like that.

Pots: OH! I shouldn't embarrass u like that. Sorry! Damn, Blood, she's serious. You ain't said one word yet and she's already takin' up for u. Got damn! Wait-a-minute, if you just want somebody to slobber over… Naw, I was just kiddin' Blood. You can go ahead. Blood, I ain't go take her from u. … I tell u, when the Lawd gave out ugly, he decided to treat Blood kindly. He made it impossible for him to look in the mirror, 'Cause he knew that if blood saw himself he'd commit suicide to keep from screamin.' Now, that's ugly. Just think Blood, everybody until tonight thought that you had not committed suicide because you're brave. They didn't know you couldn't see yourself.

I guess there must be some Blood in all of us. We all gots some ugly in us…When the God gave us the instruments with which to sing pleasure unto all to hear, they expected -- I suspect – us to use music to bring love, freedom, beauty, compassion, harmony, unity to this universe we inhabit. Yawl, understand what I'm sayin'? So when, are we going to act like its ours? When we go act like this space is here for all of us? That is, if we learn how to treat it right. That's the problem. We are not treating earth right. And, after a while, not even this earth can take any more. It can't tak no mo'! It caint take no mo'! We caint take no mo! We cain't take no'mo'.

Yawl know what I'm sayin'. We got comfortable, yawl. Good music can do that to anybody. Thang is, we now at an impasse. Ain't nobody movin' everybody just holdin' on to their position. Why? They waitin' to see what we gone do. So…

Blood: What we gone do, yawl? Let's take it to the Chief Minister, Goraka's Presidential Estate. He ain't Bad: Yo! That's our Estate. So, it's time to take it. Lets' take the Estate. Right on

Blue: Now that we've got that taken care of let us enjoy Pots. First, make sure we understand that our activity will operate primarily in three areas: Propaganda, Political, and Military. Okay,

Yoni: As Pots begins to unravel history; ironically, similar events begin to unfold in real life.

Pots: Thank's Blue. Now that yawl done acted so righteous, we gone really git down. Did you hear me? I said, we gone really git down.

Yani: The place is in a real uproar now. Then, [pause] things become so silent that you can hear a phat rat full of piss and vinegar piss on concrete.

Pots: I mean really git down to some hard-core comedy. I'm mo' have yawl laughing so hard that the bottom is gonna fall outa Gomora. They gone thank we crazy in here. I can just hear Gomora. {Now Pots gets loud.}

ATTENTION ALL GOMORANS, FOR QUITE SOME TIME NOW, WE HAVE BEEN ROUGH SHOTTED BY THESE VILLAGE BANDITS, SO-CALLED REVOLUTIONISTS. IT HAS BECOME IMPOSSIBLE FOR DECENT PEOPLE TO TRAVEL THE HIGH- WAYS AND WALK THE STREETS. REVOLUTIONARY BANDITS HAVE TAKEN OVER THE PUBLIC WAYS. THEY'RE TERRORIZING US DECENT COMMON LAW CITIZENS OF XAIRE, EXCUSE ME, GOMORA. MURDERS, KIDNAPPIN', ARMED ROBBERIES, AND THESE THUGS IN THE NAME OF THE AKUYA COMMIT HIGHWAY CRIMES.

MOST IMPORTANTLY, THEY ARE TRYING TO OVERTHROW OUR LEGITIMATE GOVERNMENT TO GAIN CONTROL OF THE STATE. WE ARE CIVILIZED PEOPLE. WE DO NOT NEED VIOLENCE TO TALK TO EACH OTHER. WE MUST BE WILLING TO HEAR AND RESPECT OUR LEGITIMATE AUTHORITY. I'LL ADMIT THAT MY SOLDIERS HAVE ACTED A BIT HASTY ON OCCASION, BUT THAT HAS STOPPED. YOU MUST PLAY YOUR PART, ALSO. BECAUSE OUR REPUBLIC IS UNDER SEIGE. NOW, IT IS NECESSARY TO CHECK EVERY VEHICLE INDIVIDUALLY, AND THOROUGHLY.

IT IS ALSO NECESSARY TO SEARCH EVERY HOUSEHOLD. WE ARE AT WAR. OUR ENEMIES ARE THOSE BANDITS OUT RUNNIN' LOOSE. YOU MUST HELP US. YOU MUST HELP YOURSELVES. I MUST WARN YOU ANYONE SUSPECTED OR CAUGHT HARBORING A KNOWN ENEMY OF THE STATE WILL BE EXECUTED ON THE SPOT. I EXPECT YOUR COMPLETE COOPERATION IN THIS MATTER.

Yoni: EVERY ONE INCLUDING BLUE IS FALLING OUT OF THEIR SEATS WITH LAUGHTER.

Pots: NOW, ONE LAST MATTER. BECAUSE OF THE NATIONAL SECURITY, WE ARE EXTENDING THE ELIGIBILITY FOR MILITARY CONSTRIPTION TO AGE OF EIGHT FROM TWELVE ON THE LOW SIDE AND AGE TWO HUNDRED AND FORTY FROM ONE HUNDRED AND SEVENTY ON THE HIGH SIDE. ALL OTHER PERSONS MUST VOLUNTEER TO DEVOTE THE PRESCRIBED TIME TOWARD FURTHERING THIS CAUSE OF THIS REVOLUTION WE ARE ABOUT. WE MUST DEFEAT THE REBELS AT ALL COSTS. HA!HA! HA!HA!AAH! HA!HA!

THIS IS YOU PRESIDENT FOR LIFE, OF THE REPUBLIC OF GOMORA, GOMORA I. HA! HAA!HA!HA!AAH!HA!HA!HA!HA!HA!HA! {Very quietly!} As Gomora, President-for Life, left the news conference with his Army of eleven thousand bodyguards; someone planted buzzers in everybody's ear. Each step taken, each bodyguard heard this deafening sound of nothingness.

Yoni: Laughter is at a very high peak with tears steaming down everybody's face.

Pots: In their effort to locate their center the bodyguards began to push inward! Inward! Inward! In panic Gomora starts to shout and scream.

Gomora: OH! MY God! They are crunching me! I am finally going to die. No!No!No!

Yoni: Now in total silence.

Pots: After half had crushed each other to death, primarily those on the inside, and presumably Gomora, the First President-for-Life in the mythology of the old country, in the process, the half remaining then moved outward into the streets of the Capital City. Out of anger and frustration, everything in their way was destroyed. You see, this was a "tribe" of bodyguards who in their six thousand years of work had never lost a ruler by assassination.]

They went mad. They were completely out of control until Blue and the Revolutionary Army arrived. By then, Gomora, bodyguards were totally disorganized. They were taking everything in sight. Burning, looting, killing, whatever fancied them was confiscated in reprisal to the death of their leader.

These bodyguards knew their fate: DEATH! It didn't matter whose hands they fell into, be it Parliament, The Revolutionary Council or tribe the came from, the fate would be the same: DEATH! So, they killed and destroyed. That brought even further shame on the tribe from which Gomora's bodyguard came. As their ward, they has inadvertently killed him, and then destroyed everything in sight while roaming the streets out of control. That was their greatest sin.

Now, let me tell you about the tribe of bodyguards. The Ukuyuebo tribe is a tribe of bodyguards who are very disciplined and reliable. No matter the stress, they never loose their cool. They will die first. Huh! Modern times, that's what it is. You can't get the same quality of service we did in the good old days. These punks punked out, and acted like uncontrollable animals in a panic.

They became a mob after realizing what they had done, or, what they were going to do. You know what I mean. Can you imagine eleven thousand bodyguards? Being squeezed to death by themselves, and ain't nothin' no body can do about it, and neither can you? Huh? Can you imagine that?....Just like that! I was gearing up for the big fight, and before I could get me a cold brew and sit down, the thing was over. Jokes like that! It took me a while to figure out what went down. Thus, the panic and I knew Gomora was dead. Just like that and it was over.

I mean, it's kind of funny. You know what I mean? There you are proclaiming yourself President-for-Life, and before you can finish, you are through. Your term has ended, and you have not even served one day in office. Why, too much attention too many people around you to protect you from your potential enemies? So, in their effort to help, you die, unceremoniously.

Not from some expert sharp shooter, or some exotic drug, no by the bodies of your bodyguards. There is something definitely......you know? I think I'm pissed......I can't tell because it all happened so fast, but I think I oughta be pissed but why? Look at what Gomora did. He had become a vicious dictator. He was said to have foreign bank accounts. He wanted to build another palace somewhere out west, but it was just too unpopular.

Really, he could not have left too soon for my money....Listen to me. This is a Civil War I'm talking about, and here I am treating it as though it is some blow-by-blow description of a prime time fight. The most brutal of Gomorans leaders is not dead, and I talk about it as though we are watching some sporting event live on visual. That's not good. What we need now is peace. Let me ask you, what did I say?

Crowd: Gomora is dead. We want peace. Give us peace

Pots: We want peace. Give us peace. Even with Gomora gone, peace did not come to Gomora. First there was an out break of typhoid, followed by cholera, then by a vicious now twelve year drought that wiped out just about all plant life: all the crops; all the domestic animals; and, all humans were suffering from starvation and political conflict. Things had to change.

Knowing their lives were at stake, Blue was elected President – a post the new Republic kept – of the House of Parliament and Chief Minister of the Council of Ministers. He deferred his Chief Ministerial responsibilities to Sharp, the Musician, but remained President of the House of Parliament. Blue later resigned from the Council altogether to devote time and energy toward healing the wombs of the country. The problem was, because the Revolutionary Council was structured and operated primarily by urban intellectuals and entrepreneurs, it did not realize that there were other peoples living in the New Republic of Gomora who felt totally neglected by all sides of the Civil War. It's not that they feel betrayed by the Revolution, they feel totally left out of the process. However, now that a "Constitutional Convention" has been called, they have made special requests that autonomy for their respective regions be written into the new constitution of the Second Republic.

The urban intellectuals and the entrepreneurs want to maintain power primarily where it is, in their hands. These are the reasons that the regions have requested that only their personally elected representatives be seated at the convention. And, only the can bid in their behalf. No problem!

All was moving smoothly when suddenly the entrepreneurs and the intellectuals objected to the idea of one of the old Monarchist's children being elected to the convention from Medina, the old commercial town of Gomora. This objection was put forward even though her constituents duly elected her. Blue intervened, and she was seated. Now, Blue has a new set of enemies because he is accused of promoting the interests of the Monarchists. None sense. Blue argues, "That this is impossible, you know what I own."

Blue went on to say that it would be funny if it were not serious because it was the commercial sector and university intellectuals who bought those titles just before the first Civil War heated up in earnest. "All they want is the maintain their hegemony."

These anti-Monarchists argue that we live in a Republic, and that titles are nonexistent here. That is true among them, but to the rest of us it is Sir Chad, lady Naime, ectera, and ectera. And, they do not plan to loose that distinction, republic or no republic.

In any case, it wasn't a real fight anyway because the anti-Monarchists and the Monarchists are so small that they are no real threat to anybody. The real fear is about those who represent the second coming as they are referred to. These are the new free entrepreneurs who are introducing these new production techniques throughout the countryside.

Pots as Sir Stead Fast: "New Enterprisers" in power, we'll loose the country to the foreign investors and the land speculators.

Pots as Captain Jingo: Yes, that's true. We must protect our on.

Sir Stead Fast: That's one thing about Gomora, he may have been kind of heavy handed and had his ways about getting things done, but he didn't let our land fall into the hands of the foreigners.

Pots: Yea! Sure! The grass is always greener when you look back, isn't it? Don't get me wrong, this was not purely nostalgia. There was much merit in the feelings expressed by the old guard of the most favored. The new policy under the New Age Alliance Party was to open up the market, to generate more capital, to encourage more adventure, adventure Capital.

Instead, things got worse. More and more peasants searched for homes in the city. In a matter of seven years, what was once a city if a quarter million, now boasted a population if over two million people. That's my guesstimate. Some say the real figure hovers around three million with a few thousand entering each week.

Everyone in power by now has admitted that things have truly become out of hand. There are not enough jobs, not enough services, not enough houses, not enough schools, food, hospitals, on forever to adequately support the numbers crowded onto the streets just at day break. At that time, human bodies are lined up to beg for "whatever you got this morning my friend. God bless you."

For those of you who have never been in this situation before, there is no picture, not even in your imagination. It is the silence. That is what you can hear most strikingly. Silence! It is the silence that raises your consciousness about the future of how you're going to live. THANK YAWL! IT HAS BEEN A PLEASURE! THANK YAWL! THANK YOU AWL!

Blue: POTS! POTS! POTS! GO ON POTS!

Audience: CLAP! CLAP! WISTLE! CLAP! CLAP! POTS! OLE POTS! STILL GOTS THAT THANG ABOUT 'EM! CLAP! CLAP!

Pots: THANK U AWL! THANK YAWL! THANKS! I LUV U! SEE U!

Yani: Pots had to be a fortuneteller because two days thiry-seven minutes and fifteen seconds after his big performance, Pots last performance; Goraka was in fact squeezed to death. No fooling I guess Pots might have said, "That simply crushed Goraka's heart."

Ironically, it was Pots murder upon leaving Global Village that set the spark. It was Goraka's untimely public news conference that allowed it to happen. However, instead of a buzzer in the ear, it was brute force of one million people pushing in on eleven thousand bodyguards. It was no contest! All of the bodyguards were crushed, and so was Goraka, presumably. I say presumably because his body has never been found.

In any case, Goraka was given s State funeral. It was agreed that a show of solidarity was important. So, all garters were represented. The unexpected in my estimation was the presence of Abdul Malik. Of course, he was received with a standing ovation when he entered the Palace Temple. If anyone would have been forgiven for not being present it was Blue. But it was Blue's idea to have a state funeral. The Revolutionary Hero he was, there was no contradiction in being here today and his personal views on the deceased.

The unexpected for me was Sharp's absence. His absence represents the true feelings about this event and it s fanfare. But, I can truly say, there was unity in the old country today, Pots was given a Hero's funeral at the Global Village Nite Spot. "The Musician" performed his suite "Meditation For some Kind of Peace" in full regalia. It was something to behold. Yes, I guess that is the only way to say it. It is truly something to behold.

One never ceases to be amazed at the Musician's genius. Incredible performance! It was like all of his soul and spiritual self were present as one. Simply incredible! A masterful performance! I cannot help but wonder will he do next? PHEW! WOW! AMAZING! That was some performance. Oh, I guess I am beginning to repeat myself.

Oh, yes what, it was recorded. Copies can be purchased at your local black market, or, from your local storyteller…..

By the way, how did you like that "it was so quiet that you could hear a phat rat full of piss and vinegar piss on concrete?" Was that bad? Anyway this is Yani, you favorite storyteller signing off.

Chapter 26

Yoni: There was no surprise as to who the next Prime Minister would be. She had already sat as head of Parliament and the Revolutionary Council, simultaneously. The choice was numerous. NAILAH! NAILAH! NAILAH! Unlike the characterizations of Pot's scenario, the 2nd republic of Xaire is not beset with famine and abject poverty. Nailah is proving to be effective because she seems to know exactly the kind of society she wants to construct. Also, she makes it a point not to appear aggressive or cocky. The thing is she she knew how listen. Most importantly, everybody has a right and the opportunity to express their views with out worrying about being put down or fired for expressing a unpopular view. What she does is to have everybody talk openly about their fears, concerns, reservations, as well as the merits of a particular project or idea or issue. This is all done before a decision is reached. Nailah can operate this very way because she has the ability to read everyone's thoughts: no one has a choice, so, everyone has decided that they might as well fess up and cooperate.

Through honest dialogue, much has been accomplished. The economy has begun to thrive again at a time when the other economies are faltering. Apparently, Nailah has combined what her opposition calls "voodoo: economic programs into viable units of operation. In fact, what Nailah has done or is doing is to sit down with each region and district until she understands the needs, desires, and aspirations of that region or district thoroughly. Then, she communicates to her staff how she wants them to approach that particular situation with a solution always the end result.

The approach has been a mixture of many forms and modes of economic organization. The results have been called a miracle. For instance, in the tropical region, she has shown the locals how to employ bambo to irrigate their crops by cutting them, making holes through the center and placing them in staggered rows so they allow the water to flow from the banana leaves into the holes of the bamboo shoots using gravity to take each arrangement to a particular bed of soil that needs irrigation.

A comparable thesis is employed in the desert region. There she show the locals how they may use the cactus and other desert plants to create more water sources by planting more in angles that take advantage of the water supply already there and create more water through rainfall. Somehow, these projects have all managed to work, or at least, appear to have worked. This allows ever region to feel that not only does she listen; she in fact carries out exactly what they have told her they want to have done.

The true test of Nailah's Administration has been the recent "energy crisis" that resulted from the drop in the price in the minerals Xaire supply to the world market. Everybody is Xaire calls it an energy crisis because they must now pay higher prices for their goods on the world market. What to do? Since energy they buy now costs more than it does to manufacture energy from agricultural products such as sugar cane and corn, Nailah has set about establishing plants that will product fuel from those products.

This is the opportunity she always wanted, i.e., it converts all energy producing produce, e.g., sugar cane, corn, soy and alfalfa, that are grown within the jurisdiction of Xaire to the machinery that can be used internally to manufacture fuels for local consumption. This she reasons will do two things simultaneously: provide more jobs, thus, putting more people to work both in the long run and in the short run; and, make Xaire less dependent on the world market for products that can be manufactured locally.

Surprisingly, it did not take Nailah long to set this project into motion because she had already allocated a larger percentage of the national budget for purchasing "relevant" research results regarding matters of national concern and development. She also had begun a project of having Xairean scientists and scholars to visit other countries and tap the brains of the best minds in other parts of the world. Allowing them to attend the best universities and institutes around the world does this.

This process is not done by catch-as-catch-can or by trial and error. No, she has calculated how many of these products are required to fulfill her mission. The mission is to create self-sustained development. So many Xairean have gone into the agricultural sciences, others have gone to study the biological and physical sciences until she now has a critical mass of trained workers to carry out her plan. They are taught not to rely on technology to retain all of their information. Her thinking is, what if they decide to take all of the technology from our learners and scholars before they leave these respective countries? Everything is brought home by memory.

The emphasis is placed on the technological equipment she is having manufactured at home. You see, engineers were the first to go away in this experiment. These engineers are now ready to implement every idea Nailah has in her brain, and there are many. The rest who go away are selected from a team of experts who are their peers. As soon as they return, they will sit down and study Goraka's "work." It is from this work that Nailah expects to obtain her greatest results.

Nationalist fever is reaching its highest peak with Nailah focusing on local initiatives while the world economy is in crisis. The motto is, we must feed ourselves first, then create a surplus for others to buy.

With this motto, Nailah is using this nationalist fever like a skilled artist. But, are they jingoists? The "chauvinist pigs" as they are referred to by the disenchanted youth. From the jingoists, nationalism in all of its aspects must be adhered to. That is their demand. Everything is expected to show some sign of nationhood. Art, culture, religion, music, polity, the economy you name it; everything has to say Made in Xaire. For instance, everybody has to adopt a name out of the old texts. No more foreign names.

The religious nationalists insist that not only should names be reflective of the rich culture of Xaire, it must personify the thinking of a Kinshasa. Everyone should be guided by the great principles of the Kinshasa's ancestors. Much pressure is being brought to bear on Nailah as Prime Minister and as the Spiritual Leader of Akuyu (the least favored who are the masses) and the Kinshasa to enact a series of laws requiring everyone to practice the Religion of the State. Nailah has refused. She calls it too doctrinaire, too parochial and extreme chauvinism of the male type. She tells them,…

Nailah: That is a non-issue, we are all Xairean people. Why do we have to wear badges telling ourselves that we are? It sounds redundant. It appears fascist. And, the last thing we need is another bout with fascism. I won't do it. We all know who we are. I have no further comment at this time.

Yani: The economic nationalists insist upon and have direct control over the operation of the market place. As the most of the most favored, that is those who occupy the ruling circle, they have designed the economy so that it is state controlled but privately run. All land rights are left as they were because no foreigners may own land or any other real property in Xaire. Besides, nobody wants to mess with Nialah's voodoo economics, while it is working that is.

The artists and musicians are basically cultural nationalists who believe that art, music; dance should express a social realism of the true believers as a way to show their belief in the true God. In this since, they are religious nationalists, too. Therefore, for them, art, music, dance, and the other performing arts should reflect the true culture of the Kinshasa in its pure form. The Akuyu led by the Musician oppose this form of nationalism on the grounds that it is stagnant. The organization he founded is called "Stagnant." The organization argues that is the very way Kinshasa culture has become obscure and out of touch with "reality."

The organization further argues that this way of producing art negates innovation and disallows creative labor from moving toward the future. Inventions will cease under this system of staged art. Culture must allow innovation of ideas to flourish.

Nailah has called all of the rival forces in to devise a contest to see who produces the best artistic expressions. This contest will offer the grand prize once per year with localities offering local contest that will lead to the finals. Now, there will be contest for the grand prize in all of the arts, creative and performing each year. A new aesthetic appreciation is called for according to the Musician.

The old guard has not taken to this notion too well. They do not like that idea at all. With Nailah's decision, this group has begun to cry for national unity. Political unity, that is. Nailah's response has been that she agrees completely, 100%, but according to how she sees it this means everybody, not simply the Kinshasa's art, music, dance, theater and other creative movements should be represented. In her speech she said,…

Nailah: I never knew that unity meant uniformity or that group because it occupies the most favored position should dominate the culture and the way people express that culture. The most favored should allow the people to show their crafts, skills and creative labor in ways that promote adventure and forward thinking. If nationalism is only for the Kinshasa people, then it might as well be called Kinshasa Ism.

Yoni: After her speech, rumors were spread that Nailah said that nationalism in Xaire should be called Kinshasa Ism. In the meantime, laughter rang throughout the chamber as the old guard sat there livid. Seeing the responses Nailah cautioned,

Nailah: We have had peace in the Second Republic simply because we chose it that way. Are we ready to change that? If we are, let our negative aggressions sit and relax for a moment. We can do without the tension that is being generated. Everyone's stress level has risen, so, I urge you to give yourselves a chance to think about it….and the price we will unavoidably pay if a conflict ensues

Yoni: Nobody could be as subtle and direct as Nailah. Nobody could be as frightening, except Blue. Why? No one ever forgot how Nailah is credited with aiming that angry Dip Ditty right at Goraka, and how Dip Ditty would have killed Goraka if the bodyguards had not killed him on the spot. The legend continues although Nailah maintains that that's not how it happened at all, it simply appeared to have happened that way.

Please, do not misunderstand me. I know how cynical we can be today. They are not afraid of her in a fearful way, except when she is attacked. No, the fear is more of an affection. Really! It is! Anyway, the old guard could not stand the scolding from Nailah in front of everybody in the House of Parliament, so they resigned en masse, all three of them. Too date, they have not been seen or heard of.

They have not posed a threat to Nailah's Government. Everyone applauded when they left. Nailah asked them to return, not to leave because everybody is needed in the struggle to make Xaire a better place to live. Paying no attention to her request, they walked out. As they moved through the aisles, the Members sat in silence. But, then out of nowhere Nailah said…

Nailah: YOU KINSHASA PEOPLE NEED TO GROW UP. YOU WANT EVERYBODY TO HONOR YOUR CULTURE AS THE ONLY TRUE CULTURE OF THIS REPUBLIC. YET, YOU CANNOT HONOR THE SYSTEM YOU CREATED. WHAT A DISGRACE! THE ORISHAS WILL PUNISH YOU FOR CREATING STRIFE WHEN THEY HAVE CAUTIONED US TO MAINTAIN PEACE…. AND, TO YOU RELIGIOUS FANATICS, NO. WE SHALL NOT INSTITUTIONALIZE ONE WAY OF TALKING WITH OUR CREATOR. ALL WAYS ARE LEGITIMATE. OLUDUMARE KEEPS ALL DOORS OPEN.

Yoni: The place rose in pandemonium. But, now it would not only be the cultural nationalists who would despise Nailah, it would be the religious oligarchy, too. Although they are few, combined they can produce bad faith. Does not matter, Nailah had her daily reading and all the signs were…

Nailah: Go for it, girl!

Yoni: Then something strange happens. What happened was this; last evening while Nailah was meditating a strange figure appeared and attempted to disrupt the flow. Although, it did not stop anything, Nailah was now aware that another force was present, and capable of operating within the same spiritual plane she could move in and out of. But, for some reason, the force backed off, a good thing too, because Nailah was set to destroy. She had already prepared to attack, and she felt the force move away.

Nailah: {Nailah is thinking to herself} (HUM! VERY SENSITIVE! IT MUST BE OPERATING ON THIS PLANE. BUT WHY? NO! WHO? HERE? THERE IS NO ONE HERE THAT I DO NOT KNOW WHO CAN OPERATE ON THAT LEVEL. SURELY, THE KINSHASA PEOPLE ARE NOT HERE. AND, THE OLD GUARD IS TOO CAUGHT UP IN RITUAL. THEY'D BE LUCKY TO CALL UPON THE LOWEST OF GODS AVAILABLE, THOSE FALSE PAGANS.

WHO WOULD KNOW? THE MUSICIAN! YES! OH! I MUST BE MORE CAUTIOUS NOW. WHO EVER IT IS CAN POSSIBLY READ ME NOW UNLESS I AM ON GUARD. FROM HERE ON, ONLY WHITE ALL THE TIME. I MUST ALSO MAKE SURE THERE IS NO EVIL WITHIN THE RECESSES OF MY CONVICTION. IF THERE IS NO EVIL THERE IS NO POINT OF ENTRY. I MUST CLEANSE MY SOUL, IMMEDIATELY! YES, I MUST SEE THE MUSICIAN. HE IS OF THE DARK SIDE. OF COURSE, BLUE MUST BE PRESENT, TOO. HIS INSUITION IS SO UNCANNY,

Yoni: When Abdul Malik arrives, Nailah and Sharp, the Musician, are already present. The percussion factory is a work making a cadence that has everybody meditative and contemplative…. Everyone is positive because each has been assured that Nailah's request is an emergency request and not a way of questioning the Orishas readings before. The Orishas have warned of nothing like this. So! What is happening?

The rhythmic pulse continues to supply the energy necessary to open the passage: the opening occurs all so quietly. A special guest is invited from Zania-on-the-Other Side, and her arrival is eminent. A humorous thing that happens is, as soon as it is time for our guest for Zania-on-the-Other Side to appear, right on time, in walks Abdul Malik. It never fails, always on time, Interesting! Very interesting. I still do not know how he does it all the time.

Sharp: HERE COMES FOLKS, ABOUT TO ARRIVE IS NONE OTHER THAN BIG MOMMA HUNTER. AFFECTION- ATELY CALLED BIG [PAUSE] MOM-MA [Drag the word…] HUN-NER.

Yoni: The instant Big Momma Hunter arrives, the crowd goes wild.

Crowd: UH! AAH! WOW! GEES! PHEW! God, she gorgeous. But, SHE'S SO HUGH. WOW!

Sharp: BIG MOMMA HUNTER!

Yoni: I'd never believe this if I were not here to see. If someone told be after and was not there, I'd say she's lying. If I did not see it for myself, anyway, the ritual is about to begin. Sorry folks, it all happens so fast… what are they about to do? Sorry folks, it is all happening so…. Oh! Big Mamma Hunter is leading the audience in a tribute to Pots – OH? No, excuse me folks, I've been corrected, that was not a libation. The tribute to Pots is about to begin. Let us see what they have to say. Maybe someone can answer some questions for us. Like, what is the purpose of this ceremony, Ms…

Usher: I am sorry sir, …

Yani: I am Mam, if you must use that authority stuff.

Usher: Yani, we say "sir" to everyone. No harm intended. Now, we must ask you to leave.

Yoni: Leave? There must be a mistake. I am a reporter. We have free access to information. That… this is our right. That is our job. We are to tell the story. That is the only way the future will know of us. Without me, you do not exist.

Usher: Not again.

Yani: Especially when it involves important events such as what is about to take place here this evening. Even more so when it involves the Prime Minister.

Usher: Yes, sir. I am aware of the Constitution. However, this is a religious worship. The right to privacy can be exercised there. We exercise that right, right now.

Yoni: But?….

Usher: Please…For Members Only. [Usher closes the door behind Yani as she leaves the Global Village Nite Spot.]

Sharp: Orishas of our ancestors, tonight we come to you as a troubled people. One of our gifts has reason to believe that a foreign body is trying to enter her person, unsuspected; the purpose of which is unknown. She believes that.

Nailah…The foreign body is not of this world. That somehow the mind of this foreign body is not the same as the other beings occupying our space; our time…there is something different that troubles me. The being seems to operate on a different energy level or source, whatever, but somehow, it's not the same.

Big Mamma Hunter: "It?" My child?

Nailah: "He" my Guardian. It is a male being. I know the force is a being, as we know beings to be. And, I know that it is male. But, it is sill far away. Yet, it generates so much energy. It generates unbelievable energy. Almost as forceful as an Orisha.

Big Momma Hunter: How flattering, my child. You could do the same thing if you got a running start, so to speak, before your launched your javelin.

Nailah: What is it my Guardian? The Lord, my light and salvation?

Big Momma Hunter: Whom should you fear, my child? I saved you, but I can't seem to give you much light.

Nailah: Yes, but this being seems to possess so much power and cunning, my Guardian. How can I fight such a life force?

Big Momma Hunter: You don't, my child. What is next, my conscious being of this world? You are still operating down here, my special child. The being as you like to call this form, this idea of yours, is operating out there.

Nailah: I am sorry, I do not understand.

Big Momma Hunter: My, my, is the Prime Ministership getting to you? You're outta shape.

Nailah: No, My Guardian, I simply forgot.

Big Momma Hunter: And almost got knocked off your little hinnie in the process.

Nailah: Yes I am sorry. I forgot, the Lord is my strength.

Big Momma Hunter:…and? Salvation…. of whom should you be afraid? My Goddaughter? Of whom should you be afraid? You must see the light.

Nailah: HUN? OH? NO ONE! Light and salvation.

Big Momma Hunter: Then, how did this force enter without your knowing? What door did the force come through?

Nailah: I don't know! I'm confused!!!! I do not know what is happening.

Blue: I KNEW IT! I KNEW IT! NAILAH IS NOT LEAVING THE GLOBAL VILLAGE TO NIGHT

Nailah: I am confused about what is going on…

Yani: I've never been so insulted. What do I do? The public is going to want to know something. What to do? Yes! I'll give them the news; I'll do a commentary. I'll explain in my own estimation what happened: on the evening of April 23, New Republic Time [NRT], this reporter attempted to attend religious ceremony in which the Prime Minister was invited guest of honor. I was allowed to remain until the ceremony began. At that point, the Usher asked me, to leave. This I might add was under protest. My question is why? Why would they not allow me to remain? What are they hiding? And why was this occasion kept secret?

This reporter, Yani, learned of the affair by accident. I just happened to be going…Well, actually folks, someone informed me from the Prime Minister's Office that something interesting was going to happen, but I was not told what it was nor was I allowed to stay. Serving the duel roll as reporter and storyteller, and all, I thought that informing me of the event meant that I could attend as an observer.

The interesting thing was, while I was there, the notorious Hip City Momma appeared out of nowhere. I am sure that it was some kind of trick, a magic trick, or something of that nature. We'll find out about that later. Right now, however, the important thing is Hip City Momma is alive and in town. The question is, where was she all this time, and is there still a price on her head? Only the Prime Minister can withdraw those charges, and the infamous reward.

In any case, Hip City Momma was seen by this reporter at the Global Village Nite Spot, former headquarters of the Revolutionary Council of the New Revolutionary Party. I shall keep you informed as new developments unfold….Meanwhile inside the Global Village Hip City Daddy is about to speak. How do I know? I was just invited to return and I am here now, than you.

Hip City Daddy: Please dear Guardian of the word, Oyu guided us safely through the passage although we knew not where we were going. You brought us safely back to our time, our space. You showed us how to open the door.

Big Mamma Hunter: Yes, but you fail to see the light. Our strength can not work all the time. We cannot continue to save you. You must see the light. Or, be able to travel on the Dark side. Which is it going to be?

Nailah: On the Dark side, On the Dark side, Where is the light?

Where is the light?, Where is the light?, Where is the light?

Big Momma Hunter: That is the question you must ponder, my child. But, remember you will seek but never find your foe until you recognize the light. Or, learn the ways of the Dark side. [Now directed toward what ever or who ever is an unauthorized presence at tonight's forum.]

And, now forces of revenge, I speak to you directly, if you choose the path of war, when the Guardians of this earth have employed you to do otherwise, you will be destroyed and brought to nothing, Isaiah 41:12.

Yani's Informant: Immediately after the Guardian has spoken to the Forces of Revenge, there is total silence and total darkness for what appears forever. Then we could hear this unusual breathing pattern working, at odds with ours: everyone stops breathing. No one has to tell anyone including me. That's how noticeable it was.

As soon as that happened, as soon as we stopped breathing, the other breathing simply went away as though it's breathing was directly tied to ours. You know what I'm saying? It's as though it's breathing was opposite, no not exactly opposite, of ours. I cannot really explain it. It was loud, but it was not dangerous. It was simply present. That's all.

On a more pleasant note, the Musician thanked Hip City Daddy for no other being disrupting the ritual. According to the Musician, Hip City Daddy brought his Guardian from the Dark side with him. I did not understand what that meant, but Hip City Daddy said…

Hip City Daddy:" Bull Shit, the musician knows that the Spirits occupy this Temple on a permanent basis.

Yani's Informant: Everybody laughed. While he keeps the audience occupied with laughter, the Musician, Nailah and Abdul Malik get into Adbul Malik's statement right in the middle of the reading Nailah is receiving from Big Momma Hunter. Their intent is to discuss Blue's statement that Nailah not leave the Global Village Nite Spot that evening.

Sharp: Abdul I know that you don't know the rules of worship, but you took a great chance by breaking in on Nailah's dialogue with Big Momma Hunter and the rest of the Orisha.

Nailah: …But, the Orishas didn't take offense. Why? They are very jealous of their time with you, usually…

Blue: Nailah means with herself. They're jealous of their time very jealous of their time with Nailah.

[Nailah laughs.]

Nailah: Blue, I didn't know that you paid attention. Now, what did you see?

Sharp: You know Blue.

Nailah: Anyway, why did you want me to remain here, and how long? Why?

Blue: When I tell you you'll say Oh! Shit! Why didn't I…

Nailah: Well, come on, what is it? What is it?

Blue: Goraka! Or, whatever his name is not dead.

Nailah: Sharp: Blue Whoa! Oh, Shit! For real? Alive? Goraka?

Yani Informant: It's as though everybody heard what Blue said at the same time, because they all said it in unison.

Blue: Check this. Watch this.

Nailah: You know, I knew it, but I couldn't figure out how he could have gotten out of there. So, rather than cause suspicion, I waited. I knew he would make his move. But, I had no idea that Goraka knew the way of the Ancients. He is definitely more learned than I imagined. Apparently, considerably more. But, I should have known. All the signs pointed that way. How did he get in the Temple? That requires mighty powers. He seems to go and come as he pleases.

Sharp: You see, that 's why I invited Hip City Daddy. He is close to the High Priest of the Dark side. There are things that operate by principles unlike any we live by, Nailah. In other words, your Magic does not work with Georama anymore. However, you do have sufficient intuitive reflexes to protect yourself as we have already seen. It seems that after Goraka, let's assume it is Goraka, was nearly killed by that crowd, he got an excellent diagram of our powers of persuasion. He also realized at that moment that if he wanted to survive, he'd better begin practicing the old art again. He really didn't realize how advanced we were until he invaded our sacred space this evening

Nailah: Yes, but how did he get in? Which door did I leave open?

Blue: Send all the ushers home, now. I think that's how he came in. Nailah has to appoint all new ushers. A whole new security force needs to be put in place. Goraka might easily have been one of the ushers. [Upon hearing the orders for the ushers to leave the Temple, the "secret force" immediately rids himself of the uniform. He then becomes the Yani Informant.]

Nailah: Wait-a-minute. I'm not questioning your judgment, I know you long enough to know that it works, but how do you know he is alive?

Blue: Goraka's Spirit never registered. No until this day, I bet.

Sharp: Damn Blue, Never thought 'bout that….

Nailah: Is that true?

Sharp: Yes! Very true! Very true!

Nailah: My God, have I moved that far away from the gift? I mean, I didn't even detect that he simply disappeared into the crowd

Blue: Hey, don't be hard on yourself. We all made that mistake with Goraka. The Musician and I too were suspicious…and, no body was ever buried? Come on, had to be. Something is definitely wrong, definitely.

Sharp: We did not want to burden you, especially with your new responsibilities, and all. It was only a hunch.

Nailah: When did you catch on, Abdul?

Blue: Tonight! You were describing this being as a male, etc., and I said Goraka, just like that. It's him! He's alive. That fucker.

Sharp: My, Blue, I didn't know you felt that way. HA!HA!HA!HA!

Nailah: AHHH! HA!HA!HA!HA!

Sharp: Okay, now what, what do you suppose we do now? What do we know about Goraka, so-called?

Nailah: I know he's not here.

Sharp: What?

Nailah: Not unless he lied to me….

Blue: About what?

Nailah: The time it takes to travel to and fro. From here to where Goraka comes from.

Blue: How much time does it take?

Nailah: Eight years.

Blue: Eight years? Goraka was serious about that?…

Hip City Daddy: That was coming this way alone. It took eight years for Goraka to arrive from Fifty-plus One, but less than a wink to go there.

Nailah: How do you know? What was that, from, where?

Nip City Daddy: Fifty-plus-One!

Nailah: And, what is Fifty-plus-One

Hip City Daddy: The New World Colony.

Nailah: And, what is that the new name they gave it? How do you know all of this? Hip City where have you been over the past……

Hip City Daddy: Eigth years???

Nailah: Has it been that long? My God, it's been eight years since I've seen my baby….You Know I'm kinda glad that Goraka ain't dead. I still might be able to see Manila, I must find her.

Hip City Daddy: Manila? Manila, who?

Nailah: Manila my baby. My daughter, the Member of Parliament who was chosen to go to the New World Colony, what do you call it? Fifty-plus-One?

Hip City Daddy: She's about twenty-two, twenty-three? Maybe? Kinda cute? Smart?

Nailah: Yes, I suppose so. She would be about twenty-three, now. And, beautiful.

Hip City Daddy: You won't believe this, but she arrived in Zania before I left. She was accompanied by a strange dude of SunRa's creation….

Sharp: I hear yea, Blood! HA!HA!HA!HA!HA!HA!AAAH!HA!HA!

[All laugh now as everybody gets the joke.

Hip City Daddy: A guy named Story Teller, her husband, Soweto, and their infant child.

Sharp: Come Nailah, sit down.

Nailah: You mean, she's alive? My daughter is alive? I want to see her. How do I get there?

Blue: Nailah! Calm down. Calm down. Too much is happening all at the same time, all at once…. So, stop for a moment and calm down….Go ahead Hip City, you were telling us about the arrival of Neptune and Manila…Damn that old buzzard is over four hundred years old isn't he? Still kicking.

Hip City Daddy: I got a joke for you. HA!HA!HA! I still don't quite know how it all happened, but the best thing that happened to us was to end up in Fifty-plus-One. HA!HA!HA! [Here the invading force puts on his act as the Yani Informant.]

Yoni Informant Impostor: As Hip City Daddy gives his impressions of Fifty-plus-One; the invisible and silent quest of the Second Republic learns what he can. He learns all their plans in the process. While observing, Goraka thinks—that's me, of course—to himself,

Goraka: They clearly do not seem to understand. I am not of this world. I am not HU-MAN. I walk on clouds; stand on raindrops and breath under water. I am definitely no HU-MAN. I can travel like lighting; give a thunder its roar. I am simply no HU-MAN. I can blow wind at the sun, light at the moon. Is that HU-MAN? I am no HU-MAN. What makes them think that I am HU-MAN? I can laugh at you now, I can laugh at you later. I am not HU-MAN. I am certainly not HU-MAN.

Hip City Daddy: Look! Look! The reporter is on fire. He's burning up. He's nothing but a flame.

Yoni Informant Impostor: I can combust spontaneously. I can recompose. I am not HU-MAN.

Nailah: So, what are we dealing with, Blue?

Yoni Informant Impostor: Blue doesn't know.

Nailah: What about you Sharp? What do you think?

Yoni Informant Impostor: The Musician doesn't know anything.

Nailah: What about you Hip City?

Yoni Informant Impostor: Hip City Daddy think he is in or on Fifty-plus-One.

Nailah: Then, what about you? What do you think? Who are you, if you are not Goraka?

Yoni Informant Impostor: I think you are funny. And, I think you are waiting your time, not that it matters. I am not your problem. You could not deal with me. I am beyond you or anything you can comprehend, even with the help of your gods.

Nailah: Orishas, not gods. We only have one Creator. Orishas are what they are called. But you would not understand that.

Blue: Then, why are you present? Why are you here?

Yoni Informant Impostor: I'm here because we have mutual interests, let us say. We have night-light, a night passage, a time mirage, and the dark side of things. The opposite of day light. Did you hear what I said folks?

Darkness is the opposite of light, not good. Darkness is not evil. Darkness is darkness, evil is evil. Thus I would argue that there are probably as many crimes committed in the light of the day as there are in the darkness of night simply different in nature, form and character. So, why are the most sinister of atrocities that have been committed are presented as having occurred under the cover of darkness, rather than the cover of light?

To continue, the cover of light is projected as offering greater objectivity. It is false reasoning, and simply a rationalization of the pleasure of seeing. We enjoy seeing, i.e., we enjoy the ability to visualize our surrounding, whatever they may be. Thus, we argue that the greatest test of existence is to see it. And, more personally, specifically I see what is seen preferably within my frame work of understanding "reality." Light is required to carry off this risk. We must specifically see the event, and officially record what was officially identified as what the event was, or, have an official reporter inform us as what happened at the time of the event recorded.

When none of these are possible, imagination seems to act as a more than adequate substitute. Example: what ever the number that could fit in the Global Village Nite Spot, the night of the "Big Event," is here. There is no standing room. The place is literally packed. So you know what's going to happen? Everybody will have a story to tell about the Global Village Nite spot: home of the Vodoun. Frankly, what is happening is too much for most attendees to comprehend. So, your encounter with me will be reported as unusual an occurrence by most who are here right now.

Thus, when everybody leaves the Temple, they will assure the rest of Xaire that they saw Nailah speak with the gods. They will say that Nailah herself is a god. That is the nature of things here. Since I am not HU-MAN, what else can I be except a god to you? No body here can prove me otherwise, so I am a god. Things like this do occur. I assure you. And, as tonight will show people will say that Global Village is a Temple of Evil and Sorcery. Others will acclaim it is a place of the gods. Those who know will simply say that the place is sanctified. That is the nature of things to come.

[After a time unknown within a space unknown.]

In case you are wondering what has happened, I have taken you some-place-else to show you that I am not bound by time and space. Remember, I am not HU-MAN. We are now looking at how everyone will view the Ritual after it is over and they are gone. I can do that, but you cannot, because you are HU-MAN. You can only live in the present. Your world is…here and now. And, Goraka is not here. So, your energies are better spent making sure that everyone here can sustain life. That is where you should focus your energies.

Chapter 27

RADIO AIRE REDIFFUSION {RAR} UPDATE

THE SECOND REPUBLIC OF XAIRE HAS ISSUED AS ITS FIRST ORDER OF BUSINESS AN OFFICIAL NAME CHANGE FROM XAIRE TO AIRE. SO, THE SECOND REPUBLIC OF XAIRE IS OFFICIALLY AND CONSTITUTIONALLY AIRE, WITH IS PEOPLE GOING UNDER THE NAME OF AIREAN. THE REASON FOR THE NAME CHANGE, THIS IS UNOFFICIAL OF COURSE, IS THE "X" IN XAIRE HAS COME TO REPRESENT AN ADMINISTRATION THAT IS TOO AUTHORITARIAN AND DESTRUCTIVE FOR THE COMMON GOOD. THE PEOPLE WILL DROP THE "X" FROM THE NAME.

THE SECOND ORDER OF BUSINESS OS THE ARIAN PEOPLE ARE TO APPROVE THE CONSTITUTION OF THE NEW REPUBLIC OF AIRE. THE NEW CONSTITUTION ALLOWS ALL OF THE FREEDOMS GRANTED UNDER THE HUMAN RIGHTS RESOLUTION OF THE UNITED FEDERATED REPUBLICS. MANY WONDER—PRIVATELY OF COURSE – WHY THESE DECISIONS WERE MADE IN THE ORDER THEY CAME? HOW CAN YOU DECLARE YOURSELF A REPUBLIC WITH A NEW NAME BEFORE YOU HAVE APPROVED THE CONSTITUTION? ANYWAY? THE CONSTITUTION INSTITUTIONALIZES SOME CHANGES ALREADY STARTED BY THE RULING PARTY, HARAMBE. ONE CHANGE NOTEWORTHY IS THE CREATION OF A ONE PARTY STATE. THE OPPOSITION PARTIES ARE WRITTEN OUT OF THE CONSTITUTION. THOSE THAT CONTINUE TO OPERATE WILL BE DECLARED ILLEGAL OUTLAWS. SOME OPPOSITION LEADERS HAVE BEEN DETAINED BECAUSE OF THE ALLEGED KILLING THAT TOOK PLACE OUT IN THE COUNTRYSIDE. PEASANT FARMERS AND THEIR FAMILIES WERE KILLED IN A NUMBER OF VILLAGES LOCATED IN THE NORTHWEST REGION OF AIRE. SINCE OVER EIGHTY PER SENT OF THE FARMS ARE OPERATED BY WOMEN WHO CARE FOR THE CHILDREN, THE DEATHS HAVE CREATED A CRISIS IN THIS YEAR'S CROP PRODUCTION, AND SCHOOL ATTENDANCE OF ARIAN YOUTHS.

IN RESPONSE TO THESE TERRORIST ATTACKS ON THE FAMERS, THE GOVERNMENT OF AIRE HAS INCREASED THE QUAN- TITY OF PESTICIDES, HERBI-CIDES, AND FERTILIZERS TO BE MADE AVAILABLE FOR SUBSISTENCE FARMING. ALSO, A BRANCH OF THE RESEARCH UNIVERSITY WILL BE FOUNDED IN THE HEART OF THE NORTHWEST REGION TO INCREASE AGRICULTURAL PRODUCTION AND MAKE CROP FARMING MORE EFFICIENT AND PRODUCTIVE. PRIOR TO THE ATTACKS, FOOD PRODUCTION IN THE REPUBLIC OF AIRE HAS INCREASED OVER EIGHT HUNDRED PERCENT OVER THE PAST THREE GROWING SEASONS.

ALONG WITH THE AIREAN GOVERNMENT GRANTING MORE AID FOR SUBSISTENCE FARMERS, RECENTLY, THERE HAS BEEN A DECLINE IN THE PRODUCTION SUGAR CANE, COTTON, TOBACCO, COFFEE, AND COCOA. HOWEVER, CASH CROPS WILL CONTINUE

TO OPERATE IN PRIVATE HANDS. THESE SUBSISTENCE FARMERS ON THE OTHER HAND WILL BE ENCOURAGED TO FORM LARGER COOPERATIVES IN ORDER TO INCREASE THEIR BUYING POWER ON THE OPEN MARKET. THIS PROCESS WILL ALSO ALLOW FOR BETTER COORDINATION OF CROP PRODUCTION ANS CROP SALES.

ON A MORE UNFORTUNATE NOTE, THE MINISTER OF AGRI- CULTURE AND COMMUNITY DEVELOPMENT WAS ASSASSINAT- ED BEFORE THE APPROVAL OF OUT NEW CONSTITUTION, SO THE POLICIES SHE INITIATED BEFORE HER ASSASSINATION WILL BE CONTINUED UNDER THE DIRECTION OF THE PRIME MINISTER WHOSE LIFE HAS ALSO BEEN UNDER GREAT PROTECTION BECAUSE OF TREATS. IN ADDITION TO A RE-EMPHASIS ON FOOD PRODUCTION IN PARTICULAR, AND AGRICULTURE IN GENERAL, A DE-EMPHASIS OUR USE OF THE MARKET PLACE OF FOREIGN LANDS TO DETERMINE HOW MUCH OUR CASH CROP FARMERS WILL MAKE IN A GIVEN SEASON WILL FOLLOW SUIT. INSTEAD, THE GOVERNMENT HAS ESTABLISHED AN AGENCY WITHIN THE MINISTRY OF COMMERCE THAT WILL PURCHASE ALL CROPS AT A FAIR MARKET PRICE. CROPS WILL THEN BE STORED TO BE SOLD AT THE APPROPRIATE TIME.

THE PRODUCTION OF OUR HIGH ENERGY MINERAL WILL BE CARRIED ON AT RATE THAT WILL PERMIT US TO HAVE OUR NATURAL RESOURCES IN PERPE- TUITY. A RESEARCH INSTITUTE AS PART OF THE UNIVERSITY OF AIRE HAS BEEN ESTABLISHED TO CONTINUE RESEARCH IN THE AREAS OF METALLURGY, GEOLOGY, GEOGRAPHY, PETROLEUM, GAS, GOLD, SILVER, AND OTHER MINERALS UNIQUE TO OUR REGION. A RESEARCH LABORATORY IS ALSO UNDER WAY TO ADVANCE THE STUDY OF TIME EXPLORATION AND SPACE TRAVEL. THIS LABOR- ATORY WILL BE CONNECTED WITH THE FAMOUS NIGHT SPOT GLOBAL VILLAGE. THE POTS COLLEGE OF MUSIC AND THE PERFORMING ARTS IS NOW THE NEW NAME GIVEN TO OUR MUSIC COLLEGE AT THE UNIVERSITY OF AIRE. FIFTEEN PERCENT OF THE NATIONAL BUDGET WILL GO TO- WARD TIME TRAVEL AND EXPLO- RATION.

NOW, TO OTHER MATTERS [Pause] THE REPUBLIC OF AIRE AND ZANIA ON-THE-OTHER SIDE HAVE SIGNED A MUTUAL AGREEMENT PACT. THE PACT IS IN THE FORM OF A TREATY: THE TREATY OF MUTUAL DESIRES AND INTERESTS. THE UNILATERALLY DECLARED INDEPENDENT REPUBLIC, FIFTY-PLUS-ONE MAINTAINS THAT IT IS IMPOSSIBLE FOR GLOBAL VILLAGE—THEIR NAME FOR ZANIA—TO MAKE FOREIGN POLICY AGREEMENTS SINCE IT IS A COLONY OF FIFTY-PLUS-ONE. THE TREATY IS THEREFORE INVALID. AIRE REMINDS FIFTY-PLUS-ONE THAT IT TOO IS A COLONY SO IT HAS NO RIGHT REGARDING THIS MATTER OF MUTUAL AGREEMENT. THE PRIME MINISTER HAS STATED IF FIFTY-PLUS-ONE WANTS TO JOIN IN THIS MUTUAL AID PACT IT IS WELCOME TO DO SO.

THE PRIME MINISTER LAUGHED AFTER HER INVITATION AND SAID THAT THE POT CANNOT CALL THE KETTLE BLACK, AND FOR THAT MATTER, THE UNILATERALLY DECLARED REPUBLIC NEW WORLD COLONY IS IN NO POSITION TO CHALLENGE THE AUTHORITY OF EITHER AIRE OR ZANIA. FURTHERMORE, SINCE, FIFTY-PLUS-ONE SO-CALLED IS STILL THE NEW WORLD COLONY UNDER THE JURISDICTION OF AIRE, AIRE MAY CHOOSE TO MAKE AN AGREEMENT WITH ANY OTHER STATE IF IT CHOOSES TO DO SO. FURTHERMORE AIRE HAS CHOSEN TO MAKE A PACT WITH ZANIA BECAUSE IT IS ABOUT TIME THAT THE TWO STATES RECOGNIZE WHAT THEY PRACTICE, OFFICIALLY.

ON LOCAL MATTERS, THE PRESENT CAPITAL MEDINA IS ENCOURAGING ZERO POPULATION GROWTH. ACCORDING THE MAYOR, IT SIMPLY CANNOT ADEQUATELY HOUSE ANY MORE RESIDENTS. A HOUSING SHORTAGE HAS CAUSED THE NEW ARRIVALS TO CAMP ANY PLACE THEY CAN FIND UNUSABLE SPACE. THIS SHORTAGE HAS CAUSED FIGHTING TO BREAK OUT IN SOME QUARTER BETWEEN THE LOCAL RESIDENTS AND THE NEW ARRIVALS, CALLED "WALLERS" BECAUSE THEY HAVE NO WALLS AROUND THEIR HABITATS.

THE MINISTER OF CAPITAL CONSTRUCTION HAS ISSUED A NEWS RELEASE SAYING THE CONSTRUCTION WILL BEGIN ON THE NEW CAPITAL SITE WITHIN THE INTERIOR OF AIRE AS SOON AS THE RAINY SEASON LETS UP. IT IS ESTIMATED THAT COMPLETE CONSTRUCTION OF THE NEW CAPITAL CITY WILL COST ONE TENTH OF THE NATIONAL BUDGET, AND THE COMPLETE CONSTRUCTION OF THE NEW CAPITAL CITY SHOULD TAKE APPROXIMATELY TWENTY YEARS.

ALL VILLAGES AND HAMLETS WITH MORE THAN FIVE THOUSAND RESIDENTS ARE AUTOMATICALLY DECLARED TOWNSHIPS IF THEY ARE WITHIN A RADIUS OF TWENTY-FIVE MILES. ALL NEW TOWNSHIPS WILL ESTABLISH SCHOOLS, PREVENTIVE HEALTH CLINICS, PAVED STREETS, WATER AND SEWAGE TREATMENT PLANTS, UTILITIES AND OTHER SERVICES RELATED TO THE INFRASTRUCTURE. A LOCAL SYSTEM OF TAXES WILL, EXCUSE ME, HAS BEEN APPROVED BY PARLIAMENT FOR THESE LOCAL JURISDICTIONS.

THE UNIVERSITY OF AIRE HAS ANNOUNCED THAT IT PLANS TO EXPAND ITS FACILITY TO HOUSE BRANCHES ALL OVER THE REPUBLIC.

THIS HAS BEEN A RADIO AIRE REDIFFUSION, RAR NEWS UPDATE.

NOW THE MUSIC SHOW BEGINS. HAVE A PLEASANT MORNING.

[MUSIC CAN NOW BE HEARD with Miles Davis playing Kind of Blue with an overlay of Bitches Brew in the background.]

Yoni: Isn't it something that it was Goraka acting as an Usher who told me that I could not observe and participate in the reading for Nailah last recently. The nerve. I suspected that something was wrong. That had never happened to me before. I knew that I should have questioned it, but… Anyway, a few days after the Government of Prime Minister Nailah of Aire issued a news release about moving the capital into the interior, the gravesite that has been identified as the site of the slain body of King-General Mathew III.

The body was uncovered when construction workers were digging the ground for the laying of the first building in the new capital city. Can you imagine that? Nailah wonders how long the body has been there. She is also questioning her decision to work through the Dark side as she attempts to bring Aire out of it slump. So far all of her luck has been bad. It obviously requires more skill than she has been able to garner so far.

The Dark side commands your total attention, your complete attention. Anyway, it is more a chance of circumstances than Nailah's inability to negotiate the Dark side that has her not knowing whether to wind her ass or scratch her watch. Excuse me, I apologize. That should read, wind her head or scratch her watch.

Who put that there? I'm gonna get somebody as soon as this expose is finished. Some heads are gonna roll. Again, I apologize for the misquote. You know how it is when someone places the information in front of you and you have no time to read it first.

Immediately after it was announced that the Akuyus discovered the King-General Mathew III's slain body in an unmarked gravesite, the Monarchists demanded that the new capital city bare his name and that he be placed in a museum named after him for permanent exhibition. A drive to reinstate the Crown has been initiated also. Fortunately, the Constitution has just been passed by plebiscite a few days before. So, Nailah has said that would require a Constitutional Amendment of two-thirds majority of Parliament and three-quarters of the voting population. She also expressed her belief that such an Amendment would be extremely difficult to pass.

Word arrived from Fifty-plus-One that if the Republic of Aire becomes a monarchy again, then Goraka I has first claim to the Crown since he is still alive and well, living in Capital District 17. Prime Minister Nailah's Press Secretary announced that it was Goraka who unilaterally declared the old country a new republic and himself President-for-Life. She stated further that Goraka is in no position to demand anything, especially since and I quote,"There is a price of one quarter of the national treasury still offered for the capture of Dr. Goraka." The Prime Minister's Office said further that "that there might be evidence forthcoming linking Goraka to the assassination of the late King-General III. If so, he will be charged with first degree murder, a capital offence."

As a matter of fact, the incumbent Prime Minister would love nothing better than to bring Goraka to trial now. That seems to be the only way to reduce the momentum to name the new capital city after Mathew III, especially out in the countryside. To that end, Abdul Malik leading a commando squad is now on his way to Fifty-plus-One via Zania. This secret mission was conceived and planned shortly after Nailah had an audience with her Guardian of the Dark side the night of the Big Event at the Global Village Nite Spot.

….UH! By the way, Uhuru that Akuyu singing band that has caused such a big wave on Fifty-plus-One, has been invited to perform at the Global Village Nite Spot. Word is, the authorities in Fifty-plus-One refuse to grant that popular singing ensemble permission to leave. Human Rights demonstrations are scheduled to take place tomorrow to protest Fifty-plus-One's violation of Uhuru's right to travel any where without being subject to restrictions.

In case you are wondering how travel between the three Republics is now possible, all of a sudden, it happened like this: one of those experiential music ensembles that goes by the name "Tomorrow" invented a new musical instrument after studying one of Goraka's equations that knows no limitations regarding time and space. Accidentally while performing their new Airean Suite #4, Tomorrow hit a cord that opened up a passage way between Aire and Zania that allowed instant travel. No one would have known except Hip City Daddy appeared at the Global Village Nite Spot, and people wanted to know how because everybody there saw it.

The Government of Prime Minister Nailah immediately declared the musical instrument a TOP SECRET upon seeing what happened with Hip City Daddy. The name of the musical instrument is forbidden for anyone to mention. TOMORROW is now employed as the musical engineers for Inner Time Travel. {As quite as it is kept, other musical groups have learned the chord plus other tones that allow them to travel, also.

This is a secret that the Government is unaware of. What the Government did not realize was it was not the musical instrument; it was the new chord they discovered with the instrument they were performing on. Ain't that nothing?} Anyway, this discovery has allowed Abdul Malik to travel to Fifty-plus-One on a special mission for the Prime Minister. Remember, Blue is the President. So this is like a reversal of roles, in my own estimation of the polity of this culture. TOMORROW cannot leave the Inner Time Travel without clearance from the Minister of Internal Security.

They too are classified. "TOP SECRET." Sort of humorous. If the matter were not so serious, TOMORROW has a hit disc out called "Top Secret?" The recording was issued before TOMORROW appeared at the Global Village Nite Spot. The concert and the discs were sold out before the day was over. The favorite tune on the disc features the new instrument. Everybody seems to enjoy the recording when played a high volume. The fascination seems to be with the fact that one can disappear by playing that particular tune and return as soon as it is complete. Everybody calls it the miracle tune. And, they agree that TOMORROW should remain under "PROTECTIVE CUSTORY" lest someone foreign or sinister character decides to "kidnap them for ransom to the highest bidder," The shit is getting funky, ain't it.

The problem is the decision to declare the new musical instrument TOP SECRET and place TOMORROW under protective custody has placed the Government in a very precarious situation, which is, by doing so; the Government is violating the civil liberties of the TOMORROW. However, TOMORROW and their public do not seem to mind, at least not for now. Interesting thing thou, the attempt by the government to collect all of the outstanding discs before they were sold has met with no success.

That effort was a total failure. No contest. And, by popular demand, no disc has been returned. I mean, come on, by issuing a recall, did the Government expect to receive any of them back out of patriotism? Come on, give me a break. Also, attempts to confiscate the new batches that were about to be distributed met with no success. Some how they were gone by the time the censors got to the spot of distribution. And, the producers of the recording label claim that they no nothing, that they ain't gots nothin' to do with it. It is out of their hands. Don't expect them to know what happen to the discs.

So, no one can explain how that is or who is responsible. Over 100,000,000 copies are reported to be in circulation as of today. The news of what the tune can do has spread like wild fire. Of course, the Government is embarrassed beyond anger. They have to laugh about it caused they blew it big time. Not only that, for them to do what they want is a violation of Article I of the Airean Constitution regarding civil liberties.

Declaring TOMORROW top secret classified and under house protection seems like a joke therefore ludicrous to the citizens of Aire and all of the other transnation-states in this part of the universe. So, the Government is in a quandary as to what to do. The enemy can pick up a copy off the net or any where within the underground economy for that matter. All the time it is the very number one tune in Aire.

Despite all of the attempts to confiscate and everything, the popularity of Nailah as Prime Minister of the Republic of Aire and Priest of Priest is at an all time high. It is very easy to become a dictator at this point under the guise of national security, but she has not even thought about it, it would seem. Maybe this is because except, for those who go to Zaria on a regular basis, few have demonstrated an interest in travelling outside of Airc. According to the Prime Minister, it is a matter of time before the people on the other side will have their own method of transferability. So, Aire has to protect its secret as long as it can, "but I'm glad that no one is interested in the time travel until our national security is assured."

As I said, it is easy for Nailah to become dictatorial but this she has refused to even contemplate. Matter of fact Nailah has forced the Minister of Internal Security to return all of the confiscated discs back to their rightful owners. I want to see how she does this. But isn't this something? The Akuyus are elated. The Aireans are elated. And, not only has she forced the return of the discs, she has demanded that an apology be given to all of the offended parities, ain't that nothing?

The nation has gone wild. Nailah called a meeting of the mass and spoke for seventeen yours. NO ONE MOVED! Over two and a half million people were reported to be present. As she spoke, Nailah dealt with everything in detail. She explained the new budget and why so much of the nation's wealth and resources are going to time travel.

Nailah: WE MUST KEEP THE SECRET UNTIL WE HAVE PERFECTED TIME TRAVEL BEYOND A DOUBT. THEN WE CAN SERVE THE REST OF PEOPLE KIND, AND SHARE WITH OUR FRIENDS THAT PORTION OF OUR GIFT THAT BEST SUITS THEIR NEEDS. WE HAVE ACCOMPLISHED MUCH DURING OUR TERM IN OFFICE. WE CAN FEED OURSELVES AND HAVE ENOUGH SURPLUSES TO SELL ABROAD. I SIMPLY THINK THAT'S GREAT, DON'T YOU? SLAP FIVE AS WE GIVE OURSELVES A HAND!

Yoni: One thunderous applause can be heard as the nation congratulates itself for a job well done: ON THUNDEROUS APPLAUSE IS BEING GIVEN BY THE NATION TO ITSELF. THE AIREANS ARE NOW TRULY A VERY PROUD NATION.

Nailah: NOW I AM HERE TO OFFER A PUBLIC APOLOGY FOR CONFIS- CATING THE DISCS BY OUR NEW AGE GROUP TOMORROW. I SAW WHAT THE MUSIC WAS CAPABLE OF DOING SO I PANICKED AND GRABBED EVERYTHING UP UNTIL I COULD DETERMINE THE EFFECT IT MIGHT HAVE ON OUR NATIONAL SECURITY. AS IT TURNED OUT, AS YOU ALL KNOW, THE PROCESS WAS COMMERCIALIZED BEFORE THE GOVERNMENT COULD ACT TO PROTECT OUR NATIONAL SECU- RITY. {EVERYBODY LAUGHS AT THE IRONY OF THINGS.} HOWEVER, WE MUST KEEP TOMORROW. {SURPRISINGLY, EVERYBODY APPLAUDS AT THIS, TOO} THEIR LIVES WOULD BE IN DANGER, OTHERWISE. AS LONG AS WE HAVE THE INSTRUMENT OF TIME TRAVEL, WE CAN REGULATE IT.

AS YOU KNOW, THE OLD WAY REQUIRED US TO BE MASTER MUSICIANS SIMPLY TO TRAVEL BACK AND FORTH BETWEEN OUR THREE/THREE WORLDS. NOW, THE WAY WE ARE ORGANIZING THINGS, YOU MAY TRAVEL TO ZANIA SIMPLY BY ORDERING ONE OF THE DISCS RECORDED BY TOMORROW. AS YOU CAN TELL, WE DO NOT NEED COMPETITORS IN THIS AREA. THIS WAY WE CAN KEEP TRAFFIC FROM GETTING OUT OF HAND…..OF COURSE, WE HAVE OPENED UP TRADE ROUTES BETWEEN ZANIA AND AIRE. AND, BECAUSE OF THE ATTACKS ZANIA HAVE SUFFERED, A SECURITY PACT HAS BEEN SIGNED BETWEEN OUR GREAT NEW REPUBLICS.

Yani: While Nailah is speaking, Blue and his commandos arrive in Zaria. Since they only have a short layover, Hip City Daddy stops by the time terminal, picks up Blue and his Panthers – as the unit is called – takes them by this hip new Nite spot called The Other Side. As they enter The Other side, a ensemble composed of Cecil Taylor, Piano, Anee Sharon Freeman, Piano, Ole Dara Trumpet and Guitar with Dianne McIntyre dancer, were embroiled in a dynamic musical exchange that defies description. The only way I can describe it is to say simply, you'd have to be here to see it yourself.

Remember, I told you that when Blue and his Panthers reach Zania, they would have to change into another kind of transport system in order to reach Fifty-plus-One secretively. Well, the jazz unit that must transport Blue's Panthers into Fifty-plus-One's Capital District Seventeen clandestinely is going through its final rehearsal of an old tune by Perez Prado entitled VOO DOO SUITE. Apparently, VOO DOO SUITE creates a sense of nothingness among the Kinshasa's when heard subsonically. Because they cannot comprehend it, they have failed to establish an effective deterrent, or put differently, a line of defense against any approaching objects when this music is playing. To them, it is simply noise.

While waiting, Hip Hop Daddy shows Blue the most effective route to Goraka's Castle. Again, because the Zarians use a totally different system of logic, it is possible for them to enter and leave undetected because their time patterns are unbeknownst to the Kinshasa. Also, the Kinshasas think that the "Noners" – as they are still called on Fifty-plus-One – are incapable of any intellectual or scientific thought. The Zanians have used this bias to their advantage in their struggle with the Kinshasa's. As they wrap up the briefing, Blue tells Hip City Daddy,…

Blue: Oh. Yes, I have one more mission to perform before we return to Aire, and I definitely need your help….

Yoni: Blue remains until the first show ends because he hasn't seen his old friend Anee Sharon Freeman in who knows when. After a few minutes of greetings and call me as soon as you return to Aire conversation, Blue excuses himself politely.

Blue: Every time I hear you play, I see that you have made another great leap forward. I must say, yawl was smokin'. I'm still flyin' up there somewhere… So, I better leave while I can. Catch you on the next go round. See you Sharon. Excuse me, Anee. I always forget.

Anee: Okay, Blue! I can't believe that you are here. What brings you this way? Or, should I leave that one alone? Hey, when are you going to finish those videos you were making? Aren't you the President of a country or something? Glad to see you thou. Good luck what ever it is. You certainly like danger and intrigue, don't you?

Blue: When we get back to Aire.

Anee: SURE!!!

Blue: Oh. I can't forget to tell you this. Lonnie Hilliard and Cris Woods were eulogized before I left Medina.

Anee: OH! I'm so sorry to hear that. Not Lonnie, he…so young. Cris, I didn't …really know…I must tell Dianne and Cecil…My next number will be dedicated in their memory. Thank you for letting us know… Sorry to hear that….

Yani: With that Abdul Malik disappears into the silence of the nightclub noise. As he moves rapidly through the Smokey crowd, Hip City Daddy catches up to him and gives a quick caveat,

Hip City Daddy: Beware of the silence. It can be deadly.

Yoni: Blue thanks Hip City Daddy for the info and keeps moving. Since he fails to ask for or give further explanation to the point Hip City just made, Au-U-Khan asks,

Au-U Khan: What did Hip City mean back there, just now?

Blue: Where we're going, the people are the complete opposite of here.

Au-U-Khan: How do they talk to each other?

Blue: We don't quite know yet. That's why we brought Roc Steady alone.

Au-U-Khan: Why?

Blue: We hope to communicate with them…Au-U-Khan: Do you mean ease drop?

Blue: Yes! That's what we need her to do.

Au-U-Khan: ROC STEADYE!

Blue: Oh, I can hear them, too. Goraka taught me when we held him up at Nailah's home during the Civil War. That's why he hates me so much. He knows when I'm near, I can read his thoughts.

Au-U-Khan: OH!!! I see.

Blue: Beware of the silence. They may be communicating right in front of us.

Au-U-Khan: Really? What do we do? How interesting?

Blue: You just listen to me…. Only me, until I say otherwise. Okay?

Au-U-Khan: Okay?

Yoni: Abdul Malik: addresses everybody now.

Blue: NOW, I WANT YOU TO LISTEN CAREFULLY. THIS LEG OF THE FLIGHT IS QUITE DIFFERENT THAN OUR TRIP TO ZANIA, ALL TOGETHER.

Blood: How so Blue?

Blue: First, we'll be traveling by different time crafts. This trip will be navigated by an old tune by Perez Prado. It's called VOODOO SUITE!!!

Blood: HEAVY!! HEAVY!! Polyrhythmic time! Hot dog!

Au-U-Khan: MULTILAYERED TIME.

Blue: Both of you are right! Anyway timing of the utmost. Noise is vital.

Angola: You mean our music, Blue?

Blue: Yes, the Kinshasa think it's noise, I'm told.

Blood: So, should we make lots of it?

Blue: Yes! As much as we can. As long as we can.

Au-U-Khan: It might not work around Goraka; he's lived around us.

Blue: It's not for Goraka.

Au-U-Khan: Oh? Then, who is it for?

Yani: Then who is the noise for? Where is the interference AIMED? Well, whatever. Blue ain't telling.

Blue: Okay, Panthers, are you ready?

Yoni: They all speak as one,

Panthers: YES, BLUE!!!

Blue: Then what are we waiting for? Let's go. It's time to make time.

Yoni: As the Panthers approach, the Jazz Unit has just completed rehearsal of the VOODOO SUITE. The bandleader speaks to Abdul Malik.

Bandleader: We are ready to transport you to Fifty-plus-One, are you ready?

Yoni: After Blue let's the bandleader know that the Panthers are ready for transport, at the last moment he takes Roc Steadye aside and addresses her privately. She looks surprised, smiles affirmatively and walks away in a fast military cadence. The Panthers look on in amazement.

What would cause Blue to send his most trusted Lieutenant away just before they are about to take off on their most dangerous mission ever? Maybe, it wasn't as dangerous as we thought it was. Maybe, it is not as dangerous as we were led to believe. What does Blue know that he is not telling us…I don't know, but out of angry frustration, another Panther speaks up?

CR16: Is Rock Steadye goin' with us, Blue?

Blue: No, soldier she is not! That is all Blood! Everybody stand at attention! I know that the policy has always been,…

Blood: SORRY! BLUE! YOU DON'T HAVE TO EXPLAIN! WE WERE OUT OF ORDER. WE READY!

Blue: At ease, get on everybody. Let's go Panthers. We don't have any time to waste.

Chapter 28

Yoni: The "attack" – more like male stealing – was so smooth and swift, that it there were any plans of deception, they never had time to materialize. Not only was Roc Steadye unnecessary, so were the rest. So it would appear. At least that is how Blood and the rest of the Panthers felt after they had boarded Goraka on their transport headed back to Zania.

Blood: Damn, we might as well stayed in Zania and had some fun. I saw some phat little momma in that club we was in. They be diggin' them some music.

Yoni: Everybody slap hands as though, "hey man, right on! I second that!" Seeing that he had an audience, here's how it all appended according to Blood. Remember, everybody's got a different version of the same happening. Blue walks out. He knows that this is going to be an all night, and. he's heard it before.

Blood: I swear man, no sooner we got on that transport we were standing around this old man. We were so close that he surrendered without a struggle or a cry for help. It's as though he was surprised, but helpless and lonely. The closeness scared him nearly to death. It seems that our closeness reminded him of when his bodyguards nearly squeezed him to death.

I didn't recognize him. I'd recognize him in a moment, I thought before we surrounded him. I'd seen him up close before. So, when we captured him, I was confused as to why we were brought along. My problem was I joined the Panthers when they had lost the now famous heroes. So I never got a chance to meet Goraka only once. You know that all of 'um were killed 'cept.

Blue. God saved Blue, he became a Muslim, changed his name and all. But we still call him Blue, and it don't bother him. He's still Blue. He'll always be Blue. But I don't have no problem with him becoming a Muslim. Abdul Malik is all right with me. So when Blue simply put his hand around Goraka's throat and said, give me one reason. I said, OH! SHIT! THE SHIT IS ON….. STRANGE! AU-U-KHAN WHY YOU LOOK SO SURPRISED?

Au-U—Khan: Well, you must admit that we did not follow the plan Blue laid out before we left.

Blood: But, we got Goraka. And, it was the smoothest action I had ever seen. Did you see what Blue did? Man, he got us so trained that all he had to do was…and we had done it already. It's finished. OVER!

Au-U-Khan: Yes, but what if one….

Blood: Yo! Hold up! Nobody fucks up in this unit. This was Blue's Panthers. We're the best! No body fucks with us.

Au-U-Khan: So, where he disappear to?

Blood: None of yo' Business. I noticed you askin' all them questions back in Zania. We checkin' you out.

Au-U-Khan: WOW! Can't even ask questions….

Blood: You can ask all the questions you like. Don't mean you gone get any answers. And, you don't question our Leader, Blue, ever. If he wants to go out, he'll let us know if he wants to. Don't fuck wid Blue. If you do, you gotta come through me. We're one…if you don't like this unit git out…. Matter of fact, why do you stay? All you do is goin' round causing trouble. {Blood now continues on with the story he was about to tell.} We snatch a man perfect! And, you were right up there, too. You were supposed to yell out, remember? And, you didn't. The noise was for you to make. All you had to do was make noise. Instead, you went right to Goraka to warn him…. And, we heard you!

Au-U-Khan: I did not know when the noise was to start….. Then someone said Music, and I got confused…. Then I heard this music for the complete journey all the way into Goraka's room and out again. As a matter of fact, it sounded something like that playing now…. and, tell me, we are not moving, why? It is like we're in suspended animation…. But, the music is still playing…. I don't quite understand…. What is going on, here?

Yoni: Blood has seen this flick so many times Au-U-Khan sounded like a broken record. WHY? WHY? WHY?

Blood: Yo! Man where you from, jJust where you comin' from?

Au-U-Khan: I live in the outer valley of the Republic. Sha Sha Faso. I am not familiar with your ways…of urbanized life!

{Blue returns to the cabin.}

Blood: UUMMM! The Outer Valley, where is that?

Au-U-Khan: The major city is Kinshahsaville.

Blood: Ain't that where Goraka's from? Originally

Au-U-Khan: Legend has it….

Blood: So, that you know bout him?

Au-U-Khan: Goraka? No more than anybody else….

Blood: So, why did you whisper into his thought? We heard you, YOU KNOW?

Au-U-Khan: I said, "don't worry about tomorrow. Tomorrow has its own problems…No need to add to the troubles it brings."

Yoni: Blue speaks for the first time since returning to the area where everyone else is located.

Blue: What does it mean?

Au-U-Khan: It was taken from St, Mathew's

Blood: Saint? The dud whispers some shit about TOMORROW, then calls the old King-General, Saint. Mathew III is now a saint. Holy Jones!

Blue: Saint? The St. Mathew is not our Mathew III….Two different stories.

Blood: Then, what about TOMORROW? I guess he wasn't talking about them either, huh?

Blue: You know, I forgot about TOMORROW being the name of a singing group, also. Excellent metaphor excellent way to pass information.

Au-U-Khan: I could have been showing compassion to a dying man. You saw him. He was listless. Yet, you wanted to kill him. What did you say General? "Give me a reason," to kill you.

Blue: I was speaking in metaphor just as you were. That was simply my way of letting Goraka know that his life was in my hands, that his only way out was DEATH, and if he wanted to die, to give me a reason, and I'd crack his nervous system without hesitation. He obviously did not want to die….

Blood: Nor, could he assume that advantage.

Blue: Now, back to you Au-U-Khan. What did it mean? Tomorrow has its own problems; don't add your troubles o it. Tell us what that meant. Are you referring to the singing group?

Au-U-Khan: Of course not! There are broader questions than the retention of a singing group.

Blood: Like?

Au-U-Khan: like the salvation of the world…I know you're not going to believe me, but….

Blood…The world is coming to an end, I know…man, where too get you lines?

Au-U-Khan: They said you wouldn't understand. The message was for all the Kinshasa's to feel.

Blood: What do you mean?

Au-U-Khan: The whole Capital District 17 could hear you and me talk to Goraka.

Blood: Why didn't they move to protect Goraka?

Blue, Au-U-Khan, Blood: They couldn't. The music froze them, so to speak.

Blue: How did you know?

Au-U-Khan: I should ask you the same question.

Blue: What did you want them to feel

Au-U-Khan: GUILT!

Angola: This is getting interesting….

Blood: GUILT? What guilt?

Angola: Legend has it that the lost family as the Kinshasa's who were never seen again are called, was sent to return and save the world one day.

Blue: Is that so?

Au-U-Khan: YES! It is true.

Blue: So, what does it mean?

Au-U-Khan: It means that the people living where we were are considered to be the saviors of humanity.

Blue: Only if they fulfil their mission.

Au-U-Khan: Yes, only when they fulfill their legend.

Blue: And, if they do not?

Au-U-Khan: Then, I am told, "May god help us, we all die as in never return again. Ever!"

Blue: No salvation?

Au-U-Khan: No redemption! No salvation!

Blue: Doom! Is that what your legend sad?

Au-U-Khan: If the Kinshasa people…

Blue: ……Fail at their task. Should all be given you? After all, I'm sure this will mean a war between our two nations….

Au-U-Khan: No! They're at fault.

Angola: Who cares if DOOM is the solution…?

Blood: Hey! Wait, yawl! Look what you doin'…this man's a spy clear and simple. That's all it is

Goraka: No! He's telling the truth.

Yani: The whole place went silent. The person everyone thought was near death now looked young and vibrant again. Goraka had spoken.

Goraka: The Creator must have looked like a fool the other day you almost succeeded in squeezing the life outta me. I must admit, I was scared. There was nothing I could do. Nothing! And, I could feel my life gradually escaping. Literally! And, there was nothing I could do. I tried to cry, no tears. I tried to scream, no noise. Then, I recalled the silence. Funny I thought I'd never get away from that again. After all, it cost us so much. Now, here I was helpless, except for the silence…Silence…. Silence…. is….

Blue: Stop!

Goraka: …and, I gradually found myself disappearing. It could not be reversed. I would survive. I had one more chance, but then I found myself back in Fifty-plus-One, with nothing to do. They had retired me with no position. I was a failure. Few visitors came by to see me, and besides, the Kinshasa people were experiencing an extreme crisis. They could not defend me even if they had wanted to. Besides, they plan to return to your republic. Why, because their present home it closing in on them. It's shrinking.

Yoni: Shrinking? How? Oh, I'm sorry.

Blue: Shrinking? How?

Goraka: TIME! We are running out of time. Our time is literally shrinking around us. So, we headed to the only places we have access to. Where we're going to, now, we call it Global Village. You call it Zania. You call it the New World Colony we call you the old country. We call ourselves Kinshasa of Fifty-plus-One. You call yourselves Aireans of the Republic of Aire. We call Akuyus of Fifty-plus-One "Noners," while they call us "rottens." All of this we've managed to do in less than a generation…this is not what we set out to accomplish. This is not the contribution the Noners were to make in our great quest for human understanding.

Yoni: While Goraka reflects, an unusual occurrence appears.

Angola: LOOK! WHAT IS THAT! THEY LOOK LIKE THEY'RE CRYING FOR HELP,

Yoni: As the questioner speaks the visual fills with hopeless souls crying out in the silence of their misery. As each person gives a sigh of relief that person's form changes to a dry rot of unusual and fascinating design. Somehow, one gets the impression that the design reflects each person's image of self. You know what I mean? Weird! Really weird…can you imagine, one moment you're a blank stare that I can't figure out. The next moment you're a piece of dry rot sculpture, now, that's WEIRD! PHEW! Now, I have seen it all. Well, maybe not. But, you get the gist of it.

Angola: What's going on out three? Where is that? Where are we?

Goraka: Those are the dying. That is the place I founded. That is Fifty-plus-One, Capital District 17, The New World Colony. The New World Colony in the Earth Life Epoch before the Great Fall From Grace That is the Kinshasa clan expiring right in front of your eyes. The Lost Family! This is what is left of it. This is what is happening to it.

Angola: This all seems like a dream. First, I see us capture a dying man. Then, I see that man given a restorative massage, a message of relief to the dying. Next, I see that dying man full of energy telling a fantastic story that invents the nightmare of my soul, our fate death so telling? So inscribed?

Goraka: Young soldier, you don't understand. That is our fate yours will be different. But, just as final. Do not be confused with how we die. That death is ours alone. Your's will be everybody's.

Angola: What do you mean?

Yani: Blue is one of those characters who no one really, but everybody knows. If you have a project that must get done, and nobody human can do it, call Blue! You know Blue, same character. Now, here is Blue down listening to his Panthers question Goraka the brilliant visionary who was not suited for the people he chose to govern although I do understand that he literally created a utopia when he founded the New World Colony. So, why couldn't he do the same at home?

Blue: Goraka, why did you betray you friends?

Goraka: Things were moving too fast. I let them get outta control. But, that's not the worst of it….

Blue: What do you mean?

Goraka: The death I described earlier is the death of the people of Aire—as you call it — now have as their fate. I not only offended Nailah, I failed to do what I was sent back to do. So, now our utopia will be as though it never existed. We shall be as though we never existed. Frightening! Isn't it? I know that you don't want to believe me, but it's true.

Blue: So, why tell us now?

Blood: Yea, the shits too late to do anything, now

Goraka: I don't think so. It's going to be more difficult, but I don't think so.

Blood: Anything to save your ass, huh! Goraka?

Yani: Goraka had to laugh at this one. His surprise laughter caused everybody to break out laughing, including Blue, who always thinks Blood's humor is hilarious.

Goraka: TRUE! But something else, too. It's really a deep reflection that was caused by the simultaneous choking and words of wisdom. When you are being given profound words of advise while someone is letting you know that your life is in their hands, it doesn't' take long to reflect on the value of what you heard and what you felt.

Yoni: The Panthers laugh again. Goraka's humor is subtle, unexpected and disarming. Except for Roc Steadye and Blue, no one else on the mission knew what Garaka looked like, let alone that he was charismatic. Now, they have standing right in front of them this handsome mahogany statute of a person offering words of vision.

Blood: Life must continue after us.

Yoni: Have we forgot why we are here?

Goraka: You se future people of this Earth Life Epoch destroy all human life forever. There is no human life on Earth after this Earth Life Epoch unless we do something…

Yoni: Goraka keeps talking about these strange occurrences, why?

{Yoni never becomes aware that Goraka was the Usher who told her she could not enter the Big Event with Nailah.}

Goraka: WE MUST ACT NOW!

Blue: Do what? You are going back to Aire so that you may stand trial, Goraka. If there is any saving the world, that'll have to come after the trial….

Yoni: Blue as always has a way of bringing everybody back to reality, doesn't he?

Blue: In case you don't know, you're being tried for treason and conspiracy.

Yoni: And, he pulls no punches in the process. Let's see how Goraka handles it. Obviously, Blue has not been sold.

Blue: That's not the point.

Yoni: What do you mean?

Blue: I have a job to-do. Goraka might very well be right, but that must be decided by a court of law. No one is above the law.

Yoni: I see! Anyway, as I said, let's see what Goraka does now that Blue has informed him why he's returning to Aire. As if he didn't already know.

Blue: And, what is this thing you keep harping on this thing about the world coming to an end?

Goraka: It is true. Unfortunately, it is true.

Blue: How do you know

Yoni: Goraka begins to explain the unusual events that convinced the Kinshasa that unless they took matters into their hands, the world is going to expel all human life forever at some point during the Earth Life Epoch. He also explained the irony of ironies: it will be the descendents of the Kinshasa people who will be responsible for this catastrophe. However, this catastrophe does not have to occur according to Goraka, if something is done, now.

Blue: What?

Au-U-Khan: That's right, what?

Goraka: Well, theoretically, that is why the Global village—excuse me – Zania was founded as a new colony.

Blood: Is that why yawl went in and attacked them?

Goraka: They did not get permission to create a new republic…

Blue: Get permission from whom? You see Goraka

Angola: …You want to preserve your cake and eat it, too.

Blood: Man, who you to talk? You under arrest for treason, and our Prime Minister saw fit not to accuse you of the other treason you committed.

Goraka: I do not understand…

Blood: The place yawl call Fifty-plus-One by right belongs to the Republic of Aire because you purchased your charter from the King-General Mathew II when he was the ruling authority of what is now called Aire. As purchase price, you were to rule in the name of the King-General as Barrister-General. Instead…you know the story better than I do. And, you ain't even been brought up on charges for doing that. No Nailah – excuse –Our Prime Minister talked the Parliament into recognizing our New World Colony, the Republic called Fifty-plus-One. Place of the Kinshasa people…. and you have the audacity to speak in the same breath about saving the world and creating colonies. Man, are you really MAD? Some have alleged in some circles that you might be. They might be right is seems.

Goraka: No, you do not understand, we must colonize. That is the only way we're going to have people in the next world after yours.

Blood: You really don't understand do you? You really don't want to understand that your colony did the same thing to you that you did to us. They formed a new republic unilaterally. We accept the fact that they exist just as we accept the fact that you exist. Both exist! It's not a question. That's one war you don't need to fight. See, we have saved the world already. So, why start a war with them…you see, I'm having' problems with your story.

Au-U-Khan: IT'S TRUE!

Angola: LEGEND HAS IT!

Blood: Legend my ass, I wanna hear this prophet confess that he's been wrong on a lotta things, including waging a war against a sovereign state like Zania. But, according to you, you attack because you are sovereign and Zania ain't. Is the moral of the story that we oughta come up to Fifty-plus-One an' kick yo' ass? Is dat the moral, Goraka? Cause if it is, I'm ready to oblige you.

{Upon seeing Blood move toward him Goraka turns toward the Mystic East and speaks to someone we can't see.}

Goraka: God, it is very difficult to do your tasks and negotiate my Earthly duties, too. What do I do?

Blood: Now, ain't this something. This mutha dun went an' dun everything under the sun. Now, he calls on Mr. G and says God, I cain't pull it off 'cause I'm weak and venerable.

Blue: Blood! Blood! Don't be so hard.

Yoni: Everybody laughs at this point. Blood was always hard on those whom he thought deserved serene criticism. And, Goraka was top of the list. You see, Blood doesn't let up. He his Goraka with one last…

Blood:…'Cause I'm HU-MAN!

Yoni: You could hear Blue clear his throat, which, although he just happen to be doing out of habit occurred at the wrong moment. Yes, indeed! The place got quiet again…. as everybody looked right dead at Goraka. Goraka obviously felt vulnerable at that moment and would have said so if asked, but they simply stared at him. Not wilfully just an objective stare right at Goraka. It was obviously unsettling because Au-U-Khan spoke.

Au-U-Khan: Tomorrow has its problems. Please do not burden it with the trials of today.

Blood: Blue, who the hell is this little twit that keeps making these, coded statements?

Blue: YO! Wait-a-minute, Blood! Au-U-Khan has a right to throw a statement like that out, if he so chooses. He was talking to Goraka just like you were. And, the point is well taken, by me at least. I'd like to know what Goraka felt at that moment. Huh, Goraka?

Yoni: PHEW! These monsters are serious. "If you say you are the chosen, if you say you have in your possession the gift, show me." That is what looks showed on everybody's face as they ignored Blood's outburst. To them, it was irrelevant as to whether or not the philosophical St. Mathew encoded statement; it was a good comment that deserves a response.

On the one hand, these elite guard that replaced the Ukuyuebo bodyguard corps that guarded King-Generals for centuries are Head Hunters. On the other hand, they are not fools. They follow Blue because they trust his leadership. They know, no matter what, Blue will be fair as he showed in the brief encounter with Blood. Blue knows that each one thinks for self, although no one else believes it. People on the outside do not know that Blue's Panthers only move by consensus. No one on the outside believes that either…. yet, here each one is interrogating Goraka in whatever way it suits the inquisitor. They know that Blood 'goes off." That is his "style." They simply go on with the business. And, the business now is…

Blue:…to know what Goraka felt at that moment…. the moment Au-U-Khan recalled his message to you from your people back home.

Yoni: Again, there is silence. No one speaks. No one attempt to fill the space, the void. An old trick they learned from Blue. But, Goraka can't take it! Suddenly, he disappears! In an instance so close to Goraka's disappearance that it appears at the same time, Au-u-Khan disappears, too.

Blue: Nobody speak! Nobody! Everybody meet me at the Score Nite Spot. Attention! On the double, move!

Yoni: Suddenly, Roc Steadye appears. Then she and Blue disappear. Blood is going mad! But, he is under orders to stay cool and meet Blue at the Score Nite Spot.

Angola: Blue said stand at attention, and head for the Score Nite Spot.

Yaoni: Everybody stays on the Score until it reaches Zania. Score is the name given the transport vehicles in Zania. The Score operates strictly according to the laws of music whereas the Time Mirage functions according to the laws of neuro-psychology. On the other hand, the instrument created by TOMORROW the pop group from Aire violates all definitions of space and time. It is the most revolutionary instrument ever invented. However, its range is still limited.

Chapter 29

Yoni: The next time we see Blue's Panthers they're sitting in the Score Nite Spot listening to Steel Pulse "talk" about the "Earth Crisis" facing the people of the three/three worlds: the three/three worlds are Aire (old country), Fifty-plus-One (New World), and Zania (Third World). Each world represents a different Earth Life Epoch. As you know, the old country is the place Goraka calls his original home, and the New World Colony is the place Goraka discovered and claimed as his new home, that is Fifty-plus-One the place founded by his people the Kinshasa. The Kinshasa's and Goraka think that the Global Village represents the future place for it to settle: a place for humanism in future Earth Life Epochs. The problem is, are the Kinshasa and the Akuyus capable of receding their differences? Is the future with its own set of problems going to greet tomorrow or will the trails of today make tomorrow only the future foretold? Will time make the difference?

……….He doesn't know how it happened, but he is still alive. This is the thought of Au-U-Khan as he assesses himself after disappearing without initiating it.

Au-U-Khan: ……What did I do? And, where am I? Let's see, what happened? I was waiting to hear Goraka's response and what I saw? What did he do? Yes, he was going out. He was fading away right in front of my eyes. And, I guess the whole thing must have awed me. So, I kept looking, and he kept fading real gradual like. To the others I guess he left an illusion until he was actually gone. What mastery! I always heard the old folks talk about people knowing how to disappear and things like that, but to see it happen right in front of your eyes, phew! Eyes? Where, where am I? How did I get here? I'm not with the others. Where am I? Where's Blue? OH! GOD!

Roc Steadye: Don't worry son, I have you in a safe place…you'll be back with the crew in a little while. First, I must do something. Don't go away.

Yoni: As quickly as aid was assured, the attendant was gone. Au-U-Khan did not know where to begin to figure out what just happened, but he knew that he was safe, but this was over his head. He did not know whether to piss in a paper bag, wipe forehead, duck, or grab his groin.

Au-U-Khan: Who was that? Was that Roc Steadye? Is that how I look? Ghee, interesting.

Yoni: Au-U-Khan did not know it but Roc Steadye had saved him from oblivion. His natural motion led him to follow Goraka, but he did not know what to do once he got there. Goraka expecting Blue, issued a death force that Roc Steadye neutralized by withdrawing all of the energy from the space with a Vacuum Pac. Goraka, startled with who it was that followed him and by the fact that his death force was neutralized, immediately disappeared further into whatever. Roc Steadye took off after Goraka thinking that blue might be in danger. After searching for a while, Roc Steadye and Blue meet up as antiforms then convert back into forms because it allows them to talk, a mode of communication they thoroughly enjoyed.

Blue: Where's Au-U-Khan?

Roc Steadye: He's okay! He's still trying to figure it all out. Think he ever will?

Blue: HA! HA! I don't know…. I was watching Goraka then suddenly I spotted Au-U-Khan dissolving, too. I said, "OH! SHIT! I didn't plan on this, where's Roc Steadye? And, PHUNGE! There you were. PHEW! I thought, I've never been so happy in all my life. Where are you come from…Oh? How are?

Roc Steadye: …They're okay. Saweto and Manila are fine. They're safe. You think that's where Goraka went?

Blue: Let's go.

Roc Steadye: Where?

Blue: To the Castle he thinks they're living in.

Yoni: Of course, by the time Blue and Roc Steadye – aka, Ife Cameron – reach the official home of the Barrister-General, Goraka is gone. But, it does give them a sense of his illness. You see, Goraka now believes obsessively that it is he is supposed to save the three worlds. And, that these three worlds salvation and redemption will come through HIS DIVINE RULE. The man is mad. He cannot deal with the fact that he is HU-MAN. That bothers him to no end. Blood made his angry! Blood had to be killed. Blood had to die. And, die he would. Brutally at the hands of Goraka.

You don't have to be a blood on the street to know that that is a declaration of war. No one in Blue's Panthers will allow Blood's murder to go unavenged…Now, ain't that madness? Goraka was told to save the three worlds and he has them on the brink of war: not just one Earth life Epoch he's threatening, but three. THREE! MADNESS! How can good intentions go so far astray? How can a desire to save humanity be so betrayed? By the fate of one man?

Roc Steadye: He's here and gone! I see he took his team with him. That could mean trouble.

Blue: Yea, we better get over to the time terminal before the Panthers become worried and do something rash.

Roc Steadye: Wait! We've got to pick up Au-U-Khan.

Blue: Oh, yes I forgot Au-U-Khan! We must hurry!

Yoni: Before Blue can complete his statement, he and Roc Steadye have dematerialised into anti form. Getting Au-U-Khan takes only the time for them to disappear. Roc Steadye explains the process as they move toward the Score Nite Spot. Blue informs Au-U-Khan that he has no choice but to learn how he did what he did because he has NO CHOICE! Their efficiency is not enough. By the time Blue and Roc Steadye arrive on the other side via the time terminal, it is too late. Everything is all over. Only Roc Steadyc's niece Angola survived the attack. Hip City Daddy arrives shortly after Blue and Roc Steadye to see what remains of the Panthers. Blue weeps openly as Roc Steadye changes colors like a rainbow until she reaches a white sizzle. Angola defuses Roc Steadye by calling her by her "real" name,….

Angola: IFE! IFE! IFE! IFE CAMERON! Do not consume yourself in your own anger. HOW RED! IFE CAMERON, you are too valuable to consume yourself with your own energy. We all loved Blood, and CR16 had all the others, but they're gone. They're gone, and the only way we can make certain that it does not happen again is to be calm and sane. Did you hear me IFE CAMERON? Goraka is INSANE! But logical and calculating! We didn't have a chance. They came our as the second band. Of course, we were right up front.

Blue: How did you survive? How did you avoid getting hit, Angola?

Angola: I had to visit the convenience station.

Roc Steadye: I'm glad! I'm happy you're alive.

Yoni: Now, for the first time Angola can see IFE CAMERON return to her calm reassuring normal self. Blue has also collected himself. His composure is as if nothing happened. But, everybody know otherwise.. And, they'll never forget it…

…..Now there is another problem, one Blue has not expected, i.e., Blue must re-capture Goraka with only three others and himself. The Panthers are definitely understaffed for this task. That's putting it mildly. Four to whatever number is in Goraka's unit is simply not enough. As Hip City Daddy inquires,

Hip City Daddy: What'll you do now, Blue? You're definitely under the required number to go on any mission to recapture Goraka. And, it's too far for Nailah to send help in time…I'll tell you what, we have a pretty tight unit we're right proud of that we'll place at your disposal under one condition, I must tag along for the ride. Okay? Oh. I forgot to tell you, the musician is here, too.

Blue: No, really?

Yoni: OH?

Blue: I wanna keep the unit tight and small, just like the previous one, Okay? I think we can take him

Yoni: Blue, don't be crazy. That is suicidal. I saw what he did to Blood Nem. It's gonna take at least one.

Hip City Daddy: Okay, just six of us. That'll be the Musician and two others plus myself, if you'd like more experience. Please excuse me soldiers, I do not intend to insult you, but, oh, I must remind you, you, are here at the courtesy of our government.

Blue:…and, as a courtesy to….

Hip City Daddy: Thus you have no choice…Just teasing to let you know that we are just as serious, and….

Blue: …that we have no choice….

Hip City Daddy: Now that we have dispensed with the preliminaries, why don't we start by telling you where all of the strong holds of Goraka's terrorists are? As a matter of fact, Goraka is stronger here and probably more safe than on Fifty-plus-One….

Blue: …Why?

Hip City Daddy: Because they have him under protective custody, 'cuse me, "had" him under "restrictive movement." But, all of his forces are here. You brought him to his stronghold.

Blue: Why didn't you tell us?

Hip City Daddy: Blue, we thought you knew: a break down in communication, someplace, obviously. We'll address that later. Anyway, we thought if anybody could take him, it would be you. I think we all under estimated his cunning, and skills. He's very adaptable when it suits him.

Blue: His brilliance! We keep forgetting it.

Roc Steadye: Oh, we might have another problem….

Blue: What?

Roc Steadye: Neptune believes that Goraka is our saviour.

Hip City Daddy: Yea, that's what I was trying to tell yawl. The dude's as nutty as Goraka.

Blue: What about Saweto our new passenger, and Manila? How do they stand?

Roc Steadye: They believe we're all INSANE.

Blue: AH! Maybe there is hope. Angola, you and Au-U-Khan will accompany us on this mission. Saweto, Manila, and the rest will remain in protective custody until we return.

Roc Steadye: Also, there is this storyteller who came along. He has some fascinating, but weird, tales to tell.

Hip City Daddy: Yea, I mentioned him to you, too… {Finally, Au-U-Khan speaks for the first time since they returned. He is stunned.}

Au-U-Khan: I'm sorry about what happened. It's really all my fault

Blue: Please! Don't! I understand! No one's to blame. NO ONE! And, the other storyteller can remain with the ones we're leaving behind. We have our own, and one is enough, really.

Au-U-Khan: So, what…. what do we do next? What is Goraka's next move?

Blue: I'm sure you've thought about it. What do you think Goraka will do next? What would you do in his place?

Au-U-Khan: Attack the time terminal. But, only after I've secured a way to Aire.

Angola: The old country will replace itself as the Global Village made up of those who escaped through the passage to the other side. THAT IS LEGEND.

Au-U-Khan: So?

Angola: If Goraka's already where legend places the future new life epoch, he would be foolish to leave…as I said, he's insane, but not crazy. He thinks very logically

Au-U-Khan: Somehow, I see Goraka wanting to rule all three worlds, in his madness. Who thinks he's capable of ruling all three…and, until then, manipulation through warfare is the order. Attrition! He thinks he has a long time to live to accomplish this deed. Somehow, a thousand eons lease is what he thinks he has on his life. That according to his logic will be the amount of time he has to gain, establish and rule this new order that will save humanity.

Angola: Yes, but Goraka doesn't have a strong alliance in Aire. Not any more, that is.

Au-U-Khan: Yes, he does! They are just quiet right now. Once they know he's alive, they'll be ready to move again. They must know he's alive first.

Angola: So, you are saying that they won't be satisfied unless they see him again. That means another civil war. Can the country take i

Blue: NO!

Hip City Daddy: NONE OF US CAN!

Roc Steadye: we've got to stop him! I hate to say this, but at all costs.

Yoni: As Blue listens to the neophytes methodically build their case, using the latest techniques in acting and courtroom logic; he decides definitely that six is the lucky number. It's not too big, and it's not too small. Besides, all for them except for the two neophytes have combat experience. Check that! All are combat experienced and very bright and innovative. They have to be, and they must strike back quickly.

Blue: WE MUST BE HARD, QUICK, AND DECISIVE! TO THE POINT! IN AND OUT, JUST LIKE THAT!

Hip City Daddy: They won't be in the way…. he won't even know they're there. Besides, we rehearsed this once before. All we need now is a small lead team, and no excuses. Now, we have both. I'll call Sharp, immediately.

Blue: Okay! How do we divide up?

Angola: Two!

Roc Steadye: What kind of pairing?

Au-U-Khan: By rhythm! And, Chemistry!

Roc Steadye: Like! Au-U-Khan…{Roc Steady stops and holds her prejudice inside. This is not the right time to doubt any one, even Au-U-Khan.}

Hip City Daddy: {Hip City Daddy says nothing either.} Blue's the boss.

Blue: And, remember, expect the unexpected. Okay, this is what we do. Hip city, I want you and Sharp to….

Yani: As Blue outlines the plan and target; Goraka wants to know how someone penetrated the castle defenses undetected. Obviously, there is a flaw within the defense system some place, and, Goraka wants it corrected, at all costs, right now.

Goraka: This means that I must change my plans. I thought I'd get here before they tried to take Saweto, my son. They must have planned that kidnapping to concur with mine. Interesting move! But, I must find Saweto.

Yoni: In the meantime, back in Aire, Nailah has dissolved the cabinet. Her new appointees include a new Minister of Agriculture and Community Development selected to carry out the Five Year Economic Development Program For Agricultural Production and Rural Preservation.

 Among the changes in agricultural program are these: Alfalfa will be grown in the western region as the cash crop for export because it feeds the soil and can be converted into fuel; cotton and corn will be planted in the southern region for export while vegetables and livestock will occupy the rest of the farm land; poultry and livestock will be raised in the eastern region for local consumption, egg and milk production; soy will be placed in the areas that need the most nutritional efficient foods; rice will be produced along the coastal region and will not be processed so that the value of the nutrients are lost. Coffee and cocoa will be grown in the hill country because they bring the best value when grown at high altitudes; while apples and pears will replace cocoa in the eastern region.

All small farms, that is, with less than 1000 hectors, are encouraged to form cooperative again for purchasing seeds, machinery, fertiliser, livestock and other vital good and services that are too costly otherwise. Also, transportation routes to market and the costal areas must be improved so that a more efficient and effective system of delivery is established. All products will be bought and sold at prices that do not put the local farmers out of business. Agribusiness must be curbed because it is now part of the problem with production, distribution, and pricing.

All mines are being nationalized to preserve the limited supply of minerals for defense purposes The old Kinshasa families that remain in Aire and who still occupy the home site of the Kinshasa's have officially requested that their elite military corps be placed at the disposal of the Prime Minister. Apparently, they think that Au-U-Khan might be in some type of trouble and his message did not get through to the Kinshasa's in Fifty-plus-One.

All known supporters of Goraka have been detained and placed on an island that is completely isolated and impossible to leave. The private elite clubs that acted as the base for Goraka in the countryside have been destroyed and/or closed. Now that Goraka is free, Nailah expects him to return to Aire with his forces. She is preparing for a surprise attack.

The opposition—what is left of it and that not in exile—claim that the Prime Minister is suffering from delusions of grandeur and a persecution complex. They also insist that Goraka is dead and everybody knows it; that the so-called evil extraterrestrial begins she talks about only point out how ill Nailah realty is. To go before a world body to request support to explore outer time is a waste of the taxpayer's money, especially a nation a poor as Aire. For her to allocate twenty-five percent of the state's budget to time exploration is ludicrous.

According to the opposition, the madness of the Prime Minister shows even more clearly when we examine how she has violated tradition by consciously educating femi persons at the same rate as meni persons. HA! What a joke. How insane they claim! She should be put to shame.

The Prime Minister is a shame they claim; AN EMBARRASSMENT to the Arian people with her wild dreams and that VOODOO MAGIC. She is the laughing stock of all humanity. Besides, that's a "mini person's job she's trying to do anyway. {The nerve of these scoundrels how dare they say such filth? Sorry about that, I just had to express my feeling here. After all, I am a femi person, too and proud of it. The dogs!}

Now ain't that nothin'! Goraka bankrupt the economy when he was in power, and Mathew III made no changes for umpteen years. My, my, ain't that something! Goraka bankrupt the First republic when he ruled, declared himself President-for-Life, murdered at random without apparent cause, lied about where the New World Colony was, forever and the opposition is so weak in its moral fibber that it said,"Oh! He wasn't' that bad. You must remember what time it was. After all,…"

To make matters worse, the unilaterally declared republic Fifty-plus-One has written into its constitution that no acquired territory can ever be released: except by an agreement in which both parties agree. Yes, Goraka recognized fifty-plus-One. This in effect gave up territory claimed by the monarch while allowing that territory it claims a new territory as its own with no regard for the original contract. And, they say, he was not that bad!

Now, you know, Nailah went off! It got so bad, Blue had to abort the first attack as he and Sharp and Hip City Daddy could talk to her She was roundly criticized for that behavior and brought up to date on the strategy they plan to employ. Blue and the others were informed about the decision of the Kinshasa to release their secret elite paramilitary unit to the Prime Minister. PHEW! Everybody was relieved now knowing that the Prime Minister was under the care of Au-U-Khan's family: honesty was their policy. And, they didn't take no shit…from nobody!

So it tuned out that was just as well anyway. The Ukuyuebo clan of bodyguards had joined Goraka's ranks, Blue's intelligence had learned via Au-U-Khan and Angola who took it upon themselves to be enterprising while Blue 'neum were conferring with Nailah.

Blue: That's why the vicious attack was launched. I couldn't remember what it was that made me so angry that I couldn't remember what I was thinking. That was it. The killers are the Score Nite spot possessed certain viciousness that was apparent in the club. It was still there. It was Ukuyuebo revenge.

Roc Steadye: Well. We don't have to change our tactics. We simply have to be more alert. Angola, au-U-Khan, don't think, ACT! You know everybody's chemistry and rhythm, here. YOU FEEL, THEN ACT! AT THAT MOMENT! YOU WAIT AND IT'S ALL OVER, FOR YOU. IS THAT CLEAR? NO PRISONERS ARE TAKEN. You know all the new dances yawl do all the time? This is what it's all about.

Angola: In other words, we throw nothing but cannons!!!

Blue: What's wrong, Angola? You were sayin' something…..

Angola: Sorry! Had a flashback. It's funny.

Roc Steadye: What

Angola: Just before STEEL PULSE took their intermission, they sang this weird song about being on a "Wild Goose Chase."

Roc Stready: And?

Angola: The words from the chorus keep ringing….

Blue: Well, tell us. What do they say?

Angola: Something about a "Wild Goose Chase." Laws of nature they just can't face ambition in the mash up place. Tell me, who shall save the human race?"

Blue: That's it, that' it.

Au-U-Khan: A Wild Goose Chase….

Blue: YES!

Roc Steadye: Of course!

Jom: While Blue outlines the wild goose chase to pull Goraka's band out into the open, Au-U-Khan unveils his own scheme to Angola. Angola laughs a funny giggle that drives Roc Steadye bananas.

Blue: Angola! Au-U-Khan! This is hardly the time for comedy. Will you please pay attention? Maybe I was….

Angola: Tell 'em.

Blue: Tell us what? C'on! Well?

Angola: Au-U-Khan wants us to play STEEL PULSE'S "Wild Goose Chase" across the airwaves.

Au-U-Khan: Yes, the part about "who shall save the human race?" We should play the chorus over and over. I think it'll get a reaction from him.

Blue: GOOD! LET'S MAKE THE PLACE THE OTHERSIDE NITE SPOT. AND, EVERYTHING WILL BE REAL…LIVE!

Roc Steadye: We don't want to endanger any civilization.

Au-U-Khan; He means it will be the illusion of being live.

Blue: Exactly! Hip City, that's where you troops come in. As I

said,….

Angola: LIVE! AND, IN COLOR!

Hip City Daddy: with surprise quests…OH! My gosh! With all the excitement I forgot to tell you. We got Black Uhuru. The Decoding Society came along, too.

Yoni: Angola and Au-U-Khan are big fans of the two groups. Angola likes Uhuru while Au-U-Khan likes the Decoding society. They grin from ear to ear. Now, they can see the groups in person. Live!

Au_U-Khan: Why don't we have those two groups over also? That'll rally blow his mind.

Blue: Okay, if we are looking to make him irrational, we had better be ready for the consequences…we seem to keep upping the ante.

Angola: Just trying to take every advantage.

Yoni: Advantage? To take advantage of! To assume the advantage! Is this a games person speaking here? What does Angola know about advantages? A whole lot, it would seem: I can recall when Angola about ten years old at the time, was given an assignment to destroy one of Goraka's Palaces; his favorite, as a matter of fact.

It was thought that if Goraka's favorite was destroyed, that might set home off and force him into making more errors. So, like a trained soldier, Angola walked into the palace undetected, placed a bomb exactly where it was suppose to go, activated it and quietly walked away completely unnoticed. As a matter of fact, no one to this day, except Blue and Roc Steadye, know who set off the bomb that destroyed Goraka's Favorite Palace. She was unbelievable.

Now here Angola is talking about advantages like an old pro. Whatever! Roc Steadye, as she much prefers to be called to the beautiful name IFE, still thinks of her as a little girl who needs her affection and protection from the forces of evil. In fact, Angola is already a trained killer who has assassinated more of Goraka's supporters than anyone alive, except Blue and Roc Steadye.

Au-U-Khan, on the other hand, comes from that wing of the Kinshasa who was opposed to the New Way of the perspective King-General was selected to found. They preferred to do it the old way. They preferred to stay at home in the old country and build their "castle in the sky" there. However, their views were in a minority. So, from that day on, they were called the "minority." Instead, they isolated themselves from the rest of the population until they realized that the Prodigal Prodigy was one of their own, and one of their own had a chance to rule the old country.

In the meantime, the "agro Kinshasa", as they came to be known because of their fine produce, perfected a style of fighting unlike anything anybody had seen before. When Goraka was elected President, they volunteered their own services to him to serve as his personal security force, free of charge to the State. That was their way of saying no hard feelings. Goraka did not even bother to respond. They were highly insulted. But, they kept their cool. As before, they went back into isolation until, now.

Au-U-Khan is their champion. He defeated their reigning champion so badly that he was declared a Master with his own unique technique of fighting. His technique is what the agroKinshasa people now employ to train the elite corps. He is the most recent addition to Blue's Panthers. He beat all the other recruits by a margin so big that shi technique is being adopted by the Panther Training Center as the official method of training their cadet corps.

Chapter 30

Nigga Dred: Every time it rains

My teardrops are dry.

Fear of fear is everywhere, everywhere.

Tomorrow, why?

Goraka: …Do you bring me so many burdens, today? Oh! I know you can hear me Blue…You want an answer? That is my answer. I must bring in tomorrow. I must rid my self of these burdens today. You understand, Blue. Ain't nothing personal. I simply cannot use you on my team. You're too radical. You wanna bring about too much change, Blue.

The people are not ready for that now. They need something else, like a father figure. The people need a daddy. You want to make them think they're better than they are. That builds false hope, bad dreams, and petty hatred. Look, if God had meant for the Akuyu to rule, he would have chosen one. But, he chose me, Goraka, a Kinshasa to rule. He gave us the Promised land. We hold title to the Lost Paradise. Goraka must rule. The Kinshasa is the Chosen. Tomorrow has its own problems, I can' burden it with today's. {I cannot quiet remember where I heard that statement, but it is true. I could not have said it better. }

Blue: Yes, I can hear you Goraka, and you hear this: the Orishas said don't ever let your position supersede your mission. And, you did just that. Now, the character Goraka is Evil. Hi is only concerned with his name and position. He wants to hold the most favored as the original position for life. The Orishas sent Goraka back to save the human race, and he has chosen to rule instead. HA!HA!HA!HA!HA!HA!HAAAAH!!

Yani: While Blue and the others age laughing STEEL PULSE BEGINS TO SING ABOUT THE "WILD GOOSE CHASE"…and "who shall save the human race." Goraka hears the song, and begins to sing along. Eventually, he starts to sing nothing but the last stanza followcd by a loud, GORAKA! GORAKA!

As Goraka calls his own name, he does in a loud and mocking robust voice while marching back and forth in a cocky stomp. The music continues over and over until Goraka becomes hilarious with laughter. After a while, with the chorus still playing, Goraka's laughter becomes an echo on top of another echo on top for many echoes in between ouches struggling with crying invading silence in between his anger with more laughter and more crying and more pure rage crying rage, mad rage…

Blue NOW!

Yani: Before blue could complete his command, the Panther sic had sprung. The timing was so accurate that although the numbers were small, they were far greater than expected: the attack was devastating. Angola and Au-U-Khan were magnificent in battle. Hip City Daddy and Sharp were their usual, they left no traces of any activity have taken place at the sight of the attack.

Roc Steadye fired and missed Goraka by accident. Angola and Au-U-Khan as a unit caused Goraka to materialize even he was in his death tumbles. Roc Steadye spotted him and fired but missed because Goraka was off balance in having to materialize and control his tumble all at the same time. It was one of those one in a million accidents that save someone's life. Ironically, as it turned out Goraka was about to aim his tumble at Roc Steadye.

In any case, Goraka's forces in Zania were nearly wiped out: all except Goraka and his military commander were wiped out. They escaped. However, with the rest one, the panthers now had time to isolate and capture Goraka.

Blue: Good job, everybody! Fantastic! No, we must isolate Goraka and capture him

Au-U-Khan: How do we do that? He seems to escape as a matter of course

Angola: By getting him to come to us….

Au-U-Khan: How?

Roc Steadye: With bait!

Au-U-Khan: What bait?

Blue: You'll see!

Hip City Daddy: the question is, will he go for it?

Roc Steadye: He'll go for it. He'll go for it.

Yoni: Goraka: went into a deep depression after the retaliatory attack by Blue's panthers. They could not have been expected to retaliate so quickly. After all, they had lost nearly everybody. There couldn't have been no more than three or four of them.

Goraka: I THOUGHT I KILLED EVERYBODY AT THAT NITE SPOT. IS THAT CORRECT DIRTY SPOT?

Dirty Spot: Apparently not, Goraka.

Goraka: Who survived?

Dirty Spot: Sir? The ones that attacked us apparently.

Goraka: APPARENTLY! APPARENTLY! How did you possibly arrive at that? Who the hell can give me some answers? I want some answers.

Dirty Spot: Yes, Goraka! At your command, SIR!

Yoni: As soon as Goraka finishes speaking, he again sinks into a deep melancholy. When he realizes it is another attack by the Panthers. Another surprise attack. Yea, you are reading it correctly. Blue senses Gorka's melancholy and strikes again. This one is a real surprise. No body expects it. Again, Goraka miraculously escapes within an inch of his life. His commander, Dirty Spot, is not so lucky.

Blue: I can't believe this being. There is no way for him to escape. No way! He should not have escaped.

Roc Steadye: I am sure he's said the same thing about you as many of us.

Blue: HA!HA!HA! That's true! But, it's almost an obsession.

Roc Steadye: With both of you….Goraka it's the rule of three worlds he feels responsible for. Yours is to stop him at any cost by any means available.

Blue: I said, almost. When this is all over, I'll put my weapons down and lead a normal everyday life.

Roc Steadye: SURE!

Blue: I just don't like to fail. And, I know what Goraka's capable of. We simply cannot afford to have him rule again. Maybe they can in Fifty-plus-One, but we cannot here, in Aire. We invested too much in the Revolution to have him come in and destroy everything. Goraka must be stopped. He must never rule again. EVER! EVER!

Yoni: By now, Blue's arch-villain is far into the bush of Zania. He cries out with great intoxication after having just finished mixing his brew of herbs to overcome his depression. What's the brew you ask out of curiosity? Locoweed! You say, why loco weed? To be honest Goraka does not know whether to wind his ass or scratch his watch. What would you do under those circumstances? Exactly, get you some good loco weed. And, pray!

Goraka: Lord, why have you forsaken me? The task you assigned makes such demands on us mental souls. I have tried the best way I know, but these enemies of yours keep appearing before me, in opposition to my and your will. Why don't you slew them, Lord, God. I've tried, but they keep coming back…

Yani:" Did you hear the mortal being? He has caused all kinds of havoc and he has the audacity to cry out the Creator, Olodumare. Ain't that nothing? In the mean while, Blue has been informed by the Prime Minister that she has received "directives" form the Council of Judges on Fifty-plus-One Capital District seventeen "requesting" that Goraka be returned to Fifty-plus-One immediately, or be prepared for retaliatory action in the form the Kinshasa people feel appropriate to protect its citizens. Nailah informed Blue that the local Kinshasa people attempted to communicate with their blood kin but to no avail…

Nailah…they are looking for a showdown, it seems, Blue.

Blue: How you know?

Nailah: They launched one of their missiles…

Blue: Where?

Nailah: Oh, it exploded way out in space above the Capital.

Blue: Was anyone hurt?

Nailah: No, but it was very impressive! Very impressive!

Blue: How do you mean? What happened?

Nailah: The explosion was so bright and loud that the United Federal Republics have asked us to surrender Goraka, immediately.

Blue: Phew! Wha? Those beach heads!

Nailah: What????

Blue: Nothin' I didn't want to curse, and that's all I could think of.

Nailah: I see! HA! HA! You have the ball, what do we do?

Blue: Well, we don't exactly have the ball in our hands, you know what I mean?

Nailah: So, you did not catch him?

Blue: Hell, no. Not after we got him outa Fifty-plus-One. He got away by disappearing and taking Au-U-Khan with him. We saved, at least Roc Steadye did, him and he is back with us, but my man Goraka got away clean. He's very slippery, you know. But, I think we may have foiled Goraka's plans of taking over Aire, again.

Naliah: How do you mean?

Blue: He had an army ready in Zania.

Nailah: A what?

Blue: The Ukuyuebos are working for Goraka again.

Nailah: You mean he still trusts them after what happened here?

Blue: Apparently!

Nailah: So that is why they are conducting manoeuvres near to our border.

Blue: Since when?

Nailah: The day I made my speech.

Blue: The day we took off. I think we been had….

Nailah: Exactly!

Blue: We gotta get somebody inside.

Nailah: WE TRIED!

Blue: What happened?

Nailah: All have been brutally murdered. Heads cut off! And, sent back.

Blue: Yes, their trademark.

Nailah: Blue, one of them is Trevor.

Blue: Trevor? Pots now Trevor. We got to do something.

Nailah: But what?

Blue: Can the elite corps handle the Ukuyuebos?

Nailah: We don't know, yet. They have not really been tested, at least not at this level of combat.

Blue: I know! Why don't you give them a test?

Yoni: As Blue outlines the test for Nailah's new elite corps. The others are wondering what their next move might be. Or, should I say, would be? Goraka, meanwhile, has regrouped.

Goraka: I cannot allow these troublemakers to take advantage of my compassion.… They have betrayed me… they have violated the law. They must be punished…But, whom can I depend on, the Kinshasa people? No! They are too caught up in their own leisure. I am of no concern to them. They placed me under house arrest as soon as I arrived, and, for what?

Yoni: For what? This is really an interesting dude, I must say. He has his nerve. He really thinks he should be invulnerable. He's mad! But, for time sake, let's try. He has not done what he is supposed to do. So what is he suppose to do? The plan: Goraka would return to the old country, claim his inheritance to the thrown, and link up with Fifty-plus-One. This would allow the Kinshasa people to migrate back home from a failing, what would you call it, a place falling apart at the seams? Time is running out.

What brings all of this turmoil about? It all begins when Goraka arrives back in the old country. After of his arrival, Goraka immediately becomes a controversy. He creates such a division within the old country that a Civil War ensues. Many claim that it is his doing. As a result if this conflict, somehow he lands on the thrown as King-General Goraka I. Immediately after taking the thrown with the strong support from Parliament, he declares the old empire a Republic and is elected President.

The presidency allows him to be progressive and creative. He brings about many needed social changes and stabilizes the economy. He presses for the recognition of the New World Colony as Fifty-plus-One. That is well received and with little opposition. Now, thing are different. Power has gone to his head. His popularity leads him to seek the Presidency-for-Life. From there it has been all down hill like a roll Acosta. Another Civil War ensues and he is oustered by his Cabinet and Parliament.

His nemesis, which he attempts to assassinate on numerous occasions, becomes President and his Cabinet Member Nailah becomes Prime Minister. Since that time, he has had a price on his head to the tune of a quarter of the treasury. That's high. He has yet to be caught. I should say, besought.

Allowed to return to Fifty-plus-One, he is immediately placed under house arrest. Living a life of loneliness, being alone Goraka begins to wither away as the life of an old flower. Then, by a miscalculation Aire decides that it is now time to bring Goraka to justice. That attention as we see right now, is all he needs. The Kinshasa people who rule Fifty—plus-One now feel abridged to enter the seen.

Up to this point, they have done nothing. Now, they are flexing their muscles and spitting fireballs. The movement on their part has changed the equation. At first they did nothing but wait and watch, with a gift offering by Blue's man stealing of Goraka, the thinking among the Council of Judges is maybe they can salvage things after all. Just maybe. Remember, no one has solved the DRY ROT plague that has Fifty-plus-One in crisis.

Added to that crisis, Fifty plus One is literally imploding as a space form. To compound matters, as we saw and heard from Hip City Daddy, Zanians have found ways of escaping the grip that has longed kept them in bondage and allowed their bodies to serve as guinea pigs, unsuccessful guinea pigs at that. Expunging the lifeblood of the Noners, so-called, has only served as a temporary relief for the Kinshasa people of Fifty-plus-One. DRY ROT is delayed for a brief moment, but it eventually sets in on all of its victims. Eventually, as they are dying their bodies assume the design of a Rorschach (ink blot) test.

Back to the main theme, Goraka has gotten the notion in his head that he is the Chosen, or as Neptune put it, Our Savior. According to his warped assessment, he is the Lord and Master of His Gift, that He is solely the Chosen, that the Charge has been given to Him all alone, that no one else has the ability and capacity to Rule, that is, Rule Divinely.

Fact: Goraka was not the Chosen, he was chosen as a compromise.

Story Teller: Hold on! Hold on! Hooold Ooooonn!

Yoni: Yes, Story Teller? Oh, I didn't know that you were here. Where did you come from? I thought…….?

Story Teller: Well, I am here. First of all, you are in my territory. Second, this is my area. I know everything you are discussing first hand. And, third, why are you telling these people things that you know nothing about except through hearsay? HUH? Who gave you permission to tell my story? HUH?

Yoni: Well, I thought that it was my job to tell it to bring everybody up to date so they will be able to follow what is about to happen.

Story Teller: Well, that's my job. So, why don't you sit here and listen like everybody else? Okay. Thank you! Now, where were we? [Pause]The plan was this: Goraka would return to the old country, claim his inheritance to the thrown, and link up Fifty-plus-One with the old country thereby allowing the Kin-Sha-Sha people to migrate back home.

Yani: Story Teller, I was told that the name is Kinshasa not Kin-Sha-Sha. Now what is it?

Story Teller: I started this story. I gave them the name Kin-Sha-Sha, so that's it, at least, as far as I am concerned. Thank you.

Yoni: Yes, but Stellar Four said

Story Teller: …Stellar Four can kiss my place where the sun don't shine. Get my drift?   Now where was I? After all, tine was run out of Fifty-plus-One. Instead, Goraka took the thrown after a civil war – which many claim he started – changed the empire into a republic and announced that he was recognizing the new world colony as a republic officially called Fifty-plus-One, The Kin-Sha-Sha people were too pissed to do anything rational. So, they did nothing bur wait and watch. Finally, the opportunity came. Maybe, they could salvage things after all. Just maybe!

 Goraka had failed with his little adventure to set up a Banana Republic type government under his authority (control) as a President-for-Life. Now the opportunity came around again. If they blew it this time, that's is! But, the Kin-Sha-Sha people needed Goraka back. With him running loose, they would never be able to carry out their mission.

The position had simply gone to his head: I'm sure being back in the old country didn't help matters very much. He was now a liability. He could not be trusted any more. He was too power hungry. Thing was, the New Way required a consensus of the Council. Goraka wanted to act unilaterally. We wanted to go it alone. Be the master of his own fate.

Somehow, Goraka had gotten the nation in his head that he was the Lord and Master of His Gift: that he was The Chosen that the Charge had been given to him alone; that no one else has the ability and capacity to rule, rule divinely, that is. Knowing all of this, Goraka was not chosen. He was a compromise. And, besides, he was the heir apparent to the King-General Mathew III, so compromise it would be. They had no choice. If anyone else were sent to rule, the old country would reject him or her outright. The Kin-Sha-Sha did not like being in this type of predicament.

They were an innovative and ambitious people who had produced most of the intellectuals and scholar-scientists as well as most of the art forms of the old country. Did they now deserve the right to rule? Now, Goraka had almost ruined the chances of the Kin-Sha-Sha people because of simple greed and arrogance.

Sure, he was selected at an early age to follow in the footsteps of the King-General, the Emperor, if you will, but that was a gift from the Kin-Sha-Sha people. They had changed the rules so that combat would not be a determinant of who the Next King-General would be. Otherwise. Goraka never would have gotten it.

Everybody knew that Goraka got the charge because the two leading candidates neutralized each other, but times were changing. The old country needed to modernize a bit,

Yoni: …A bit? HA

Story Teller:…and Goraka was probably the only one capable of carrying out the process. And, thanks to the Kin-Sha-Sha people, this is exactly what he got a chance to do. Under Goraka's leadership, the old country moved into the forefront of modern technology. Also, as of now the old country has a name, and, most importantly, anyone may try for the Prime Minister ship: amazing advancement in such a short span of time. Now, even the masses – called the Mass or the Akuyu – may seek public office. Yes, for that everyone must thank Goraka.

Ironically, it was the most favored that orchestrated the rise and fall of Garaka. Well, that's not quite right. Let me try that again. The Kin-Sha-Sha people had released the tide that brought about Goraka's rule, and the most favored reaped the great majority of the benefits from that effort. S, although the most favored reaped the majority of benefits of this modern rule, advancement of technology and a regulated market, the Kin-Sha-Sha people never really moved very far from the positions they have come to occupy over the centuries. For a brief moment, it would appear otherwise.

When the prodigal prodigy was finally crowned King-General Goraka I, the Kin-Sha-Sha people in the old country and Fifty-plus-One partied like none had ever partied before. Remember, music was still outlawed in Fifty-plus-One. So, that must have taken some doing…

Yoni: ……I wonder what the hell they were doing…

Story Teller…Things would be different, now. The new system invented by them – NO! GORAKA, HIMSELF! – Would now spread like wild fire. No one would ever rule over them again, ever!

Everything was going well. Then for some reason unapparent to anyone except Goraka, he brought the Akuyus into his Council. Remember these were the least favored people in the old country. We did not mind the transition from an empire to a Republic. That was a natural happening that could not be stopped. The movement demanded change. And, besides, that's exactly what the Kin-Sha-Sha people wanted.

   A republican form of government would assure the most favored, now the so-called middle classes, if not the Kin-Sha-Sha rule specifically. This it was assumed would remain in place as long as there was a Republic. But, to bring an Akuyu into the Cabinet was unthoughtful. To choose a femiperson was unpardonable and unforgivable. Further more, to select a name of unpopular origin for the Republic showed poor judgement and a lack of character.

   How could Goraka so such a thing? How could he make so many errors of judgement in such a short span of time? Did he not realize that is was the Kin-Sha-Sha people who made him the master of his time? No one else held that honor. Did he not recall the Night Passage? The Time Mirage? The Other side? …. What got into him?

   So, when Goraka was deposed, he was brought back to Fifty-plus-One to account for his misdeeds and errors of responsibility. Some say that he should have been left to die at the hands of the Akuyu; that he would be less trouble; that he could be given a hero's funeral; a monument to his name as one of the original founders of Fifty-plus-One, and put to rest peacefully forever. Times had changed, they say. Goraka was antiquated. Old Timer! This was a New Time. A New Day! It required new thinking.

This was not to be, however. Instead, Goraka was saved at the last moment. A moment he shall never forget, ever. He still has nightmares over that day. Hot dry sweat still pours down his body as he screams silently in terror. He can still feel all of those bodies crushing against him. Squeezing life from his limbs. He can still recall being too scared to scream. Ironically, that's what saved his life. His silent scream.

Goraka: AHHHHHH!AHHHHHHHHHH!AHHHHHHHHHHHHHHHHHHHHHHHHHHHHHHHHHHHHHHH! PLEASE DON'T LET THEM KILL ME! DON'T LET THEM KILL ME! SAVE ME! I DON'T WANT TO DIE LIKE THIS! PLEASE, OH GOD OF MERCY, HAVE MERCY ON ME AND DON'T LET ME DIE LIKE THIS! PLEASE!

Story Teller: When they rescued him, Goraka was near death. A few squeezes more, and…. But, this is Goraka, and like many times before, he would survive. Somehow, he has survived. In shock! In pain! Both mental and physical! Insane! And, drunk with fear, he is still alive. Now he has been found and kidnapped right under the eyes of the Kin-Sha-Shas. The question is, what to do?

Yani: Finished? Okay! For Goraka, the answer is simple. Go home, back to Aire and soon. The Ukuyuebos are ready and waiting for the word when to strike. They are not rulers, except at home; they are the most peaceful people you ever saw. Elsewhere, they were servants-with-arms. Some call them hired guns; others refer to them as mercenaries. Then, there is always the name professional killers. What ever their reputation, they are notorious and deadly. And, now twice, they have lost their comrades to Blue. The first was enough. The second is too much. So? Why haven't they attacked and assassinated Nailah?

One.   They only move on orders of their payed employers.

Two.   They are not yet aware of the other losses.

Three: They do not know where Goraka is.

Four: They do not know where Blue is.

Five: They have been warned by the Orishas not to mess with Nailah under any circumstances.

   Funny thing is, it is not Blue who frightens them as much as Roc Steadye and Nailah do. They are not human. They are not femi-persons, they are demons. They are waiting to hear if Blue's Panthers, especially Roc Steadye, have been defeated. Why concern about Roc Steadye? She is a born killer. The way they are. Instinctively, she knows when to kill and how best to do it. That is the same way they are. That frightens them to no end to have a like kind working as the opposition.

Story Teller: I sure you already know what their plans are don't you? you knoe the plans Yani?

Yani: No!

Story Teller: Oh? Well, if you must know. Their plans are already laid out: Roc Steadye, Blue, and Nailah are to be assassinated if they are not already dead.

Yoni: But, you said that the Orishas told them not to mess with Nailah and that Roc Steadye brought them fear.

Story Teller: Look, the trade mark of the Ukuyuebos is assassination. That is how they protect their employers. Their motto is "the best defense is a dynamite offense, no pun intended." After they say it, they break out into this curiously crazy laughter that only the Ukuyuebos are famous for and think is funny.

Yoni: Wait, you said that they have been warned not to mess with the femi persons. Why would they violate the warning?

Story Teller: Demons have no ethics, no morals, no conscious, and no fear. So, they have respected the Orishas up to this point, but now they have reason to believe that they can pull this off without repercussions. Besides, if a few have to die to fulfill a mission, so be it.

Yoni: But that is in Bad Faith. What if they fail at these attempts?

Story Teller: They are dead any way. No one is to return home alive from an unsuccessful mission. So, to reinforce their demonic qualitative, they go by such names as: Skunk; Nose Snot; Dirty Rot; Slop Jar; Joy Juice; Smelly Phartz; Pique; Stinky Dink; Stinky Pee, Mean Machine; Crazy Brains; Skull Dungaree; and, Lost Cause.

You can see, forever. Life for the Ukuyuebos is a fantasy to be enjoyed by whatever means that suits their employer. Their fancy primarily is to see others – their enemies – die as strangely as can be imagined. For them, the greatest honor to bestow upon an Ukuyuebo is to die while making love. They have this saying, "what better way to go than while you are cunin."

Yoni: UH! How gross?

Story Teller: Check this, they do not stop there the above statement is followed by that wild laugh only they can give, and a high five that sounds like two Rams head butting each other simultaneously.

Physically, the Ukuyuebos are unusually large and tall. The average weight is about 375. Their height runs from 7" to 8"5' for meni demons. The femi demons are 6"9' and weigh in at about 295 up ward and they grow as tall as the meni demons. Mind you, this is all muscle and quick reflexes.

They are sharp eyed and can hear distances up to five miles given the right location. Their sense of smell is the envy of the beast of the wilds. No one has poisoned them in anybody's memory. Up until they ran into the one million people squeeze against their eleven thousand bodies, they had not been killed in mass before. Again, when they ran into Blue's Panthers, no one defeated them in a firefight either, but that's another story.

By now, the Ukuyuebos have found out what happened to the Panthers while they were sitting in the Score Nite Spot. And, what happened to Score Nite Spot and Goraka shortly after. So, they begin to plan their next move. The point is to go after Nailah. The question is, how to find her.

Yoni: Want that be a mistake for them? Do the demons really want to materialize the Orishas? Do they really?

Story Teller: Yani, femi-person, you are right on time, almost too late because while you are asking these questions, listen to this commentary by yours truly,

While the Ukuyuebos are plotting their next moves step by step, plan by plan, detail by detail, they are hit with a surprise that seems to come out of no where. BAM! ZOOM! POW! POW! BOOM! ZING! WHOP! ZIP! POOF! AHHHHH! And, leave without a trace except a bunch of dead bodies lying everywhere. Although the losses are extremely heavy, it is the surprise that surprises everybody.

I see! The strategy is to do the unexpected. The same way they were surprised at Score The Nite Spot, Blue and the Panthers are following the same blueprint. Hit hard and run like hell before anybody knows what just went down. This worked out well for Nailah's forces because there is no declared war on anybody's part, legally that is, between Aire and the Ukuyuebos. She has managed to even avoid a border dispute between he two forces. As a matter of fact, her forces are over a hundred kilometers from the border before the attack is launched in order not to arouse any suspicion or give the Ukuyuebos a ready target to vent their RAGE.

So, the Ukuyuebos are caught totally by surprise. And, the test that Blue has set for the elite corps has provided the answers they need. Nailah is so happy with the results that she decides to celebrate. What she does not know is that the assassins left Ukuyuebo Land before the attack, and are headed in her direction. What she does not know also is than the assassins are not Ukuyuebos at all. The Ukuyuebos figure that everyone will recognize them if they set foot in the capital because of their size, so, they employ their cousins, the Wimps, to perform this vital task.

What makes the Wimps so effective is the fact that they can blend in with the local population no matter where they are. They are ordinary looking creatures that may be mistaken for any being regardless of origin. They are ordinary looking creatures in other words. The only difference is, they have this penchant for killing.

They are called Wimps because just before they strike their victims, they make this funny wimpy sound that chills up the spine. The sound is like a sad cry or moan that seems to sound like weeping for the dead. So, they are called Wimps. With the Wimps on their way to attack Nailah's Palace, by the time the elite corps of the agroKin-Sha-Shas finish their job in Ukuyuebo Land, the wimps are already making their way into the capital, one by one…. By now, the security is tighter, and the surveillance is tough. Everybody who enters the borders is searched from bottom to top, in and out, no exceptions.

Security: Where are you headed? What's in the vehicle? What is the nature of you business? Will you please step out? Thank you! May I have the keys, please? Do you have anything to declare? May I look, please? Excuse me; will you kindly open that container for me, orders from the Ministry of Internal Security, simply precautionary measures. Thank you! You may move on. Next…

Yani: The Wimps are aware that armed patrols are everywhere. How could you miss it? The closer you get to the interior, the more layers you have to go through to get closer inside. By the time you reach ten city blocks from the Prime Minister's Palace, a twenty-four hour curfew is in effect. Anyone not on official business to or from the Prime Minister's Quarters or the Parliament is detained first and questioned later.

With all off these precautions, and the surprise attack across the border, Nailah feels safe for the first time in a long time. Nailah decides to relax for a moment. Besides, it's her birthday. She is 278 years old and has not relaxed for quite sometime; over a century it seems. She really wants too, so nobody wants to stop her. She has really earned this brief moment of relaxation.

What Nailah really wants right now is to see her baby, Manila. However, she's willing to imagine that she's safe with Blue, and will be home some time soon, with the help of her Orisha. The Wimps realize that after they reach as close as they can legally, that it is impossible to get any closer to the Prime Minister without being arrested. To counter that difficulty, alternatives are put in place.

The Wimps operate from the basic premise that no one singular Wimp is given the assignment to assassinate any particular political figure. Each has the same order. All are expected to get in a position to calmly move out the order successfully. The objective is to penetrate. So, each starts to improvise until one reaches the target. Thus, while the patrol is searching all incoming vehicles a diversion is set into motion, this diversion it to be one of many. All timed to be activated at the appropriate moment. The purpose is to pull the troops further and further away from the city center, the target area.

No one is better trained at deception than the Wimps. In other words, no one can blame the soldiers for rushing away from their stations to cover the explosion here, another there, and some more elsewhere. They may be criticized as undisciplined later, but at the time, now, they are simply trying to keep everyone from becoming a mob.

For now, they would be irresponsible to try and protect their stations when all life is falling around them: that is exactly what they are doing. Soldiers and civilians are running and screaming and firing their weapons at would be villains. Nobody seems to be sure who the enemy is at this point with soldiers and civilians firing at each other. It appears to be an all out revolutionary attack.

With such a successful diversion, the Wimps move closer to the target. Then something happens. Out of nowhere, all of these femi persons dressed in white appear. ODD! Thousand upon thousands of femi persons all dressed in white surround the Prime Minister's Palace. It is a sight to see. But, why are they here? Do they expect to protect the Prime Minister? With what? I see no visible means of protection. What do they expect to do? FIGHT? To further compliment matters, the soldiers are confused and dumfounded: what to do? Shoot them? The orders said no one should be on the streets. Period! Did that mean the persons not fighting dressed in white, too?

Security: Sir, we have thousands of femi-persons dressed in white surrounding the Prime Minister's Palace. What are we to do?

Yoni: Before the question is answered, the femi-persons are now walking and singing. What are they saying? Let me see if I can make out the words:

Femi-persons-in-White:{Singing} Exodus, movement of Jah people! Exodus, movement of Jah people. Exodus, Exodus, Exodus, Exodus, movement of Jah people.

Yoni: With all of the commotion, the Wimps seize the opportunity to move inn.

Cry Baby: MOVE! WEEP! WEEP! MOVE! WEEP! WEEP!

Yoni: The Wimps are as efficient as clockwork. Before the guards can do anything, the Wimps approach the Prime Minister's residence with a full-scale attack is launched. You can hear wimps and cries and sobs as the Wimps strike upon the landscape. There is no way for anyone to come out alive. No way!

The elite corps of the agro-Kin-Sha-Shas arrives just as the Wimps have completed their sobbing. Angered at their own delay in returning the elite strike fast and hard, Every Wimp in sight is killed: no prisoners taken alive. After all is over, the agroKin-Sha-Shaa sits down and weep tears of sorrow. Where did they go wrong? Should they have stayed? Had the Orishas betrayed them? Again? Now, they have lost the Prime Minister. It is all their fault, shame!

Chapter 31

Yoni: After the agroKin-Sha-Shas had finished mourning their loss, their failure to protect the Prime Minister, they followed their usual ritual by putting things back in order: exactly the same way things were when they first arrived at the Presidential Palace, recently named Efon Alaye Presidential Palace. Then, they made the long trek back to the Out Country.

Wimps who were on the look out immediately returned to the Ukuyuebos to report the good news. You thought I said, all the Wimps were killed? I did. These Wimps are the Look Out Wimps. They are never to engage in combat. Their only role is to report back to their employer a blow by blow of what happened, period. And, that's exactly what they did.

Look, See & Tell: Nailah is dead.

General Too Crazy: Are you sure?

Look, See & Tell: Positive

General Too Crazy: How do you know? Did you actually see the dead body? Give us the details. Leave nothing out. Nothing!

Yoni: Following their instructions, Wimps Look, See & Tell began to tell the story, detail-by-detail, from beginning to end. They left nothing out, even added a few gruesome details to increase the interest. Not that it was necessary. However, when Wimps Look, See & Tell completed their, General Too Crazy said,

General Too Crazy: Did you see the body? Did you actually see the body

Yani: Wimps Look. See & Tell thought, how preposterous.

Look, See & Tell: I mean, give me a break. The whole place was annihilated. Everyone inside was destroyed. That, I am certain of.

Yoni: As usual, all Wimps spoke at the same time, and told the same story; they were not about to back down, now.

General Too Crazy: I don't trust that. I want to see the body. Didn't you tell me that the agroKin-Sha-Shas wiped out your Wimp Force…I don't trust them? I want to see the body. I want some concrete proof. Nothing less.

Look, See & Tell: Wait, now! Contract is contract! We did everything you agreed to. We want…

General Too Crazy: Don't give me that bull sh….

Yoni: The moment General Too Crazy makes his statement, and before he can complete the last part of it, Wimp Look slips out a blade and stabs him right through the heart. Dead, just like that! The only warning, the sob comes at the exact moment of impact. Immediately, the hands of the Ukuyuebo standing nearest to her crush Look's skull. See and Tell pull weapons from their fake note pads and begin firing at the remaining soldiers. Although they wound most and kill other Ukuyuebos soldiers, the hands of the Ukuyuebos manage too crush them.

Following the incident, the Ukuyuebos High Command announces that the deal is off. The Wimps retort by demanding full payment for the assassination of Nailah. The High Command said that it would oblige them and open fire point blank, killing every Wimp there to observe Look, See and Tell.

Now, that was a mistake, a serious mistake, to say the least. Goraka has suffered great set backs but this is his greatest to date: Wimps do not like to be betrayed. A contract is a contract and they fulfilled their end of the contract. They expect to be paid in full immediately. The Wimps declare war on Ukuyuebo Land. For the first time ever, the Wimps and Ukuyuebos are mortal enemies. Even in times of victory, Goraka seems to suffer defeats. But, at least, Nailah is dead. Without her official protection, that will make it easy to eliminate Blue and Roc Steadye.

Stellar Four: While all of the activity is going on Aire and Zania, the council of Judges on Fifty-plus-One has been observing very intently. Don't forget, they have their own agenda for Aire. With Nailah out of the way, it should be easier to capture Goraka, and erase him from the picture, if you get my drift. "If those fools – meaning Blue's Panthers – had left well enough alone, things would have not gotten out of hand."

That might very well be so, but what about the shrinking time problem of the Kinshasa of Fifty-plus-One are facing? And, the DRY ROT plague? Those are the most important two matters of concern, at least in my own estimation.

Council of Judges: Stellar Four, there you go again. Opinions are not what we promote in our storytellers. Mind your business and tell the story accurately. Thank you.

Stellar Four: As I was going to say, the Kinshasa's must abandon ship very soon, so to speak. If the shrinking time does not kill us, the DRY ROT will. Why? Well, there is no cure for DRY ROT, although there was a false alarm at one point: it was thought that since the Noners – you probably remember them as the Akuyus who were in captivity here – did not suffer the same disease, they might be used as guinea pigs to find a cure.

After much experimentation and the loss of many untold lives, no real cure has ever been found, to date that is. But, at least, the Night Passage is open again. The new mode is still not as advanced as the "TOMORROW MACHINE" used by Blue and his Panthers to get to Fifty-plus-One via Zania. With the proper innovations our travel can arrive in Aire without going through Zania, something TOMORROW cannot do. Also, the two capsules still operate according to different principles: Aire's uses music while Fifty-plus-One requires biopsychology.

We are still going to take the slow passage for the most part because it has been determined that this will allow the Council to establish a new government and socio-economy. That loud multi rhythmic music will be the first to be outlawed. No more music! Good riddance. Tranquility based on silence will be the definition of a harmonious life. Pacification will be the way people are expected to live.

A democracy of the Kinshasa will be practiced whereby each group will be allowed to participate as soon as that group is functionally ready. Of course, the Kinshasa will determine when and who is ready. Local Kinshasa will or should be able to participate immediately if they cooperate. That does not include the minority, the agro Kinshasa, however. The will be tried as traitors. The leadership of the Akuyus will be arrested and executed upon arrival and the Noners will be encouraged to return to the homelands that will be reserved for them. Otherwise, they will impede progress.

Council: Or, migrate to Zania, Stellar Four.

Stellar four: Of course, my error. Excuse me, an omission. My omission.

Yoni: Now, ain't that nothin'? These are the chosen. They are here – or there whatever! – To save humankind, and they sound exactly like the people they are suppose to save. Humanity must have a better recourse – an alternative—than either of the platforms on the floor at this moment. There must be something more humane than what we see-taking place before us. There must be another way, a better way than this.

Hip City Daddy: Blue! Blue!

Blue: Yes, Hip City?

Hip City Daddy: Come with me. I want you to meet someone who just arrived from Fifty-plus-One.

Blue: Damn, Hip City, yawl are pulling them ottah the hat fast?

Hip City Daddy: Yes, but this is a bit different. He's one of our operatives there. He has to get back before they miss him, but I want you to speak with him before he leaves. He has some important matters I thought you might like to hear.

Blue: Okay, let's go. Roc Steadye, I want you to find out what you can about the trip Manila and Neptune. Maybe you can get some vital information.

Yoni: Blue has no idea of who is going to meet, so, the visit is as much an honor as it is a surprise.

Blue: Lightnin' and Blin' Lemmon? WAW! I've been a fan of yours for…

Lightnin': Don't tell us. We'd rather forget how long we've been at this business. Singing' blues is a business, you know?

Yoni: Everybody, including Roc Steady who has joined the party, laughs a hearty laugh…. Now, down to business.

Blue: So, what's up?

Blin' Lemmon: Go ahead, Lightnin'!

Lightnin': No! You first Blind….

Blin' Lemmon: Well, you know I've been on Fifty-plus-One since me an' Lightnin' an' Hip City was pulled there way back when, you know how long that is.

Lightnin': Hey man, cut all the prelims, git to the chase.

Yoni: Lightnin' said jokingly as Blue acknowledges that he knows without showing any impatience. Blin' Lemmon continues without responding because that's exactly where he plans to be right at this moment in his delivery.

Blin' Lemmon: Yea! Anyway, the Kinshasa's plan to invade Aire and Zania and take over both places simultaneously.

Yoni: Whaa??

Blue: Blue Yea, we suspected that.

Lightnin': But, listen…that ain't all.

Blin' Lemmon: Yea, they plan to arrest everybody and set up their own government…. and, they're leavin' soon. All leaders of the Akuyus are to be tried and executed immediately

Blue: How soon?

Hip city Daddy: Tell them how soon

Blin' Lemmon: Tomorrow!!!!

Lightnin": You see, they know what happened in Aire.

Blue: What do you mean?

Blin Lemmon: You know, with the assassination of Nailah.

Hip City Daddy: So, it worked.

Blue: Apparently! Now, they've shown their hand.

Yoni: As Lightnin' and' Blin' Lemmon delve into the here's and there's pros and cons, etcetera, of what the Council of Judges of Fifty-plus-One plan to do, it becomes clear to Blue that something has to be done, and fast.

    Then as suddenly as they are finished, zip, they become DRY ROT right in front of Blue, et al. Lightnin' takes on the form of an acoustic guitar while Blin' Lemmon like a being searching to see where he is. Blue is even more convinced now, something has to be done, and soon is not fast enough.But, Goraka is still on the loose. "Well…

Blue: That just has to wait for the moment. There are more pressing things to do on this far away illusion that only Aired and Zania are attached to.

Yoni: Come on, now! We saw what these monsters can do as a demonstration of their power and weaponry when they caused that Hugh explosion aver Aire, Blue's Panthers might be tough, but they are hardly any matches for the technology the Kinshasa's have developed. Besides, Blue's forces are – excuse the pun – undermanned. Even at full strength the commandos are no matches. With six people, that 's out of the question.

Blue: come, Hip City, we have to make some tracks. We've got to get over to where the others are. We need to talk to their informants

Hip City Daddy: Blue, I know the Panthers are tough, at how?

Blue: I don't know, but we've got to do something. We've got find a way to stop this planned slaughter. It's bad enough dealing with the forces on earth, but to have to deal with some lunatic tribe that thinks by killing everybody will save life on earth is beyond earthly reason…we must do something.

Hip City Daddy: Yea, but what?

Yoni: That is the question. Uh! Huh! As blue and Hip City Daddy head over to meet the six, Blue can't help but remember how he always enjoyed listening to Lightnin' and Blin' Lemmon when he was a young lad. Now, they are dead from serving their country as spies in some far away territory that no on can envision even in their wildest imagination.

Blue: Oh,shit! I forgot something. Didn't you tell me about how the storyteller paid close attention to the experiments they were carrying on while she was there?

Hip City Daddy: Yes, that's right, but I thought that's why you wanted Angola and Au-U-Khan to speak to everybody who came down with Manila.

Blue: Yes, that's true, but I didn't know what to instruct them to look out for, what kinds of questions to ask. I had no way of understanding what they are doing.

Hip City Daddy: Still don't!

Blue: That is true, but I'm getting better. (I hope!)

Hip City Daddy: I know this may sound like it's coming right from the hip, but we have only one choice.

Blue: What's that?

Hip City Daddy: We have to force their time to collapse round them while they are in travel.

Yoni: PHEW! That' heavy! Wow! That's really heavy, but, how?

Blue: What's that?

Blue: Yea, but we don't have time. We don't have the means.

Hip City Daddy: MAYBE! MAYBE NOT! LET'S SEE!

Blue: Obviously you have something in mind. What?

Hip City Daddy: TOMORROW!

Blue: What about it?

Hip City Daddy: Oh, how can you forget them. The musicians, singing group, you know TOMORROW!!! They made it possible for us to get here in record time. But, this is as far as we can go. To get to Fifty-plus-One we have to rely on your system. I don't know…maybe we can use them together. Maybe, somehow we can put the two together as one unit. An integrated unified form.

Blue: It's worth considering. What do you have in mind?

Hip City Daddy: Let's go home.

Blue: HA! HA! Yea, let's call home, but after we talk to the rest.

Yoni: In the meantime, Blue and Hip City Daddy stop by to visit Angola and Au-U-Khan to see if they talked to Story Teller who sat in on the experiment that was conducted on Neptune. As expected, although the information is somewhat dated, what Story Teller has to see serves to reinforce everything Hip City Daddy and Blue have just learned from Lightnin' and Blin' Lemmon.

Au-U-Khan: Boy, he can certainly talk, can't he?

Angola: He sure can. But you must admit that he has some interesting tales to tell.

Yoni: Little do they know, there is not a single tale to tell if it is coming from Story Teller?

Au-U-Khan: And, almost believable!

Angola: I know! I never would have believed them if I had not seen a lot of it myself.

Au-U-Khan: But, I wasn't aware the population was so large.

Angola: I know!

Au-U-Khan: How did it grow so fast?

Blue: Well, they obviously made many mistakes when they were perfecting the Time Mirage.

Hip City Daddy: That's how I ended up there with Lightnin' nem.

Au-U-Khan: PHEW! But over thirty million people in one city alone. Phew! I can't even begin to imagine it.

Hip City Daddy: Take my word; it was no paradise, at least for us Noner's.

Blue: Can you imagine how they'll threat us? Excuse me, our people back home. We won't even be there if they can help it.

Hip City Daddy: Tell me' bout it.

Yoni: By the time Blue and Hip City were ready to move out, Saweto asked to speak to them. Isn't it funny, through all the mayhem Blue had not spent time with Saweto, the official Governor-General of Global Village. I guess he wanted to avoid him. But, now Saweto wants to talk.

The problem is so does Neptune. And, Blue does not want to hear any shit about Goraka being the savior. Dumb shit, he says. This savior is trying to destroy their republic and his followers want to create a new social order in their own image.

Damn that! If the world were going to end at some unknown future date, it would simply have to be, but now, all the Aireans and Zanians knew was their personal lives were at stake and they wanted to survive. Besides, the way the Kinshasas were handling it, they would have time. Not much, but what's the difference? These foreigner invaders are not going to destroy them for future preservation of humanity. It would be a fight to the death. You can bet on that! Yes sir, you can bet on that. You can bet your life in that!

Saweto: I'd like to rerun to Fifty-plus-One. Manila and I have discussed the matter, and we think that I might be able to reason with the Council. After all, I am still an official member of that August Body.

Yoni: Blue did not expect that, so he had to play it by ear.

Blue: And, what do you expect to accomplish?

Saweto: Dialogue!

Blue: Dialogue? What type of dialogue? They have had many opportunities for dialogue. What makes you think….

Saweto: I know them. They are afraid, now. They've been isolated too long. They need to talk to someone they know and trust.

Hip City Daddy: And, what about Manila?

Saweto: She stays with you, of course: Manila and the child….they're acting tough because their world is collapsing around them. Literally! They are afraid. What would you do?

Hip City Daddy: Look; we don't have time for philosophical dialogue about the fears of the Kinshasa's…

Blue: NOT ANYMORE! YOUR FATHER SAW TO THAT!

Saweto: I know where we are. I know that we haven't left the Castle. I know about the illusion you've created around us. I, I should say we—we also know that my father and Manila's mother are mortal enemies, and that my father is probably insane; suffering delusions of grandeur: a megalomaniac is what you call him if you were being kind.

Hip city Daddy: Probably? SH…!

Manila: we also know that Nailah is supposed to be dead.

Blue: And?…. You call your mother Nailah?

Manila: This is politics now, she is my mother but she is or was as you would like for us to believe, Prime Minister. We know that she is not. Don't worry, if we wanted to betray your plans, we could have done so long time ago. Look!

Yoni: All three, Manila, Saweto and Makeba disappear like it was nothing. Just like that! Presto! And, they were gone. Obviously Blue and Hip City Daddy have to listen, now. What choice do they have? Either that or…

Saweto: Well? What do you say?

Blue: Why didn't you escape before?

Saweto: To where?

Yoni: Neither Blue or Hip City want to seem stupid so they let the question go as a rhetorical one. My, my, why do things become so complicated? Here the elders are funning around zapping each other like flies and two youngsters have things all figured out. Or, do they?

    Now is it one of those things we are quick to tell our youngster, "You don't understand. You just don't understand." In any case, Saweto though tactful is firm. Manila – whose seat in Parliament has never been occupied by anyone else – reinforces Sweat's determination to intervene with,…

Manila: After all, it's our future you elders are destroying. We ought to have something to say about what. Don't you think so, Abdul? Don't you Tendi?

Yoni: UH! HUH! The M.P. has spoken.

Manila: Not only that, I am disgusted that you spent all this time fighting and killing and have not spoken to us once. NOT ONCE! Did you hear me, not once have you bothered to check on us. That's disgusting!

Yoni: Did you hear that? First, Blue excuse me, Abdul and Hip City Daddy, Ops, Tendi, have to adjust to being called Abdul and Tendi: she is always proper. Then too, you have to account for their negligence. That's right, pure adultrated negligence. Blue and Hip City Daddy have done what many elders tend to do, they assume that they know best. And, you know what they say about assuming things: to assume is to make an ass-uh-me.

Manila: Now that you have finally bothered to ask, we might as well be candid

Yoni: And, candid they are. It is both refreshing and amusing to hear two young people – relatively speaking, that is – speak so fluently, directly and knowledgably about "Adult Problems" Abdul and Tendi – Blue and Hip Ditty –sit, pace, stand patiently while they are chastised masterfully by this skilled Parliamentarian. She in fact takes over and speaks her mind. No one can say anything, because what she is telling them is so true.

So accurate, so correct, so indicting, so insightful, so spellbinding yes, sir, this is Nailah's daughter all right. When the Panthers finally arrive back at the Headquarters the others want to know what took so long. They become worried. Everyone is amazed to see whom they bring with them as company.

Blue: There's a change of plans.

Yoni: Well, ain't that nothing'. This is it. Are these warriors on the frontline willing to sacrifice honor and heroism – pronounced either! HER-O-ISM OR HE-RO-ISM! Whichever! You get the point, for another way of life?

Roc Steadye: What has happened to change your minds? I must hear this! HA!HA!HA!HA!HA!

Angola: Do you mean? HEEE! HEEE! HEEEEE

Blue: Now what….?

Hip City Daddy: WHO…..?

Roc Steadye: OH?

Yoni: Now Roc Steadye – A.K.A. IFE Cameron – has been in many firefights with Blue. She knows him like a book. You really have to be convincing to change his mind about anything. Blue is stubborn about anything he has already made up his mind about so, what is this?

Humorously, they all smile when Roc Steadye makes her subtle, OH? OH! Then they break out into a grand laughter that everybody seems to need. The laughter is almost like therapy. The laughter is so hard that IFE Cameron, then Abdul, then Tendi break out in tears…..How long? How long has it been at this war? No one can remember anymore.

Chapter 32

Goraka: What are you doing here? Where'd you come from? How did you find me? How did you get here?

Lost Scholar: I thought that I waited long enough. Don't you think?

Goraka: For what?

Lost Scholar: OH! You forgot. That is right, you have been very conquering. Is that right?

Goraka: Forget what?

Lost Scholar: Do you not remember? You were reading that book to us.

Goraka: Book? What book?

Lost Scholar: You remember, it was the Puritan Invention. You know, The New Native: A Puritan Invention. I think that was the title. You were reading it to us, then you were called away to return to the capital again, I believe. You promised to return and complete it for us.

You said something about this being the book you had returned to find, and what a lucky coincidence that you ran into me, and I said, "again" to myself because we were meeting for the second time. We had met before, long ago. Now, it is our third. ….The book was supposed to help you avoid all of the pitfalls of modern civilization. You remember! You said that was the key. Yes, I think those were your words exactly, were they not?

Goraka: Look! I don't know! That was so long ago! So many things have happened since then, and that was only a book. A silly old book that I am sure nobody but me ever read.

Lost Scholar: Partially read! You did not finish it, remember?

Goraka: Phew! Why are you bothering me? Can't you see, I'm Goraka. I have a mission to accomplish. I must save the world from destruction.

Lost Scholar: Oh? Whose destruction?

Goraka: World destruction! You know, it was all written in the book.

Lost Scholar: It was? Obviously you never read that part to me. And, that is why I am here.

Goraka: Man, are you serious? Do you know who I am? I was….

Lost Scholar: Please, spare me! I know all of those exploits; you told everybody and failures that you kept to yourself. You know, you've done the impossible. You've single handedly caused a three world war? Not one, not two, but three! I do not know of any of our other creatures that have ever done that before, do you? Did you hear me?.... And, where did you choose that horrible name from? Goraka? HUH! I just shiver every time I hear it. I mean, couldn't you have been a bit more creative? I mean, give me a break!

Yani: What do you suppose you were doing?

Goraka: What do you mean?

Lost Scholar: What do I mean? What do I mean? HA! HA! HA! HA! HA! You are funny. Crazy, but funny. You do know that you're insane don't you? You are insane, you know.

Goraka: How did you get here?

Lost Scholar: How did you get here is the question?

Goraka: I cam…..!

Lost Scholar: Please! Do not bother! I know the story! Anyway, it was a theoretical question. No response was necessary…Anyway that is not why I am here.

Goraka: Then, why did you come?

Lost Scholar: I told you. You never finished the book you started. And, besides, you were the only person I know who can read this esoteric language. I am sorry. It is not my fault. It has to be you. Sorry!

Goraka: Am I really crazy? Am I seeing things? Are you real?

Lost Scholar: HA! HA! HA! HA!

Krishna: At this point, Goraka—whatever! – disappears only to find the lost scholar right beside him, then in front of his face, as if to dare him to do something, anything.

Lost Scholar: Because I am the lost scholar does not mean that I will suffer abuse, not even at the hands of a tyrant.

Goraka: What if I…..!

Lost Scholar: There you go again with your nonsense. Spare me! I told you, I am not leaving until you finish reading the esoteric book to me. You know I can't read it. So, stop stalling and start reading.

Krishna: By now, Goraka's temper has flared, but he must contain it. However, this is too much for Goraka. The thing is, what to do? Goraka has found a way to get rid of this lost scholar or whatever he is.

Lost Scholar: Do not even try it! I know what you are thinking, so, do not even try it. I told you, I am not leaving until you finish reading that esoteric book to me.

You promised and I expect you to live up to your promise. After all, you owe it to me. Don't you think? In any case, I have waited all this time, what is a little time? The point is, I ain't leaving. I'm not going any place without you that is, and that's that.

Look, do not even try to get angry. It is not even about that. So, it is not going to work…I know about those people you have had murdered, so, do not bother with threats. I just might get pissed. You do not want me pissed. You do not want me pissed off. I will mess you up!

Krishna: The lost scholar must have lost his cool because as soon as he said that, he demonstrated his skill by kicking Goraka right in the groin. Yes, you heard me, right smack dab in the balls, and hard, too, but not too hard to do him any permanent damage.

Lost Scholar: Do not mess with me. I will mess you up for life'. What life' you have left, that is. So you better treasure it. Or, I'll….

Goraka: NO! Don't! Don't!

Krishna: At that point, Goraka starts to weep, openly weep just like a baby. But, the lost scholar shows no mercy.

Lost Scholar: Please, Goraka! Save the tears. I am not impressed.

Goraka: Look, why don't you go away? Please leave! Can't you tell, I am in no mode to engage in any scholarly endeavors, now?

Lost Scholar: Goraka that is what you want to be called is it not? I did not tell you to get yourself in all the mess you are in. That it you're doing. That is not my problem. My problem is getting you to finish this book.

Goraka: Look! I know I can't whip you, what ever your name is, but if you help me get back to your time, I'll read you the whole goddamn thing…

Lost Scholar: HA! HA! HA! HA! I told you are funny. For what? What for? Have you not been listening? Did you not hear? Your thugs are now fighting each other. To the death all of them. They are as mad as you are, if that is possible.

Krishna: By now, Goraka is totally dejected! He feels like a total mess. He is a failure. But the lost scholar does not let up. Not at all!

Lost Scholar: Hey man, you are not getting any sympathy, empathy or anything else outta me, except as ass kicking, if you mess with me.

Krishna: Now folks, tell me, what do you do when you are faced with this kind of impasse? {I didn't know they use bad words? Curse words?}

Lost Scholar: I ought to take you back myself. I would if I thought it would do any good.

Krishna: PHEW! For a while, Goraka thought that might be the next move. At least he does not have to worry about that now

Lost Scholar: Do not be so sure.

Goraka: What was that?

Lost Scholar: You heard me, I said do not be so sure. I may still take you raunchy ass back. You deserve it. You sleaze! You louse! The only reason I have not, is I know what further turmoil it can cause, and Aire – whatever! –Does not need any more bloodshed…

Do you know how many objects of the old stories you have destroyed? Do you know how many lives you are personally responsible for taking out? Do you? I won't boast your ego by telling you how many… and, what became of those diplomats who you were suppose to transport to Fifty-plus-One? UH? HUH? You thought nobody would remember with all of the fracas going on, did you not?

Krishna: Goraka looks shocked as he stares in the direction of the lost scholar while looking into his nothingness of abyss. While looking at the lost scholar Goraka begins to turn dark brown, black, blue, purple, red, orange, yellow, white, ash grey, back to a recomposed self, a beautiful indigo no ebony, well it is very hard to tell, complexion: just like those objects he has destroyed. ……Goraka is truly puzzled about his informant. Who is this being? What is it?

Goraka: How do you know about that? Who are you? How do you always happen to find me, at the most surprisingly interesting times? Just who are you?

Lost Scholar: You would be surprised to know what I know about you and all your crap.

Krishna: It is not even an impasse anymore. Goraka has been out manoeuvred, out classed. He has nowhere to turn. All of his cards have been played and he is now left standing alone. All alone!

Lost Scholar: Is it not lonely being alone when you have betrayed all of your friends? You have no one to turn to?

Krishna: Goraka simply looks at the lost scholar. By now, he has so many thoughts running through his head that he can't even hear anymore. He then becomes so numb that he can't even think anymore.

Goraka: Why don't you leave me alone? Why don't you find someone else to, to pick on……

Krishna: Goraka breaks down.

Lost Scholar: Look at you! Just look at you. Crying like a baby. Big strong, Goraka is crying like a baby.

Krishna: With that comment, Goraka attempts to strike the lost scholar with all of his might and skill only to miss him completely and fall on his face.

Lost Scholar: Look at you! Can you not think straight anymore? ….Serves you right! I ought to smack you just for good measures. You are no good…..Please! Let me chill out. You will have me acting crazy like you after a while…..It's contagious; you know…..Back to the subject at hand. The book! Are you going to read it to me or not?

Krishna: When it rains, it pours, does it not? Goraka has lost his position, his army, his faith, him humanity. He is now left with nothing, so it seems.

Goraka: What do you want from me, to say that I am sorry? Is that what you want? IS THAT WHAT YOU WANT? Give me a break.

Lost Scholar: HO! HO! Listen to this tough guy. Obviously, you can give it, but you cannot take it. ……No Goraka, I do not expect you to say I'm sorry. I only expect you to do what is right. And, right now, in my book, you ain't right….God don't like ugly.

Krishna: UH!UH! I think Goraka had better be cool. He obviously did not know what he was getting into when he picked up this stranger on the roadside on the way to the country that day long ago. He obviously never expected it to come to this. Nor, did he expect to see him again and again. As a matter of fact, Goraka has forgotten this stranger long time ago.

    Now, here he is haunting Goraka over a past better forgotten, better left out of history, better referred to as pre-history, better thought of as a historical fiction, a crime worth forgetting. A phase of humanity we'd rather deny ever existed. Don't you remember, to recognize is to create a state of non-recognition? One does not exist without the other. That is how denial operates. It is not that what is does not exist we simply refuse to recognize it. We deny it! We write it out of history.

That is what Goraka wanted to do. He had hoped that somehow, someway, he could rewrite the past, and everything would be okay. Now, without fore warning, the most insignificant aspect of his past is here to haunt him. And, ain't nothing he can do about it. When it rains, it pours.

Lost Scholar: All I ever ask of you is for you to read the book to me. Nothing else! You said that you would and that is what I expect, nothing more, nothing less.

Krishna: I mean come on, now. This guy has been through holy hell. He doesn't have any inclination to read to anybody at this point. I mean isn't this kicking a po' dog while she's down? Give the meniperson a break – like he said.

Lost Scholar: And, whose side are you on, here my Story Teller?

Krishna: I beg your pardon? Were you speaking to me? I'm a reporter. A storyteller! I am not a character.

Lost Scholar: Did anybody else say anything?

Krishna: Well, No! I….

Lost Scholar: Then, I am speaking to you. Where do you fit into the picture, here?

Krishna: I don't!

Lost scholar: Then, leave your commentary to yourself. I am not in the mood.

Krishna: I was only trying to make the story interesting…Now, wait-a-minute, you can not talk to me like that. I'm not….

Lost Scholar: I cannot do what? Apparently, you have not understood me clearly. I said, I'm not in the mood. Period!

Krishna: Yes, Sir! I get your point!

Lost Scholar: Thank you! I thought you would understand.

Krishna: Look yawl, it's a j-o-b. I ain't gone get my butt kicked over a job that pays what I make. It ain't worth it, you dig? This cat's as crazy as Goraka or those fools up on Fifty-plus-One. Anyway, as I was saying, Goraka has gotten himself up a tall tree out on s long limb with no support. Is that right? Sir?

Lost Scholar: It is better! Just stick to your job. That is to tell the story correctly, just the way it is happening. Let us deal with Dr. Goraka.

Krishna: Doctor? Yes, Sir! You got it. Anything else you want, Sir?

Lost Scholar: Cut out the bull and get on with your work.

Krishna: Well, obviously folks, I am a bit taken aback by the reaction by the reaction of one of the characters in my story. So, if I make a few mistakes here and there, give me a little time and I am sure that I will be back on track. Now, uh,uh, where was I?

Oh, yes. Goraka, er! Is now facing one of those offers, you know what kind! The question is how will he handle it?…..Folks I am no sure that I can continue under these circumstances. I am simply too upset to be of any help tot the story. I am sorry, but I must go. There is simply too much pressure, too little pay, and not enough respect given, I 'm sorry.

Sir, will you get someone else to tell the story? I 'd appreciate it. Thank you! Sorry folks! I hope you don't judge me too harshly.

Lost Scholar: Look Krishna, your name is Krishna is it not? Yes, Krishna, I did not intend to hurt your feelings. I apologize! You are really good, you know. No! Really! You are! Do not leave on my account. Stay! I insist! STAY! STAY! You are going to stay? Good! Thank you! I appreciate it! Hey guy! You got a raise. How's that? How much do you want? No problem! You got it!

Krishna: Gee! Thank you, Sir!

Lost Scholar: Okay! Now, go on with the story, please!

Krishna: I really do not know what to say.

Lost Scholar: No problem! I shall talk to Dr. Goraka a while. You, get yourself together. Okay? Good! Okay, Goraka, the scholar, the intellectual, nobody knows you have a doctorate of laws do they? Or, is that a LL.D. or a Ph.D.? Which one?

Goraka: Both!

Lost Scholar: Okay, good doctor, what is it going to be?

Goraka: What do you mean?

Lost Scholar: Come on Goraka, fun and games are over. WE HAVE SOME INFINISHED BUSINESS TO DISCUSS.

Goraka: Who are you? You are not the lost scholar?

Lost Scholar: You are not Goraka, either. But, That is not the point. The point is, I am the being you met on the road back in the old country. I am the one who returned the missing book to you. I am also the one who gave it to you, the second time we met. You lost it! I found it and stopped you, again. You told me it looked like Greek to you. I t was not Greek, however, you said. Years later, I saw you again….

Goraka:….and, what business do we have to discuss?

Krishna: PSSSSST! PSSSSST! Sir, I am ready… [Pause] Even now Goraka is ignorant. He still does not know the point being made. So he raises the last question, he opens the door to the unfolding of his future. Little does he know that while he is out making war in the name of peace, killing in the name of salvation, destroying nature in the name of humanity, ad infinitum, the lost scholar was watching. Every move, every step Goraka took was being weighed by his observers…And, who are these observers? Check this, they are the ones who offered Goraka the gift. Now, they want an account given as to why he chose to road he did. The path he took, so to speak. They are inquisitive. They are Goraka's inquisitors.

Lost Scholar: Wh

Goraka: Why what?

Krishna: Just a small point before we go with the story, lost scholar? I want to put thing in a way that these mortal people will comprehend, understand. They paid for his education at the best universities of the universe. With that funding he was allowed to obtain or attain two doctorate degrees. That is a lot of money invested in my man. You get, now? Okay, lost scholar, thank you. I just needed to bring everybody up to speed. I think some might have got lost some place around the turn.

Lost Scholar: Thank you, Krishna. Hey man, I told you don't make me angry. You know, I don't think you're taking me seriously.

Krishna: At this point, the lost scholar knocks the wind out of Goraka by faking a straight kick to the groin followed by a leg sweep that knocks Goraka off his feet leaving his midsection vulnerable for an elbow right to the solar plexus. The motion is so fact and fluid that Goraka does not have a chance to react let alone defend himself. Goraka gets angry as hell. When he recovers, Goraka attempts to use his inner vision to attack the lost scholar's consciousness. That does not work either, now he cannot move. Goraka tries again only to find that not only can he not move, he is totally paralysed. He is also psychologically at a loss as to what to do. Befuddled is how I would describe it.

Lost Scholar: You see, that is exactly why you shit don't work no more, to put it bluntly.

Krishna: Now, able to speak, Goraka asks,…

Goraka: What do you mean? How are you?

Lost Scholar: You really do not know? You really do not know me? You have abused every power and advantage we gave you and you do not know who the lost scholar is. My, my, haven't we become narcissistic with a neurosis of grandeur. If you do not remember me your fate is sealed, and there is no turning back.

Goraka: WE?

Krishna: Goraka is truly befuddled at this point. Has he been so self centered that he does not remember the one who raised the existential question of where are you going?

Lost Scholar: Yes we,damn it! And, check your tone of voice out from here on. We will not tolerate insolence, not even from you, especially from you. So, you had better show some respect when you speak to us. We are tired of your silly false arrogance.

Man, you ain't got nothin' now. You dig?

Krishna: Modesty is a virtue that Goraka lost long time ago. It would be hard for him to regain it n

Lost Scholar: He had better learn some soon, because I am this close to taking him out. …. I do not play that shit. Now, if he wants me to git nas-tee. If you wants me to lay some black on yo' ebony/mahogany body, what ever! I am willing to oblige you. I have been waiting to kick you're na-va-re-o ass for a long, long time. Too long!

Krishna: I hear yea! And, he means it, too. At this point, everything begins to sink in –I hope. Goraka realizes that he is dealing with a force greater than anything he has ever encountered before; that includes Roc Streadye, Blue and Nailah. As a matter of fact, they are not even in the same league with this frail looking scholar. Nobody I have seen so far is for that matter. And, I have watched some folks pull magic tricks that'll make you wonder where you've been all this time. So, obviously this is a different ball game all together. Goraka is being asked to explain a few things to a higher authority, so to speak, if you know what I mean. Sure you do. UH! HUH!

Lost Scholar: By the way, while we are at it, what was that bull about you being "the savior" and NOT HUMAN??? Where in hell does that come from?

Goraka: But, I thought!!!!!

Lost Scholar: You thought! You, thought? No Goraka, you did not think. If you had, I would not be here, now.

Krishna: All Goraka can do at this point, look silly. You know how you look when your mom catches you in the cookie jar? Yea, that's it.

Lost Scholar: I mean, did you not ever think that someday you'd be asked to account for these actions on your part? Did it eve occur to you that your gift is not yours to abuse? Do you not recall the tale of the seeds, you know, you reap what you sow? That is no fantasy tale. You know…

    Instead, you take the gift and loose the book. I bring you the book again thinking you got a little careless. Then, you run off somewhere and get involved in who knows what…What seems to be the problem, Goraka? Where are you going? Tell me, just where are you headed? I am going to give it to you straight your only saving grace is Saweto.

Goraka: My son! I want to see my son. Please let me see my son?

Lost Scholar: You had every opportunity to see him, but you were so dead set on revenge that you blue that, too.

Goraka: What do you mean? Blue had kidnapped him from the castle before I got there.

Lost Scholar: You see what I mean? Goraka, Saweto never left the castle.

Goraka: Then, how…

Lost Scholar: Roc Steadye took advantage of you blind hatred and used your energy to create the illusion. Saweto, Manila, and Makeba – their little girl – and Neptune – your first disciple – saw everything you did from there.

Goraka: That is not fair! What about Blue and the rest? Why didn't you let them see them, too, that is not fair.

Lost Scholar: They did! And, frankly they think you are all insane. I agree unfortunately. Frankly I really wonder why we even bother? Maybe, I should say, ever bothered.

 Goraka: To do what?

Lost Scholar: You are really not that bright, are you? To save humanity as you like to call it. I frankly wonder if you are worth, the effort?

Goraka: Why do you say that?

Lost Scholar: Do you realize how much life – I am not simply referring to human life – you have destroyed. I mean it simply seems a matter of principle for humans to destroy nature's life: all of nature's life forms I am speaking of. That is what I am talking about. One way or another, you find a reason to destroy what you will, all in the name of progress.

Krishna: As the lost scholar discusses the "death Wish Principle" in full, Goraka finally begins to get the real picture. Every species that we have been directly or indirectly responsible for killing was listed. The list – I am embarrassed to say -- is enormous. My God, I thought, we've actually taken trillions of lives, in the name of human understanding. I am glad that I am privy to this conversation because I am learning so much. And, to think, I wanted to quit.

Lost Scholar: I understand! I have wanted to quit myself, sometimes. The point is you didn't. But.

Krishna:. ...Goraka did!

Lost Scholar: Exactly! And, that's why I am here, to find out why? To see what we did wrong, or, did not do it.

Krishna: Lost Scholar, I hope you don't mind, but do you think that possibly your choice may have been wrong? This is just a question, Sir?

Goraka: I beg your pardon?

Lost Scholar: No, I don't mind. Goraka, you have lost all rights to speak with any authority…Yes, Krishna, that is a question we continue to ask ourselves, over and over.

Krishna: And, what have you come up with?

Lost Scholar: Maybe we ought to allow this Earth Life epoch to go the way it is headed, learn from our mistakes, and create a more perfect being on the next go round.

Krishna: And, where does that leave us?

Lost Scholar: Is that a rhetorical question?

Goraka: No, it is not.

Krishna: Your tone, Goraka.

Goraka: Dr. Goraka to you my unsuspecting pest.

Lost Scholar: {Ignoring Goraka.} Thank you! That leaves you out of the next picture. I am speaking of Goraka, not the idea necessarily. HA! HA! HA! HA! HA! AHH! HA! I like that! The frame! AHHH! HA! HA! HA! HA!

Goraka: I fail to see the humor

Lost Scholar: You failed, period.

Krishna: Tell me, Lost Scholar, are all of you this blunt? [Pause] This candid?

Lost Scholar: Oh! I suppose! More or less! It depends! Not all of us!

Krishna: So you cove the range like we do? I hope you do not mind all these questions. After all this maybe my only opportunity. Sorry Goraka, excuse me, Dr. Goraka.

Lost Scholar: Oh, that's okay. I welcome them. Somebody seems to have some sense around here. Maybe we ought to do this more often…yes, I suppose we come in all forms, so to speak. HA! HA! HA! HA! HA! And, do not worry about Goraka. His fate has already been voted on.

Krishna: OH? OH!

Goraka: OH???

Lost Scholar: Yes, Goraka! That is why I am here, to give you the vote. The decision was, to ask to read the book just one more time. Everyone but me said that you would read it this time because you would realize the seriousness of he request, coming a third time, that is. I said no he will not even remember the document. My exact quote, He will ask, "What book?" And that is exactly what you did.

Krishna: Well, what is it?

Goraka: I am supposed to…I 'm the one who should be asking. I want the storyteller out of her. If you are here to give me the vote, I should have the choice of learning about it before the reporter does.

Krishna: Storyteller!

Lost Scholar: You need not apologize to Goraka. It was unanimous!

Goraka: UNANIMOUS?

Krishna: UNANIMOUS!

Lost Scholar: Come on, Goraka. You had to know something like this was in the making; it was coming sooner or later. Come on, Goraka…In my mind, it should have been soon, but that's hindsight, Monday morning quarterbacking.

Goraka: So, what is the decision?

Lost Scholar: You'll find that out later. Right now, I am to warn you not to attempt anything rash….Also, you may not see your son…By the way, send those diplomats home, immediately. That is my charge to you.

Krishna: Now folks, I took this job not really knowing what a storyteller does. Here I am now seeing this kind of action first hand. A reporter's dream. I never imagined that I would ever be a party to this kind of action, first hand. Goraka, once a ruler of two worlds two different worlds now being…..

Goraka: Three worlds!!! It was three worlds! ….If you gonna tell it, tell it right! It was three worlds.

Krishna: Sorry Dr. Goraka! Three worlds!!! It was three worlds….Now in disfavor with the Orishas. Although his fate has been determined, we were told that the actual sentencing might come later, if at all. There may not be any sentencing. Is that right, did I get that right, Lost Scholar?

Lost Scholar: Yes! And, I would like to add that the delay in awarding a sentence is because we would like to see what the outcome of Saweto's trip would be?

Goraka: Saweto? Where is Saweto going?

Lost Scholar: He's requested to return home.

Goraka: For what?

Krishna: TONE! Dr. Goraka, watch your tone.

Lost Scholar: He does not know it, but to be the one to determine the fate of the rest of you, yawl picked a duzzie. I take that back, he knows what he's doing.

Goraka: Isn't it too late?

Lost Scholar: Goraka, I am surprised! Nothing is too late! Unless, that is, it has already happened.

Goraka: Then, I must…. Excuse e; I 'd like to go…

Lost Scholar: ABSOLUTELY NOT! THAT IS OUT OT THE QUESTION! NO!

Goraka: Why? My fate is determined, and you can come along for safe measures.

Lost Scholar: NO! I am afraid not. Saweto and the Kinshasa must work this out – or fail! – among themselves.

Goraka: But, that's not fair. That is unfair. Besides, I am not….I was not always this way. I like to make up for all my mistakes. I can change! Honest! Honest!

Lost Scholar: NO! NO! NO! NO! NO! I am sorry those are the rules. If matters fail, it won't be because Saweto did not try. It was not an easy matter getting Blue to allow it, but he did….and, Manila did quite a job. We would rather leave this one to the youths. They have been left out of the picture too long. And, besides, you elders have done nothing but botch things up….They certainly cannot do any worse.

Who knows, they might even pull this one off. It certainly will speak well for the future if they do. And, it they fail, humanity will have earned its fate; and you have some heroes to celebrate if they do not. After all, if the future leadership cannot convince its elders to stop killing humanity and other life forms, what reason do you have for continuity? None, we can think of. Sorry to sound so cold, but that is how we see it….And, this is not to be taken lightly, we do still have the final word.

Krishna: I hate to sound philosophical folds, but limitations of free will are being tested to the max, here. Apparently we do possess the freedom to determine whether we live as social beings or not. The question is, in our drive to understand our universe; will our desire to conquer nature outstrip our will to live? Will our hatred toward each other supersede our love for survival? Will our eventual downfall be our hunger for power and wealth?

    Well, folks, I must sign off….This is your storyteller, Krishna coming from Zania some where out in the bush. Hope to see you again. It was a pleasure talking to you.

Chapter 33

Saweto: This is Saweto calling, requesting special permission to enter Capital District 17 of Fifty-plus-One, Over…Do you read me? This is Saweto calling, requesting special permission to enter Capital District 17 of Fifty-plus-One, over…

Comptroller: This is Capital District 17 of Fifty-plus-One, we read you. What is your request? Over!

Saweto: This is Saweto calling, requesting special permission to enter Capital District 17 of Fifty-plus-One, over.

Comptroller: This is Capital District 17 of Fifty-plus-One, what is the nature of your business? Over!

Saweto: This is Saweto calling, requesting permission to speak with the Council directly. Over.

Comptroller: This is Capital District 17 of Fifty-plus-One, are you coming alone? Over!

Saweto: This is Saweto calling. Yes, I am coming alone. The vessel I arrived in simply acted as my mode and means of transport. Over!

Comptroller: This is Capital District 17….Permission is granted to enter alone, over.

Saweto: Thank you, over!

Yoni: About a decade ago, New World Time, when Saweto and Manila decided at the spur of the moment to elope, they had figured that such a day might come when they would be required to utilize all of their skills to prevent a conflict between what is now separate peoples living in the three separate worlds. Each had hoped that although their fears that an impending conflict was inevitable, they were wrong.

Unfortunately, they were right. Now, here is Saweto requesting special permission to enter his home state hoping that it is not too late to prevent a three world war, i.e., wars occurring in three worlds simultaneously. The question is, what will Saweto do? What will he say?

At this point he has no idea. So he will do what he has learned following the outlawed music, improvise. First, he needs to determine their mood. Second, he needs to secure their trust. Third, he needs time. And, time is no literally at a premium, i.e., new world time is moving at a record velocity while old world time is still operating as it always has. So, he has to talk fast, and make his points clearly.

Being able to communicate silently Saweto hopes will make the last proposition easier. Only time will tell, however. Now that permission is granted, he will find out first hand. It is already established that the phantom time colon is running out of time: time is literally collapsing around them. Word has it that Commercial district 33 has already collapsed, totally, killing all of its inhabitants.

So, the Kinshasa are desperate, to say the least. They do not like the idea of invading their homeland anymore than Saweto does. but what else can they do at this moment. Besides, not everybody wants to settle in Global Village, I have been informed.

Saweto is very much aware of the invasion plans because he was present when Lightning' and Blin' Lemmon told about the plans. Also, he knows that is how the Kinshasa people operate. Have a problem to solve? Attack it with full force. That is why they are so efficient and disciplined.

He knows that the Akuyus are no match for the technological prowess the Kinnshasa people will bring with them to Aire. He also knows that "if" they invade and win, unless they exterminate all Akuyus, there will be permanent warfare, or, until the two can learn to live together side by side and integrate through intermarriage and cross mixing. That seems improbable not impossible, but improbable.

Obviously what Saweto needs is a miracle, and miracles are not in the cards these days. Saweto will have to make his own miracle. So, Saweto is left to his own wits, intellect, imagination, improvisation and persuasion. He really wishes that Manila were there. That is impossible because Manila has her own mission to perform, and her's is as impossible as the one he has chosen to undertake.

Anyway, Saweto wishes Manila well, and hopes the same for himself. I guess you might say hope is the major factor in this equation. And, hope is an unknown variable, as you know quite well. There is no way of measuring the outcome: One can only hope that everything turns out okay. Hope is wishful thinking, and a wish may not come true no matter how much hope is there; if neither party is unwilling to cooperate.

Lord knows that cooperation is what is needed now. The question is, cooperation in doing what? Not leaving a dying planet colony built on borrowed time and space? That is out of the question. No right thinking people will give up their lives on a dying proposition if they have choices in the matter: the Kinshasa people feel that their only choice is to invade Aire and colonize Global Village.

So, here we are at the crossroads again. As Saweto makes his way across the platform headed for the vehicle to take him to the Council Chambers to a meeting that has been convened at his request. After all, Saweto is still a member of the /council given tht post before he migrated to dare I say Zania. And, anyone of the members may convene a special meeting simply by requesting it.

Stellar Four: Okay everybody, the meeting is about to begin, so let us beam down to the Chamber to see and hear (HA! HA!) what transpires?

CEO: What is the nature of your request Saweto? The body is sure that you did not make this long sojourn in an enemy vessel just to pay your farewell to a place that will never exist in the minds of anyone after today.

Saweto: I have come on a peace mission. I want the fighting to stop, now. We cannot continue living this way. Besides, our constitution opposes attacking a foreign nation unless provoked.

CEO: Obviously you are aware of your father's kidnapping?

Saweto: I am aware of the kidnapping, but what does that have to do with anything? You know my father has been ill for quite some time, and besides, you had him under house detention yourselves, so what is the point?

CEO: a foreign invader violated our territorial integrity.

Saweto: Come on, that sound like a frightened people pulling at straws. You know I do not buy that. That is pure rubbish.

CEO: Rubbish or not, we feel offended

Saweto: By whom? How?

CEO: Please, let us not continue along these lines, state the nature of your request. Time is of the essence.

Saweto: I know time is of the essence, that s why I am here.

CEO: Do you have a proposal to make?

Saweto: Yes, I do.

CEO: What is it, please?

Stellar Four: Now, we know that Saweto must have pulled that out of a hat, because he had no idea of what he was going to say before he arrived here just a short while ago. His manner of speech gives that away.

Saweto: Damn it, we need time!!!!

Stellar Four: For some reason, the statement must have amazed everybody because they all burst out in a great Kinshasa laughter only moments after sitting there with their mouth open for a while. They cannot believe it. Here they are sitting there waiting for this grand proposal that will let everybody off the hook, and all Saweto can say is, "we need time." Now that is an understatement, if there ever was one.

CEO: Young man, we have no time. We need space also because we do not have any of that either…And, somehow optimistically we had hoped that in you brilliance and with you father's wisdom that you might provide us with a way out of this grand mess…

It appears somehow, however, that you have no sense of what to do anymore than we do. If there is nothing more, I'll entertain a motion to adjourn this our last meeting as a Council here in Capital District 17 Fifty-plus-One Another Dimension. It has been properly moved and second, a call for the question, all in favor? Adjourned!

Look Saweto, we all know how you must feel. We know you mean well, but things are no longer in our hands. Now, we must act.

Stellar Four: Is fate that deterministic? That's cruel? Is there really no hope for humanity at this point? Must we all stop in our faith that life will go on? Now, Saweto looks dejected and defeated. How can fate be so cruel? So, what is the purpose of it all?

Saweto: Why my brothers and sisters? How can the Orishaa place so many responsibilities on the shoulders of only one people? Now, all humanity rests on our shoulders. NO! NO! NO! NO! I will not accept it. That is wrong! Something is not right! I refuse to believe that we, the Kinshasa's should be given such a burden. I simply refuse to believe it. I refuse! I refuse! I REFUSE!

Stellar Four: By now, the Council Members are looking at Saweto. One Elder goes over and tries to console him, He, too, looks and feels betrayed. Somehow, the Orishas have played a cruel hoax on everybody. To give them hope then withdrew that hope at the wink of an eye does not give one much faith, anymore. Should they have placed their faith so blindly in these Orishas?

Saweto: GOD DAMN YOU! GOD DAMN YOU! ALL OF YOU! GAD AND ALL!

Stellar Four: Gradually everybody begins to go their separate ways, heads bowed, shoulders slumped. For the first time, their ages begin to show: the one walking out the door is 395 years; that one over there is around

421 years; the one with the long nappy locks hanging all the way down to her ankles is 560 years; while that every beautiful femiperson who manages to keep the order and who serves as the CEO for the Council is reported to be over 900 years. Unbelievable!

Now, they must go and tend to their duties. As Saweto so aptly put it, time is of the essence…

……….If only we could have done something different…

Judge, the Confessor: Like what? Look, when you have a gift you do not know its true value until somebody else comes along and shows you how valuable it is. I am sure that you recall someone you knew once who was really talented at what he or she did, you know what I mean!

Stellar Four: Yes! Sure!

Judge, the Confessor: Now what happened to that talent? Nine times out of ten, unless, someone who understood the value of the gift challenged him or her, that individual never truly realized the potential. Of course, that individual may have beat everybody on the block, but the true potential was never realized.

For us, it was that way. We, either by accident, or whatever, come upon this passage that to us at the time is a dream come true. At last, we have reached the Promised Land. So we think! None of us wise intellectuals realize that there is a different type of work that has to be done. We think that all we have to do is work hard and study the sciences. We do not know that we have to do things another way altogether.

Again, this brings us back to the local talent. I am sure that all of you knew this "super star" and got angry when that person's turn came to perform, because no matter what, that person could always do better than everybody, no matter how much work all of you put in before the "big event": always so smooth with such skill and grace. You know what I mean!

Well it was the same with us. Man. HA! We could sail anywhere. That is what we called it then. ANYWHERE! Time? That was no problem. We arranged time to suit our wishes. We had plenty of it, distance, no problem. We went here, there, everywhere. And, I mean everywhere! We saw everything! Creation! Destruction! Creation, again! Destruction, again! Then, we realized that after a while there was something missing. There were no people all of a sudden.

"Oh shit! Ain't no people here, " somebody realized. We got scared as hell. You remember? Se we sat down and calculated exactly to the period what life epoch that was, and we realized without a doubt that this was the period after the life epoch we had originated from. "That's our life epoch," again someone recognized. "What to do?"

So we sat down and began to work out this plan to save humanity from extinction. Day and night around the clock we worked. All of our greatest were put to work. Everybody had a purpose. Everybody had a reason to exist. Awards were granted to the scholar-intellectual who discovered how to this, and how to do that. Wealth was spent on science and technology. In the meantime, although we did not know it, we had used up the gift. Not completely as it turned out, but enough to keep us from doing what we wanted. We did not panic. We figured that with what we had, we could still save humanity from extension. Then, someone came up with this wise idea that we were the chosen,….Am I boring you, Stellar Four, I know you like to talk a lot.

Stellar Four: HUH? UH! NO! NO! Continue! By now everyone leaving the Council Chambers is standing, listening…

Judge, the Confessor: I do not remember which came first. Maybe that did. I cannot remember anymore, but anyway, the idea was propagated that we were "THE CHOSEN." And, that did it. We knew we had arrived. We had the gift, and, we would save humanity.

Then Goraka -- we call him our child—remembered this book he had come across during one of his many expeditions around the world. He said that it contained the key. Of course, we had never seen it, but we took his word. After a while he became so obsessed with finding it that he insisted that he had to return to his—our—place of origin, the old country. The rest is history. Or, I should say, HIS-STORY!

Stellar Four: WAIT! THERE MUST BE MORE!

Judge, the Confessor: Of course, there is, but time is….

Stellar Four: ….I know, "of the essence"….But, go on. We have nothing to loose, now. And this may prove valuable later on.

Judge, the Confessor: Yes, of course it will. Sure it will. Anyway, his insistence on returning to the old country was vehement that we finally gave in.

Stellar Four: What about him being next in line for the throne?

Judge, the Confessor: OH! Yes, that was true. All true! And, that is really what caused us to give in. After all, he had discovered the original night passage, so called, and we were very grateful. Goraka was brilliant! I said, was, I am sure that he still is, but his mind went bad, or something.

I mean really bright! You see all of those degrees he has behind his name. That is real. He earned all of them. I have forgot how many there were, are. He was truly bright. So, we—the Council – agreed. But, we knew that if he turned up now, everybody would be suspicious. So, we decided to tell them – that he should tell them – that we had settled this New World Colony that we had originally been granted a charter for.

The problem was how to explain the distance, and why they had never been able to find it. You see, it was originally scheduled for what people on Earth now call New England. However, when we arrived there, we saw, the Algonquin speaking people, so-called, already inhabited it. I understand that they have been pretty much exterminated. How sad. Anyway, we decided to move on elsewhere.

By now we were tired and weary, having been travelling for god knows how long. Frankly, we were ready to give up, and out of nowhere, it happened. One night while everybody was asleep, Goraka came through like a town crier and worked everybody up talking about this miracle, and that our prayers had finally been answered, People said, "Yes sure, go back to bed," but Goraka insisted. Some of us went with him and low and behold, there it was. It was like a dream come true.

Stellar Four: How did he find the passage?

Judge, the Confessor: Goraka said that a little mini person and femi person from the Algonquin people showed it to him before, but he could not see it until when he called us.

Stellar Four: Did you ever find them, and thank them?

Judge, the Confessor: NO! As a matter of fact, we did not. I suppose we should have. Who knows, that might be one reason we are going through these hard times. You never know when it comes to the Orishas. It might be a simple thing like not remembering to say, "thanks."………. You know, I never thought about that. Ain't that something?

Stellar Four: UH! Excuse me , "Yani says, 'ain't that nothing.'

Judge, the Confessor: Oh, I knew it was something of that sort, but thank you. Yes, a simple thank you, and we forgot. I'll be damned! ….Well, I gotta go, time……

Stellar Four: YES! I know!

Judge, the Confessor: Oh, thanks for listening. I think I just needed someone to talk to. Someone not involved. Thank you! I appreciate if for what its worth.

Stellar Four: Thank you! As my informant disappears into nowhere, I can't help but think, PHEW! Is this what life is all about? Thank yours and hellos and goodbyes?…So much for the digression. Now it's time to get back to work. I make sure that there are other matters to cover before we abandon this collapsing time colony. Excuse me! Excuse me! I am trying to locate Saweto. Has anyone seen Saweto? Excuse me, sir, did you see which way Saweto went?

Passer-by: Yes, I believe he went back to the time terminal.

Stellar Four: Thank you! Oh, there he is. SAWETO! Saweto, may I speak with you for a moment? I know you must be in a rush.

Saweto: Yes, as a matter of fact, I am. What may I help you with? I really don't have much to say right now. I feel so despondent, may be at another time.

Stellar Four: Another time? I see you listening to music right now. Isn't that kind of unusual? Kind of out of place, so to speak, where music is outlawed?

Saweto: NO! Not really! Really, the mood I am in right now, I think it's kind of appropriate. It's relaxing.

Stellar Four: Do you mind telling me what it is you're listening to?

Sewato: No, not at all! I'm listening to Eddie Grant's music. You know, "Walking on sunshine." It seems appropriate, especially the cut, "Living On The front Line."

Stellar Four: Well, I must say you do have a sense of humor during these grace times.

Saweto: Obviously, you haven't heard this particular cut.

Stellar Four: NO! I 'm afraid I haven't.

Saweto: You should listen to it sometimes. Then, I think you will get my drift. That is, get my point.

Stellar Four: Yes, I 'll do that sometimes. At another time, I suppose. Maybe we can sit and enjoy it together.

Saweto: Now, you have a sense of humor.

Stellar Four: How do you mean?

Saweto: Don't you know? If my people invade the Aireans, that'll mean war.

Stellar Four: Yes, but there should be peace again, someday, maybe, then?

Saweto: Hey, you're weird! You're really weird!

Stellar Four: I don't understand. What did I say wrong?

Saweto: You don't know? This improbably is for us, at least.

Stellar Four: Oh, you don't believe all of that junk about life ending on Earth, do you? I hardly believe such is the case.

Saweto: I hardly believe that you are with us. I mean, where are you? This is it, if we don't stop the invasion.

Stellar Four: You mean return home?

Saweto: Whatever! It is going to mean holy war. None of us can afford that.

Stellar Four: So, why did you have such difficulty convincing the Council?

Saweto: Because I did not have any alternatives to give them.

Stellar Four: Then, what about everybody going to Zania, Global Village as we call it here? Why did you not purpose that? Did the Council realizing this day might eventually come not create it?]

Saweto: Not everybody wants to go there, apparently. Also, our transportation system is really inadequate to handle all of these people with life support systems and everything. Besides, people have been leaving for the old country and Global Village now for the past decade.

Stellar Four: That means they are due to arrive at anytime, now.

Saweto: Exactly! And, neither country is prepared to receive the numbers arriving.

Stellar Four: How many would you put that number at?

Saweto: I haven't the slightest idea. I suppose it is in the millions.

Stellar Four: Yes, but haven't millions already died in some of the Districts of Fifty-plus-One?

Saweto: That is what they tell me. I understand that Commercial District 33 has totally collapsed, and…

Passer-by: So have about sixty other Districts.

Stellar Four: Sixty Districts, sixty other Districts?

Passer-by: Probably even more by now, everything is happening so fast. Everything seems to be speeding up.

Saweto: So, you see. Millions of people are dying around us, mostly Kinshasas, and you think there is hope.

Stellar Four: And, what is you plan now Saweto?

Saweto: I must find manila. She went home to Aire hoping – I have never used one word so often to express faith – to get the Arians to find some way to receiving their old relatives back home.

Stellar Four: Are you optimistic?

Saweto: NO! But, I only hope that she is more successful that I!

Stellar Four: Saweto, would you say that you handled that meeting properly, and everything.

Saweto: What do you mean? I don' understand you question.

Stellar Four: Well, I'm sure you have something in mind when you made that proposal about time…

Saweto: NO! I didn't have anything in mind except to create some kind of dialogue.

Stellar Four: Dialogue? What kind of dialogue?

Saweto: I really have no idea. Look, time is short, and I really must leave. They were kind enough to allow me to return, and I really don't want to wear out my welcome, okay?

Stellar Four: Sure, but, one last thing….

Saweto: I really must go.

Stellar Four: But, I want to get your opinion on how you see the war going.

Saweto: You know, you reporters really get me. You are overbearing and inconsiderate. Now, here we are almost at war, and all you can do is disrupt people's lives. You seem to have no sense of responsibility whatsoever. I mean, don't you know we are trying to make the best of a terrible situation? Where is you humanity? Don/t you have any gumption? My goodness, gee!

Stellar Four: But, I'm a storyteller, not a reporter.

Saweto: Storyteller? Storyteller? Then, what the hell are you doing asking me those questions. You should solve this mystery that plagues us at this time. It is your story. You solve our problem and let us go home. If not, why aren't you off telling somebody some stories or something? Meniperson, excuse me, femi person; you are all just the same. Always prying, and giving misinformation. Excuse me, I must go. I have a score to catch. YO! Get those people away from the craft.

Stellar Four: But, …Well, folks, I can understand Saweto's impatience. He does have a score to catch…I still don't know why they keep calling us storytellers reporters. We're not at all like them…anyway, to wrap things up here folks; this is a very historic occasion like none you ever witness again. The story of the fall of this great society is as fascinating as its rise. This is your favorite storyteller signing off, forever. HA! AH! I hope you like my sense of humor. Bye!

Blue: Did you have any success?

Saweto: NO! I really didn't know what to propose. I've failed.

Yoni: What is the old saying? What you don't know won't hurt you? Well, what Saweto did not know was that the moment he boarded the Score vessel, and gave him his answer – which was expected to be negative –Blue had used that new instrument developed by Tomorrow to cause a total collapse of Fifty-plus-One.

{My god, they didn't! Have they gone mad? The Kinhshasas could have killed them at worst or could have arrested them and placed them away forever. They chose to do neither. Were they thought to be fools because they were Akuyus? Were they thought to be weak or fools? What would prompt such a decision to take such drastic action? Knowing Blue, he thought that is was simply an error on the part of the Council that was to good to pass up.}

Yoni: Unbeknown to Saweto, the reason the sixty districts had already collapsed while he conferred with the Council was that same machine, Tomorrow. He had already started to close out the place, as they referred to it, while Saweto was on his way back to the Score. Blue figured that there was no way for all of those people to fit into the old country, Aire or Zania. They would wipe out everybody. His first loyalty was to the Republic of Aire and the Arian people: there were no other loyalties.

The attack was so effective that the Council did not even suspect what was happening. They thought that is was simply the process speeding up sooner than they had calculated. Most would defend that same argument in the future even if contrary information were provided. They would never believe that the old country could develop so rapidly: it was impossible for Aire to have technology superior to Fifty-plus-One. So, Blue slipped it on them. The Council thought it was simply a matter of time coming to a close. After all, they had never experienced it before. Now, the main jurisdiction, Capital District 17 was about to collapse. Thirty million or what was left of them would die and never know what befell them.

As the attack was being carried out, Blue could not help but thin, "too many lives are at stake back on earth, wherever!" What he did not count on was Soweto realizing what had happened. But, Saweto did not speak. He had other matters to attend to, like to find Manila and Makeba. Besides, the Kinshasa's were planning their attack and wanted Blue there so as not to present some resistance back in Aire or Zania. They thought that it would be poetic for him to return home to a liberated Aire; why waste literature by destroying the anticlimactic ending was how the Kinshasa people reasoned: looks as though Blue would have the last laugh.

Saweto could only think, when will it all ends? And, would there be enough time? Only time would tell. After all, this is a matter of time and these are the masters. Blue and Roc Steadye now feel a sense of relief. PHEW! We finally did it. We have finally brought the war to an end. We were able to avert a holocaust. We did it! We did it! At last, the war is won. All that is left now is to capture Goraka. Aire along with Zania may open new chapters. This HA! HA!HA!HA!HA! WE SHALL CALL THE END OF THE BEGINNING. HA!HA!HA!HA!

CHAPTER 34

Yoni: The way Soweto and Manila had mapped things out, he would go to Fifty-plus-One while she would travel to the Republic of Aire. If anything happened, they were to find their way back to Zania, and carry out their plans from there. Why Zania? Very simply, Zania exists apart from either Aire or Fifty-plus-One. And, no matter what, the Zanian side of the world will exist no matter what the other worlds do to each other.

This place called Zania was discovered to contain virgin land that travelled for thousands of miles in space beyond where we are right now: all of this was discovered through mind travel; if only they could get there. That would require a new set of equations that must be addressed later on. Right now, the concern is with the safety of the family.

Saweto and Manila had been through plenty together, and had learned to live in isolation during the time they spent travelling on the time mirage, and while under siege in Goraka's Castle as it came to be know for reasons no one to this day can explain. They had also learned that a castle was well constructed and would probably be left alone after both groups had sufficiently neutralized each other. The other thing is they are the only ones who know how to use it to travel. The team that showed them how it worked was killed in a surprise attack one night long ago.

The irony is the team that showed Saweto and Manila how to work Goraka's Castle was suppose to be a hit team that had arrived on Zania to assassinate Hip City Daddy. Obviously, they failed, or better still, never got the chance. Hip City is still around and the team is gone, having never succeeded in making the New Colony, "Global Village."

It remains the Republic of Zania 'til this day. In the meantime, Saweto and Manila, et al, have been in confinement for quite a while. Living that way has allowed them to learn each other's ways and raise Makeba without any of the inhibitions of the Kinshasas or the fears of the Akuyus. It has also allowed them to teach Makeba the skills of silence and mind travel beyond anything humans had known up to that point.

Now, it is possible for them to attach their waves to any communication devise or network millions of years apart like right now the way Saweto is doing as he checks with Manila to see if she's okay. She is okay. That is how they have known what is going on all the time. That is how they learned that Goraka is suffering from megalomania and narcissism; something they swore to fight against. No human is justified in being power hungry.

The problem is Saweto has not been able to communicate with Goraka since he went into hiding: something Saweto finds strange. Some strange force—a very powerful force – is able to keep them from communicating, from determining his whereabouts. Yet, somehow they know that he is alive. Strange, isn't it? But, who could do a thing like that, except? NO! It couldn't be.

With the possibility of Saweto not seeing his father again, he began to ponder how difficult it was for his to avoid his father when they were both in the castle. As it were, Saweto realized that either his powers were increasing or Goraka's were waning because at no time did Goraka realize that Saweto was so near. That hurt Saweto, but it also made him aware of what they have to do.

All three worlds apparently have gone mad. Everybody is talking about fighting everybody else: Martial law; conscription, and, National Security are top agenda items for all three nations. Peace is never placed on the agenda for discussion. Matter of fact, any one who speaks of peace is immediately placed under arrest as a traitor to the motherland. Peace, it seems, is a bad word. War is a normal activity. Assassinations and attempted coups are as commonplace as eating brown rice and breadfruit.

Saweto is despondent while Manila is happy, for the first time in God knows when, when Manila and her mother are together again: they are so close that it is painful to think that they have been apart for so long, odd how things can bring people together. Manila and Nailah became close after that accident that killed her father tragically along with about 700 other Akuyus. After the accident,

Manila grew under the watchful eye of her mother, Nailah, the Priest of Priests. Manila has acquired many powers during that tenure with her mother. It was possible for Manila at age five to lift a person the size of an Ukuyuebo bodyguard off the ground and move him about at will. This she did with her mind. This is one of many skills she has taught Makeba.

Enough background information, what about Nailah now? I thought she was assassinated. How did she survive? Where is she? Well, Nailah decides to retire after that attempted near assassination at the Prime Minister's Place a short while ago. Her reasons are very single, the New Prime Minister —- also a femi person – is an able and capable honest person. She is also a first rate orator and smooth political. Besides, Roxahn loves the job. "It is time for me to get out of the job and let someone else run the show."

The way Nailah got involved in politics was criticized at first as being pussy politics, but she knew what she was doing. Show knew that as long as she was there, Blue would remain alive. She had made sure of that: Nailah is reported to have told Goraka that if anything happened to Blue, she would hold him responsible, personally responsible.

Goraka is said to have got madder than bees on the warpath. It did not matter to Nailah. She was serious! And, Goraka knew it. Nailah never understood why Goraka wanted Blue dead. To this day, she finds that so odd, especially since it was "Blue who saved his ass," as Nailah always refers to it. "That's deceit for you." Nailah never forgave Goraka for that. Set gets angry every time she thinks about the incident.

But, this is not a social call. This is a call involving life and death. Manila now knows that Saweto has not accomplished what he optimistically had set out to accomplish; and, that Blue has acted militarily and closed down the phantom colony, killing everybody there. She also realizes that Aire has developed by leaps and bounds to possess such a massive weapon. Manila and Saweto thought the same thought, "my God, there seem to be no limitations to this weapon called TOMORROW." The weapon TOMORROW has obviously changed the equation considerably.

As a matter of fact, if Saweto and Manila had known the extent of this instrument, their proposal to Aire and Fifty-plus-One might have suggested ways of using it constructively: too late, now! What Blue has in his possession can compete with the awesome weapon the Kinshasa of Fifty-plus-One demonstrated to convince the people of Aire that they better surrender, or else. There seems no way to stop an all out war now. Both people will be destroyed. Nobody will be left to run anything.

The question remains, what to do? No matter that blue has closed of Fifty-plus-One, a force is already on its way to Aire, and will be within Aire time-space every soon. Blue knows that. That is why he acted so decisively. Saweto thought, so cruelly! One would never think that these are really the same people with the same bloodline. They certainly do not act like it, do they? Nor do they believe it anymore. They act more like neurotic infidels than civilized people. What is the old saying, no one can be more brutal than when brother fights brother. Well, this is it.

So, what happened to that combat to the death that we are so accustomed to seeing on the visual so often? Isn't that the point? And, what about this noble cause to save humanity?

Nailah: Honey, the Orishas have just about given up on humanity this time around.

Manila: What do you mean, mama?

Nailah: Honey, the Gods don't like ugly, and humankind has gotten too ugly to do anything any good. It's all Goraka's doing. That meni person just ain't right. Something went wrong with him somewhere. He just went off. Child, the meni person is crazy. The Orishas are really gonna have a grand time with this one. They're gonna fix him.

The problem is, he has dragged us all down with him. He has made us all evil doers. Do you know that I've had to request a hearing twice within six months, alone? They are really upset. I do not know what they are gonna do about the rest of us. We should not have allowed this to happen. Blue calls that place he came from hell. He says that all of 'em are evil. Of course, I do not believe that. They just got caught up in time, that's all.

Yoni: PHEW! Manila is glad to hear that addendum.

Manila: Blue's shut off fifty-plus-One, mama, killing everybody!

Nailah: Did he kill Goraka?

Manila: No, mama! No body knows where Goraka is.

Nailah: The Orishas will find 'em if they haven't already done do by now. I am sure that they certain that they have.

Manila: What are we going to do now? …Mama?

Nailah: Honey, all we can do now is wait just wait! If the sign comes, we'll move the way they tell us. It's all a bad dream, simply a bad dream. I should have killed him when I had the opportunity, and we never would have gone through all these troubles. If I ever had a mistake that I would ask to take back, it would be not killing that Goraka beast. Something is wrong with that man. Terribly wrong! He is a traitor to humankind. He ain't no meni person. I d not know what he it.

Manila: What are we going to do, mama?

Nailah: I'm gonna see that you and your family are safe. Then, after that I'll leave it up to them. It seems like you have a real fine husband. It is hard to believe that he is an offspring of that evil man, that death force.

Manila: You really do despise him, don't you mama?

Nailah: Yes, child, and it has been eating away at me, too. I have had to ask forgiveness so many times!….. I'm so happy that they spared me so that I could see you again, babe. That's really why I kept him alive.

Manila: What do you mean, mama?

Nailah: The meni person lied! He told me one thing about the trip, and I found out later on that it was untrue. So, I felt I had to keep him alive. He's the only one who knew where you were.

Manila: Thanks, mama!

Nailah: You are welcome child…That's enough about that for a while. I want to hear about you and my beautiful grand child. HA! HA! HA! HA! I feel so happy for you. And, I see you are carrying another one. I bet its gonna be a little meni person. …..I just love the name Makeba.

Manila: Yes, mama! Well, Saweto thinks….

Yani: As Nailah get down to shop talk!,…

Krishna: Blue, Roc Steadye and Saweto – who said nothing during the whole trip back to Zania – enter the time terminal in Zania and are met by sharp and Hip City Daddy.

Hip City Daddy: So, what's up?

Blue: Well, I don't quite know, yet

Sharp: What do you mean?

Krishna: Saweto speaks for the first time.

Saweto: He means that I failed, and he destroyed Fifty-plus-One.

Hip City Daddy: Is that right Blue? Did you do it? Did you do it? Hot damn!

Blue: I do not know! Have you picked up any signs of the enemy approaching?

Sharp: Not yet, Blue! And, that's strange, too. They should be arriving soon.

Blue: I know, that's why I high tailed it back to Zania as soon as I could.

Sharp: so, do you think the storyteller was right?

Blue: I hope so!

Saweto: Right about what? What did the storyteller say?

Blue: NO! I'll tell him. The storyteller noticed something while he was there that reinforced what Hip City Daddy said he'd finally figured out.

Saweto: And, that was what?

Sharp: That the time mirages were able to travel because they used people to act as the driving force.

Saweto: How?

Blue: Silence! The silence allowed a sort of a brain drain, so to speak. The energy used to drive your time mirage operated on a totally different principle from our score crafts. The Kinshasa people employed the principles of psychology – or mind control, i.e, a use of the energy from the brain cells to drive the time mirage – while we employ the principles of music to power our score. That is, until a whole new system was accidentally discovered by one of our music ensembles.

Saweto: Oh? Who was that?

Blue: I am sure you know them…TOMORROW! TOMORROW created a new musical instrument. That musical instrument as it turns out, knows no bounds, no limitations regarding time and space. The problem is, we had only perfected it to allow us to travel as far as Zania. But, we could use it in other ways.

Saweto: Like, collapsing Fifty plus-One?

Sharp: Yes, but that's only they exploded a bomb right about Aire to intimidate us to capitulate. You are well aware that they plan to take over Aire and Zania for their own needs and to exterminate those of us left after the attack. We had no choice in the matter. We simply took advantage of an opportunity presented to us by your insistence on returning home.

What we did work only because Fifty-plus-One operated as a time mirage. You operated in time almost to the exclusion of space. Your space was almost non-existent…so, when we discovered that your transportation system operates according to the unusual principle of mind control mind movement, we thought that we might have a way of stopping the invasion. That is why I did not waste time destroying your terminal.

Saweto: [Thinking to himself, is this how the DRY ROT comes about? Once the brain cells are used up, dried up, so to speak, the body can do nothing but decompose. I wonder if that is what happened to us?] What do you mean?

Blue: Well, if you were right in assuming that the time mirage has left eight or so years ago, it would bad a waste to destroy the time terminal alone…. like closing the gate after the cattle are gone. However, if we made a successful strike against the capital district – which, by the way, is where the power emanated – then we might be lucky and stop the whole advance.

We know that we cannot compete against your advanced weapons system. I t is too far advanced, but if we struck at its heart that might incapacitate the whole system. After all, that is really what we fear. You see, the whole system is what is/was driving the time mirage toward our nation. That was all done in silence. Time requires none of the engines required to transpose space. Any transport done in time can move in silence.

Saweto: Virtual silence!Krishna: [Blue does not really hear, that is, process what Saweto has just revealed continues as though nothing was said, he acts as though he was never interrupted…]

Blue: If no one makes any sound. That is, if nobody said anything, they learned that the silence would conserve energy. That energy could be converted into a sort of fuel not in the usual since that we think of fuel, but for lack of a better term, the fuel emanated directly from the brain.

Saweto: Waves. They were waves more like you might see in a large ocean. The brain waves are what propelled the time mirage. They were not fuel, they were waves. The waves created the movement.

Krishna: Again, Blue seems not to hear Saweto. He is so engrossed in telling his thesis, he does not realize that Saweto is filling in the missing hole, the missing pieces, so to speak. [Why are we all saying," so to speak?" What is with this, "so to speak?" I must be mindful of it next time. HUM!]

Blue: The behavior of not speaking allowed the time mirage to serve as a transport vehicle. Very unusual way to transport matter – people. And, for long distances, e.g., millions of years, the whole system, people, individually, were rotting wherever they were at the time.

Saweto: Not quite that way, you are a bit off in your analysis at this juncture. Matter of fact you have been off for quite some time. However, I am impressed at what you have learned not being any where near to the source.

Krishna: Still unaware!

Blue: amazing! Simply amazing! Can you imagine how much sacrifice that takes? One can easily understand the dry rot that occurred. The whole system, people, individually, was rotting wherever they were at that time. Not slowly! Very abruptly it would happen. One day a normal looking person, the next, dry rot struck to the feller, the ground, what ever. But, it worked.

It worked so well that it transported one individual back to his own time to live out his life, so he said,…
Saweto: Actually, Blue inadvertently has explained what I have attempted. Now, I see what happened. The waves each brain produced was so draining for that particular individual that all of the fluid was drained out of each body so activated. I would guess that it simply went through the brain into the time mirage simultaneously to the dry rot occurring. There was no fluid left to maintain the body, so it collapsed as an ink spot.

Khishna: Readers, I must apologize. Blue was not ignoring Saweto. He could not hear his thoughts, but I could. I made the mistake of thinking because I hear him Blue and the other do, too. I am wrong! I apologize! I'm sorry!

Blue: Anyway, their system is crumbling and the people need some place to go. Somehow, they got locked into our time, our space. This is ideal, but how? Ho can they take over? The Kinshasa's decide that they will allow Goraka to return as the lost prodigal. He will establish a rule in the name of the Kinshasa's. As I said, their own system was crumbling faster than they could repair it. It fortunate if Goraka agrees to return.

Saweto: Goraka will not be ruling anybody. That has already been decided.

Blue: There is one problem, however. The people already have a ruler. If they attempt to install Goraka, they will make the same mistake here that they made with their Global Village idea. They assumed.

Saweto: And, what was that?

Blue: That there would be no opposition to your rule. As it turned out, you never left the castle; living under virtual house arrest. Simply put, the Kinshasa's have both options blocked as home sites. They want to come to Aire, but that is not feasible. So, large percentages are chosen for Zania as the new colony Global Village. Only thing is when they arrive what will they do? You are not in power. Zania has its leadership in tact.

Saweto: Abdul Malik, you tell us this fantastic story about some phantom place you call Fifty-plus One. Can you prove that this place you say we call Fifty-plus-One exists? Or, has existed?

Blue: For me, that is hardly a problem. If you want to say that it never existed, no problem! No problem!

Saweto: does that relieve you of guilt?

Blue: No! You do it and don't think about it. If you do, you'll never be able to do another job, for another mission. That can be dangerous. So, you don't think about it. In my case, if you had not made your comment, I'd still feel the same. It doesn't mean that I must not atone myself for the death of these people. I know many of them are Akuyu people; that they are innocent bystanders who were treated like slaves. In fact they were slaves. One of them is standing right here before you. But, I had to do what I had to do.

If I had blown up the terminal only, since the signal emanates from other locations also, we would have delayed some death charges, but the others would have still reached Aire. By forcing the whole nation to collapse instantly—relatively speaking – maybe none of them will reach Aire. I had to take the chance. I had no choice.

Saweto: So, tells Abdul Malik, give me one good reason why I should trust you, and the others like you? My Council betrays me, and you betray me. They use me. You use me. What's the difference? Neither of you have proven trustworthy.

Sharp: Look, we understand your feelings.

Saweto: No, you don't! You do not even know what I am talking about.

Sharp: Tendi, I am speaking of the future?

Sharp: What about the future?

Saweto: Will you, will we solve our problems this way?

Sharp: I don't know, that's up to you.

Saweto: GOOD! WE WILL NOT SOLVE THE PROBLEMS THIS WAY, IF I CAN HELP IT.

Sharp: Hey kid, it's your old man's fault.

Saweto: Why did you not leave him in Fifty-plus-One while we was under house arrest? You gave him his exit. It was you in here that started this mess. Oh, I know all too well what he did. I included him with the rest of you.

Roc Steadye: Don't be cynical, now!

Saweto: All of you used me to do something you wanted – which was to destroy each other – and you tell me, don't be cynical. I am not to be cynical. I am not cynical Mr. Marimba; I'm only describing what you collectively are doing.

Roc Steadye: It may appear that way, but it isn't.

Saweto: OH, another illusion, just another illusion?

Blue: NO! It is not an illusion. Neither is Fifty-plus—One. Not that anybody will give a damn tomorrow. Speak about tomorrow. Gonna recommend that they be removed from the National Security Rick list, and be allowed to perform public ally again.

Krishna: This is after the State has gotten what it wants out of their instruments, that is, the ability to apply their techniques for the military destruction of another society completely. Why, not lift the ban?

Saweto: What was that? You held the TOMORROW BAND, too. Are there no limitations to this madness?

Blue: It is indicting, I'll admit. It was a whole sense of paranoia. Goraka had us killing each other like mad. I cannot understand that menipeson.

Saweto: What was wrong with my father?

Blue: Nobody knows! Except, Nailah maybe! None of us know.

Saweto: He was suppose to come back to save humanity. Where did he go wrong?

Blue: He should not have become King-General, but that was his destiny. That was his dilemma. You cannot do both. Save humanity and want power. They don't love each other very much. The problem is, it seems that you need power to save humanity because no matter how big we get or how strong we become we cannot resolve our differences without fighting and killing. Or, fighting to kill, I should say. I said, "it appears." I don't really know! I'm not a soothsayer, or one who knows how to save humanity.

Saweto: But, you do know how to employ power and force.

Blue: Tactics and strategies!

Saweto: Deception!

Blue: Surprise!

Saweto: Whatever! You are very good at what you do.

Blue: As long as we limit this dialogue to military matters, I would say we could hold our own with the best.

Saweto: Now that you have defeated my father, what will you do with those skills? Or, better still, what will the Republic of aire do with you?

Blue: Me, personally, I'll retire as soon as this mission is officially completed and retire and maybe write a book.

Saweto: And, what will you do for a living? OH! FUNNY! FUNNY! I own a rather large piece of land out in the country. I'll probably try my hand at farming. I'm going to grow plants for fuel. And, maybe grow some loco weed as a hobby.

Saweto: Fuel? Locoweed?

Blue: And, other things. But fuel and locoweed seem to be where the wealth is. Don't you think so, Hip City?

Krishna: Hip City and everybody else break out in laughter.

Blue: Farming seems to be where I should place my stock for the long haul.

Saweto: Oh?

Blue: With proper legislation to encourage development, of course. Then, I want to write a book, my memoirs. I think that should be interesting.

Saweto: Memoirs? What about?

Blue: Goraka! I shall entitle it, Goraka's Memoirs of Infamy. I kinda like that don't you?

Saweto: And, what will be the purpose of this book?

Blue: To show those of you in the future how not to mess up society in the name of national security.

Saweto: Why would anyone want to read that?

Blue: I don't know! I really don't know. It would be about how Aire was attacked by Goraka's emigrants from Fifty-plus-One.

Saweto: But, why would anyone want to attack Aire, now?

Blue: To take what we have!

Saweto: How will it end?….

Blue: …do not know! I really do not know the ending, yet.

Saweto: I take! You defend! How will it end?

Blue: Oh, in that case, that depends!

Saweto: On what?

Blue: Your ends! What do you want to accomplish, toward the end? Toward what ends?

Saweto: Save humanity from total annihlation. You just successfully annihilated nearly everybody on earth, our time, could you write a book on how that might be avoided next time?

Blue: Look, that wasn't a question. I was simply letting you know how many simple things, many factors; some beyond your personal control determine what you do.

Saweto: Oh! I know! But, my question is can you write about how that might be avoided. You seem to know how to deal with the cattle after they have left the corral. I think that was your analogy. How do you prevent the cattle from leaving the corral to cause a stampede before it happens? How does one prevent war? How does one contain death and destruction?

Blue: Oh! I understand you point, now. I don't have the answer to that existential question. Certainly not by killing off your enemies. But, other than that, I haven't the faintest clue.

Saweto: Why not?

Blue: Because somehow you must account for that your self.

Saweto: And, what will your accounting be?

Blue: Me, personally? It might not be anything. For the nation as a whole, I don't know. I don't really know. You never know how things will work out. You never know those things.

Krishna: with everybody's attention directed toward Blue, Saweto disappears. Blue and the others disappear also trying to catch Saweto, but to no avail. At the same time manila and Makeba disappear fro Aire. Nailah does the same, but more to find Blue than Manila. Nailah feels that Saweto and manila and Makeba and TOMORROW and Neptune and the minority agroKinshasas and story Teller will make it. It is Blue Nailah is worried about.

    Why does everybody disappear? Well, Blue is correct in his logic. He leaves out one variable, however. Human emotion! And, at that moment, i.e., the moment of impact, the Kinshasas were emotionally charged because they were acting as the engine for the time mirages headed for Aire and Zania.

    The collapse of the time based nation-state impacted directly on the emotional Kinshasas. That forced more energy out of them than otherwise possible. This extra lift, if you will, caused the time mirages to reach their destinations as perfect missiles for of TNT: enough to destroy Aire and Zania totally.

    Blue has committed the perfect fiasco. Ironically, he will ever know this. Neither he nor anyone wise will ever know how the three worlds collapsed to nothing, relatively simultaneously all in complementarity.

Ain't that nothin'? In Blue's determination to close down Fifty-plus-One before it has any time to complete the launch phase of its time mirages inadvertently provides the exact amount of energy to spring board the death wish human cargo directly onto the targets they wanted to reach, Aire and Zania. If he has only waited! Fifty-plus-One would have been completely destroyed, but Aire and Zania would have survived. But that is academic now. 'Cause ain't nobody around to notice the difference. So, what difference does it make?

Chapter 35

The Shadow: There are survivors of the three worlds war. Only the disappeared can claim that privilege, however. The way the disappeared survived the holocaust is to remain in a state of anti-matter for the entire six days the three worlds need to undergo their respective reformations.

This mode of survival has its drawbacks. As an example, the reason is, as Nailah is searching for Blue, everyone is scattered to every part of the globe still inhabitable. They are placed in different parts of this new planet to be. Oh, boi!

For instance, the newly adopted family of Saweto and Manila settle in a valley along what the offspring will call the" Nile Valley." The agroKinshasas on the other hand end up further south in an area they name Zimbabwe. Angola and Au-U-Khan, who have remained in Zania, end up in what they will name Ethiopia.

Manila and Makeba make it to Zania from Aire. There they meet up with Saweto. As reported before, they end up the Nile Valley. Neptune, Yani and Krishna the storytellers decide to settle in you guessed it, Angola.

To make sure her daughter is taken care of, Nailah is able to get Alaya to recompose in the Nile Valley. Alaya will serve as Manila's midwife as Saweto and Manila prepare for the delivery of their second child. Alaya is fortunate because Nailah saw fit to recompose her companion Azania to keep her company as they settle in and reproduce their own family.

Nailah feels happy now. Very happy! This femi person has successfully passed on the matrilineal process in a manner the Orihsas of Oldumare said things must be done for her birth line to continue and flourish. What she wants to do is find Abdul Malik and IFE Cameron and Tendi and Marimba to tell them that the war is over; that they can now rest in peace. That they now must rest in peace.

Where they settle, she has not quite decided. However, she knows that it will be far away. Maybe they will find the lost trail. Yes, that seems like a good place. This will be a land where the practices of the dark side will be honored. HA! HA! HA! Ain't that nothin'! Nailah has finally learned how to control her movements on the dark side. That's why she prefers being down under. Some how it provides a better geography for the type of telepathic development she wants to enhance.

Nigga-Dred: Down under will be her Home.

There, she will never be Alone

There, her people will roar

Down under will be

Nailah's home.

Chapter 36

DyingSoul:AAAAAAAAAAAAAAAAAAAAHHHHHHHHHHHHHHHHHHHHHHHHHHH!!

The Merciful: My son, you will listen to every silent scream of every single body of life in all three worlds you destroyed. The screams at first will appear to be the same, that is, one continual scream. But, as you become more proficient in learning how to listen to each scream separately, you will begin to hear each life being as it ends its life. After each scream, you will repeat, "thou shall not kill." As you repeat, "thou shall not kill," you will never see the peacefulness that death brings. You will only see the agony of what you caused.

You will weep at every death, but for only a brief moment because you cannot miss a count, a single death count. During your weep, your victim will personally scorn you by asking. "How could you?' You will want to answer/scream will always be right at the tip of your tongue, but it will never come. It will always be there, but you will never have the pleasure of feeling and hearing that response.

Instead, you will thus feel dual agony and physical pain simultaneously. The physical pain you suffer will take you as far as the transformation of your body with your mind always intact and alert, the same way each individual is transformed from life to death, except you will always return to live the next death.

To give you an example of what I am saying, on fifty-plus-One you will suffer each DRY ROT and physical expression of the personality each DRY ROT leaves on its victim, only to do the same for the next victim. Since you cannot die, your personality will witness each transformation as it occurs through all of your senses: you will retain consciousness at all times; you will be aware of all suffering at all times. you will be there at all times.

Goraka: Oh, Merciful?

The Merciful: Repent, my son?

Goraka: Yes, oh merciful, I want to repudiate my sinful ways. I was wrong. I can see that was wrong. May I ask forgiveness?

The Merciful: Forgiveness, my son?

Goraka: Yes, Oh Merciful!

The Merciful: And, what are we to forgive, my son?

Goraka: My crime against humanity! I want to repent my crimes ask for forgiveness, and seek salvation. I was only trying to carry out your word.

The Merciful: First, let me explain, my child! The Merciful are no longer in power. The stewards replaced them during the last election. The scientists are running things now. If it is an appeal you are making, you must seek their attention. I am only a researcher.

You see, we have no precedent for what has happened here. You are the first to accomplish this feat. To destroy all life forms in three worlds virtually simultaneously. That is a feat we have no records of, any precedence for. You are the first.

The scientific body decided unanimously that we should not proceed further until we can figure out what went wrong. You see, as I said, you are undergoing the most rigorous testing we can provide, so that hopefully one day we may have a species of intellectual beings who can think and communicate in a common language with the rest of life without trying to impose its will.

Life is not just people! What makes you think that you can claim exclusively of the right to determine what lives and what dies? You are only one of many life forms on earth. When you collected your intellect, no one said, "okay, lets make humans our representatives. They will destroy all life forms in our behalf." I mean, who gave you that idea? …. The idea that you could decide on a personal as well as a universal basis who or what life was measured at what value is what we are trying to understand. What gall! Where did the idea come from? We want to know.

Goraka: Are any of the others undergoing the same testing I am undergoing at this point?

The Merciful: NO! I am afraid not!

Goraka: Why?

The Merciful: No one else claimed the gift. You did, and I might add you even claimed immortality.

Goraka: But, I guess I was not adequately prepared to accomplish the mission I set out to accomplish.

The Merciful: You might be right. At least, that is one of the theses under consideration now. That is one reason I am to test your reaction to death. We want to know why killing for you was so enjoyable. We assume that it had to be for you initiate it on the scale you did.

Goraka: But, you don't understand, I needed power. How else can I save humanity? Oh, UH! Could have?

The Merciful: Shit! All you better worry about at this point is your ass. You better leave that power thing alone….You don't want that issue brought to the floor. But I understand how that might create a dilemma for you. That is, to have a mission, salvation, challenged by a desire for power. We want to know why it was so extreme with you? We still think of you as rational, so your intellectual faculties are of importance to our research.

The most amazing thing that we saw is, there is no reason for that entire killing, simply, no reason. The other thing was no matter the reason given to rationalize the killing – suicide or homicide – the end result was guaranteed to always be the same, the human cause of death….Not symbolic death –which we thought you might consider – but the actual taking away of life in an organized and glorified fashion. It got to the point where the highest honor could be bestowed upon an individual was heroism on the battlefield of warfare. How irrational!

You know, what you did was like a satire on the Orishas. It is as though you said, "we may not be able to make life, but we certainly can take life. You make it we take it. "I dare you! You stop us! What are you going to do about it?"

Was there an apparent void, and you assumed command over the dominion? Seemingly you said that life was expendable and that you were willing to take full responsibility for your actions to suspend it. By doing that, you added a whole new set of variables to the equation of earth's ecobalance; and you upped the ante. We found your logic interesting at first, so we said, "hey go at it, and come what may!" Then we criticized our liberalism and opened up the floor for other options.

Eventually the proposals started to come forth. One was to look into the possibility of selecting a group to assume as their responsibility the salvation of humanity. Everybody said, "Good idea!" I'll volunteer to work on this idea."

And, the project was ready to go. We knew that the body did not care one way or the other about what was happening on earth. "Where the hell is earth?" So that was no problem getting the idea legislated. "If earthlings live, good! If not, no problem."

Earth suffers from being away form the center of power. It is really far away, you know. Besides, it is so insignificant in the universal politics that earth is not noticeable. That is unless some one decides to scan the rest of the universe and accidents upon the place. , "Look there's earth. What are they doing?' So on and so forth!

Goraka: I'm sorry! My thoughts were elsewhere. I missed your point…..What did you say?

The Merciful: Come now, my son. I am sure you can do that and listen at the same time. Don't you want to know how we got involved? Well, whether you do or not, you are going to be told the whole story from complete to finish.

Goraka: Yes, Oh Merciful, I shall try.

The Merciful: Yes, that's another emotion we must understand. In the meantime, you "try" to listen to me talk while you count.

{At that moment, another conscious being appears and asks,….}

Balid au Sudan: Why does the meni person keep calling you "Oh Merciful?"

The Merciful: I do not know? I do not rightly know?

Goraka: Because you offered to kill me. Death could be no worse than this.

The Merciful: DEATH? You are immortal! Do you not remember? You told Neptune that you are immortal.

Goraka: Yes, Oh Merciful, but I didn't know that to become immortal all one has to do to declare oneself immortal.

The Merciful: Is that why you took other's lives?

Goraka: I do not understand, Oh Merciful? [113,695,weep! Thou shall not kill!]

Balid au Sadun: What your questioner is asking you is did you think that the only way for you to become immortal was to kill everyone else off? –How intelligent are you?

The Merciful: I really do not know! But they do reason to some degree.

Goraka: Yes, I do understand your guest ion. NO! I had not really thought of it that way. I was simply trying to survive. They were trying to kill me, you know. [157,321, weep! Thou shall not kill.]

Bilad au Sudan: I wouda been tryin' to kill yo ass, too. Did you see all the things you did to earth?

Goraka: I got bored! What can I tell ya? [164,191, weep! Thou shall not kill']

The Merciful: Bored? What's bored?

Balid au Sadun: I do not know. What is bored?

Goraka: It's when you start to get restless because nothing is happening [193,152, weep! Thou shall not kill.] That interests you.

Bilad al Sudan: Interesting!

The Merciful: Very interesting!

Goraka: NO! BORING! [211,438, weep!,,,,,,,,,.]

The Merciful: HA! Ha! Ha! HA! AH! HA!

Goraka: [………kill.] I wasn't bringing humorous, I was being honest. [274,632, weep! Thou……]

Bilad al Sudan: He does have a sense of honor….But, isn't that interesting? Every time he invents a new word, he automatically creates it opposite.

The Merciful: How do you mean?

Garaka: ..kill] He means as soon as I show honesty, I have assumed that there is untrustworthiness around. [304,727; weep! Thou shall not kill]

The Merciful: You see why we have not been able to think in terms of laying out punishment.

Bilad al Sudan: Yes! And, lose the opportunity to learn so much from these creatures Yes, I see! How old are these species? And, what are they called?

The Merciful: Oh, A few million years their time, maybe 25 million or so.

Bilad al Sadun: MY! And, they have progressed this far. I thought they were doing quite well. But, I never understand why they used so little pf their thinking processes.

The Merciful: I think you might be confusing them with the Calypsonians.

Balid al Sudan: No!…..PHEW! GHEEA! WHAT WAS THAT ODOR?

Goraka: [573,374, weep! Thou shall not kill.] [593,…]

Dying Soul: How can you?

Goraka: [Thou shall not kill. Please, forgive me, 184,405,993,…] These are not the Calypsonians. They are from that other water planet.

The Merciful: Excuse me , Balid al Sudan. I see you remember what to do. Very good! Next time, say," please forgive me" after the Dying Soul asks, "How can you?" Not after "Thou shall not kill."

Balid al Sudan: ……They sure did!…'Beginning to remember now. These are the earth people.

The Merciful: Yes, do you know something about them?

Bilad al Sudan: Well, it's been some time back a ways, but I do recall observing the earth people. Whatever! Oh! I see! You know, I never had earth people. Whatever! Oh! I see! You know, I never had a chance to get back to finish my observations. Funny, I never would have thought they would have ended it so soon. HUM! I'm usually right about these things. So, what happened?

Yombe: As the lost scholar – or, Oh, Merciful as Goraka has chosen to call his inquisitor – unfolds the past covering three earth life epochs of 26 million years each, Goraka becomes aware of one vital point, his name will never be mentioned again in his presence. EVER!

Goraka: In my presence! Make that clear. We don't know what they say when I am not there, do we? When they discuss me, they must identify me somehow. Maybe, then! [735,940, sniff, please forgive me. Thou shall not kill.]

Yombe: Goraka continues to maintain some array of hope. He does this by maintaining some attachment to his name.

Goraka: What's in a name, the basis of a claim. The basis of my claim, that's what's in a name.

Yombe: But was their thesis, without a name one has no basis for a claim? Was this their attempt to erase from memory the sin of us all? What ever! Goraka counted, heard the scream, wept, asked for forgiveness, and received the question, however! He was learning. Eventually it became count,

Goraka: 1,065,476.

Yombe: Receive the question….

Dying-Soul: AAAAAAAAAAAAAAAAAHHHHHHHHHHHHHHHHHHH!

Yombe: Weep!

Goraka: Sniff! Sniff! Sniff! Weep! Weep!

Yombe: Ask for forgiveness….

Goraka: Thou shall not kill! Please, forgive me, Oh Merciful!

Bilad al Sudan: Why is he asking for forgiveness?

The Merciful: That's an innovation on his part.

Bilad al Sudan: Like, Oh, merciful??

The Merciful: Exactly! The same!

Bilad al Sudan: What does he expect, to gain something, maybe?

The Merciful: They believe in emotion in the subjective tense. He believes that at some point there must be forgiveness, compassion, and understanding.

Balid al Sudan: And, then what?

The Merciful: I shall set him free.

Bilad al Sudan: Really? Did you tell him?

The Merciful: I told him! You were here.

Bilad al Sudan: And, he's still doing it? Obviously he doesn't believe you. If he's depending on that, he'll be here forever. How long are you assigned to this research project?

The Merciful: I was told, "Take as long as it takes." So, it'll be at least for three earth life epochs.

Bilad al Sudan: That's' not so long, considering, but, how you goin' to do that?

The Merciful: I'll run them side by side simultaneously.

Bilad al Sudan: Yea, but won't that be a bit taxing on him?

The Merciful: How do you mean?

Bilad au Sudan: I mean, he's going to be counting three earth life epochs at the same time. Isn't that a bit taxing?

The Merciful: Oh, I hadn't thought of it that way.

Yombe: Can you imagine doing that for the rest of forever? Where is the distinction between punishment and testing here?

Goraka: There is none! [1,764,58, weep, etc.]

Yombe: Excuse me that was really a rhetorical question directed at my audience, sir. I am not allowed to talk to you. I'm sure you know that. I 'm sure you understand. After all, you are…..

The Merciful: NO! NO! Go ahead! Let my child explain. I would love to hear his answer.

Goraka:…..Merciful.] Well, as far as I can determine…

Yombe: The moment Goraka [he can't hear me now.] said, "determine" something very unusual happened. I have the lone scholar here to tell us what happened.

The Merciful: "LOST SCHOLAR!"

Yombe: Yes, lost scholar here to tell us what he just did. Go ahead, sir.

The Merciful: Well, basically what I did was to place my child right in the middle of the radiation showers for a parsec, and then I removed him.

Yombe: I see! And, the purpose of which was?

The Merciful: The purpose was to give my child a frame of reference for understanding the difference between punishment and testing…

Yombe: [Let us see what Goraka has to say about this reference he was just given.] Yes, sir! And, you were saying? I think you were speaking and you stopped at "determine," what was that?

Goraka: There is a noticeable difference…Take the word. If you don't take my word on anything else, take my word there being a difference between punishments and testing. [2,002,002, weep, thou shall not kill,]

Yombe: And, what about your original statement, do you retract it?

Goraka: Oh!] Yes! Without reservation! [2,347,…,…

Yombe: Without a doubt?

Goraka: ….weep! Thou shall….] There is no doubt what ever.

[Oh, Merciful….]

Yombe: And, how would you account for this sudden change?

Goraka: Thou…] It is unbelievable. The pain is too painful to ever imagine any circumstances, by anyone of us. [3,…

Yombe: And, if you have a choice?

Goraka: 3,486,979, weep. Thou shall not

ill.] That is too hypothetical!

Yombe: Yes, but if you have a choice?

Goraka:….3,834,720,….]

DyingSoul:How can you? AAAA AA H HHHHHAHAHAHA

Goraka: Sniff! Sniff! WEEP! WEEP! THOU SHALL NOT KILL! PLEASE THANK YOU, OH MERCIFUL! 4,365,418/3,857,968/3,827,030]

Yombe: The most interesting outcome of this unusual story is for the first time, a small insignificant planet in a far away galaxy in a far away solar system kept alive by a small star is receiving attention. All kinds of studies are being conducted on earth, the live planet. Not only that, the Council has voted to establish live planets throughout the rest of the multiverse.

The number has not been agreed upon yet nor have such things as a carbon based life forms. That's an argument I understand that Goraka's researchers are making; that the live bodies of minerals should contain the same approximate proportion of ingredients as that found on the planet earth.

The experimentalists will challenge this proposal, I am told as being too deterministic. They will argue that the council needs to experiment with other forms and means of life before deciding on one organization, and one arrangement as is now the case on earth.

Yes, this is I your little storyteller. I got a little promotion after me and that so-called "lost scholar" – see how I gave him that little dig there by calling him the "lost scholar—see how I gave him that little dig there by calling him the "lost scholar. HA! HA! HA! AH! – Got into our run in. Now, travel everywhere looking for interesting stories to tell. I tell you folks; this is an exciting time to be a part of.

My stories are now heard on thirty-two planets and number of clusters operating around ten major planets operating with intelligent life forms. Oh, I have not forgotten, you want to know about the case of the Grand Infamy. You want to know finally happened to Goraka and Nailah. I know!

You see, there's only Story Teller, Stellar Four, Yani, Jom, Krishna, Yom, and me, Yombe left from the old storyteller corps. So, naturally we three have as affinity going. The problem is, we don't get a chance to get together often, but we keep in touch. When we hook up the first thing they want to know is, how is he doing? And, I tell them about his latest whatever. They just laugh!

Last time we spoke, we were all trying to do the same thing: each was organizing a school to train our new recruits, so we have a ready-made corps of storytellers. Our worlds are gone now, and we need some able and willing listeners to transmit what's going on to the rest of us. In the meantime, I guess you'll have to guess what's going on in most places. Jom, the storyteller, always a supporter of Goraka said, "Goraka 'offed' 99% of the storytellers, damn."

So we have to start from scratch. Krishna has chosen the old engung way, Yani is open to whatever works, and I have decided to take advantage of this new SciTech the Calypsonians have mastered. I am sure you can tell that we hardly see each other. Not seeing each other regularly, and using different modes of communications has kept us from getting all of the exciting stories to you. Sorry about that!

As for Goraka, he's doing about as well as can be expected under the circumstances. I don't men to laugh, but every time I see Goraka ccountin' then become the most grotesque being I have ever seen, I think, "PHEW! I AM SO GLAD IT AIN'T ME DOIN' THAT." But, can you imagine, they have a punishment more cruel than the tests he's been undergoing?

Can you imagine that? Before Goraka was placed in the radiation showers for that parsec, I did not believe Krishna when he reported that they went through a similar process. Krishna called it hell in real time with no virtual meaning ever apparent. It was reported that Neptune yelled out so loud that the whole earth trembled.

That's what I thought about when I asked Goraka what he might do if he had a choice. Did you see what he did? He simply continued to count, weep, repeated the commandment like he was telling me, "I do not want to talk about. I shall ignore you question as though it was never asked."

When I finally got him to discuss it, his only comments were, "it was a qualitatively different experience. The two can never ever be compared. You saw what he did, didn't you? I simply kept countin' " Now, that I think about it, Goraka was about ready to talk about anything at this point. So, I asked him, "How does it feel? Each death suffered?

Goraka's answer was, and I still don't know how he was able to talk and count, etc., "each death is a separate occurrence that I must witness and feel each time it occurs, every death, I suffer!"

Well, maybe Goraka has repented after all. Even so, he continues to look very fit. You think that his mind was sharp when he was President? You should see him now. Unbelievable! Goraka attributes this swiftness of girt to the repetition of counting the dead. Because of the added abilities, Goraka ways that he can one cream while he counts; that his favorite dream is about the first time he visited Nailah as her home.

Chapter 38

Phantom: I guess the only way to put it is everybody seemed surprised when they heard that is was Goraka that Nailah was in love with or that it was Nailah that Goraka pursued. Everybody within Nailah's circle always figured that if Nailah fell in love with anybody, it would be Abdul Malik. Her circle adhered to this notion even though the two always denied that anything hanky panky was going on between them.

So, when word got around that Nailah had this mysterious visitor boarding with her, it was communicated that Blue was very upset, to put it mildly. The mysterious meni person was it turns out was Goraka, and Abdul Malik was not angry. As a matter of fact, it was because of Blue that Goraka was living on Nailah's estate. No one believed this, however.

It's probably a good thing too because no one eve suspected that Nailah's new boarder, whose assumed name hid the fact that he was the "wanted" Barrister-General from the Phantom New World Colony called Fifty-plus-One, was to be the next King-General of the old country. However, we are no interested in that matter here. That has been addressed elsewhere.

What we are interested in here is the romance. Yes! The romance! To let everyone tell it today, as it turned out, I was wrong. Everybody did know that Nailah was ripe for a romance. After all, her husband had been killed in a tragic mining accident over a decade before Nailah became involved with her new guest. And, her effort to court Blue had fallen on deal ears, etc., etc., etc., with Blue taking up with Ife Cameron. And so the gossip went.

The fact that Abdul Malik and Goraka and the Musician, aka, Marimba, and Nailah would laugh themselves into hysterics every time a new version of the love train game was unfolded by Marimba not with standing. So, I was wrong! In any case, whose versions you choose to accept is you own decision. I can only report what those involved agree happened. None involved say that Blue and Nailah ever had a love affair passive or negative. They were simply very good friends. Okay! Now, back to the romance.

And, romance it was! As it turns out – all agree – Nailah and Goraka –so-called – fell in love almost the instant they saw each other. It wasn't that love at first sight, no, this was and I want to physically consume you, romance. At least, that's what it was for the first fourteen months. Then Nailah began to ask questions about her daughter's where abouts and the Barrister-General began to accuse her of carrying on an affair with Abdul Malik. However, those fourteen months were heaven on earth. That is, if heaven is a place where pleasure and desire are rewarded with more pleasure and desire.

For the Priest of Priests and the barrister-General, this was a castle in Ife's Garden. No pleasure went unfilled in the garden. No desire was left unattended! All of loves pleasures were explored as though tomorrow would always take care of tomorrow. "Love is ours today as all of the passions of ours should rush to the fore as great streams of rhapsody."

This love passion would last days on end. One such encounter is reported to have begun at 7:00 p.m. one Friday evening and ended at 7:00 p.m. the following Sunday. When they finally took a break to get something to eat, Nailah reported that her passion flowed from the moment they began to the moment they finally took a reluctant break; that it began again the moment she started eating; and, that she cums just thinking about it.

The Barrister-General swears that he is still ready for "dome now action." Yet, he claims that the stimulations he received were so pleasurable he didn't want to cum for fear of loosing their pleasure. So, he simply enjoyed! Each angle! Each position! (How many were there?) Every hold created more desire, more desire in pleasure, and more and pleasure. I am sure that you get the point.

Nailah simply laughed when she thought of the things they did; all of the ways they did these things. The laugh was always a pleasure to watch because you knew no matter what, these would be memorable moments that will always bring pleasure, but never duplicated. It's like no matter how much you may enjoy your next pleasure, that occasion is one that you know will never be out classed.

So, you don't even try. And, in the process, you discover more pleasure with equal desire. That's when you realize that it is not in the pursuit, but in the actual activity of loving that the greatest desire for pleasure is fulfilled. That is how Nailah and the Barrister-General fell in love at first sight.

Nailah: Now, who could that be waking me up at this time in the morning? I hope it's not something awful. Oh, my God! I hope it's not about my baby…..Be calm Nailah. Everything's gonna be okay, simply calm down. You know you don't need to get excited.

YES! WHO IS IT? WHOSE THERE? HOW MAY I HELP YOU? IS THERE SOME TROUBLE?

Sharp: Nailah! It's me Marimba! Open the door! Please, hurry!

Nailah: SHARP? MARIMBA IS THAT YOU?

Sharp: Nailah! It's me! I have Blue with me. Hurry, let us in! Blue's in danger.

Nailah: [Nailah, without thinking, rushes to the door in her nite gown.]

Oh! Wait! Never mind! [Damn, I should have put on something.] COME ON IN! ……. Hi Marimba! [Nailah kisses everybody.] Hello, Blue! How you doin'? [Pause!] Why, hello Mr. Barrister-General.[Change voices, Nailah asks Sharp,..] Who is that standing out there in the shadows? Wha..?

Sharp: Oh, that's Blood. He's with us. He's not comin in… I didn't know you two knew each other…Thank's Nailah!

Nailah: For what? I haven't done anything, yet. [All the while, Nailah is watching her new guest.]

Sharp: Oh, let intro…. Let me explain why we're here.

Nailah: Yea! Sure! Let me see you explain to my neighbors tomorrow why you were at my door at who knows what time it is in the morning. What time is it?

Blue: About 4:00 O'clock!

Nailah: Is that A.M. or P.M.?

Blue: A.M. Sorry! It's an emergency, really.

Nailah: I am sure that it is. [Eyes still on the Barrister-General.]

Sharp: Let me explain! Tonight – this morning, I mean! Blue's hideout was raided. All were killed except for a few. Abdul, Roc Steadye, Blood, and Goraka here survived.

Nailah: WHO?

Sharp: Goraka, the Barrister-General.

Nailah: Oh, I did not know you had a name. I always thought that your name was Mr. Barrister-General. [Everybody laughs.]

Sharp: YEA! [Rather embarrassed.] He prefers to be called Goraka.

Nailah: And, I'm Nailah. Simply Nailah! Now, what do you want me to do? I don't think you woke me up at what time is it, blue?

Blue: 4:30!

Nailah: A.M. or P.M.?

Blue: That's A.M., Nailah!

Nailah: Just to show me that Abdul Malik is alive? A simple message would suffice. Don't you think so? HUH, Blue?

Blue: Yea, Nailah. You do have a point, as usual.

Sharp: Nailah, please! Lighten up! Give us a break

Nailah: I let them in and the Musician says, "Give us a break!" I'll give you a break, all right.

Sharp: Anyway, we wanna ask you to put up Goraka fir a while. The King-General is after his head.

Nailah: What while? How long?

Sharp: Not long, we hope; maybe only a few days but no more than a 'til the end of the week.

Nailah: Yea, sure! The way the Revolution is going, think you are being a bit optimistic. Don't you. Blue!

Blue: I hope not, but you are probably right Nailah. I don't know!

Nailah: And, what about Blue and, the rest? Where is Roc Steadye? Don't they need hiding, too? Obviously, your shit is tight. Why else would you wake Nailah up at what?

Blue: Time is it, Blue? 5:00 A.M.! And, we'd better go! We've got more stops to make. They truly put a hole in our movement this morning. Anyway, will you do it? You know I wouldn't ask if it could be done otherwise. You know that…

Nailah: Yes! I know, Blue. And, you know how I worry about you.

Blue: I know! Thank's for caring! But, we….

Nailah: Have to go…

Blue: Yes! Let's move, sharp! …See, you Nailah! [Blue embraces Nailah.] Take good care of our new King-General, now.

[Now Blue turns toward Goraka.] "G" take care! And, don't listen to what she advises about food. HA! HA! AH! HA! No, really. You can learn a lot from this High Priest of the Akuyu people. [As Goraka smiles, Marimba bids farewell to Nailah.]

Sharp: And, you must tell me about how you and your new houseguest know each other…. Take care! ….Goraka, couldn't be in better hands.

Yombe: Goraka still says nothing. He simply smiling approvingly at Abdul Mali and Marimba as he shakes their hands while they are moving toward the door. After Blue and Sharp move out into the daybreak, Nailah and Goraka take time to get acquainted. Amazingly, things are too not awkward. Nailah and Goraka hit it off very quickly. Many say that has to do with Nailah's character. Others say that it's her personality. I think it's probably a combination of the two…. In any case, the relationship is right on time, so to speak. You know, at the right moment for both of them.

Nailah: Well, Mr Barrister-General, I am sure that you are tired after such an eventful night. Are you hungry, too? Shall, I prepare an early morning breakfast? What time is it? Yes, I think I shall. I am going to fix us some nice duck eggs, some hot biscuits, some harmony grits, and…. do you eat red meat? What are you grinning about? The whole time you're been here. What's on your mind?

Yombe: If you see Nailah, now you'd immediately know why Goraka is smiling. Nailah now 267 years new world time is very sensuous and appealing. There are not many people Nailah does not turn on, meni or femi-persons. It isn't her beauty – although she is extremely beautiful, too – or the fact that she is attractive. The Akuyu people are said to have to most beautiful femi-persons. No! It is something else. It is her sensuality that turns people on. To Nailah this is simply natural. Nothing contrived! Nothing special! Simply Nailah! It is nothing she does. It is just her, period. And, that is enough, too much for most, but just enough for her.

Goraka: Nailah! I must apologize for staring at you the while back, there.. I could not help but recall our first meeting. I thought you were the most beautiful femi person I had ever seen, and you still are.

Nailah: It is not the beauty that turns you on Mr. Barrister-General, it's my charisma…

Goraka: Goraka! Please call me Goraka. Oh? And, all along I thought it was your beauty, my, my, what a revelation.

Nailah: …….And, boldness that does the trick. [Goraka laughs.]My, what a funny laugh. HA! HA! HA! You laugh as though you've laughed before. What a funny, where'd you get that laugh? WAW!

Yombe: At that point, Nailah burst out into a laughter that was to romantically funny that Goraka began to laugh again, also. Once he got started, there was no stopping him. You know Nailah laughed even more. It wasn't like he was over doing it or she was making fun of him. No, it was just plain fun.

Oh, they laugh until the sun rose. It was now sunup. The new weekend begins. The time is now 7:00 A.M. In the meantime, Nailah had been treated to a gourmet breakfast, lunch and now for dinner we are going to get a surprise. Realizing that Nailah not going any place for the weekend, Goraka decided to get ambitious and ask,

Goraka: What are we having for dinner?

Nailah:…What…?

Goraka:……Dinner is served! A La Carte. Why don't you allow me to carry the dinner into the dining room?

Nailah: At your pleasure, M Chef.

Yombe: As Goraka lifts his serving into this phantom plate; he feels serge of energy that makes him feel as though a thunderbolt is ready to strike. The energy level is so high that Goraka is transformed into a new person. The transformation is so literal that for the first time, Nailah sees him as Goraka. The newness in him is a change heretofore unexpected in beings of consciousness. Yet, it comes about so naturally, so poetically, so enticingly delicious, Nailah thinks.

{Nailah's voice is so low that one can hear her sigh after each kiss as though his name and the sigh are all one.}

Nailah: Oh, Garaka!

Yombe: Her voice so softly precedes each kiss with a calling of his name again and again and again and again and again and again and again and again. "Go-Ra-Ka!" As they reach the dining room, Nailah is still wrapped in her beautifully colored robe, is placed on the table. Goraka's motion seems effortless, his desire insatiable. Dinner is ready it be served.

Goraka: Dinner is ready!

Yombe: And, how! As Nailah lies upon the table waiting to be served, her robe which she has managed to secure after closing the door behind the behind the revolutionists naturally falls open from around her gorgeous thighs. There Nailah's pubic fluff gradually reveals the true nature of her beauty. The beauty is so stunning, Goraka, who prides himself on being cool, has to be guided like a missile into the wonders of her pleasure. It is not only Nailah who has not done it in a long time, you see.

Nailah: A little rusty, huh, Goraka?

Yombe: Once there, once inside the wonders of pleasure, Goraka returns to his old and unusual form. Oh, what form! As I said, Goraka is guided by the vibrations of the gravitational pull of Nailah's blackhole of her nasty continues to pull, pull, pull him deeper into bliss. Once inside, after overcoming the initial shock of bliss, Goraka regains his sense of balance. That is when the real pleasure treasure is realized.

Goraka:OOOOOOOOHHHHHHHH HHHHHH!OOOOOOOHHHHHHHH! BABIE! GIVE IT ALL TO ME!! OOOOHHHH! Yes!

Nailah:OOOOOOOOOOOOOOOOOOOOOOOOOOOOOHHHHHHHHHHHHH! YESSSSSSSSSSSSSSSSSSSSSSSS! AUHHHHHHHHHH! DON'T STOP! DON'T STOP! DON'T STOP! RIGHT THERE BABIE! JUST PUT IT RIGHT THERE BABIE! OH, YES, YES, BABIE! RIGHT THERE! OH, YES! YES!

Yombe: Nailah and Goraka carry on a though the stars are falling, and the world is in its greatest beauty, e.g., when Nailah begins to chant, don't Stop! It's rhythmic pulse sends Goraka into trance like movements. Now he is possessed with the delight of the treasure pleasure. After they reach a height neither thinks possible and still have not cum, Nailah and Goraka both know that bliss is simply the beginning of the trip they are about to take, and that Cumming is simply one to many parts of their total pleasure. It is also one of the many pleasures of their total pleasure. It is also one of the many pleasures of their total desire. Oh, what desire! And, what pleasure! What desire! What pleasure!

Nailah: Oh, Goraka, I don't know how you put me in this mood, but I certainly need it. It feels good having someone inside of me, having you inside me.

Goraka: If anything turns you on that I do – listen to how I'm talking backwards – it must be my staring at you lustfully. I want you so badly, I can…

Yombe: Before Goraka can finish his sentence; he has withdrawn his missile and begins to suck her toes. Each toe one by one, crack by crack. The he starts to suck he big toe as though it is the only pleasure spot in her luscious body and she cums and cums and cums and cums while he moves into the arch of the foot. The right foot! His tongue lingers as a soft sensation while she cums some more simply from cuming. As Goraka massages Nailah's feet with a foot massager, Nailah sucks on Goraka's missile until he is about to explore the withdraws her mouth and inserts it into Ife's Garden.

Nailah: My god! What a super hard cock! You are as hard as a missile standing on the run way ready to explore its energy in a take off. Oh, but you feel so goood! It feeel sooo goood!

Goraka: Oh, yes, it does! Oh, yes it does.

Yombe: This time Nailah assumes the top position – a position neither maintains for very long before a leg is placed on the floor while the other lies across the missile range within the rounds of his two rather long muscular legs. As she stands on one leg, she begins to try every spot within reach of her vaginal senses. Her movements are always rhythmic. This feat simply makes Goraka's missile even harder, if that is at all possible, would you believe, it gets harder?

Nailah: My god! I don't believe it! It feels do gooood! It is so deep. Your head is so large! Oh, it feels good! Just hold it right there. Right there! Don't move!

Yombe: Goraka's missile causes Nailah to become turned on even more. Yes, it is possible. So, she tells Goraka to get down off the table and enter her from the rear, i.e., through blossoms passage because she thinks the experience might be interesting. He does!

Goraka: Does it hurt? Is it in? I never thought it would be so easy. You are so elastic. So refined! So good!

Nailah: I just do what comes natural. I do what I feel. The more it turns you on, the more I get turned on.

Goraka: It is simply how you do it!

Yombe: By now, Nailah is leading Goraka up the stairs. When she reaches the top of the staircase, she beckons Goraka to lie down with his head on the top of the staircase facing upward, she then stratals his face only to change her mind and moves into a powder puff position while squatting. She just feels like teasing him, now.

After a while Goraka's tongue begins to create a sensation around Nailah's clitoris that causes her to desire more. To obtain more, Nailah changes back to massage Goraka's face with Ife's Garden until she moves to far on one occasion and Goraka sticks his tongue onto the tip of blossoms passage.

The sensation is so stimulating and evoking that Nailah decides to allow Goraka to stick his tongue into blossom's passage while he massages her clitoris. Without warning just as Nailah is preparing to let out a burst of orgasm, Goraka withdraws his tongue and thrust his missile right into Ife's Garden. He continues to massage her clit with left finger while she increases the movements of both into a dynamic rage of ecstasy.

They are moving so fast and powerfully – now on top of the upstairs floor – that the explosion drive both of them into further and further ecstasy. By now, Albert Adler is blowing one of his improvisations so wildly that the whole place seems to be in ecstatic turmoil ready to violate the most passionate of passions.

As each moves through the ecstasy, neither can help but see the beautiful love gods (inclusive) sculptures stationed throughout and around the Indian Garden as seen in her bedroom. Each motion brings into a view another position of a different statute of another set of gods always in pairs, always doing something another way: making love as in a play den of desire. Suddenly, without any warning, Nailah leads Goraka by his missile into her guest bedroom.

Nailah: I've always wanted to make love in water. Come!

Yombe: Goraka, who is still amazed at his rate of recovery, follows Nailah into her Hugh bathroom smiling and without question. However, he cannot help but wonder what next? As they enter, Goraka sees the large bathtub with multilayered waterfall of continually running water. What he does not see, at first, are the love stones that are stones carved into statutes of people making love all the way up the waterfall? They are so life-like that they look like lovers making love in eh rain.

Goraka becomes so turned on by the love gods that he begins to massage Nailah's lower back in such a way that she orgasms in a slow flow of juices streaming down her thighs: what wetness she feels. After a while it becomes too much. Nailah simply melts into the waterfall bathtub as one of those love gods with pleasure written across her pose. In other words, her pose would make a dead man rise to the occasion.

Goraka sees Nailah in this love pose created by the mini-orgasms he elicits and gets turned on even more. Nailah's behavior encourages Goraka to try yet another pleasure sensitive spot on her body. He, thereby, tries to find a spot that arouses her, but in another way so different than the last that she….

In so doing, Goraka accidents upon the armpit with his exploratory tongue. Although this does not cause Nailah to cum, it excites her to no end.

Nailah: Baby, please? Put it in? Please? Auhhhh! Yes! Slowly! Slowly! Oh! It feels gooood inside me. I could leave it there all night. Oh, yes.

Yombe: Eventually, Nailah and Goraka locate a suitable spot underneath the love falls that allow them to receive the constant drops of water while they remain inside each other all night. The drops are so meditative that neither can remember sleeping, but they are rested, and are not sore.

As a matter of fact, after Goraka finds himself saying how he did recall sleeping, that he feels fresh, the two find themselves making love again. By now, it is Saturday morning, 9:00. And for the first time, they approach the bed. Neither feels that they have missed anything not "making love on the bed."

By now, the fragrances of the incense Nailah has stationed throughout the lovely small estate – thirty-three rooms, to be exact! – Were making their rounds past Goraka's nostrils.

Goraka: My, where do you burn all of these different fragrances? And, how do you get them to be so separate and so distinct? I can smell each room. That's all! I think you might be beginning to recognize each fragrance, now.

Goraka: TRUE! So, what is that one that just went past my nostrils just now?

Nailah: That was cinnamon mixed with ginger. The one you can smell now is opium peach. This one coming by is…

Yonbe: As Nailah proceeds to give Goraka the names of all the fragrances they can smell; she symmetrically untangles the two bodies. Then she walks over to a cabinet-marked "herbs" and begins to fool around with the contents inside.

Goraka: What are you doing?

Nailah: I gonna give you something for your taste buds now that you have experienced my incense. I am trying to decide what combinations to introduce to you first.

Goraka: Oh? What does it do?

Nailah: That depends!

Goraka: On what?

Nailah: Your state of mind.

Goraka: What do you mean?

Nailah: Oh, you'll see. Are you game?

Goraka: Sure! Blue told me to follow your lead. Isn't that right?

Nailah: It sure is!

Yombe: As Nialah mixes the contents from her herbal cabinet, and places them into a flat tin can; Goraka stands by and looks on intently.

Goraka: "ERB," to smoke?

Nailah: You'll see! I thought we might smoke up a pipe, now. I think you are ready, now

Goraka: Ready, ready for what?

Yombe: Goraka is now even more apprehensive, but Nailah refuses to acknowledge that his fears are anything but that,

Nailah: I don't know! What ever your heart's content.

Goraka: Should I be scared?

Yombe: The unknown can be a bitch!

Nailah: NO! NO! This is nothing like that. I don't engage in frightening stuff. That's bad for your spirit, your body, your soul. Such things are disengaging. We are engaging here. We are engaging in the pleasures of desire.

Goraka: Dark side? Anything like that?

Nailah: NO! Don't enter with negative vibes.

Goraka: Negative what?

Nailah: "Vibes!" Vibrations…simply relax and enjoy your thoughts.

Yombe: As Nailah ends with that thought she passes Goraka an ivory pipe with an ebony mouthpiece. He takes the ivory pipe, places the ebony mouthpiece into his mouth and inhales a mild tasting herb referred to as "lamb's bread." By now, Nailah is seemingly wandering on another plain. By the time Goraka begins to say,

Goraka: I don't feel anything….what should we be on the look out for?

Yombe: He is laughing hysterically.

Nailah: Then, why are you laughing?

Goraka: I don't know, it's just funny.

Nailah: What's funny? HA! HA!AH!HA!HAAH! HA!AH!

Goraka: [Goraka is really laughing, now. That silly laugh when you are high on locoweed.]

Nailah: You're really high! How do you feel?

Goraka: I feel good!

Nailah: I feel good? Mr. Barrister-General, I feel good? Yes, maan, you are high.

Goraka: Yes, I guess I am!

Nailah: Good! I gonna fuck you until you cum all over creation.

Yombe: By now, Goraka is hysterical with uncontrollable laughter, with tears rolling down his mahogany cheeks.

Goraka: You are? HA! HA!HA!HA!HA!AAAH! HA!HA!

Yombe: As Goraka holds out his long strong arms, he grabs Nailah and pulls her into an embrace. From that moment, he gets the fucking of his life. He is now enjoying physical sensations of pleasure beyond anything he recalls ever experiencing before. You remember those call recall songs you often hear in today's music? That's what Nailah and Goraka now sound like.

Nailah: Is it good to you?

Goraka: Yes, baby it's good.

Nailah: I said, is it good to y

Goraka: Yes'm baby, it's good to me.

Yombe: with the call and response in full form now Nailah is riding Goraka as though he is a wild horse on the plains of Aire. Goraka in turn acts as though this is the pleasure of a lifetime. So, without realizing it, the pleasure has driven Nailah and Goraka into an Aretha Franklin kind of funk blues love ballad with Nailah singing,

Nailah: Is it good to you baby

Yombe: And Goraka answering,

Goraka: Yes, baby, it's good.

Yombe: The rhythmic movement gets so good that they start to change up with Nailah taking turns for a while, then Goraka taking the lead. As each assumes the lead, that person sets the tone for what is to happen next. As timing will have it, An Afro-Cuban tune by Perez Prado called VOO DOO SUITE comes screaming across the airwaves.

It is Nailah's turn to invent the next movement. Nailah gracefully eases her body away from Goraka's embrace and begins to dance to the rhythm of the VOO DOO SUITE. Her movements are simply poetic and lyrical. They are simply unbelievably hypnotic. While carrying on this movement, Nailah does everything. I mean everything. Nailah has to possess the most fluid naturally rhythmic movements in all of the old country.

For instance, Nailah stands in one spot and moves her body away from Goraka's embrace and begins to dance to the rhythm of the new movement of the suite. She remains in that one spot and moves her mid-body from her waist to the realm of her knees as though she is giving a clinic on the technique of body control through movement of the center. She accents each beat as though she is the composer/arranger of this suite. In the meantime, Goraka looks on in total admiration and amazement. WITH AWE!

Goraka: My god, how do you do it?

Nailah: Move your body with so much fluidity, with such grace!

Yombe: Still moving from the waist down Nailah asks,

Nailah: Do what?

Goraka: Move your body with so much fluidity, with so much grace?

Nailah: I don't know. It just comes natural.

Yombe: Yea, sure. Run it Nailah.

Nailah: I hear the music, if it turns me on, I simply move in rhythm to the music. See!

Yombe: Nailah now demonstrates an on the beat body movement, then she shows off by demonstrating an offbeat movement that counters they next movement of the suite. No one knows how much practice it took to reach that level of perfection. Yet, as she moves, she never misses a beat on or off the beat, a movement of the hips, or a step as she continues to dance, dance, and dance.

By now, her pelvic section is moving while she rolls her belly. Goraka gets turned on without realizing it. He is so turned on that he jumps up and begins to imitate Nailah as closely as his untalented ways allows him to approximate her movements. Nailah greatly amused begins to encourage Goraka to do more and to come closer.

Nailah: come on, baby. Come on! Oh, yes baby, come on.

Yombe: Goraka is fired up now that he's a high as a Georgia pine. His inhibitions long gone, Goraka moves closer and closer as Nailah is beckoning him,

Nailah: Come on baby, do it to me, do it to me baby. Come on in.

Yombe: At this point Nailah has turned her ass of a behind toward Goraka while she moving it, Goraka still naked moves in closer. As a matter of fact, he's so close not that his only option is to put it in or back off. He opts for putting it in.

Although he aims for Ife's Garden, his missile lands in Blossoms Passage. Nailah simply bends over waist down with her hands holding her ankles with her legs spreads apart as though the other part of the clinic has just begun. In this position, Nailah begins to do the funky grind, or the dog as it is called today. Goraka, although he has other intentions, finds himself simply holding on for dear life as he gives Nailah a straight thrust with emphasis. Before he realizes it, he's touching every nook and cranny inside Nailah, Blossoms Passage. The feeling is so good that Nailah starts to moan and groan,

Nailah: Sock it to me baby. Sock it to me. Sock!

Yombe: Goraka is caught up in the activity of intercourse that all he can respond with it is,

Goraka: Okay, baby. I'll give it to you. Yes, baby. I'll give it to you. Here baby! How's this? HUH? Baby? Can you handle this? Can you feel this? Can you feel it baby?

Nailah: Oh, yes baby. I want all of it. Give me all of it, Mr. G. Give it all to me, if you can. Oh, yes! Oh, yes! Yes! Yes! I want all of it inside of me.

Yombe: The next thing Goraka knows is Nailah has taken the missile from Blossoms Passage and placed it in Ife's Garden and is starting to slide closer and closer to the floor as her legs spread further and further apart. Goraka say,

Goraka: WAIT!

Yombe: The moment Goraka cries, "wait" he places his hands above his head and moves into an all fours position, commonly referred to as a back breaker. A back breaker is so named because once your hands reach the floor your stomach is forced upward thus arching your back as though you are the Gateway to the West in St. Louis.

Now with Nailah's legs spread and Goraka's missile spring boarding to the highest elevation possible at the moment, they both remain stationary for a little while as Goraka's missile throbs like a bass drum being beaten by a drum stick on both sides of the drum.

Most importantly, now the most infamous missile to all humankind is trying to but cannot explore in Ife's Garden. To accommodate the impasse, Nailah mounts the missile with her spread legs a though she is about to ride a hop pie horse. Pressing down on the throbbing missile slowly and with great accuracy, Nailah's expressions are,

Nailah: GHEE! PHEW! WOW! You are really very hard. I can feel you all the way down the shaft, all the way inside of me. It's as though you are in my stomach.

Goraka: Do you want me to move?

Yombe: HA! Is he serious? How?

Nailah: No! No! Don't try to move. Just stay there. Just stay…there, right there.

Goraka: Are you sure

Yombe: Is he serious? She gives him a break knowing that there is nothing else he can do but remain in the position he has placed himself, and he asks,

Goraka: Are you sure?

Nailah: Goraka don't be funny. You know you can't move, I know you can't move so you no good….you don't know how this feels being inside this way, from this angle. But, it feels so good. And, besides, I can control everything now. All you have to do is stand there.

Goraka: You mean, this feels good, or, how good this feels?

Yombe: Nailah plays along with the humor because it really feels good,

Nailah: Oh, how good it feels to be in control. Anyway, what ever, just do not move. I have it the way I want it.

Yombe: At this moment Nailah find herself in the right position to move just enough to drive Goraka mad with this focused tease. Slow and show! Or is that slow and sure?

Goraka: Oh, shit that feels good. Too good! GHEES! PHEW! WOW! OOOHHHH! GOSH! DAMN! GEE WIZ! My god, this feels good, real good.

Yombe: On each descriptive note, verse, what have you; Nailah accentuates the movement with just enough to produce another round of descriptive language that produces poems, prose of lust and singular concentration on Goraka's part. To add fuel to the fire, Nailah begins to add her own verbal sounds of ecstasy. Yup! That's right, another song. By the time they get the call response together,

Nailah's new position allows her even more control over the movement of both parties. In doing so, she spreads her legs jus enough to keep the movement and allow the rest of the missile to enter her silo from an angel she has always wanted to try but never had the opportunity. Now's the time, seize the time. The missile is in the silo, Ife's Garden, for safe keeping until it is ready to release it payload.

The key words here are "safe keeping" and "release its payload" as you may have surmised. Why? Because the depth the missile has reached is just enough for both to enjoy themselves totally without either cumming. Thus, no need to release any payloads, no need to leave the silo, no need to stop making love a pleasure, a desire fulfilled. With all of that happening, there is no motive to explode the missile….

Unbelievable, it is now Sunday evening. Wait-a-minute, did I say that it's Sunday evening? Unbelievable! Nobody can do it that long. No way! Especially, no one as old as you say Nailah and Goraka are, No way! Wait-a-minute, you did say how old Goraka is didn't you? Or, did I? I don't recall.

Now, Monday morning, Nailah is required to return to her weekly chores, selling her incense, oils, hand crafted jewelry and whatnots. That is done mostly. That is done mostly because she loves it; mostly to let the Akuyu people know that she is still Nailah although her teaching, i.e., her discs, dvds/cds have made her rich and famous. Disc? DVD's? CD's? What discs?

Nailah: Goraka, I'd like for you to give me your impressions of my personal space, especially my library that contains my erotica collection. My thesis is, it's the sound that creates the mood. You'll see! Oh, by the way, no sex during the week. Save it for when both of us can enjoy it. Agreed? Bye! Hope you enjoy yourself. See you!

Goraka: YEA! SURE! NO PROBLEM! Oh, well what the fuck? What the fuck? HA! HA!HA! HA!AHH!HA! What the fuck HA! HA! HA!HA! What the fuck? HA! HA! HA!HA!HA! WHAT THE FUCK? HA!HA!HA!AHH!HA!HA!

Yombe: Goraka finally laughs himself into tears,

Goraka: She can't do this to me. I mean, that's mean. She has been so enjoyable. So fulfilling! Yes, that's the word I am searching for, Fulfilling! So, why not wait until it's fulfilling for both? That makes sense. How thoughtful! I still want…don't think about it. It's not even necessary. Anyway, what is that Nailah wants me to examine?….Something about esoteric books? Or, something! Now, let me see, where are the books? Where is this library?

Yombe: After checking every room and admiring its uniqueness and creative beauty, Goraka finally stumbles onto the library.

Goraka: My god, I did not know it was this size. But, so large! And, look at the volumes! I wonder what is on these discs Nailah is telling me about. Let's see, how do you work this contraption? Oh, okay. I see! Now, let's see what disc do I want to drop into the player?

Yombe: It takes Goraka a while to learn how to use the videodisc machine, but finally he has it. He turns it on only to find out that he has the wrong disc transcription combination. After spending some time figuring it out, he discovers that there is more to the process than simply a disc into the player. There are combinations of things that must be coordinated.

You see, Nailah has taken the opportunity to leave this great wealth of information on the art of creating peace through pleasures and social enjoyment. It is a topic that interests Nailah immensely. She has researched it as part of her religious and spiritual training. Her research has led her to "write" this masterful encyclopedia on the ART OF LOVE THROUGH PLEASURE. The Text is placed on videodisks so that it will be more assessable to the average households. Nailah has become filthy rich in the process.

So here Goraka is about to see the footage that no one else has had the opportunity to view. With the introduction, Goraka is told the story about how Nailah got the idea of creating the first series of videodisks on sex and pleasure and peace meditation.

After Nailah completes the introduction, she explains to the viewers that there are some preliminary things they must do before they can expect to become proficient in the "art of love thought pleasure." Number one. One must take great care of the body. This according to Nailah is cardinal to the whole process.

The ultimate of this holistic approach to life according to Nailah is the desire for peace and harmony. This is simply amazing to Goraka. He has never given much attention to pleasure in the past. He has never given so freely of himself, so willingly. What is she? Peace through love and pleasure?

What an interesting concept. What an interesting name, Nailah. Pronounced, Na-ee-lah. Just who is this "High Priest?" This Priest of Priests? Apparently what she has transcribed must come from high authority. Whatever, in any case, she has produced a most interesting and enlightening discourse.

Nailah has written, directed, and produced a fifty part series on how to establish and maintain peace through love and pleasure long before the idea became fashionable to so. This is the trendsetter. This is what world governments will embrace only when they have no choice, only when it is too late.

These are the discs that everyone will have to respond to when they "write" their discourse on love and peace and pleasure, pro or con. While Goraka ponders the question of how he never connected the name to the person, Nailah walks in.

Goraka: I'll be damned!

Nailah: What happened?

Goraka: Oh, I did not hear you enter. I must have gotten caught up in my thoughts. Your video discs!.....

Nailah: Oh, how do you like them?

Goraka: ……My thoughts?

Nailah: Oh, my lover has a sense of humor. HA! HA! HA! HA!

Goraka: Oh your discs! Great! /simply great! I would like to have this on Fifty-plus-One as soon as possible.

Yombe: By now, Doug Carn's "We are a mighty, mighty people" is racing across the airwaves as Nailah demonstrates the exercise on can do to such music. My, my what technique. It 's like dancing.

Nailah: The key is in the movement. If you put a little rhythm to your movement visually it adds on a new dimension. Just to see someone who has excellent "moves" may turn the other partner on.

Yombe: Goraka get turned on immediately.

Goraka: I thought you were nit going in any lovemaking until the weekend?

Nailah: We're not!

Yombe: Nailah is still taking her exercise to Doug Carn's music.

Goraka: Then, why are you getting me excited?

Nailah: Oh? My exercising excites you? How exciting!!

Goraka: Then, why are you getting me excited

Nailah: Oh? My exercising excites you? How exciting!!

Yombe: That moment, the music changes to a basa nova rhythm. Nailah changes right in stride, not loosing a beat, simply changing emphasis, or, should I say, changing her emphasis.

Goraka: You know these movements are stimulating, very stimulating.

Nailah: Yes, I know! But, I am amazed that they turn they you on.

Goraka: Oh! I mean sexually stimulating! Watching you makes my joint hard!

Nailah: Oh, really?

Yombe: Nailah continues to exercise. This excites Goraka to no end so he joins in the exercise. Nailah continues her routine totally unaffected by this new convert. Not caring, Goraka gets loose. Nailah finding it fascinating changes the pace again. Goraka follow suit.

By now, the rhythm is midrange so Nailah is moving. Goraka in unbelievable fashion, doubles his rhythm movement. Nailah continues to exercise at her pace while she checks it out. His rhythm is perfect. Absolutely perfect! But, mechanical!

After completing her exercise, Nailah took a shower, and Goraka treated her to a gourmet style menu that used peanuts as base of preparation. This was done by candlelight and music and video and talking.

Nailah: So, tell me about your phantom colony.

Goraka: There's not a lot to say. We began very small….never expected to find what we did.

Nailah: What was that?

Goraka: The phantom colony as you so aptly put it, Fifty-plus-On

Nailah: What a funny name for a colony.

Goraka: No funnier that "old country."

Nailah: Defensive, huh?

Goraka: "Old Country," that's no name for a country.

Nailah: True! I never thought of it before.

Goraka: When I become King-General, I am going to give this country a name.

Nailah: What will you call it?

Goraka: Xaire. I shall call it Xaire.

Nailah: Xaire? Why Zaire?

Goraka: Xaire was always the place of the Kinshasa people.

Nailah: So why not name your colony, Xaire?

Goraka: I suppose wee never thought of it. We were caught up in symbolism that we forgot the obvious. In any case, I realized the error and thought no, it should be the old country. Xaire should be the name of the old country, not the New World Colony.

Nailah: So you claim the old country as part of your heritage?

Goraka: Of course! It is well known that we are form the old country. Legend has it! The records are documented.

Nailah: Why do you think you'll be King-General? Mathew seems to be in full control.

Yombe: Nailah has not bothered to tell Goraka that the King-General's Army is everywhere looking for him, but somehow, he senses that this is the case.

Goraka: Mathew has his Army everywhere, I take it?

Nailah: Yes, everywhere!

Goraka: That could mean tow things: that he is defeating Parliament; or, he is loosing control over the populace.

Yombe: Goraka could not have read things more accurately. But, which way is it going? Who is winning the war?

Nailah: Well, we have not seen Blue yet, so this could be positive. Or, they could be bad. In any case, I seem to have no problem moving around. All of the action is centered on the Headquarters of the King-General's bodyguards. I understand things are changing fast....

Goraka: Yes, but everything is at an Impasse.

Yombe: so it seems! And, gossip is rampant. Gossip has it that the Barrister-General is dead. It also has it that his body was destroyed in the fire that killed Blue and his Panthers. Following that line of reasoning, the King-General Mathew III is staging a clean-up operation. The rebellion should be put down within the next few weeks.

Even Nailah recognized that this is not what was happening. She noted to Goraka that they had been living together for a few months now and there seems to be no end to the fighting. The Civil War seems to never end. So, what Mathew thought would end in a short while is now taking a turn against him and the entire monarchical empire. Yes, things are taking a turn fir the worse. That is, if you are one of the supporter of Mathew.

For the first time in six years, it seems like a matter of time the war will come to an end. The problem now is getting Mathew to concede defeat. He keeps holding on, saying that those troublemakers will pay for their treason. Out of touch are the words utilized to describe the delusional soul. The King-General could not invasion ever loosing his reign over the empire, the old country and all of its colonies scattered all over the three worlds.

Now, virtually powerless, Mathew is unwilling to concede defeat. For the first time, however, he really looks old and tired and in poor health. His will, based on his delusions of grandeur, is still in tact. Will or no will, the signs of change are already apparent.

Poster and graffiti art of social realism are everywhere. People are now very open with their criticisms. For instance, one old lady—about 473 years old – is said to have gotten close enough to the King-general Mathew III to spit on him and did. It is also reported that her head was cut off in front of everybody. The people rioted for the next forty-eight hours.

Mathew thus has become a virtual prisoner in his own castle. No one has seen him since the incident in the square. Word has it that he is drunk all the time. As I said, this is only a rumor. Regardless, nothing is going well at this point although Parliament has made it a point to be very visible, and to keep the political machinery working. Matter of fact, the old country is working quite well without the presence of Mathew. This has caused the "radicals" to openly contend that the country no longer needs a King-General, that a Republican form of government is more in order.

In the meantime, Nailah continues to treat Goraka royally. After all, he is her houseguest. By now, they have experienced every position demonstrated on Nailah's erotic discs, the statutes, and corresponding "books." By now, they have realized that it is possible to enjoy making love no matter how often they do it. Each occasion is a new experiment.

Each experiment is a new experience. Each experience is a new revelation. Each revelation provides further enlightenment about the inner workings of their bodies. Each being is now free to move as the self dictates. And for Goraka this movement mans: "Glory is my reward! Glory is my reward! Glory is my reward!

As the Hugh crowd affirms its desire for a new King-General, it is also feeding the ego of Goraka. The simplest way to put it is Goraka is in his glory, and who is standing there beside him? Abdul Malik, Marimba, and Nailah. Nailah is visually stunned by the remarks of Goraka, but she remains reserved. So does Marimba, the Musician. Abdul Malik in the other hand is furious. How dare he become arrogant? Not on the first day, before he is sworn in. How arrogant! What is his problem? Is he crazy?

Goraka is visually shaken by Blue's remarks. He is angry! But, he continues to enjoy his glory. He also swears revenge upon Abdul Malik if that is the last thing he does.

Goraka: GLORY IS MY REWARD! [WHO DOES HE THINK HE IS? WHO DOES HE THINK HE IS? I WILL DESTROY HIM!] GLORY IS MY REWARD!!!!.

Yombe: And, so it began. Nothing Blue did from that point could satisfy Goraka. His name was forbidden in Goraka's presence. Goraka's first act was to make it impossible for Blue to be elected to the New Parliament. The Republican's Republican was outlawed from public office. Then, there were attempts upon Blues life.

This occurred after Abdul Malik officially laid down his weapons. After unsuccessful assassination attempts, Blue went underground. He became invisible. Only those he wanted to see saw him. Yet, he kept up with Goraka's every move, every decision.

In other words, Abdul Malik had well oiled information networks. Other than the feelings of insult and betrayal, and the inability to be vocal and openly participate in making the new society, Blue took his setback/defeat in stride. Everyone was shocked, including Parliament. But, no one said a word.

Nailah: Do you think it was necessary to force Abdul Malik underground?

Goraka: I DO NO'T WANT TO DISCUSS IT!!!!!!

Yombe: And, that was that! From here on, everyone tried to be accommodating: one never mentioned Blue's name in front of Goraka. But, somehow, the name came up, always. And, it was always Goraka who brought it up. Case in point:

Nailah: Goraka, baby, let's relax tonight, and for the rest of the weekend. Just the two of us. Just you and me. You look tired.

Goraka: Okay! I could use a good relaxing weekend.

Yombe: By now, those who think they're in the know are angry. What is Nailah up to? I thought you and Blue was ace boon coons why is she selling Blue down the drain? Damn! That's sexual politics for you. Etcetera, etcetera, ectera.

Nailah: Baby, I'm going to cook you an excellent meal tonight.

Goraka: But, our chef can….

Nailah: NO! NO! I have it all arranged. We're going to go away. Out to the country. You haven't seen this part of Xaire before. It is beautiful and tranquil.

Goraka: You've thought of everything.

Nailah: I think so.

Yombe: While Nailah and Goraka are traveling out to the country, they start to reminisce about their first love encounter. The thought turns them on, so before long, before they know it, they are rolling on the carriage floor like young lovers. First, Nailah lands on top. She takes the opportunity to remove her beautifully colorful long flowing gown. Then Goraka ends up on top, He does the same. Both are now buck-naked. For a while, each takes time to admire the other's beautiful body. For a while! They smile at each other lovingly while Goraka slides his missile inside of Ife's Garden.

Goraka: Oh! So smooth, SUH! It feels so good.

Nailah: Awe! Ohhh! Baby! Baby! How are you? How are you? HUH? Is this what my baby wants?

Goraka: Yes, baby!

Nailah: Well, give it all to me. Oh! Yes, right there baby.

Goraka: Oh, yes baby! Oh, yes! How is this baby?

Nailah: Oh yes, right there baby. How's this baby?

Goraka: Oh yes, baby, right there baby.

Nailah: Tell me it's good , baby.

Goraka: Oh yes! It's good baby.

Nailah: Tell me how it feels, baby.

Goraka: Oh yes, it feels good baby.

Nailah: Say its good, baby.

Goraka: Oh yes, it feels good baby

Nailah: Tell me!

Goraka: Oh yes, give it to me baby.

Nailah: Say its good, baby.

Goraka: Oh, yes! It's good baby!

Nailah: Is it good to you, baby?

Goraka: Oh, yes. Right there baby!

Nailah: Tell me! OOO OOO OOOH HHHHHHH! OOOOOOOOHHHHH! OOOOHHHHHH!

Goraka:OOOOOOHHHHHHH! OOOOOOOOOHHHHHHHH! OOOOOOHHHHH!

Nailah: Oh! Yes! Right there baby! I'm cumming!!!!!!!!!

Goraka:MMEEEEEEEE!TTTTTOOOOOOOOOOO! OOOOOOHHHHHHH!

YES! YES! YES!

Yombe: By the time Nailah and Goraka get though carrying on, the have reached the country. Good thing too because although the carriage is sound proof and concealed, Nailah was about to let out one of those great screams that was coming to the fore when she came in the carriage. In other words, Nailah was ready! She intended to enjoy this weekend. She planned to have her self some fun. So, the carriage was simply a warm-up. Preliminaries!!!

Goraka: Goddamn! Goddamn! Goddamn! OOOOOOOOOO OHHHHHHH HHH HERE IT COMES!!! HERE IT COMES!!!! HERE IT COMES!!!!!!!!

Nailah: Yes, baby! Yes, baby! I can feel it baby. I can feel it, baby. It feels so good. Oh, yes! Oh, yes!

Yombe: Like I said, this was the prelims!!!! The real stuff was not about to begin. . .Goraka now finds himself remembering the passage where King Solomon asks God for wisdom.

Solomon: Lord God…you have made me king over a people who are as numerous as the dust of the earth. Give me wisdom and knowledge, that I may lead this people, for who is able to govern this great people of yours?

God: Since this is your heart's desire and you have asked for the death of your enemies, and since you have not ask for long life, but wisdom and knowledge to govern my people over whom I have made you king, therefore wisdom and knowledge will be given you. And I will also give you wealth, riches and honor, such as no king who was before you ever had and none after you will have…

Goraka: Time to have some peace. Every time the same. No matter who's to blame? Every time the same. Gotta have some peace. 1stworld: 136,758,937,830. 2ndworld: 183,736 656,423. 3rd world: 516,627,545,170. Weep! Weep! Weep! Thou shall not kill. Dying Soul: How can you? Nigga Dred: Before it rains. No clouds in the sky. No life on the plains. Our wells are dry. Before it rains. Our forests cry. My window of tears that dry. After it rains. What will I try? Oh, my what pains. Will I ever really die?

THE END

www.ingramcontent.com/pod-product-compliance
Lightning Source LLC
Chambersburg PA
CBHW082023050526

44107CB00101B/631